TERRORISM TODAY

The Past, the Players, the Future

CLIFFORD E. SIMONSEN

JEREMY R. SPINDLOVE

Prentice Hall

Prentice Hall, Upper Saddle River, NJ 07458

Library of Congress Cataloging-in-Publication Data

Simonsen, Clifford E.
    Terrorism today: the past, the players, and the future/
Clifford E. Simonsen, Jeremy R. Spindlove.
        p. cm.
    Includes bibliographical references and indexes.
    ISBN 0-02-301731-7
    1. Terrorism. 2. Terrorism—History. 3. Terrorism—Prevention. I.
Spindlove, Jeremy R. II. Title.
    HV6431 .S53 1999   99-15762
    303.6′25′09—dc21   CIP

Editor in Chief: *David Garza*
Acquisitions Editor: *Neil Marquardt*
Managing Editor: *Mary Carnis*
Production Editor/Interior Design: *Glenn Johnston*
Director of Manufacturing and Production: *Bruce Johnson*
Manufacturing Buyer: *Ed O'Dougherty*
Associate Art Director: *Marianne Frasco*
Senior Design Coordinator: *Miguel Ortiz*
Cover Design: *Amy Rosen*
Cover Illustration: *Rick Lieder*
Typesetting: *Janet Bolton*
Marketing Manager: *Shannon Simonsen*
Marketing Assistant: *Adam Kloza*

 © 2000 Prentice-Hall, Inc.
Upper Saddle River, NJ 07458

Printed in the United States of America
10   9   8   7   6   5   4

ISBN 0-02-301731-7

Prentice-Hall International (UK) Limited, *London*
Prentice-Hall of Australia Pty. Limited, *Sydney*
Prentice-Hall Canada Inc., *Toronto*
Prentice-Hall Hispanoamericana, S.A., *Mexico*
Prentice-Hall of India Private Limited, *New Delhi*
Prentice-Hall of Japan, Inc., *Tokyo*
Prentice Hall (Singapore) Pte., Ltd.
Editora Prentice-Hall do Brasil, Ltda., *Rio de Janeiro*

This book is dedicated to the millions of people who have died and continue to die at the hands of state, religious and individual terrorists. It is sincerely hoped that the Twenty-first Century and a new millennium will someday see a world free from acts that threaten those we love and those we don't even know.

CONTENTS

PART II: TERRORISM AROUND THE WORLD   73

Chapter 4: British Isles and Western Europe   75

Chapter 5: Central and Eastern Europe   117

Chapter 6: North Africa and the Middle East   133

Chapter 7: The Persian Gulf   169

Chapter 8: Central and Southern Africa   191

Chapter 9: Southern and Southeast Asia   213

Chapter 10: The Pacific Rim   235

Chapter 11: Latin America   249

FOREWORD

SIR BRIAN HAYES CBE QPM

Although I have read dozens of books on terrorism and worked for many years on the subject in the police service, I have never previously been asked to write a Foreword. However, there was some logic in doing so for *Terrorism Today*. One of the co- authors, Jeremy Spindlove, had served in the Surrey Constabulary during the mid-seventies, when the IRA bombed two local pubs, killing and maiming innocent customers. I joined Surrey Constabulary in 1977 as an Assistant Chief Constable, coming from a strong anti-terrorist background in London. I was to be the Chief there in the late 1980s when the four IRA members convicted and imprisoned for those bombings were released on appeal due to improprieties in the original investigation

In the years between the mid-70s and the dawn of the new Millennium, Jeremy has become a close colleague of Clifford Simonsen, the other co-author. The two men have a wealth of experience combining the military, policing, private security, loss prevention, correction and investigation. Clifford Simonsen, a former full colonel in the US Army Military Police Corps, is already an accomplished author in his own right. Your two authors have enormous experiences in the "University of Life," which they have drawn on copiously in producing *Terrorism Today*.

It is absorbing to read this book and link it to one's own knowledge and experience and to note how some aspects of terrorism have changed over the years whereas others have remained comparatively constant. For example, when I was involved at operational level in anti-terrorism work—mostly in the 1960s and 1970s—it was the age of the aircraft hijacker. This is graphically illustrated by the authors' detailed description of the Dawsons Field incident in Jordan. Small terrorist units were highly active internationally and often operated as an offshoot or extension of a much larger organization. Thus the Baader Meinhoff gang, the Japanese Red Amy (IRA), the Red Amy Faction (RAF), Black September—all mentioned in the current book—were causing havoc, mostly to Western European democracies. The Irish and Spanish Separatists (IRA and ETA) were in full flow. Western European forces of law and order were uniting to fight the growing threat to political and commercial stability.

Not surprisingly, as soon as I was asked to write this Foreword, I scanned the newspapers to see what was current on the terrorist scene. The English press was full of the increase in kidnappings in Chechnya and Yemen, particularly because British "hostages" had been killed in both countries. Eight hostages, including Britons and Americans, had just been murdered in Uganda. The Irish violence, on the British mainland at least, has halted since the Easter 1998 Peace Accord ...but the men of violence are still carrying out beatings, knee-cappings and other summary punishments in Ulster. To me, this typifies the absolute link between terrorism and criminality, which is well clarified in *Terrorism Today*.

It has always been a personal issue for me to underline all terrorist acts as out and out crimes. All terrorists should be viewed as criminals first and foremost and terrorists second. I have never felt that they should be accorded any form of celebrity status. This was particularly relevant in the early 1970s because Interpol, the worldwide police organization, struggled to deal with terrorism within its charter, which precluded its involvement in issues of a religious, political or racial/ethnic nature. Terrorist acts almost invariably fall into one or more of these categories; in Europe we had to develop other means of communication to circulate operational terrorist intelligence between law enforcement agencies. We eventually resolved most of the problems by classifying and prosecuting offenses committed by the main terrorist protagonists under the normal criminal law. Thus assassinations were murder, hostage-takings were kidnapping and so on. Almost all of our terrorist targets were guilty of immigration and passport offenses. Caution was still needed, however, because some of the Interpol member states were either sheltering terrorists or organizing training on their territory.

In those years, between the 70s and the 90s, various established terrorist groups spread their tentacles even further afield and copycat groups sprang up. North America, as your authors point out, remained insulated from terrorism at home for many years...although it was soon to suffer violent attacks on US military and diplomatic targets abroad. The bombing of the World Trade Center in New York in 1993 and the Oklahoma bombing in 1995 brought the problem into the USA's own backyard. During the 1970s I had a steady flow of FBI and other US law and order personnel through my office at New Scotland Yard, thirsty for information on current terrorist trends in Europe and methods of combating them. The subjects were then rather academic to them, but that all changed dramatically as *Terrorism Today* illustrates.

Terrorism Today is a massive and brave attempt to chronicle the whole of terrorist activity across the world since the problem first reared its head sorting each country, group or individual in the appropriate historical context and seeking to explore and explain their "raison d'être." The authors rightly recognize the danger of superficiality in attempting a "tour d'horizon" of such a vast subject. They firmly make the point in the Preface that this is an introductory text on terrorism, recognizing that they have taken on a daunting task leading logically to a broad brush coverage. The authors attempt to counterbalance this with a very useful preface, previewing the main content of each chapter. Those 14 chapters in turn are each supported by a list of Terms to Remember, Review Questions, and Endnotes.

This is a long book but it achieves the authors' objective of being written in an easy to read, flowing style. By its format and content it is also intended as a didactic volume, geared to teachers, students and the casual reader alike. For me, it is not a book to plough straight through, but rather to pick chapters or even sections of chapters to concentrate on which are of particular current interest to the reader.

This is where the "terrorism bytes," "terrorism briefs" and "terrorism players" are very useful little icons in the text, giving examples and illustrations of particular groups, individuals and incidents. Additionally, the experiences of the two authors blend the operational and the academic/intellectual to render the subject matter light and enjoyable, informative and instructional. Having consumed a diet of books and articles on terrorism produced by the established authors and commentators on either side of the Atlantic, including those such as Richard Clutterbuck, Paul Wilkinson and David Yallop, all of whom are quoted from in *Terrorism Today*, I had to adjust to such a broad compendium of information gathered in one volume. But despite that difference, indeed almost because of it, *Terrorism Today* merits its place in the library of teacher or student and in the booklists of anyone seriously interested in extending their knowledge of this absorbing subject.

Sir Brian Hayes
London
March 1999

Sir Brian Hayes served as a police officer in England for nearly 40 years, retiring in April 1998. He rose to the second most senior post in The United Kingdom, that of Deputy Commissioner in the London Metropolitan Police Service, commonly know as "Scotland Yard." Sir Brian has lectured on terrorist matters in England, Scotland, Europe and the USA. He currently works as a management and security consultant and was Knighted by Her Majesty The Queen in 1998 for services to policing. In the same year, he was also awarded the Meritorious Police Cross by the Spanish Government for services to Spanish Policing.

PREFACE

When one decides to write an introductory text about a subject that is as complex and rapidly changing as terrorism, it becomes a daunting task very quickly. The concept of Terrorism connotes such a wide range of activities that the most difficult task is to make a text short enough to be comprehensible to students, but long enough to satisfy colleagues, professionals and practitioners that it at least covers an acceptable depth of this fascinating field. We have to admit that at times it seemed like we were trying to paint a moving bus, with the players, organizations and operations changing faster than the words could be written down. This text, written in an admittedly and intentional broad-brush manner, examines where terrorism came from, where it is today, where it seems to be going as we enter the new millennium and some of the issues that require specific countermeasures to prevent getting there. The student will soon appreciate that there is no easy answer to the question, "what is Terrorism?" It will become apparent in the course of reading this text that most terrorism actions are often poorly articulated groups of fanatics, dissidents or crazies, often with conflicting goals and little interface. However, it will be shown that many of them are carefully planning to upset the feelings of security and safety for persons, places and things. This knowledge we provide is intended to stimulate students to seek out ways to understand methods to offer better safety and security to all persons worldwide.

Your authors have attempted to provide a clear overview for many of the sectors and operations that comprise the broad term of terrorism. We explore some of the subjects in greater depth than others in an attempt to cut redundancy and cover as many differences and similarities as possible. The text is presented in the firm belief that a learning experience should be enjoyable as well as educational. For the instructor, a text has been offered that is organized and written with the goal of making the teaching and learning experience as effective and interesting as possible. This is accomplished by covering the essentials of the subject with a large array of pedagogical tools.

Security is an ancient need for humans, a basic rung on the ladder of Maslow's hierarchy of needs. But is only in recent history that mankind's sense of security has been shaken so badly by terrorist acts abroad and at home. As with most fields of human endeavor that are just entering the stature of an academic discipline, the material that is available that present scientific theory, literature and research is not very extensive in the field of terrorism. The materials available for developing an introductory text have come from a large band of resources found on government sites on the internet, along with a few articles, news clips and textbooks dealing with specific historical areas of interest. Much of the information and data came, therefore, from where the rubber meets the road and the action is in terrorism. We continue to challenge our colleagues in academia and in the operational security, law enforcement and the military to conduct the basic research, collect the data, and develop the theories that will transform terrorism into a true subject for academic debate and research.

THE TRADITION CONTINUES

The methodology for textbook development, used in the past for several other successful texts, will be the foundation for this one. It will build on the comments of instructors and students to provide a text that works well for both, such as:

- An engaging writing style, resulting in a book that is highly readable and effective as an informational, teaching and learning tool;
- A balanced treatment of practical examples, technology, history, and data from available documents and academic research;
- An eye-pleasing design for easy reading, with features such as clearly understood current and past examples, of current and historical photographs, illustrations, and other supplemental materials to augment the basic text;
- A systems approach to exploring the varied elements of terrorism, terrorists and the various motives for terrorist groups as a potentially integrated and interrelated series of subsystems;
- An unbiased presentation of a wide range of topics makes for a text suitable for instructors and students from many disciplines and points of view;
- In-chapter and end of chapter materials that augment the textual materials with examples of events, persons, stories, terms to remember, review questions and bibliographic suggestions for further reading;
- An Instructors Manual which features test banks and other aids for the busy instructors, many of whom are adjuncts who are tilling the fields of law enforcement, security or the military in a full-time capacity.

ORGANIZATION OF THE TEXT

This text has been divided into three major "Parts" and fourteen chapters that build from an historical background to predictions about the Twenty-first century for terrorism. It should be noted that materials in "Terrorism Bytes," "Terrorism Briefs" and "Terrorism Players," and endnotes are carefully selected for their content and applicability to the subject matter being covered. These should be considered as important as the textual materials themselves for presentation and study. The materials selected come from the best and most current available sources in the field and the authors choose to keep and present them in their original form or blend them into their own writing to minimize confusion.

PART I: THE HISTORY AND EVOLUTION OF TERRORISM

An in-depth historical look at terrorism and its origins, types and history will provide the student with a background necessary to understand the background of yesterday and the evolution of terrorism today.

Chapter 1: Defining Terrorism

This chapter will set the basic historical foundation for the following chapters and allow for the student to understand the difference between terrorist acts and ordinary criminal acts. Definitional issues, operational definitions, useful typologies, forms of terrorism, and tactics of terrorism will be explored and used to develop some tentative model definitions. Terrorism as criminal behavior and the use of this as a method of action is covered. These will include such acts as Ambush and Assassination, Arson, Bombing, Hijacking, Hostage taking, Kidnapping, Blackmail and Protection.

Chapter 2: A Brief History of Terrorism

The chief theoreticians for terrorism, such as: Mao Tse-Tung, Beria, Heinrich Hedriech, Carlos Marighella Abimael Guzman Reynoso will be examined in light of their historical and operational impacts. The Inquisition, the Holocaust, the PLO, The Phoenix Program Tiananmen Square and guerilla warfare are among the examples examined to see how individual terrorism can grow into a national or religious crusade. The student will be presented with examples such as: the Christian Crusades, Iran and the Ayatollahs, Iraq and the Kurds, Israel and the Palestinians and India and the conflicting religions there. Major terrorists acts from the King David hotel to the bombings of the US Embassies in Africa will be discussed and shown as key events in terrorism's development as a sophisticated method of changing opinion and politics.

Chapter 3: Terror as a State or Religious Strategy

This chapter explores the motives and methods employed by individual terrorists or groups with some perceived agenda as compared to the motives of a state for suppressing dissent and revolution. It explains the concept of state sponsored terrorism that supports terrorist groups and individual terrorists with weapons, money and supplies to achieve their goals. From the Crusades to the frictions between religions around the world today, this section discusses how these got started and where they seem to be today.

PART II: TERRORISM AROUND THE WORLD

The student will be brought up to the events of the Twentieth century in general terms that will lead into the discussions of terrorism from both the left and right wings. The right wing factions of various countries and regions will be examined and discussed and the difference shown as to goals and objectives. The left wing factions of various countries and regions will be examined in a similar methodology and contrasted with the right wing's goals and the difference discovered as to goals and objectives. Regions and nations are covered by the investigation of terrorism and the many different factions and their interrelationships.

Chapter 4: British Isles Western Europe

The background for the "Irish Problem" is detailed and brought up to date with examples of friction and terrorism on both sides of the issues. This long chapter provides a model for the student in examining the others terror spots of the world. It shows how similar and yet different the use of terrorism is in meeting political or religious goals. The French have used or supported terrorist acts and the student sees that the Germans are a race that thrived on terrorism and was able to be led into blind obedience and violence many times. Use of terrorism by the Mafia, and Mussolini's fascist thugs demonstrate the changing political patterns of the Italians over the centuries. The turbulent history of Spain from the Inquisition to the fascist reign of terror under Franco is examined along with the many terrorist activities in Spain, especially the Basque separatists.

Chapter 5: Central and Eastern Europe

The sad history of the multi-racial, multi-religious region formerly known as Yugoslavia is examined from the standpoint of partisan terrorism and German terrorism in WW II to the broken up state that has seen inter-racial and inter-religious fighting since the breakup. Terrorism will be shown to be one of the main weapons in these battles for ethnic purity. The Russians are examined as having a long history of national terrorism to keep the populace in control, from the Czars to the Soviet Union and the murders of fifty million countrymen by Stalin. Afghanistan and Chechnya after the fall of the Soviet Union display continuing tactics of terror.

Chapter 6: North Africa and the Middle East

An examination of an area of the world where terror is the primary weapon in local and international conflicts gives the student the "big picture." Slowly the realization is that the conflicts are all similar and terror is the primary weapon used by either side. The 3000 year battle between the Jews, Christians and Arabs remains the hot bed of terrorism and is covered in detail as to the problems faced in this ancient feud for land and minds. Algeria, Libya, Egypt and other hot spots of state sponsored and religious terrorism are covered as well.

Chapter 7: The Persian Gulf

The nations of the Persian Gulf states have either involved active warfare or constant terrorism, (religious or political). This most valuable source of the world's petroleum remains a hot bed of violence and terrorism today. The persecution of the Kurds in Iraq, the use of oil revenue to sponsor worldwide terrorism and use the constant fear of the use of nuclear, biological, and chemical weapons stir the pot of terrorism in this area. The Gulf War and Saddam Hussien's constant tricks keep it boiling. The struggles for prominence among the states that ring the Persian Gulf are examined in some detail.

Chapter 8: Central and Southern Africa

From the long struggle for freedom from apartheid in South Africa, to the quite different struggles in Zimbabwe, the Dark Continent is shown to have suffered many trials. The genocide in the Congo, Uganda and Rwanda are explored as well as the tribalism that divides most regions. The threat of right-wing directed warfare against the new Black governments is a new and rising problem that is shown. The great potential for this region, with great problems as well makes this area and its nations the hope for the future.

Chapter 9: South Asia and Southeast Asia

India has a long history of terrorist tactics in it's past. The war against the United Kingdom taught them that terrorism works. Following independence, India has had to fight many terrorism attacks from religious factions and from rebel causes. Pakistan and India have a long-standing state of war and the Punjab has used terrorism to try to gain independence from India. Sri Lanka, formerly Ceylon, has an ongoing war of terrorism by the Timal Tigers and other splinter groups so peace is far from certain. The terrorism used by the rest of the world has found many locations in Southeast Asia and the local conflicts, religious and ideological, seem to echo the same themes as elsewhere on the globe. From the Khymer Rouge in Cambodia to the guerilla fighters in the jungle of Malaysia and Indonesia, terrorism has found a home in Southeast Asia.

Chapter 10: The Pacific Rim

China is shown to have passed the terror-filled times of the period following the ascension of communism to power in that ancient land. Terror as a philosophy can be traced all the way back in Chinese history as a viable means to control that vast nation. From the Huks at the turn of the century, to WW II and the Japanese occupation and on to the terrorist tactics of the Marcos regime, the Philippines has shown the use of terror to be a useful tool in controlling a large and poor country. Japan has been hit with fanatical terrorism that extends back into history through the occupation of China and the Pacific islands in World War II up to use of chemical terrorism in the present. Indonesia and Malaysia are shown to have many terrorist groups.

Chapter 11: Latin America

The so-called "Banana Republics" have had long struggles against terrorism against the people by repressive dictators and terrorism by rebel causes against the government. Major conflicts are examined in terms of past history and present status. The roles of Mexico and Cuba in these struggles are pointed out to the student. The "other America" is shown to have been rife with terrorist activities for a long time, from the Shining Path of Peru to the "disappeared" in Brazil and Argentina. The drug cartels in Columbia and political upheavals have shown this region to be very violent and dangerous as suppressive governments invite terrorist organizations to emerge. Even Mexico is shown to have a long history of terrorism and revolution against governments internal and external.

Chapter 12: North America and the Caribbean

The student examines the American Revolution as a terrorist plan to overthrow the colonial government by fighting as guerillas and using terrorist tactics. The student will see familiar terrorist schemes in light of the actions of the American colonists. Terrorism was surely one of the major ways of fighting in the Civil War. Terror and brutality have always controlled slavery and the United States is no exception. These tactics are examined in light of the students better understanding of what terrorism is. The kinds of terrorist group found in Canada are discussed and their battle with French and English origins. The two general types of terrorism in the United States are examined and analyzed to see how the previously examined paradigms of terrorism stand up when compared with those in the most prosperous country in the world. The United States is shown as free from the violent terrorist actions of the rest of the world for too long. The peaceful and idyllic islands of the Caribbean are seen to have been impacted by the drug terrorism as shipping stops and participants in the narco-terrorism in their homelands and in the United States.

PART III: COUNTER TERRORISM

The last part will discuss the kinds of efforts being expended around the world to find ways to deter or discover terrorism and find other ways to deal with it. The final chapter will examine what the future might be in the 21st Century as far as terrorism is concerned.

Chapter 13: Countering Terrorism around the World

Efforts, political and operational are examined to determine which are effective and which have failed. These range from national paramilitary groups to local activities by regular citizens. The importance of intelligence gathering, the cycle of intelligence, and the proper uses of intelligence against terrorism are studied in detail. A model of the intelligence cycle is developed and presented. Worldwide types of anti-terrorist groups and strategies are examined, from the Delta Force in the United States, to the Mossad in Israel, the Special Action Squads in the United Kingdom and many other highly organized and effective agencies. The strategies of the United Nations and regional governments are discussed and analyzed as to their success or failure.

Chapter 29: A Modest Look at the Future of Terrorism

The authors will make an attempt to predict the most likely spots where the pressure from terrorism will be found at the start of the 21st Century, and what possible effects will be felt in doing away with terrorism for a number of regions around the world.

ACKNOWLEDGEMENTS

How do your authors begin to acknowledge those persons whose support, encouragement, assistance and belief in our dream have allowed us to develop, refine, and produce a book that attempts to cover an encyclopedic and world view of terrorism? To try to acknowledge each of them individually would take several pages and we shudder to think we might miss some of them. The list begins with our families and close personal friends; then our colleagues and international friends in academia, as well as professionals and practitioners in terrorism at the international, federal, state and local levels. Perhaps most important were the efforts of Sir Brian Hayes, Mr. Eddie Garcia and Dr. Harry Allen who took the time to read the early manuscript and share their reactions and comments with us. To each of them and the rest of you we extend our deepest appreciation and gratitude for encouraging and assisting us in putting together a text about this important topic that seems to work.

We would, however, like to single out a few of the special persons who helped the authors turn their prose, ideas, and concepts for a book about terrorism into a textbook which will greatly assist the users, professors and students alike. First, our senior editor, Neil Marquardt, gets kudos for leading us through this first complete edition with minimal problems and a lot of positive support. Neil fought for our ideas and concepts about using new concepts and techniques, rather than just staying with the status quo. Paula Baird, our copy editor, gets a special "thank you." She used her "magic red pencil" to good advantage and helped turn the words of two authors into a book that we hope reads like the words of one. Glenn Johnston, our production editor, was a calm and professional center in the midst of what became a frantic effort to stay on schedule. This text also received excellent support from Adele Kupchik our senior production editor, who listened to our sniveling about schedules, photos and permissions then inspired us to try to meet them. Marianne Frasco, the art director, helped us understand the importance of the visual effect of this new edition and made the book graphically appealing. Shannon Simonsen, the marketing manager, got the word out to the sales staff and will be a great factor in making this text successful in a very competitive field. Ed O'Dougherty, the manufacturing buyer, made sure that everything was in place for final production. We hasten to mention Cheryl Adam, who was the ringmaster of this three-ring circus. We enjoyed working with her as an editor and know she will continue to help us in future editions.

We offer continuing thanks to the last, but by far not the least, of those who provided support and solace...our families, friends and relatives. While they will enjoy with us whatever modest success we may have with this text, they have also had to put up with the periodic absences and the frequent bouts of frenzied revisions and changes...conducted in the heat of deadlines and often from long distances on E-mail. We have found out that writing is a lonely task, especially when it involves a very specific field, and often not easy to discuss in the frantic throes of revision. We deeply appreciate the understanding and support we have gotten in these periods over the past period of hard work and love you all for understanding and caring.

ABOUT THE AUTHORS

Jeremy R. Spindlove

Jeremy Spindlove is presently the Regional Director in Loss Prevention, Health and Safety for a world leader in third party logistics management. He has spent thirty years in both public and private sector security operations and administration on an international scale. During his police service in Great Britain he was the first officer on the scene at the now notorious Guildford pub IRA bombings. During his service as an aviation security expert with British Airways, he was assigned to trouble spots in Europe, North Africa and the Middle East, spending two years in Baghdad and extensive duty in Beirut. Jeremy Spindlove also served as the Director of Security for the Vancouver International Airport Authority in British Columbia. He has presented seminars on aviation security to IAMTI at the University of British Columbia. He has collaborated on this text with Clifford Simonsen, a career military police officer, criminologist, writer and teacher. This has allowed the combining of a unique blend of writing experience and acumen with first hand knowledge and personal experiences. Jeremy is an active member of the American Society for Industrial Security.

Clifford E. Simonsen

Presently the President of Criminology Consultants International, Clifford Simonsen has over forty years of experience in criminal justice, security and law enforcement. As a career Army Officer, he retired as a Military Police Colonel. His background includes a Ph.D. in Public Administration, (with an emphasis on criminal justice administration and deviance), from Ohio State University and a Masters in Criminology from Florida State University. He is also a graduate of the Army War College and the Industrial College of the Armed Forces. Dr. Simonsen is the author of dozens of articles on the fields of crime, criminal justice, delinquency and security and is the author or co-author of several texts in a broad range of disciplines. These include Corrections in America: An Introduction (8th Ed), Juvenile Justice in America (3rd Ed), Private Security in America and Security Administration. Dr, Simonsen has taught at several universities, full-time or as an adjunct. He is an active member of the American Society for Industrial Security (Lifetime Certified Protection Professional), the American Correctional Association, the Academy of Criminal Justice Sciences and the International Association of Professional Security Consultants. Dr, Simonsen is pleased to be associated with Jeremy Spindlove and share in his depth of experience with terrorism on both a local and international scale.

PART 1

THE HISTORY
AND EVOLUTION
OF TERRORISM

The terrorist bombing of Pan Am flight 103 over Lockerbie, Scotland shocked
the world on December 21st, 1998. CP Picture Archive (AP Photo)

CHAPTER 1

DEFINING TERRORISM

"Kill one, frighten one thousand."

Sun Tzu

OVERVIEW

Terrorism, if only used as a "bogeyman" phrase, constantly impacts upon the lives of major governments and common people worldwide. It hangs over us everywhere, from the way we conduct our personal lives to the way corporations transact business, even the conduct of national and foreign affairs. Fear of terrorism supports a massive security industry aimed at protecting individuals, tourists, travelers, institutions and industries. This constant specter of doom requires the expenditure of huge sums of money to protect us from the threat of dangers by those mysterious criminals we call "terrorists." In travel today, especially by air, this threat has forced large delays and drastic changes in our planning, scheduling and timing for a trip, especially a trip abroad. The news media, both legitimate publications and tabloids, immediately inform and frighten us about horrible terrorist acts around the world. Novels and movies are written and produced, replete with terrorist plots, characters and themes.

Who is this larger than life creature that we call a "terrorist"? What are terrorist acts? Can we protect ourselves against them? How do we define this activity we casually refer to as "terrorism?" Combs discusses this problem:

> ...terrorism is a political as well as a legal and a military issue, its definition in modern terms has been slow to evolve. Not that there are not numerous definitions available–there are hundreds. But few of them are of sufficient legal scholarship to be useful in international law, and most of those which are legally useful lack the necessary ambiguity for political acceptance.[1]

Defining terrorism is a difficult but not impossible task. The term must be carefully constructed so that it projects the meaning intended. A **terrorist incident** is a violent act that can escalate as the purpose and intention become better known. What it is and is not called hinges on a commonly understood meaning of the term "terrorism." This chapter will lay a foundation that will assist the student throughout the rest of this text. We will start by defining the term from a number of perspectives. These include understanding the concept of behavior as a continuum and the role of folkways, mores and laws in developing societal groups.

Behavior as a Continuum and the Development of Laws

The student is about to embark upon a journey into the fascinating phenomenon of terrorism and terrorists. In order to understand these concepts, we must explore together the historical context and specific rules society has developed as a factor in defining the use of criminal and antisocial acts to meet political or social goals. But, before we do, it is useful to look at **social control** from a behavioral viewpoint. Prior to the establishment of social groups, in which people gathered together for companionship, reproduction, group hunting and crop growing, we humans probably just wandered around the countryside like all the other animals. Meeting the needs of the reproductive drive and managing to eat while not being eaten fully occupied our distant ancestors' days and nights. However, with the development of the concept of **territoriality** and **personal property**, as well as group social relationships, humans began to worry about the protection of their persons, their places, and their status in early tribal societies. From this simple concept has evolved a vast system of controls and processes that define who gets what, and attempts to dictate the behavior of those who would lead others into antisocial acts in order to change or control their society, or sometimes to prevent change.

Behavior in social groups, whether they are primitive tribes or complex modern nation-states, can be regarded as points on a simple continuum, as shown in Figure 1–1.

In even the most primitive societies, certain acts or groups of acts have always been universally forbidden, discouraged, or **proscribed**. Such acts include murder, rape, incest, kidnapping, and treason (or some form of rebellion affecting the group's safety and authority). By contrast, most societies have encouraged, sponsored, or **prescribed** other behaviors such as having children, marrying, hunting, growing food, and other actions that benefit the common social welfare.

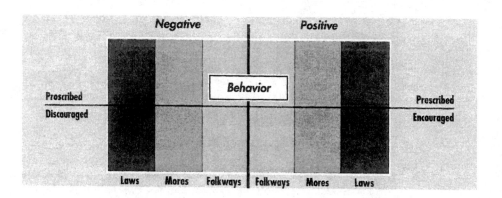

Figure 1–1
The Continuum of Behavior

Behavior that is situated toward the center of the continuum is usually controlled by a set of simple social rules called **folkways**. These rules are enforced by means of mild disapproval (i.e. the raising of an eyebrow, staring, frowning or a look of shock) or by mild encouragement (i.e. no negative reaction, applause, or a smile).

Behaviors that move to the areas a bit farther out toward either end of the continuum shown in Figure 1 are those which serve to either:

1. Threaten the group's safety or social order on one end of the scale or
2. Contribute to the group's improved existence on the other end.

These are generally controlled by a stronger set of rules called **mores**. In early human history mores were enforced by means of strong social disapproval (i.e., verbal abuse, beatings, temporary ostracism, banishment, or even death), or strong encouragement (i.e., dowries, advancement in social or financial status, huge weddings and fertility rites). Many of these informal controls still protect certain mores today.

As societies became more complex, they were required to devise more structured sanctions in order to prevent violation of the mores (*morals*) that were most essential to the group's survival. These sanctions have generally developed into codified forms of written rules, or **laws**, which formalize and describe certain boundaries of behavior and outline specific punishments for their violation. The reward for respecting and obeying laws is simply the ability to continue as a productive member of a social group. Simplified definitions of these social controls are as follows:

- *Folkways*: traditional social customs, including ways of thinking, feeling, or acting common to a social group of people.
- *Mores*: binding moral attitudes, habits, customs, and manners of a particular group of people.
- *Laws*: rules of conduct formally recognized as binding, defined and enforced by a controlling authority.

Terrorism often falls into the range of behaviors that are not only violation of laws, but violation of the politics and practices (*mores*) of a social group or an organization. Often the violation of codified *law* requires that a person call a public safety officer to effect an arrest. All of these aspects are related to the ways that social groups or subcultures chose to respond to transgressions.

Retaliation

The earliest remedy for wrongs done to one's person or property was simply to retaliate as an *individual* against the wrongdoer. In early primitive societies, personal retaliation was accepted and even encouraged by members of the tribal group. This ancient concept of personal justice or revenge could hardly be considered "law." Yet it has influenced the development of most laws and legal systems, especially English Common Law, from which most American criminal and civil law has been derived.

The practice of personal retaliation was later augmented by the **blood feud**, in which the victim's whole family or tribe took revenge on the offender's family or tribe. Because this form of retaliation could easily escalate and result in an endless *vendetta* between the injured factions, some method of control had to be devised to make blood feuds less costly and damaging. Thus the blood feud could be perceived as the earliest form of terrorist activity.

The practice of *physical* retaliation began to develop into a system of criminal law when it became customary for the victim of the wrongdoing to accept *money* or *property* in place of blood vengeance. This custom, when established, is usually dictated by tribal tradition and the relative social status and power of the injured party and the wrongdoer. Custom has always exerted great force among primitive societies. The acceptance of vengeance in the form of a payment (such as cattle, food, or personal services) was usually not compulsory, and victims were still free to take whatever vengeance they wished. Legal historians Albert Kocourek and John Wigmore described this pressure to retaliate:

> It must not be forgotten that the right of personal revenge was also in many cases a duty. A man was bound by all the force of religion to avenge the death of his kinsman. This duty was by universal practice imposed upon the nearest male relative, "the avenger of blood," as he is called in the Scripture accounts. [2]

The need to find better ways to deal with retaliation and prevent its escalation in tribal warfare forced the development of the custom of atonement for wrongs by payment to appease the victim's family or tribe. This custom became known as *lex salica*[3] (or *wergeld*,[4] in Europe). It is still in effect in many Middle Eastern and Far Eastern countries, with the amount of payment based on the injured person's rank and position. *Friedensgeld* was the practice of paying restitution to the Crown, in addition to the injured individuals, for crimes. It later replaced payment to individuals and became the system of fines paid to the state. With fines, the victim disappeared from the criminal justice system, becoming the ignored component of the crime, a player only recently gaining more of a role in the legal process.

Fines and Punishments

How did these simple, voluntary programs become part of an official system of fines and punishments? As tribal leaders, elders, and later kings and emperors, came into power,[5] they began to exert their acquired authority on the negotiations. Wrongdoers could choose to stay away from the proceedings; this was their right. But if they refused to abide by the decided upon and imposed sanctions, they were declared to be outside the law of the family, tribe or nation, literally *outlaws*. There is little doubt that outlawry, or exile, was the first punishment imposed by society,[6] and it heralded the beginning of criminal law as we now know it. Only the goals and objectives they espouse, and the means they use to accomplish them, separate outlaws from terrorists.

Criminal law, even primitive criminal law, requires an element of public action against the wrongdoer, as in a pronouncement of outlawry. Before this element of public action, the backgrounds of criminal law and sanctions seem to have been parallel in most legal systems. The subsequent creation of legal codes and sanctions for different crimes either stressed or refined the vengeance factor, according to the particular society's group values and willingness to enforce the decisions.

Babylonian and Sumerian Codes

Even primitive ethics demanded that a society express its vengeance within a system of regulations and rules. Moses was advised to follow the "*eye for eye, and tooth for tooth*" doctrine stated in Exodus 21:24, but this concept (**lex talionis**) is far older than the Bible. This concept appears in the Sumerian codes and in the code of King Hammurabi of Babylon,[7] compiled over five hundred years before the Book of the Covenant.

Ironically, the area of the Middle East we call Iraq, which we have seen in recent decades as a major source for state-sponsored terrorism and constant wars, was where many scholars agree recorded history, as we know it, began.

In ancient times, the land area now known as modern Iraq was almost equivalent to Mesopotamia, the land between the two rivers (Tigris and Euphrates). The Mesopotamian plain was called the "Fertile Crescent." This region was the birthplace of the varied civilizations that moved us from prehistory to history. An advanced civilization flourished in this region long before those of Egypt, Greece and Rome, for it was here in about 4000 B.C. that the Sumerian culture flourished.

The people of the Tigris and the Euphrates basin were the ancient Sumerians. Using the fertile land and the abundant water supply of the area, they developed sophisticated irrigation systems and created what were probably the first cereal agriculture and the earliest writing. Called cuneiform, this writing was a way of arranging impressions stamped by the wedgelike section of a reed stylus into wet clay. Sumerians invented the wheel in 3700 B.C. and developed a math system based on the numeral 60, which is the basis of time in our modern world. Sumerian society was "matriarchal" and women had a highly respected place. Banking originated in Mesopotamia (Babylon, from "Bab-ili," meaning "Gate of God"), where temples and palaces provided safe places for the storage of valuables. Initially, deposits of grain were accepted and later other goods including cattle, agricultural implements, and precious metals followed.

Land was cultivated for the first time in this area, early calendars were used and the first written alphabet was invented there. Its bountiful land, fresh waters, and varying climate contributed to the creation of deep-rooted civilization that fostered humanity. Mesopotamia is suspected as the location for the "Garden of Eden." Ur of the Chaldees, just north of the traditional site of the Garden of Eden, is about twenty-five miles northeast of Eridu, at present Mughair. It was a great and famous Sumerian city, dating from those early times.

Predating the Babylonian era by about 2,000 years, Noah is believed to have lived in Fara, 100 miles southeast of Babylon. The early Assyrians, some of the earliest people there, were known to be warriors, so the first wars were fought there. The land has been full of wars ever since. The Assyrians were in the northern part of Mesopotamia and the Babylonians more in the middle and southern parts.

After the collapse of the Sumerian civilization, the people were reunited in 1700 B.C. by King Hammurabi of Babylon (1792–1750 B.C.), and the country flourished under the name of Babylonia. Babylonian rule encompassed a huge area covering most of the Tigris-Euphrates river valley from Sumer and the Persian Gulf. King Hammurabi extended his empire northward through the Tigris and Euphrates River valleys and westward to the coast of the Mediterranean. After consolidating his gains under a central government at Babylon, he devoted his energies to protecting his frontiers and fostering the internal prosperity of the Empire. Hammurabi's dynasty, otherwise referred to as the First Dynasty of Babylon, ruled for about 200 years, until 1530 BC. Under the reign of this dynasty, Babylonia entered into a period of extreme prosperity and relative peace. Throughout his long reign he personally supervised navigation, irrigation, agriculture, tax collection, and the erection of many temples and other buildings. Although he was a successful military leader and administrator, Hammurabi is primarily remembered for his codification of the laws governing Babylonian life. Under Hammurabi, the two cultures which compose Mesopotamian civilization (the Assyrians and the Babylonians) achieved complete and harmonious fusion.

Hammurabi was a king and a great lawgiver of the Old Babylonian (Amorite) Dynasty. His law code was produced in the second year of his reign. Many new legal concepts were introduced by the Babylonians, and many have been adopted by other civilizations.

These concepts included:

- Legal protection should be provided to lower classes;
- The state is the authority responsible for enforcing the law;
- Social justice should be guaranteed;
- The punishment should fit the crime.

The Hammurabic Code concept of "An eye for an eye, a tooth for a tooth," is also known as Lex talionis (the law of the claw) and is found in Exodus 21:24. This book covers the exodus of the Hebrews (not yet Jews) from Egypt and the efforts of Moses to lead the tribes toward an understanding of God, as well as forge them into one people.

When people who are fighting injure a pregnant woman so that there is a miscarriage, and yet no further harm follows, the one responsible shall be fined whatever the husband demands, paying as much as the judges determine.

If any harm follows, then you shall give: Life for life, eye for eye, tooth for tooth, hand for hand, foot for foot, burn for burn, wound for wound, stripe for stripe.

As early societies developed more refined language and writing skills, they began to make permanent records of the laws of their leaders, elders, and kingdoms. The Hammurabic Code is viewed by most historians as the first comprehensive attempt at codifying social interaction. The Sumerian codes[8] preceded it by about a century, and the principle of lex talionis was evident in both. The punishments under these codes were harsh and based on vengeance (or talion), in many cases inflicted by the injured party. In the Babylonian code, over two dozen offenses called for the penalty of death. Both codes also prescribed mutilation, whipping, or forced labor as punishments for numerous crimes. It was felt that the severity of the punishment would act as a general deterrence to violation of the codes. Then, as now, this seldom worked, except on the specific individual being deterred. The kinds of punishments applied to slaves and bondservants have been cited by many scholars[9] as the origin of the punishments that in later law applied to all offenders. As historian Gustav Radbruch stated:

> *Applied earlier almost exclusively to slaves, [the mutilating penalties] became used more and more on freemen during the Carolinian period (A.D. 640–1012) and specially for offenses which betokened a base and servile mentality. Up to the end of the Carolinian era, punishments "to hide and hair" were overwhelmingly reserved for slaves. Even death penalties occurred as slave punishments and account for the growing popularity of such penalties in Carolinian times. The aggravated death penalties, combining corporal and capital punishments, have their roots in the penal law governing slaves.[10]*

The early punishments were considered synonymous with slavery; those punished were often required to even have their heads shaved, indicating the "mark of the slave."[11] In Roman days, the extensive use of penal servitude was spurred by the need for workers to perform hard labor in the construction of the great public works demanded by the emperors. The sentence to penal servitude was reserved for the lower classes and usually meant life in chains, working in the mines, rowing galleys of ships, or working on the massive public works of the empire. These were generally a sentence of slow death by hard labor. These sentences carried with them the complete loss of citizenship and liberty and were classified, along with exile and death, as capital punishment. Penal servitude became known as **civil death**, which meant that the offender's property was confiscated in the name of the state and that his wife was declared a widow, eligible to remarry. To society, the offender was, in effect, dead. From the Emperor's viewpoint, many of the historical accounts of uprisings by slaves who wanted freedom, justice and a role in society could easily have been labeled "terrorism."

Crime and Sin

Punishment of the individual in the name of the state also included the concept of superstitious revenge. Here crime was entangled with sin, and punishment in the form of *wergeld* (payment to the victim) or *friedensgeld*[12] (payment to the state) was not sufficient. If society believed the crime might have offended a divinity, the accused had to undergo a long period of progressively harsher punishment in order to appease the gods. Over time the boundaries between church law and state law became progressively more blurred, and the concept of personal responsibility for one's act was combined with the need to "get right with God."[13] Early codes were designed to make the offender's punishment acceptable to both society and God.

Roman and Greek Codes

In the sixth century A.D., Emperor Justinian of Rome caused a vast code of laws to be written, one of the most ambitious early efforts to try to match an equitable amount of punishment to all possible crimes. Roman art of the period depicts a female goddess holding up the "scales of justice" (from Justinian). This metaphor tried to show that codes could be devised that allowed the punishment to perfectly balance the crime without the need for human deliberation. Justinian's effort, as might be expected, bogged down in the morass of administrative details that were required to enforce it.[14] The Code of Justinian did not survive the fall of the Roman Empire, but it left the foundation upon which most of the Western world's legal codes were finally built.

In Greece, the harsh Code of Draco[15] provided the same penalties for offenses by both citizens and slaves, incorporating many of the concepts used in primitive societies (for example, vengeance, outlawry, and blood feuds). To this day, the term "Draconian" is understood to mean harsh and cruel administration of punishment. The Greeks were the first society to allow any citizen (not just the victim) to initiate a complaint and prosecution of an offender in the name of the injured party, clearly illustrating that during that period, the public interest and protection of the social order were becoming more important than individual injury and individual vengeance. It is probably just such Draconian treatment by some social/tribal/religious groups that became the catalyst for early terrorist acts.

The Middle Ages

The Middle Ages were a period of general disorder and chaos. Vast changes in the social structure and the growing influence of the church on everyday life resulted in a divided system of justice. Reformation was viewed as a process of religious, not secular, redemption. As in early civilizations, the sinner had to pay two debts, one to society and another to God. The ordeal was the Church's substitute for a trial, until the practice was abolished in 1215. In trials by ordeal, guilt or innocence was determined by subjecting the accused to dangerous or painful tests in the belief that the innocent would emerge unscathed, whereas the guilty would suffer agonies and die. The brutality of most trials by ordeal ensured a very high percentage of "convictions." In other words, the suspect usually died.

The church expanded the concept of crime to include some new areas, still reflected in modern codes. During the Middle Ages, many sexual activities were seen as especially obnoxious or sinful. Sex offenses usually involved either public or "unnatural" acts, and they provoked horrible punishments, as did heresy and witchcraft. The church justified cruel reprisals as a means of saving the unfortunate sinner from the devil. The zealous movement to stamp out heresy brought on the **Inquisition**[16] and its use of the most vicious tortures imaginable to gain "confessions" and "repentance" from alleged heretics. Thousands and thousands of persons died at the hands of the inquisitioners. Spain and Holland were especially devastated, two places in which these methods were the most extensively used. Punishment was not viewed as an end in itself, but as the offender's only hope of pacifying a wrathful God.

The main contribution of the medieval church is the concept of **free will**. This idea assumes that individuals *choose* to take their actions, good or bad. They could thus be held fully responsible for them. The religious doctrines of eternal punishment, atonement, and spiritual conversion rest on the assumption that individuals who commit sins could have acted differently if they had chosen to do so.

The early legal codes and their administration were usually based on the belief that punishment was necessary to avenge the victim. In early small tribal groups and less complex societies, direct compensation to the victim was used in place of revenge to prevent disintegration of the social structure through extended blood feuds. When those groups began to concentrate their power in a king or similar leader, the concept of crime as an offense against the victim gave way to the idea that crime, however lowly the victim, was an offense against the *state*. In the process, *wergeld* was replaced by *friedensgeld*, and the administration of punishment became the responsibility of the king. Concentrating that power also led to a tendency to ignore victims and their losses, while concentrating on the crime and the criminal.

Punishment

The most common forms of state punishment over the centuries have been death, torture, mutilation, branding, public humiliation, fines, forfeits of property, banishment, transportation, and imprisonment.[17] These acts, and numerous variations on them, have always symbolized retribution for crimes.

The death penalty (killing of the offender in the name of the state) was the most universal form of punishment used among early societies. There was very little knowledge of behavior modification and other modern techniques to control violent persons, and often the feared offenders were condemned to death by hanging, crucifixion, stoning, burning at the stake, drowning, and any other cruel and unusual method the human mind could conceive. As technology advanced, methods for killing offenders became more sophisticated. In the belief that punishment, especially death, would act as a deterrent to others, societies carried out most executions and other lesser punishments in public. The last public execution in the United States took place in Owensboro, Kentucky, on August 14, 1936.

Torture, mutilation, and branding are found in the general category of **corporal punishment** (any physical pain inflicted short of death). Many tortures were used to extract a "confession" from the accused, often resulting in the death penalty for an innocent person. Mutilation was often done in an attempt to match the crime with an "appropriate" punishment. (A liar's tongue was ripped out, a rapist's genitals were removed, a thief's hands were cut off, and so on.) Branding was still practiced as late as the nineteenth century in many countries, including the United States. Corporal punishment was believed to act as a deterrent to other potential offenders.

The public humiliation of offenders was a popular practice in early America, utilizing such devices as the stocks, the pillory, ducking stools, lynching, and branding. The most significant aspect of those punishments was their *public* nature. Offenders were placed in the stocks (sitting down, hands and feet fastened into a locked frame) or in the pillory (standing, with head and hands fastened into a locked frame) and were flogged, spat upon, heaped with spoiled fruits, vegetables and garbage, and reviled by all who passed by.

The ducking stool and the brank were used as common public punishments for gossips. The ducking stool was a chair or platform placed at the end of a long lever, allowing the operator on the bank of a stream to repeatedly dunk the victim. The brank was a birdcage-like instrument placed over the offender's head, containing a plate of iron with sharp spikes in it that extended into the subject's mouth. Any movement of the mouth or tongue would result in painful injury.

Flogging (or whipping) has been a common punishment in almost every Western civilization. The method was used particularly to preserve discipline in domestic, military, and academic settings. It was usually administered by a short lash at the end of a solid handle about three feet long or by a whip made of nine knotted lines or cords fastened to a handle (the famed "cat-o'-nine-tails"), sometimes with sharp spikes worked into the knots. Flogging was a popular method of inducing confessions at heresy trials, as few victims could stand up for long under the tongue of the lash.

Deterrence

As noted, the extensive use of capital and corporal punishment during the Middle Ages reflected, in part, a belief that public punishment would deter potential wrongdoers. This cherished belief has been strongly refuted over the passing years. "It is plain that, however futile it may be, social revenge is the only honest, straightforward, and logical justification for punishing criminals. The claim for deterrence is belied by both history and logic."[18] No matter how society tried to "beat the devil" out of offenders, in most cases the only criminal deterred was the one tortured to death.

Emergence of Secular Law

Christian philosophers who insisted that law was made in heaven compounded the problem of drawing up a set of laws that applied to the actions of men and women in earthly communities. In the fourth century A.D., St. Augustine recognized the need for justice, but only as decreed by God. The issue was somewhat clarified by Thomas Aquinas in the thirteenth century, when he distinguished among three kinds of law:

1. Eternal law, or lex externa
2. Natural law, or lex naturalis
3. Human law, or lex humana[19]

All were intended for the support of the common good. The last, *lex humana*, was considered valid only if it did not conflict with the other two.

As time passed and the secular leaders (kings and other monarchs) became more powerful, these rulers wanted to detach themselves from the divine legal order and its restrictions on their personal power. In the early fourteenth century, many scholars advocated the independence of the monarchy from the Pope. Dante, the Italian poet and philosopher, proposed the establishment of a world state, completely under the rule of secular power.

England's Lord Chancellor, Sir Thomas More, opposed the forces advocating the unification of church and state and died on the executioner's block as a result of his beliefs. He refused to bend ecclesiastical law to suit the marital whims of his king, the fickle Henry VIII. Sir Thomas More was out of step with his era in another sense as well. As an advocate of the seemingly radical theory that punishment could not prevent crime, he was one of the first to see that prevention might require a close look at the conditions that gave rise to crime. In the sixteenth century, unfortunately, this line of thought was far ahead of its time. But Sir Thomas More's ideas persisted and eventually contributed much to the foundation of modern theories in criminology and crime prevention that are the basic principles of modern law and justice.

> The idea of punishment to repay society and expiate one's transgressions against God explains in part why most punishments were cruel and barbarous. Presumably, the hardships of physical torture, social degradation, exile, or financial loss (the four fundamental types of punishment) would be rewarded by eternal joy in heaven. Ironically, those punishments did little to halt the spread of crime: "Even in the era when extremely severe punishment was imposed for crimes of minor importance, no evidence can be found to support the view that punitive measures materially curtailed the volume of crime."[20]

As has been shown, the state and the Church always seemed to devise punishments for perceived wrongs in early societies. The agents of these sanctions, those designated to observe, detect, and respond to violations of societal codes, have formed the basis for law and order throughout history.

Changes in Behavioral Definitions

What is considered right or wrong has been shown capable of being placed on a behavior continuum from prescribed to proscribed. The balance point of the behavioral continuum is not constant, however, and often changes over time, at different times, and in different societies. An example of how changes can be observed *over time* in regard to the folkways, mores and laws about what is considered pornographic material. It was not that long ago that material found on sale at almost every grocery store and bookstall today would have previously gotten the publisher burned at the stake. As attitudes toward the viewing of the human body gradually changed, however, this was reflected in what appeared in print and how society reacted to it in plays, movies, and dress as well. Eventually groups challenged these changes in court with different attitudes about what could and could not be shown. Attempts were made to legislate and regulate such material. The values of the society as a whole are continuously subjected to challenges that test the limits of taste and acceptance. A clear example is the growth of the Internet by leaps and bounds and efforts by concerned citizens and government to balance the right to access pornographic material against denial of access by concerned parents.

In regard to reaction to behaviors at *different times*, one need look no further than the Eighteenth Amendment to the U.S. Constitution, commonly referred to as the Volstead Act (or the Prohibition Act), which in 1919 prohibited the sale of alcohol under punishment of law. Prior to 1919 alcohol was legal to sell and consume in

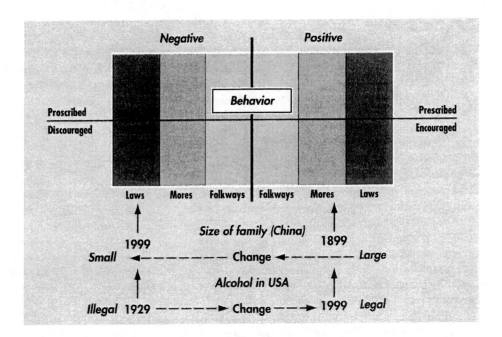

Figure 1-2
Behavior changes
along the continuum
over time and as
conditions vary.

the United States. From that date on, until repeal of prohibition in 1933, sale was illegal but *consumption* was legal. This created a flourishing criminal industry supplying "bootleg" alcoholic beverages for those persons who did not agree with the law. How we can relate this to the continuum of behavior is shown in Figure 1-2.

In the first example, the folkways and mores of the society changed over a long period of time and its members came to agree that the previously strict pornography laws were unnecessary and needed to be relaxed. In the example of legal prohibition of the sale of alcoholic beverages, a minority of private interest groups was able to get the Eighteenth Amendment passed. But since the *law* was not in sync with the *folkways* and *mores* of the society upon which police agencies were told to enforce prohibition, it was generally ignored. As a result, the majority of the people continued to get their alcohol from illegal sources until the laws were finally repealed. It is easy to see that the attitudes within a subculture of a larger society could make a case for terrorism, as a legitimate way to meet their specific needs. This could happen despite the illegality or immorality of the acts if the group could move the pivot point of the continuum of behavior far enough in the direction of *prescribed* behavior. Different societies (as noted, sometimes even subcultures within societies), move the acceptance level on the behavioral continuum based on their perceived needs and wants. For example, the birth/death ratio in the United States is almost even with or below replacement. The growth of industrialization, incredible increases in the productivity and replacement of manual labor with machinery in factories and farms, along with social welfare programs that secured old age make it unnecessary to have large families to provide a workforce and old age security for family heads. As a result, family planning became encouraged and family size shrank. However, in many third world nations, high infant mortality and the lack of provision of social welfare by the government cause great concerns. Large families continue to be the primary means of supplying a large unskilled work force and at least some security for the senior members of their family groupings.

Right or Wrong?

So, what is the appropriate definition of "right" and "wrong?" Why is it "right" to take pencils and paper from the office for your children to use in school, but "wrong" to use that same company's vehicles and fuel for your personal use as a self-awarded "perk"? Societies are constantly faced with the conflict between subgroup ethics and standards and societal ethics and standards. While many say that one must follow the societal "Golden Rule" (*whoever has the gold makes the rules*), this simplistic statement falls into the trap of **situational ethics** and hardly denotes a sense of ethical behavior. The individual is often encouraged by less ethical colleagues (or more passionate advocates of their subgroup goals) in a dissenting minority to "go along to get along." This usually means making a compromise of personal standards in situations that are clearly unethical, immoral or even illegal for the benefit of some higher cause. We all receive a constant barrage of sordid investigative journalism about unethical behavior in the media disclosing scandals by our Congress, televangelists, police, bankers, doctors, teachers, businesspersons, financial advisors, union leaders, and even national leaders. It is therefore not surprising that terrorists are less than vigilant about their own ethics. It is always easy to say "everyone is for doing it" or "everyone is against it" and look the other way from such behavior, or even join in.

As they come to an end, the 1990s may be remembered as a time in history when ethics were often scoffed at, bypassed or ignored. Terrorists often have basic ideals and ethical standards for themselves and their comrades to a very high degree. Governments are charged with "guarding the chicken coop." They must not let themselves succumb to the temptation to become a *fox*. It is critical that the leadership of society provides a positive example, no matter how difficult it may become. Having laid a foundation, we can now move on to the definitions of terrorism in a more enlightened manner.

A View Over Time

A historical perspective may help define the term "terrorism" in regard to a specific time and particular locale. First, we must accept that terrorism, in one form or another, has been around throughout the history of man and society; it did not suddenly appear as a whole new concept in the twentieth century. The statement that "one man's terrorist is another man's patriot" must always be related to the time and location in which it is occurring. We have seen many examples of yesterday's terrorist becoming today's national leader in the historical, political and economic context of change in which terrorism must be operationally defined.

History has used the ideologies of both the left and right in the application of what has been loosely termed "terrorism." The understanding of ideological pressures over time allow us to deal with the reasons put forth for terrorist acts in the twentieth century and those on the horizon of the twenty-first. The ideological commitment of the perpetrators of terrorism can be seen more clearly in this context. The bombing of an airliner over Lockerbie, the slaughter of tourists in Egypt and the Oklahoma City bombing all are seen in a common thread when viewed from the perspective of the terrorist. This in no way justifies such acts. But it leads to a better understanding of the political, religious, and ideological fanaticism that creates a terrorist and leads to terrorist acts.

Some states even sponsor and finance the commission of terrorist acts to provide surrogate warriors for their own agendas without the direct involvement of their people or politicians. Libya, Syria, the former Soviet Union, Iraq and Iran participated in state-sponsored terrorism by surrogates for decades. The relationships and similarities between state-sponsored terrorism and other kinds of individual and group terrorism will be developed throughout this text. We will always be asking about terrorist financing, goals and targets. The study of this topic begs the question of whether or not nations can or want to completely eliminate terrorism. If not, how much is just enough or too much and to what purpose should it be supported? This is why we must look at the many definitions of this age-old practice and apply the right ones at the right times on the continuum.

Terrorism: A Search for a Definition

It is easy to use the terms "terror," "terrorism" and "terrorist" about acts that shock the senses of reasonable people. The *Regime de la Terreur* (**Reign of Terror**) that took place in France has been accepted by most as the first general use of such terms. During the bloody French Revolution, from 1792–1794, those who resisted that revolution faced arrest, imprisonment, and death by guillotine. Most of these actions were without the benefit of trials or legal procedure. Brutal members of the revolutionary group took steps to eliminate every possible threat. They eventually sought out those with even moderate to mild opposition to their cause. Those who considered themselves possible targets of the revolutionaries were finally motivated to take counteraction for their own self-preservation. On July 27, 1794, members of the Jacobin dissenters murdered Robespierre and his council of supporters. The Reign of Terror, in which over four hundred thousand "suspects" (including many women and children) had been imprisoned and thousands hanged and guillotined, finally came to an end. But the seminal concepts of terror tactics as a part of political strategy arose from these bloody episodes.

From this bloody beginning, terrorism and terrorist acts became defined as the systematic application of violence to establish and maintain a new political system. Such a definition might be difficult to use today, primarily because it fails to separate terrorism from other acts of aggression that use terror as only a small component.

For example, terror in conventional warfare between nation-states is a natural byproduct of the violence and confusion of combat. Military objectives are chosen in order to effect the quickest elimination of the enemy force and the destruction or disruption of its command, control, communication, support and supply networks. Victory is decided by force of numbers, skill at arms, weapons superiority, strategy and tactics, or a combination thereof. Terror is not intended to be the *primary factor* in such military actions.

Those soldiers (in war) or citizens frightened into surrender or compliance, but not physically injured, are the real targets of terrorism. Other casualties are easily classified according to the way they were injured or killed. A tentative definition of terrorism is offered for consideration by Rosie:

> "The use and/or threat of repeated violence in support of or in opposition to some authority, where violence is employed to induce fear of similar attack in as many non-immediate victims as possible so that those so threatened accept and comply with the demands of the terrorists."[21]

Within this wordy, but necessarily so, definition we can develop a methodology for describing the behaviors of terrorists acting upon a variety of motives. At the same time, this definition remains neutral with regard to the great variety of individual traits that characterize particular groups. This definition can be applied to political terrorism, revolutionary terrorism, state terrorism and others. It eliminates the need for suggesting a particular type of motivation as part of the definition of terrorism and the temptation to infer that all terrorism is politically motivated.

The placement of a bomb in a department store or the shooting of doctors and staff at an abortion clinic are acts calculated to induce fear and anxiety in a large number of people, a far larger number of people than are likely to be injured by the acts. The perpetrators of the act believe that by such means clients and purveyors can be coerced into abandoning certain commercial practices or medical procedures. Their acts are most definitely acts of terrorism, but are not necessarily politically motivated in the larger sense.

This definition of terrorism is also able to exclude acts of violence in which the terror component is incidental or secondary to some other primary objective. The death of the owner of a major logging company may be the goal of extremists that wish to silence his voice or his particular quality of leadership. The owner could be about to influence some item of legislation that is opposed to the extremist group's goals. The fear generated by the killing is of secondary importance to the actual silencing of that individual. This act should be labeled as "murder" or "assassination" rather than terrorism. If the extremist group were also to issue a statement of demands, however, and threaten that more industrialists and even private citizens would be attacked if demands were not met, then it would be fair to refer to such a group as "terrorists."

It is clear that categorizing someone as a terrorist does not preclude also categorizing that same person as a madman, guerrilla, ideologue, or a revolutionary. A grocer who plays baseball on weekends can be called a baseball player, but he has not stopped being a grocer. The fact is that members of the IRA (Irish Republican Army), PLO (Palestine Liberation Organization), or ETA (*Euzkadi Ta Azkatasuna*) can be seen as **"freedom fighters"** to their sub-group in a political system. At the same time, to others in the system they remain "terrorists." Clearly, without some reference to established definitional parameters, such labels are purely a matter of value judgment. If the person making the judgment does not agree with the objectives of the group using such methods to gain some goal they will describe the group as "terrorists." The group thus categorized immediately denies this, of course, and calls itself a "national liberation army," a "workers' army," or some similar term. The conclusion is that a terrorist group has no legitimacy and therefore its aims have no validity. The label of "terrorist" then becomes a term of derision, and obscures whatever legitimate complaints have inspired the use of terrorist tactics.

In order to understand the phenomenon of terrorism, one must always assess the divergent views of what exactly constitutes terrorism and the definition in use. Reaching a general consensus on the definition of terrorism has generated many debates in the social sciences. No one definition seems to satisfy the broad interpretation of what terrorism is.

Terrorism is a special type of violence. It is a tactic used in peace, conflict, and war. The threat of terrorism is ever present, and an attack is likely to occur when least expected. A terrorist attack may be the event that marks the transition from peace to conflict or war. Combating terrorism is a factor to consider in all military plans and operations. Combating terrorism requires a continuous state of awareness; it is a necessary practice rather than a type of military operation. Terrorism is a criminal offense under nearly every national or international legal code. With few exceptions, acts of terrorism are forbidden in war as they are in times of peace.[22]

Some Approaches to Defining Terrorism

In addition to the broad definition used above, the following are some samples of the diverse definitions used to describe terrorism:

Simple: Violence or threatened violence intended to produce fear or change

Legal: Criminal violence violating legal codes and punishable by the state

Analytical: Specific political and social factors behind individual terrorist acts

State-sponsored: Terrorist groups used to attack Western interests

State: Power of the government used to terrorize its people into submission[23]

In his book *Political Terrorism* (1983), Alex Schmid surveyed one hundred scholars and experts in the field and asked for a definition of terrorism. This analysis found two characteristics of the definition: first, an individual being terrorized and second, the meaning of the terrorist act is derived from its target and victims. Schmid's analysis concluded that the following elements are common throughout the one hundred definitions surveyed. They are as follows:

- Terrorism is an abstract concept with no essence.
- A single definition cannot account for all the possible uses of the term.
- Many different definitions share common elements.
- The meaning of terrorism derives from the victim of target.[24]

Terrorists, the perpetrators of terrorism, believe their cause to be altruistic and serving to better society. Bruce Hoffman, in his most recent work, *Inside Terrorism* (1998), states that the terrorist is fundamentally a violent intellectual, prepared to use and indeed committed to using force in the attainment of his goals (p. 43). He also adds that by distinguishing terrorists from other types of criminals and terrorism from other forms of crime, we come to appreciate that terrorism is:

- ineluctably political in aims and motives;
- violent—or, equally important, threatens violence;
- designed to have far-reaching psychological repercussions beyond the immediate victim of target;
- conducted by an organization with an identifiable chain of command or conspiratorial cell structure (whose members wear no uniform or identifying insignia); and perpetrated by a sub-national group or non-state entity.[25]

Once we accept, however, that terrorism is simply a means to an end, we can apply the term without the inclusion of moral beliefs and sociological or political mumbo-jumbo. The operatives of the PLO are terrorists, but that fact, standing alone, does not mean that their aims and objectives are without validity. IRA members can be described as freedom fighters, but they must also accept being terrorists in their methods of reaching that goal.

Obviously it is easier for one to perceive a long established, freely elected (even dictatorial, religious, or royalist) regime as "legitimate" than it is to accept that a handful of individuals with views significantly different from those of the majority might deserve the same classification. This is especially so if the methods used by the handful of individuals provoke moral indignation by horrific actions against a sanctioned "legitimate" target—the government. When an indiscriminate "enemy" label is applied to those not actually supportive of a dissenting aggressor's objective, the situation becomes far more disturbing, because the aggressors frequently use violence as a means to their ends. Wearing no uniforms to indicate their presence, they employ weapons that they need not personally fire or activate (mail bombs, car bombs, time bombs, etc.). The result is unknown aggressors killing unknown victims for reasons that will not be made clear until after the event.

There will always be some "bottomline" considerations, of course, even when the targets are acceptable "enemies" in the eyes of many onlookers. Violence against former Soviet-backed regimes, for example, finds more favor among Western observers, even when such strikes are easily definable as terrorist actions. But if the nature of the assault transgresses certain unwritten but widely accepted boundaries of "decency" or "fair play," then condemnation is more neutrally applied. The downing of a Russian helicopter gunship by elements of the rebels in Chechnya, for example, is interpreted by all save supporters of the Russians to be more acceptable than the downing of a civilian airliner by the PLO. The deliberate slaughter of armed soldiers in an ambush is more easily accepted than is the slaughter of small children. In descending order, "fair game" for terrorists or dissenters might be depicted as follows:

1. Military personnel
2. Government officials
3. Civilians unconnected in any way with the continuance of the policy against which the terrorist is fighting

This same attenuated sample list might constitute the basis of a target selection for almost any military offensive. On the other hand, an actual terrorist group would consider the following order to be more appropriate for maximum impact:

1. Civilians unconnected in any way with the continuance of the policy against which the group is fighting
2. Government officials
3. Military personnel

This seemingly illogical order is very logical for terrorism because maximum fear and anxiety can be generated by attacks against noncombatants. This demonstrates to the populace as a whole that the targeted regime is unable to protect them. Such actions are generally a far safer technique for the terrorist group than trying to prove that the regime cannot protect itself. Terror groups will frequently have to outrage and cause revulsion in their target audience in order to maintain the required level of terror and anger at the government.

We now have an understanding that while strategies incorporating acts of terrorism in the past centuries have changed somewhat in delivery and methods, the basic purposes of terrorist acts have generally remained constant:

- To bring attention to a perceived grievance or cause by some act or acts that are shocking and attention getting
- To use the media by getting coverage of such acts in order to get the widest possible dissemination of their message
- To contain reaction by the public at large through fear and intimidation and
- To coerce change and destabilize opponents through the threat of further and continued acts until these grievances or causes are recognized and acted upon

Jenkins argued a quarter of a century ago that, "...terrorism is theatre; therefore terrorists do not want a lot of people dead...they want a lot of people watching and listening."[26] This watching and listening has ranged over the centuries from a few villagers who stood by while terrorists acted or gave their speeches to live television coverage of the most vile acts, piped into millions of homes. It is seldom that one hears of the barbarous acts committed in third world countries on the evening news in other than a passing sound bite. But let a few thugs take over a major airliner and the media flock like flies to stand and listen to the demands of the terrorists and broadcast them around the globe. This chapter begins our study of this thing we call "terrorism" and examines the difficulty in deciding just what that means. George Rosie highlights this difficulty:

> Terrorism is a complex, multi-faceted, and often baffling subject. The organizations involved have a way of emerging, splintering, disappearing and then reappearing which makes it very difficult for the average reader to follow. Individuals come and go, are jailed, die, go underground, or apparently vanish. Counter-terror bureaucracies are formed then reformed, names are changed, and leaders are shuffled around as they are promoted, demoted, forced to resign, or put out to pasture. Incidents proliferate across the world, some of which can trigger a chain of events that will destabilize a whole region and bring nations to the edge of ruin. At the same time major terrorist actions can shock for a short while, and then be quickly forgotten (except by those affected by the inevitable tragedy). Treatises are written, theories propounded, grievances aired, tactics discussed, occasionally to some effect, usually not. Causes are picked up by the world's media, examined, probed, and then all too often overlooked, until the next bomb explodes, or the next airliner is hijacked.[27]

We continue our examination of what terrorism is with a few more commonly used definitions. Acts of terrorism conjure emotional responses in the victims (those hurt by the violence and those affected by the fear) as well as in the practitioners. Even the U.S. government cannot agree on one single definition. Listed below are a few more common definitions of terrorism:

- Terrorism is the use or threatened use of force designed to bring about political change–Brian Jenkins
- Terrorism constitutes the illegitimate use of force to achieve a political objective when innocent people are targeted.–Walter Laqueur
- Terrorism is the premeditated, deliberate, systematic murder, mayhem, and threatening of the innocent to create fear and intimidation in order to gain a political or tactical advantage, usually to influence an audience.–James M. Poland
- Terrorism is the unlawful use or threat of violence against persons or property to further political or social objectives. It is usually intended to intimidate or coerce a government, individuals or groups, or to modify their behavior or politics.–U.S. Vice President's Task Force, 1986
- Terrorism is the unlawful use of force or violence against persons or property to intimidate or coerce a government, the civilian population, or any segment thereof, in furtherance of political or social objectives.–FBI definition
- The calculated use of violence or the threat of violence to inculcate fear; intended to coerce or to intimidate governments or societies in the pursuit of goals that are generally political, religious, or ideological–Department of Defense definition[28]

Marine Operations Center. A truck bomb killing–Beruit. CP Picture Archive (AP Wirephoto).

The FBI Construct

The FBI seems to have developed a most useful construct of what is to be considered terrorism in the United States. This issue concerns foreign-power sponsored or foreign-power coordinated activities that:

A. Involve violent acts, dangerous to human life, that are a violation of the criminal laws of the United States or of any state, or that would be a criminal violation if committed within the jurisdiction of the United States or any state

B. Appear to be intended to:
   - intimidate or coerce a civilian population
   - influence the policy of a government by intimidation or coercion
   - affect the conduct of a government by assassination or kidnapping

C. Occur totally outside the United States or transcend national boundaries in terms of the means by which they are accomplished, the persons they appear intended to coerce or intimidate, or the locale in which their perpetrators operate or seek asylum

The FBI investigates terrorist groups in the United States and acts of terrorism directed at Americans overseas. The Bureau received these responsibilities through a series of presidential decisions and legislative acts. The most important of these include the following:

- In April 1982, then-President Ronald Reagan signed a National Security Decision Directive giving the FBI the responsibility of investigating terrorism in the United States.
- The Comprehensive Crime Control Act of 1984 addressed the FBI's role in responding to hostage taking.
- The Omnibus Diplomatic Security and Antiterrorism Act of 1986 expanded the FBI's jurisdiction to include investigating acts of terrorism directed against Americans overseas.

- In 1995, President Clinton signed Presidential Decision Directive 39, entitled U.S. Policy on Counterterrorism, that further articulated and defined the roles of members of the U.S. Counterterrorism Community, including the FBI.

Investigating acts of terrorism overseas includes interviewing victims, collecting forensic evidence, and apprehending terrorist fugitives. The FBI coordinates all overseas investigations with the U.S. Department of State and the host foreign government.[29]

The U.S. Department of Defense (DOD) Construct

Terrorism, as defined by the DOD, is normally considered to be calculated. This simply means that terrorists generally know what they are doing. Their selection of a target is planned and rational. They know the effect they seek. Terrorist violence is neither spontaneous nor random. Terrorism is intended to produce fear in someone other than the victim. In other words, terrorism is a psychological act conducted for its impact on an audience.

The DOD definition, noted earlier, also addresses goals. Terrorism may be motivated by political, religious, or ideological objectives. In a sense, terrorist goals are always political, as extremists driven by religious or ideological beliefs usually seek political power to compel society to conform to their views. The objectives of terrorism distinguish it from other violent acts aimed at personal gain, such as criminal violence. However, the definition permits including violence by organized crime when it seeks to influence government policy. Some drug cartels and other international criminal organizations engage in political action when their activities influence governmental functioning. The essence of terrorism is the intent to induce fear in someone other than its victims to make a government or other audience change its political behavior.

Terrorism is common practice in insurgencies, but insurgents are not necessarily terrorists if they comply with the rules of war and do not engage in those forms of violence identified as terrorist acts. While the legal distinction is clear, it rarely inhibits terrorists who convince themselves that their actions are justified by a higher law. Their single-minded dedication to a goal, however poorly it may be articulated, renders legal sanctions relatively ineffective. In contrast, war is subject to rules of international law. Terrorists recognize no rules. No person, place, or object of value is immune from terrorist attack. There are no innocents.

This situation did not always prevail. Throughout history, extremists have practiced the attack on and killing of political and religious leaders to generate fear and compel a change in behavior. Frequently, terrorism was incidental to other forms of violence, such as war or insurgency. Before the nineteenth century, terrorists usually granted certain categories of people immunity from attack. Like other warriors, terrorists recognized innocents, people not involved in conflict. Terrorists usually excluded women, children, and the elderly from target lists. For example, in late nineteenth century Russia, radicals planning the assassination of Czar Alexander II aborted several planned attacks because they risked harming innocent people. Old-school terrorism was direct; it intended to produce a political effect through the injury or death of the victim.

The development of bureaucratic states led to a profound change in terrorism. Modern governments have continuity that older, charismatic, royal or inherited governments did not. Terrorists found that the death of a single individual, even a monarch, did not necessarily produce the policy changes they sought. Terrorists reacted by turning to an indirect method of attack. By the early twentieth century, terrorists began to attack people previously considered innocents to generate political pressure. These indirect attacks create a public atmosphere of anxiety and undermine confidence in government. Their unpredictability and apparent randomness make it virtually impossible for governments to protect all potential victims. The public demands protection that the state cannot give. Frustrated and fearful, the people then demand that the government make concessions to stop the attacks.

Modern terrorism behavior offers its practitioners many advantages. First, by not recognizing innocents, terrorists have an infinite number of targets. They select their target and determine when, where, and how to attack. The range of choices gives terrorists a high probability of success with minimum risk. If the attack goes wrong or fails to produce the intended results, the terrorists can deny responsibility.

Ironically, as democratic governments become more common, it may be easier for terrorists to operate. The terrorist bombings of the World Trade Center, the Oklahoma City Federal Building and the embassies in Kenya and Tanzania prove how easy it is for terrorists to operate in a free or democratic society. Authoritarian governments whose populace may have a better reason to revolt may also be less constrained by requirements for due process and impartial justice when combating terrorists.

As national leaders and politicians address terrorism, they must consider several relevant characteristics. First, *anyone* can be a victim. (Some terrorists may still operate under cultural restraints, such as a desire to avoid harming women, but essentially, there are no innocents these days.) Second, attacks that may appear to be senseless and random are not. To the perpetrators, their attacks make perfect sense. Acts such as bombing public places of assembly and shooting into crowded restaurants heighten public anxiety. This is the terrorists' immediate objective. Third, the terrorist needs to publicize his attack. If no one knows about it, it will not produce fear. The need for publicity often drives target selection; the greater the symbolic value of the target, the more publicity the attack brings to the terrorists and the more fear it generates. The media often inadvertently provide just the notoriety desired and wanted by the terrorists by covering the event.

Finally, a leader planning for combating terrorism must understand that he cannot protect every possible target all the time. He must also understand that terrorists will likely shift from more protected targets to less protected ones. This is the key to defensive measures.[30]

Motivations of Terrorists

Terrorists are inspired by many different motives. One could separate them into three categories: rational, psychological, and cultural. Many combinations and variations of these factors may shape a terrorist. Rational terrorists think through their goals and options, making a cost-benefit analysis. They seek to determine whether there are less costly or more effective ways to achieve their individual or group objectives other than terrorism. To assess the risk, they weigh the target's defensive capabilities against their own capabilities to attack. They measure the group's capabilities to sustain the effort. The essential question is whether terrorism will work for the desired purpose, given societal conditions at the time. The terrorist's rational analysis is similar to that of a military commander or a business entrepreneur considering available resources and courses of action. Groups considering terrorism as an option ask a crucial question: Can terrorism induce enough anxiety to attain its goals without causing a backlash that will destroy the cause and perhaps the terrorists themselves? To misjudge the answer is to risk disaster.

Psychological motivation for resorting to terrorism derives from the terrorist's personal dissatisfaction with his/her life and accomplishments. This individual finds a reason to be involved in dedicated terrorist action. Although no clear psychopathy is found among terrorists, there is a nearly universal element in them that can be described as the "true believer." Terrorists do not even consider that they may be wrong and that others' views may have some merit. Terrorists tend to project their own antisocial motivations onto others, creating a polarized "us versus them" outlook. They attribute only evil motives to anyone outside their own group. This enables the terrorists to dehumanize their victims and removes any sense of ambiguity from their minds. The resulting clarity of purpose appeals to those who crave violence to relieve their constant anger. The other common characteristic of the psychologically motivated terrorist is the pronounced need to belong to a group. With some terrorists, group acceptance is a stronger motivator than the stated political objectives of the organization. Such individuals define their social status by group acceptance.

Terrorist groups with strong internal motivations find it necessary to justify the group's existence continuously. A terrorist group, as a minimum, must commit violent acts to maintain group self-esteem and legitimacy. Another result of psychological motivation is the intensity of group dynamics among terrorists. They tend to demand unanimity and be intolerant of dissent. With the enemy clearly identified and unequivocally evil, pressure to escalate the frequency and intensity of operations is ever present. The need to belong to the group discourages resignations, and the fear of compromise disallows their acceptance. Compromise is rejected, and terrorist groups lean toward inflexible positions. Having placed themselves beyond the pale, forever unacceptable to ordinary society, they cannot accept compromise. They consider negotiation dishonorable, if not treasonous. This may explain why terrorist groups are prone to fracturing and why the splinters are frequently more violent than their parent group.

Such dynamics also make any announced group goal nearly impossible to achieve. By definition, a group that achieves its stated purpose is no longer needed. As a result, success threatens the psychological well-being of its members. Therefore, when a terrorist group approaches its stated goal it is inclined to redefine it. The group may reject the achievement as false or inadequate or the result of the duplicity of "them." Terrorists groups often suffer from fear of success. One effective psychological defense against success is to define goals so broadly that they are impossible to achieve. Even if the world proclaims the success of a political movement, the terrorists can deny it and fight on.

Cultural concepts also shape values and motivate people to actions that seem unreasonable to foreign observers. Americans, for example, are generally reluctant to appreciate the intense effect that cultural factors have on behavior. They accept the myth that rational behavior guides all human actions. It is easy to reject as unbelievable such things as vendettas, martyrdom, and self-destructive group behavior when they observe them in others. There is disbelief that such things as the destruction of a viable state can be done for the sake of ethnic purity, especially when the resulting ministates become economically unstable.

The treatment of life in general and individual life in particular is a cultural characteristic that has a tremendous impact on terrorism. In societies in which people identify themselves in terms of group membership (family, clan, and tribe), there may be willingness to accept self-sacrifice seldom seen elsewhere. At times, terrorists seem to be eager to give their lives for their organization and cause. The lives of "others," even strangers who they perceive as being wholly evil in the terrorists' value system, can therefore be taken with little or no remorse.

Other factors include the manner in which aggression is channeled and the concepts of social organization. For example, the political structure and its provisions for power transfer shape and level of violence. In some political systems there is effective nonviolent means for the succession to power. A culture may have a high tolerance for nonpolitical violence, such as banditry or ethnic turf battles, and remain relatively free of political violence. The United States, for example, is one of the most violent societies in the world, yet political violence remains a rare aberration. By contrast, France and Germany, with low tolerance for violent crime, both have long histories of political violence.

A major cultural determinant of terrorism is the perception of "outsiders" and anticipation of their threat to ethnic group survival. Fear of cultural dilution or extermination leads to violence that, to someone who does not experience it, seems irrational. All human beings are sensitive to threats to the values by which they identify themselves. These include language, religion, group membership, and homeland or native territory. The possibility of losing any of these can trigger defensive, even xenophobic, reactions.

Religion may be the most volatile of cultural identifiers because it encompasses values and beliefs deeply rooted in their cultural paradigm. A threat to one's religion puts not only the present at risk but also one's entire cultural past and future. Many religions, including Christianity and Islam, are so confident they are right that they have used force to obtain converts or to eliminate nonbelievers. Terrorism in the name of religion can be especially violent and is discussed in Chapter 3. Like all terrorists, those who are religiously motivated view their acts with moral certainty and even divine sanctions. What would otherwise be extraordinary acts of desperation becomes a religious duty in the mind of the religiously motivated terrorist. This helps explain the high level of commitment and willingness to risk death among religious extremist groups.

Terrorism as Criminal Behavior

The broad field of violent activities we try to label as "terrorism" can now be seen as difficult, if not impossible, to define in some simplistic and universal way. There are some specific acts that seem to straddle the behavioral continuum in such a way to cloud the distinctions between criminal acts and terrorist acts. Some so-called terrorist acts are so specific and localized as to be outside the scope of the broad definitions. We shall examine a few of them that seem especially relevant as we enter the twenty-first century.

Hostage-Taking

Taking hostages, whether for political reasons or for extortion of funds to support terrorist groups, is a tactic often used. The policy of the U.S. government, for one, is to make no concessions to terrorists holding official or private U.S. citizens hostage. It will not pay ransom, release prisoners, change its policies, or agree to other acts that might encourage additional terrorism. At the same time, the United States will use every appropriate resource to gain the safe return of American citizens who are held hostage by terrorists.

Hostage-taking is defined under international law (International Convention Against the Taking of Hostages, adopted December 17, 1979). "The seizing or detaining and threatening to kill, injure, or continue to detain a person in order to compel a third party to do or abstain from doing any act as an explicit or implicit condition for the release of the seized or detained person. This activity is also a criminal act in most countries around the world, as a part of extortion or kidnapping for profit."

Basic Premises

It is generally accepted in the international community that governments are responsible for the safety and welfare of persons within the borders of their nations. Terrorist threats and public safety shortcomings in many parts of the world have caused the United States to develop enhanced physical and personal security programs for U.S. personnel, and to establish cooperative arrangements with the U.S. private sector to help warn and protect business travelers. Bilateral counterterrorism assistance programs and close intelligence and law enforcement relationships have been instigated with many nations to help prevent terrorist incidents or resolve them in a manner that will deny the terrorists political or financial benefits from their actions. The United States also seeks effective judicial prosecution and punishment for terrorists and criminals victimizing the U.S. government or its citizens and will use all legal methods to these ends, including extradition alone and, hopefully, in cooperation with other governments.

After many serious incidents, the U.S. government concluded that paying ransom or making other concessions to terrorists in exchange for the release of hostages only increases the danger that others will then be more subject to be taken hostage. U.S. government policy is to reject any demands for ransom, prisoner exchanges, and deals with terrorists in exchange for hostage release. At the same time, every effort will be made, including contact with representatives of the captors, to obtain the release of the hostages without responding to the demands of the terrorists. United States policy also strongly encourages American companies and private citizens not to respond to terrorist ransom demands. It believes that good security practice, relatively modest security expenditures, and continual close cooperation with embassy and local authorities will lower the risk to Americans living in high-threat environments.

While the U.S. government is concerned for the welfare of its citizens, it cannot support requests by companies that host governments violate their own laws or abdicate their normal law enforcement responsibilities. On the other hand, if the employing organization or company of a hostage works closely with local authorities and follows U.S. policy, U.S. Foreign Service posts can be involved actively in efforts to bring the incident to a safe conclusion. This includes providing reasonable administrative services and, if desired by the local authorities and the American organization, full participation in strategy sessions. Requests for U.S. government technical assistance or expertise will be considered on a case-by-case basis. The full extent of U.S. government participation must await an analysis of each specific set of circumstances. Again, we see the problems involved with making precise definitions of who can do what in a situation which may or not be terrorism.

Legal Issues in Hostage Taking

Under current U.S. law, 18 U.S.C 1203 (Act for the Prevention and Punishment of the Crime of Hostage-Taking, enacted October 1984 in implementation of the U.N. convention on hostage-taking), seizure of a U.S. national as a hostage anywhere in the world is a crime, as is any hostage-taking action in which the U.S. government is a target or the hostage-taker is a U.S. national. Such acts are, therefore, subject to investigation by the Federal Bureau of Investigation and to prosecution by U.S. authorities. Actions by private persons or entities that have the effect of aiding and abetting the hostage-taking, concealing knowledge of it from the authorities, or obstructing its investigation, may themselves be in violation of U.S. law.

Assassination

Terrorists like Osama bin Laden, the alleged leader of the bombings of U.S. embassies in Kenya and Tanzania, create fear that they will strike at the United States again. This increases pressure in Washington and around the talk show circuit to reconsider assassination as a method of solving problems with leaders we consider dangerous. The old argument is, "How many lives would we have saved if Hitler had been assassinated in 1938?" This argument is strong, and for a long time many countries have ordered "extreme sanction" on leaders of countries or criminal or terrorist organizations. To cut the head off the snake was considered a good response to perceived danger. But ordering an assassination today would mean straying from long-established policy and practice. This issue is noted in Terrorism Brief 1-2, written after the bombings in Africa.

Time will tell whether or not the United States can garner the backing of the international community to head into a sure to spiral path of assassinations to meet perceived solutions to growing problems. The problem is similar to that of euthanasia. Who decides when a person is so bad or in such bad health that elimination is the only alternative? This issue will have a long discussion period in times when cooler emotions prevail.

Terrorism and Weapons of Mass Destruction

The fact that it is possible for terrorists to mount an attack on a U.S. city with nuclear, chemical or biological weapons, as in the actions of such renegade despots as Saddam Hussien or Muammar Qaddafi, seems to worry few. According to the findings of a nationwide Pew Research Center survey, the public interest or concern on this issue is low. Senator Richard Lugar made this the central issue of his failed Republican presidential campaign in 1996 and did not get much interest from the voters.

Sentiment was mixed in the wake of early terrorist actions in the United States as to whether civil liberties will have to be curbed in order to combat terrorism in this country. By an almost two-to-one margin, Americans first believed that it will not be "necessary for the average person to give up some civil liberties" to curb terrorism. In more recent times, however, more citizens thought some sacrifice of civil liberties would be required. This turnaround was probably influenced by the rhetoric that took place during the standoff with Iraq over their buildup of chemical and biological weapons of mass destruction.

Abortion Clinic Violence

When and how does legitimate protest in a free democracy become terrorism? On January 3, 1997, the peace of the new year was shattered by bomb blasts and injuries at the Northside Family Services Clinic in Atlanta, Georgia, rekindling fears and memories of the bombing at the Summer Olympics in that stately southern city. The

TERRORISM BRIEF 1-2
ASSASSINATION: NEEDED OR NOT?

The FBI, which is investigating the U.S. embassy bombings in Africa that bin Laden allegedly masterminded, says the exiled Saudi multimillionaire undoubtedly will launch another terrorist attack on an American target.

"We can predict with some certainty that we will see a reaction by bin Laden and his organization," FBI Director Louis Freeh told the Senate Judiciary Committee on Thursday. The potential targets are not limited to embassies overseas. "We've identified people in the United States or people who have transitted the United States who are associated with him," Freeh said. Bin Laden, Freeh said, poses "about as serious and imminent a threat as I can imagine."

Against that backdrop, committee members asked Freeh to consider the legality of assassinating bin Laden and other suspected terrorist leaders. "What is present law with respect to their takedown?" said Senator Dianne Feinstein, D-Calif.

Senator Joseph Biden, D-Del., said, "I would very much like a legal memorandum from the FBI, stating whether or not the prohibition against assassination of heads of state applies to organized crime units, and/or terrorist units." While the senators said they were not ready to advocate assassination, even consideration of the idea marked a sharp departure from the long-standing U.S. policy against assassination, a policy driven by pressure from Capitol Hill against the CIA in the mid-1970s.

In an interview after the hearing, Senator Arlen Specter, R-Pa., said the rules forbidding assassinations do not apply to situations in which the United States is virtually at war with an international terrorist organization. "If you're undertaking a military action, there's no limit" on the use of force, Specter said. The United States could send commandos to try to arrest bin Laden, he said. "There's always the possibility that you'll have a firefight. When you have a warrant for someone's arrest you can use whatever force you have, including lethal force," Specter said. Freeh said that while the prohibition against killing heads of state is clear, he was unsure about the legality of assassinating others and would study the question.

In 1976, after extensive hearings that exposed CIA assassination plots, President Ford signed an executive order prohibiting U.S. officials from plotting or engaging in "political assassination." The prohibition was broadened by Presidents Carter and Reagan to state: "No person employed by or acting on behalf of the United States government shall engage in, or conspire to engage in, assassination."

The prohibition is not limited to assassination against heads of state, said Steve Aftergood of the Federation of American Scientists, a Washington-based watchdog group that follows intelligence matters. The legalities of killing a specific person in a military strike are less clear.

Former CIA Director James Woolsey, who also testified before the Judiciary Committee, said, "There's a difference, even though it's a subtle one, between an air strike going at facilities when you know an individual might be there, and going after a single individual." Still, Woolsey said he opposed a deliberate assassination campaign. "First of all it's hard to do. The United States isn't good at it," citing bungled plots in the 1960s to kill Cuban leader Fidel Castro. "It would make it more likely that one or more groups would come back with an assassination attempt aimed at the president."

Following the August 1998 U.S. embassy bombings in Kenya and Tanzania, the Clinton administration planned and executed a cruise missile strike on alleged terrorist assets of bin Laden's in Sudan and Afghanistan. The timing of the strike on was pegged in part to intelligence indicating bin Laden would be at the Afghan camps that day. Officials now believe bin Laden left the site hours before the missiles struck.

"We have to think in a different way than we thought before," Feinstein said. "It's a very dicey thing to get into a situation where you're going to have licensed hit squads. At the same time we need to find ways to be proactive."

SOURCE: JOHN DIAMOND. "SENATORS QUESTION ASSASSINATION LAW." INTERNET WEB SITE: WASHINGTON TIMES. (ASSOCIATED PRESS, WASHINGTON, DC, FRIDAY SEPTEMBER 4, 1998 1:55 AM EDT)

---

first blast occurred at 9:30 AM, while the second blast was set and deliberately delayed to catch federal agents, firemen, ambulance attendants, and clinic workers as they responded to the scene forty-five minutes later. The second blast resulted in major and minor injuries and serious damage to the five-story building less than a week before the twenty-eighth anniversary of the Supreme Court's decision in *Roe* v. *Wade*, which had legalized abortion. Was this explosion simply individual rage and violence or was it a terrorist act?

Terrorism is a technique, a way of engaging in certain types of criminal activity so as to attain particular ends. It is a process by which a group can create an overwhelming fear for coercive purposes. Such fear will then be raised not only in the immediate victims but also within the broader community or society. Such thinking fits nicely within the parameters of the violence used against abortion clinics by extremist pro-life movements across the nation. The technique used in the Atlanta bombings is one well known from the efforts of terrorist groups like the Irish Republican Army (IRA). This method is referred to as the "congregate effect." The goal is to get people to gather around or near the first bombing and then explode the second or third device with devastating impact. Such planning is not typical of a random act of violence by a single person.

As we mentioned earlier, terrorism can be defined as the unlawful use of force or violence against persons or property to intimidate or coerce a government, the civilian population, or any segment thereof, in furtherance of political or social objectives. The acts of violence against abortion clinics by those who wish to have the Supreme Court reverse *Roe* v. *Wade* seem to fall neatly within this definition as well.

SUMMARY

Terrorism is a complex, multifaceted, and often baffling subject. The players involved have a way of rising to prominence, splintering, disappearing for years and then reappearing. Counterterror bureaucracies are formed and reformed, names are changed, and leaders are shuffled around as they are promoted, demoted, or forced to resign. Incidents proliferate across the world, some of which can trigger a chain of events that will destabilize a whole region and bring nations to the edge of ruin. At the same time, major terrorist actions can shock for a short while and then be quickly forgotten (except by those affected by the tragedy). Treatises are written, theories propounded, grievances aired, tactics discussed, occasionally to some effect, usually not. Causes are picked up by the world's media, examined, probed, and then all too often overlooked, until the next bomb explodes, or the next airliner is hijacked. With the various definitions and application of them to specific events, the student now has a good foundation for the study of terrorism and terrorist acts as they shock the senses and promote fear and concern around the world. In the next chapter we shall take a short look at the major theoreticians and practitioners of terrorism and the success and failure of their application to the events of the years since France's "Reign of Terror" in the late eighteenth century. The next chapter will provide a brief history of terrorism, in order to give the student a longer perspective on this issue than just the headlines and television sound bites. The term "the past is prologue" will be the standard throughout the rest of the text, as the student is provided some of the historical underpinnings of the issues that result in terrorism throughout the world. Terrorist causes are often looked upon as bizarre when seen in a context of the present, but most issues (political, religious, racial or ethnic) have a past that needs to be understood. We believe that the student who understands the historical foundations of issues will never be able to view the evening news in the same way.

Terms to Remember

terrorist incident	social control	territoriality
personal property	proscribed	prescribed

Terms to Remember (continued)

folkways

blood feud

free will

corporal punishment

mores

lex talionis

Reign of Terror

civil death

laws

the Inquisition

freedom fighters

Review Questions

Trace the concepts of social response to violence from retaliation through the development of codes and laws.

How did the Inquisition contribute to punishment of offenders of those times?

What are the advantages and disadvantages of vengeance?

Discuss the pros and cons for the use of assassination.

What are the differences between criminal behavior and crime?

Endnotes

1. Cindy C. Combs, *Terrorism in the Twenty-First Century* (Prentice Hall, NJ, 1997), p. 6.
2. Albert Kocourek and John Wigmore, *Evolution of Law, Vol. II: Punitive and Ancient Legal Institutions* (Boston: Little, Brown, 1915), p. 124.
3. *Lex salica* was the fine paid for homicide, and it varied according to the rank, sex, and age of the murdered person. In general, *lex salica* refers to a payment for death or injury.
4. *Wergeld*, which means "man-money," originally referred to the death of an individual and the individual's supposed value to his or her family. It later referred to personal injury as well.
5. Ronald Akers, "Toward a Comparative Definition of Criminal Law," *Journal of Criminal Law, Criminology and Police Science* (1965): 301–6.
6. Kocourek and Wigmore, *Evolution of Law, Vol. II*, p. 126.
7. The Code of Hammurabi is estimated to have been written about 1750 B.C.
8. The Sumerian codes were those of Kings Lipit-Ishtar and Eshnunna and are estimated to date from about 1860 B.C.
9. Thorsten Sellin, "A Look at Prison History," *Federal Probation* (September 1967): 18.
10. Gustav Radbruch, *Elegantiae Juris Criminalis*, 2d ed. (Basel, Switzerland: Verlag für Recht und Gesellschaft A.G., 1950), p. 5.
11. Slaves were also marked by branding on the forehead or by metal collars that could not easily be removed.
12. *Friedensgeld* was the practice of paying restitution to the Crown, in addition to individuals, for crimes. It later replaced payment to individuals and became the system of fines paid to the state. With fines, the victim disappeared from the criminal justice system, becoming the ignored component of the crime.
13. This religious requirement brought the two issues of sin and crime into the same arena and broadened the scope of the church courts. The offender was obligated to make retribution to both God and the state.
14. Emperor Justinian I A.D. 483–565 was a great preserver of Roman law who collected all imperial statutes, issued a digest of all writings of Roman jurists, and wrote a revised code and a textbook for students. His *Corpus Juris Civilis* became the foundation of law in most of continental Europe.

15. Draco, ruler of Greece in 621 B.C., drew up a very harsh and cruel code that used corporal punishment so extensively that it was said to be written not in ink but in blood.

16. The Inquisition was a tribunal established by the Catholic church in the Middle Ages with very wide powers for the suppression of heresy. The tribunal searched out heretics and other offenders rather than waiting for charges to be brought forward (somewhat in the manner of former Senator Joseph McCarthy, who rooted out "Communists" in the early 1950s). Emperor Frederick II made the Inquisition a formal institution in 1224, and it came to an end in 1834.

17. Walter C. Reckless, *The Crime Problem*, 4th ed. (New York: Appleton-Century-Crofts, 1969), p. 497.

18. Harry Elmer Barnes and Negley K. Teeters, *New Horizons in Criminology*, 3d ed. (Englewood Cliffs, N.J.: Prentice-Hall, 1959), p. 286. For a more recent update on deterrence, see Steven Klepper and Daniel Nagin, "The Deterrent Effect of Perceived Certainty and Severity of Punishment Revisited," *Criminology* 36 (1989): 721–46. [bk1]

19. Edwin H. Sutherland, *Criminology* (Philadelphia: Lippincott, 1924), p. 317.

20. Reckless, *The Crime Problem*, p. 504. There is no evidence that increased use of incarceration will lead to lower levels of crime. See David Biles, "Crime and the Use of Prisons," Federal Probation (June 1979): 39–43.

21. George Rosie, *The Directory of International Terrorism* (Paragon House. New York. 1987), p. 7.

22. See, for example, the Hague Regulations of 1907 and the Geneva Conventions of 1949.

23. U.S. Army Field Manual 100–20, "Chapter 8: Combating Terrorism," *Stability and Support Operations* (U.S. Department of Defense, U.S. Government Printing Office, Washington, DC, 1993), Chapter 8.

24. Alex P. Scmid, 1983, *Political Terrorism.*

25. Bruce Hoffman, 1998, *Inside Terrorism.*

26. Brian Jenkins, *International Terrorism: A New Mode of Conflict* (Los Angeles: Crescent, 1975), p. 4.

27. U.S. Army Field Manual 100–20, "Chapter 8: Combating Terrorism."

28. Ibid.

29. Editors. "FBI Counterterrorism Responsibilities." *FBI Website, Appendix Two.* (U.S. Government Printing Office, Washington, DC. Department of Justice, 1996.)

30. Jonathan R. White, 1991, *Terrorism: An Introduction.*

CHAPTER 2

A BRIEF HISTORY OF TERRORISM

If we suppose that humans are by nature wicked, then kindness and love need special explanation. If, on the other hand, we think that the depth of our soul knows only good we must provide an account of wickedness and violence.

John Lachs

OVERVIEW

When did terrorism begin? As noted in the previous chapter, the word "terrorism" was coined during the French Revolution and the Jacobean Reign of Terror. However, this does not mean that individual and group acts of what we might classify as terrorism cannot be traced back into the earliest activities of humankind. Animals make themselves appear to be bigger and more dangerous by puffing up, shrieking or roaring, making false charges and waving arms, flapping ears, and expanding feathers to frighten sexual competitors and dangerous predators. This chapter will examine human violence and how it came to be incorporated into terrorism today. We shall examine the evolution of humankind into the behavior that we have defined (with some difficulty) in Chapter 1. This will give the student a different perspective on the behavioral aspects of violence and violent actions as just another point on the continuum of behavior that was presented in the previous chapter.

VIOLENCE AND TERRORISM

What are the conditions that can generate violence? What is it that allows a person, or group, to apply violence to a situation and believe it to be such a probable, logical or natural response? Violence is the application of great power that results in measurable harm by a conscious decision of the individual committing the act. Violence in this sense has had broad usage in the world, demonstrated by the application of great force to achieve specific short-term goals by agents acting alone, in mobs or as part of an organized group of like-minded individuals.

...if we think of the paradigm of violence as the fury of a wounded or humiliated man, we can readily see that violence, or something very like it, is not even a uniquely human possession. Animals also release their energies in violent and destructive ways; in fact it is its similarity to the behavior of brutes that makes violence so distasteful to the human mind.[1]

In the earliest social groups violence could be controlled by the approbation of the rest of the tribe, all of whom were intimately known to one another. Violent behavior was quickly dealt with by individual or group retaliation. Violent people were considered to be like animals and banished to the wild to live as such. As societies grew in size, close group violence was dealt with through a system of mores and laws. Probably the earliest examples of what might be called terrorist behaviors and acts were those intended to frighten another group into running away or surrendering with the threat of violence (e.g. painting oneself in bright patterns and colors, brandishing weapons and shouting threats, killing enemies and placing their heads on poles, etc.). The point was to so shock the other people that they would either go away or submit to the will of the perpetrators.

Modern societies have huge populations, complex bureaucracies, restrictive laws and procedures. They are composed of diverse religious, ethnic, and racial groupings that often seem out of contact with the power structures. When frustrations peak, use of one-on-one violence as a way to bring attention to an individual (or group) grievance becomes difficult. When a busy and hectic life makes a public official inaccessible, it is a natural temptation for a frustrated constituent to burst into that person's office and pound on his or her desk, sometimes with a weapon. If that is not possible, the constituent might stalk the official, and perhaps seize and shake him or her at a shopping center or in the extreme, find some way to kill him. When an unwilling or uncaring bureaucracy fails to respond to a **perceived grievance** or to right a wrong, it is understandable that the aggrieved, in desperation, may resort to some spectacular and destructive act. This does not mean that shooting a politician or destroying public property is a rational choice to rectify the aggrieved person's situation. The motivation to do something has grown from a sense of anger, frustration and hopelessness. The hapless "victim" begins to see all of society as a single, monstrous machine. It is against this background that the distraught and frustrated person thinks a blow must be struck.

Another aspect of today's global society that tends to make violence an attractive, attention-getting solution is that most significant creative actions are social in nature. There is not that much constructive, autonomous and well thought out action open to those who are not writers, doctors or self-employed professionals. The accomplishment of virtually anything worthwhile today usually includes the cooperation of countless persons or groups. Acts of violence and destruction, however, are among the small number of things a single individual can still resort to. One needs no assistance in shooting at drivers and passengers from a freeway overpass, or driving a vehicle into a group of pedestrians. The natural desire to do something can, for this reason, be easily channeled into a violent act. The frantic and fast-moving nature of modern society makes us feel that it is more important to do something, whether or not what we do is humane or good. The catch phrase so often heard is, "Don't just stand there...do something!" But this concept is meaningless without a clear idea as to whether that something needs to be violent or nonviolent, verbal or physical.

Violence, precisely because it is usually initiated as an individual decision, is something we can do that leaves us feeling active and involved. The act of violence can be fragmented into a logical progression: (1) **formation of intent**, (2) execution and, (3) immediate consequences, all taking place in microseconds within a single individual. The feeling that whatever we do is not something of our own design has been rectified and is replaced by the satisfaction that what we mean, do and observe taking shape are all unique and individual to us.

Violence perpetrated for ideological reasons and for a systematically promoted cause or complaint is much different, however. Organizations in the business of doing such things frequently suffer the problem of too much discussion and very little action. In the mind of an individual person, however, the satisfaction of being told to blow up some representative target does not nearly match the rush of an act both conceived and performed alone. Action planned and ordered by others is something that comes from the group's justification of a cause, or from the release of group anger and resentment. Individuals taking violent action on their own, by contrast, take satisfaction in the unity, rightness and self-empowered nature of their acts. This is obvious in the readiness with which they accept responsibility for their acts and take personal pride in their actions. Acts of violence planned and executed by a group always dilute the credit, and blame is spread so broadly that it fails to satisfy a "righteously angry" individual. If such individuals seek secrecy, it is usually to make sure they won't be caught and can continue their violent behavior.

Lachs presents a surprisingly positive side to the horrors of war. "Many people report that great danger leads to an exhilaration that renders experience vibrant. Some say they can never recapture the keen sense of being alive they felt in battle, or even when they merely supported the war effort."[2] The predictable regularity of most individuals' daily lives seems to validate such claims as believable and natural. Living in a routine and in the cocoon of a safe society eventually makes life seem dull. War makes one contemplate death, feeling its nearness and finality with crystal clarity. Something akin to this effect happens in connection with violence. In these outbursts the adrenaline flows in quantity, the eyes focus tightly into **"tunnel vision"** and blood rushes to the brain and other vital organs. Any soldier in combat or policeman in a shootout can describe this effect. The use of violence, especially physical action that threatens damage, heightens experience. Life's triviality is erased and the person is suddenly standing face to face with the core of human existence, the finality and irreversibility of what might happen. This is a "drug" not available on the street or in a pharmacy, but once experienced is just as addictive.

When Did Violence Become Terrorism?

By definition, at least to the ancient Greek democracies and Roman republics, the **assassination** of Julius Caesar in 44 B.C. was an act of terrorism. This holds true as well, insofar as a modern political assassination is defined, as terrorism.[3] Modern political scientists generally treat assassination, the murder of a head of state or other state official, as a terrorist act whether by an individual acting alone (as Hinkley acted with President Reagan) or in concert with a group (as in the shooting of President Kennedy).

Group terrorism, as opposed to individual acts, became more common as early as the Middle Ages. In fact, the word "assassin" comes from an Arabic term *hashashin*, which literally means "hashish-eater," or one addicted to hashish. It was used to describe a sectarian group of Muslims who were employed by their spiritual and political leader (the local caliph) to spread terror in the form of murder and destruction among religious enemies, including women and children. This was enhanced by the promise of instant acceptance and transport to Paradise if killed themselves.[4] Marco Polo's travel journals included lurid tales of murder committed by these assassins. These early terrorists were motivated not only by promises of eternal reward in the afterlife, but also by unlimited access to hashish and other drugs. Even the Crusaders made mention of this group of fanatics and the terror they inspired.[5]

The region from which the original Assassins emerged was Persia, present-day Iran. In modern times, the Ayatollah Khomeini became the religious leader of the Shi'ites in Iran during its revolution in the late 1970s. It is widely accepted that the young men in the Iran–Iraq wars were told that they would go directly to Paradise if they fought bravely and died for Allah. Stories have been reported from that war of fifteen- and sixteen-years olds walking in waves into the guns of their enemies, the Iraquis, unarmed and unafraid. The potent combination of religious and political fanaticism is the legacy of the Brotherhood of Assassins.

From a deadly combination of religious fanaticism and politics in the 1890s another Brotherhood of Assassins emerged in the Sind region of British India. The **Hur Brotherhood** resembled the earlier Islamic Brotherhood of Assassins and was supressed after considerable bloodshed. Yet another Hur rebellion occurred in Pakistan in the mid-twentieth century. Indeed, much of Pakistan's terrorism comes from its Sikh minority and religious and political dissatisfaction with Muslim Pakistan's leaders continues to take innocent lives in this turbulent region of the world.

Islam, Christianity, Judaism and Hindu are not by doctrine violent religions. Generally speaking, this is true of the other major religions. However, the mixture of religion and politics has quite often resulted in violence, frequently against innocent victims, which makes it, according to the definition suggested in the preceding chapter, terrorism. The Middle East, as the home of three major world religions, has been plagued by a variety of violent sects. The creation of these violent sects, whose blending of religion and politics is similar to the Brotherhood of Assassins, continues to keep the flames of violence burning.

Religion is the "narcotic" which both motivates terrorist actions in its name and deadens consciences to the horror of the slaughter inflicted upon innocent persons. History enables us to examine such motivations in a larger context, gaining a more logical understanding. But retrospect has not helped governments or terrorist organizations to prevent the explosion that occurs when they combine such potentially lethal elements.

Tyrannicide

Over time, assassination became both an ideological statement and a powerful political weapon. The doctrine of **tyrannicide**, the assassination of a political leader (tyrant), was widely practiced throughout Italy and other European countries during the Renaissance. During the Age of Absolutism, Spain and France advocated this solution to the problem of tyrannical leaders. We see much of the same political justification used by leaders of national liberation movements today. Mariana asserted that people necessarily possessed not only the right of rebellion but also the remedy of assassination, stating that "if in no other way it is possible to save the fatherland, the prince should be killed by the sword as a public enemy."[6] Only ten years after Mariana's words were uttered, the monk Francois Favaillac assassinated King Henry III of France. Many leaders since that time have been struck down by persons who have claimed to have acted as instruments of justice against a tyrant. Even President Lincoln's assassin, John Wilkes Booth, saw his act in such a light, as evidenced by his triumphant shout, "*Sic semper tyrannis!*" (Thus always to tyrants!)[7]

Like those committing murder in the name of religion, political assassins have frequently believed they were acting as **"divine instruments"** of justice. Such assassins have viewed themselves as the chosen instruments of a popular legitimacy, rightly and even righteously employed in the destruction of tyrannical rulers. Like the religious fanatics, political assassins have no hesitation in acting as judge, jury, and executioner, spurred by the power of a higher will and authority.

At the end of the eighteenth century and the beginning of the nineteenth, the theory that kings rule by divine appointment began to lose its political grip on Europe. This weakening of the king's divine right to rule allowed those who carried out political offenses such as tyrannicide a more benign atmosphere in which to act. If such terroristic acts were perceived as a way to "right the wrongs" committed by government, then the political assassin was no longer regarded with universal disfavor. Vidal, a leading French legal scholar, has noted that:

> *Whereas formerly the political offender was treated as a public enemy, he is today considered as a friend of the public good, as a man of progress, desirous of bettering the political institutions of his country, having the laudable intentions, hastening the onward march of humanity, his only fault being that he wishes to go too fast, and that he employs in attempting to realize the progress which he desires, means irregular, illegal, and violent.[8]*

Not until the middle of the twentieth century was the murder of a head of state, or any member of his family, formally designated as terrorism. Even today, those who commit the "political" crime of murder of a head of state can often enjoy a type of special protection, in the form of political asylum.[9]

STATE TERRORISM

The use of "irregular, illegal, and violent means" was not, of course, limited to lone political assassins. As we have noted before, the execution of Marie Antoinette on October 16, 1793, and the public guillotining of enemies of the revolution were some of the first incidents to actually be called terrorism. In this instance, the terrorists were not trying to overthrow the government. They were the government!

Therefore, modern individual and group terrorism derives its name from a perfect example of **state terrorism**. This is usually considered to be terrorism committed by a state or state agency against defenseless victims. States have been and continue to be involved from time to time in a wide variety of violent acts against their own citizens and those of other nations.

Guerrilla Warfare

With so many definitions (see Chapter 1), it has become increasingly difficult to differentiate between terrorism and guerrilla warfare. Guerrilla warfare is essentially an armed protest, implemented by means of **"selective violence."** To the extent that the violence in guerrilla warfare remains "selective" it can be considered different from terrorism. The main selective factor is the choice of targets that are military rather than civilian.

"Guerrilla," means "little war," a term which evolved from Spanish resistance to the invasions of Napoleon in 1808. In this war on the Iberian Peninsula, Spanish "guerrillas" aided British military in mounting successful attacks on French encampments. This method of maneuver became the prototype for the twentieth century wars of national liberation. In contemporary guerrilla struggles, indigenous vigilante groups are often supported openly or covertly by the military of other nations.

Ideology and nationalism combined with terror-violence in the **Internal Macedonian Revolutionary Organization (IMRO)**, a group that made its first appearance in 1893. For several years the IMRO waged guerrilla warfare, sometimes employing terrorist tactics, against the Turkish rulers of their region. As in the Iberian conflict, other nations both assisted and interfered in the struggle. Bombings and kidnappings, as well as the murder of civilians and officials, were frequent in this nasty **"little war."** Violence escalated into the Saint Elliah's Rebellion in August of 1903, which was ruthlessly dealt with by Turkish authorities. This struggle left thousands dead on both sides, at least 70,000 homeless, and 200 Macedonian villages in ashes.

Turkey's suppression of similar nationalist struggles on the part of its Armenian population in the early part of the twentieth century helped to create Armenian groups willing to engage in terrorist activities today. These activities, which include bombings and murder reminiscent of the IMRO, have been directed less by nationalism than by a desire for revenge for the ruthless suppression of that earlier nationalism. In this case, savagely suppressed nationalism has spawned vengeful terrorism, whose perpetrators' demands are perhaps even harder to satisfy than were those of the nationalists of earlier decades.

Events in the 1990s in the former Yugoslavia give credence to the concept that repressed nationalism can, in a resurgent form, exact a bloody toll on innocent civilian populations. In the turbulent years before the outbreak of World War I, the Balkan states were engaged in a wide variety of revolutionary violence. Terrorist brigands, calling themselves *Comitatus* ("Committee Men"), covertly sponsored by Greece, Serbia, and Bulgaria (which was also involved in the IMRO struggles), roamed the countryside. In the worst, not the best, tradition of revolutionaries, these brigands terrorized their own countrymen by burning, murdering, and robbing all who stood in their way. The incredible destruction and genocide taking place in the Balkans at the end of the twentieth century exceeds even this pattern.

World War I was, in fact, triggered by a transnational assassination that had its roots in revolutionary terrorism. A secret Serbian terrorist organization, popularly known as the **"Black Hand,"** was both an organization employed by the Serbian government as an unofficial instrument of national foreign policy and a lethal weapon of political protest against the Austro-Hungarian Empire. On June 28, 1914, a nineteen-year-old Serbian trained by the Black Hand murdered the heir to the imperial throne of that empire, Archduke Franz Ferdinand, in Sarajevo. This assassination was the catalyst for a series of events which, within a month's time, grew into a global conflagration. Revolutionary terror-violence triggered international devastation on a scale unprecedented at that time.

Conflict in and around Sarajevo in the late 1990s is partially explained, too, by this early pattern of revolutionary terror-violence. At least twice within the twentieth century, revolutionary terror-violence has been unleashed by groups, governments, and militias against a civilian population, This type of violence makes reconciliation extremely difficult, if not impossible, to achieve. Memories of violence against women and children within families are hard to erase. And repetition of such violence within less than a century makes the creation of a sense of common identity (nationalism) and reconciliation between populations within that region an almost impossible goal.

Revolutions are not by definition terrorist events. Indeed, some have been successfully carried out without resorting to terrorist tactics. It is increasingly difficult, however, for an untrained and sparsely equipped indigenous army to wage a successful guerrilla war against a national standing army. With mounting frustration in the face of apparently insurmountable odds, it is increasingly easy to resort to terror-violence to achieve by psychological force what it is not possible to achieve by force of arms.

Nowhere else in this century has the role of liberationist combined more thoroughly with that of terrorist than in the actions of the militant group usually known as the **Irish Republican Army (IRA)**. This group's guerrilla campaign of murder and terror, growing out of the Sinn Fein political movement in 1916, provoked the British to respond in kind, with a counterterror campaign. This struggle offers insights in several historical respects. In addition to being, in part, a blend of nationalism and terrorism, it is also a contemporary example of the potent mixture of religion and politics. Catholic Ireland has long resented Protestant Britain's domination of its politics. Northern Ireland, which remains under British rule, is predominantly Protestant, with a large Catholic minority.

Thus, the lines of battle are drawn along both nationalistic and religious lines. Catholics in Northern Ireland have tended to support a unification of those northern provinces with the Irish Republic, whereas Protestants in Northern Ireland have demanded continued British rule. The legacy of hatred and mistrust bred by generations of violence is so bitter that an end to the violence seemed, until the end of the twentieth century, unlikely. The cyclical nature of violence can indeed create a deadly spiral. (See Chapter 4 for details.)

CYCLICAL NATURE OF TERROR

Terrorist violence has too often created a cycle of violence, with those against whom the terror-violence is first carried out becoming so angered that they resort to terrorism in response. Each violent act frequently causes equally violent reactions. When the violence is unselective, when innocent people are victimized by car bombs and random violence, the reactive violence is also likely to "break all the rules" in the selection of targets, and become another form of terrorist violence. "Round and round it goes and where it stops nobody knows," seems to be the theme song of terrorism.

Most revolutionary groups assert that it is terrorism by the state which provokes, and justifies, acts of terror-violence by nonstate groups seeking to change the government or its policies. The relationship between terror-violence by the state and that of nonstate groups and individuals is evident in the history of many modern nation-states. But the nature of that relationship is still the subject of many debates.

Perhaps the most prominent proponents of individual and collective violence as a means of destroying governments and social institutions were the Russian anarchists. These were revolutionaries within Russia who sought an end to the Czarist state of the late nineteenth century. "Force only yields to force," and terror would provide the mechanism of change, according to the Russian radical theorist Alexander Serno-Solovevich.[10]

In the writings of two of the most prominent spokesmen for **revolutionary anarchism**, Mikhail Bakunin and Sergei Nechaev, one finds philosophies often echoed by modern terrorists. Bakunin, for example, advocated in his National Catechism (1866) the use of "selective, discriminate terror." Nechaev, in his work, Revolutionary Catechism, went further in advocating both the theory and practice of pervasive terror-violence. He asserted of the revolutionary:

Day and night he must have one single thought, one single purpose: merciless destruction. With this aim in view, tirelessly and in cold blood, he must always be prepared to kill with his own hands anyone who stands in the way of achieving his goals.[11]

This is surely a very large step in the evolution of a terrorist from the use of a lone political assassin in earlier centuries. Even the religious fanatics of the Assassins were arguably less willing to kill "anyone" to achieve a political objective. But this difference may well have existed more on paper than it did in practice. In spite of this written willingness to kill "anyone" who stood in the way, even the Socialist Revolutionary Party resorted primarily to selective terror-violence, and took special pains to avoid endangering innocent bystanders. For instance, the poet Ivan Kalialev, who assassinated the Grand Duke Sergius on the night of February 2, 1905, had passed up an opportunity earlier that evening to throw the bomb because the Grand Duchess and some of her nieces and nephews were also in the Grand Duke's carriage. Although an attempt was made to kill Tzar Alexander II as early as 1866, the first generation of Russian terrorists generally resorted to violence only to punish traitors and police spies, or to retaliate against brutal treatment of political prisoners.

With the creation of the *Zemiya I Volva* (the Will of the People) in 1879, political assassination of a wide range of targets began to become a normal form of political protest, becoming part of an intense cycle of terror and counterterror. This revolutionary group believed that terrorism should be used to compromise the best of governmental power, to give constant proof that it is possible to fight the government, and to strengthen thereby the revolutionary spirit of the people and its faith in the success of the cause.[12]

A blending of revolutionary and state terror-violence began to take place during this time. The assassinations of Tsar Alexander II in 1881 and of First Minister Peter Stolypin in 1911 were incidents that produced periods of counterterrorism (in the form of state repression). This repression probably accelerated the revolutionary movement responsible for those assassinations. Terrorist acts of assassination, inspired by brutal repression in the Czarist state, provoked further state terrorism, which in turn the inspired revolutionary movement to further acts of violence.

The **Union of Russian Men** formed to combat the growing revolutionary movement "by all means" was not only sanctioned by the Tsar, but granted special protection by him. This reactionary group engaged in a variety of terrorist activities, including but not limited to political murders, torture, and bombing. The Okrana (the Czarist secret police) also used vicious counterterror against the militant revolutionaries in an unabated attack until World War I began.

George Kennon, commenting on the rising tide of terrorism in Russia during the last half of the nineteenth century, explained the relationship of state and revolutionary terrorism in this way:

> Wrong a man...deny him all redress, exile him if he complains, gag him if he cries out, strike him in the face if he struggles, and at the last he will stab and throw bombs.[13]

Some of the seeds of a more widespread and random terror-violence had been sown in the revolutionary and anarchistic movements of the late nineteenth century. But, by the beginning of the twentieth century, terror-violence was still principally directed toward political assassination. Between 1881 and 1912, at least ten national leaders lost their lives to assassinations.

The cyclical nature of terror is also evident in the events surrounding the creation of the state of Israel. The terrorism spawned in Nazi Germany helped to create a cycle of violence that still grips the Middle East today. After losing World War I, the Central Powers collapsed and the Armistice Agreement of November 1918 was signed. Within Germany, however, a large number of right-wing paramilitary organizations began to grow. In ideology, terrorist method, and political role, these groups were in many respects the historical heirs of the Brotherhood of Assassins. They were also the nucleus for the German Reichswehr.

Under the leadership of the **Reichswehr**, Germany began to commit the greatest atrocities the world had ever recorded. Organized state terrorism reached its zenith in Nazi Germany, and produced victims numbering in the millions, the majority Jewish. Many Jews sought to flee the terror and emigrate to Palestine, which at that time was under British mandate and, by 1940, was engaged in closing the gates to Jewish immigration. Palestine was, in fact, already occupied by Arabs. As the population balance began to swing away from the indigenous Arab population toward the immigrant Jews, the British government sought to stem the tide of refugees.

The Haganah, a Zionist underground army, and the Irgun Zvai Leumi, a Zionist militant force willing to use terrorist tactics, pursued terrorism against the British forces in Palestine. Bombing, murder, and assassination became the order of the day, as British counterviolence met with escalating Haganah and **Irgun** terrorsim. (Around and around...) When the Irgun bombed the King David Hotel, in which many innocent persons died or were seriously injured, British determination to quell the rebellion waned.

But during the struggle to gain a homeland free of Nazi terror, the Irgun had also committed terrorist acts against the indigenous population. Israel finally declared itself to be an independent state in 1948. Then, some of the dispossessed people within its borders and those who fled to surrounding states began a terrorism campaign against the new nation of Israel, whose terror-violence against the Palestinian people sparked a conflict which continues to rend the fragile fabric of peace in the Middle East today. Born in bloodshed, violence, and desperation, Israel continues to struggle against the terrorist violence that its very creation may have evoked.

THE KU KLUX KLAN: AMERICA'S HOME GROWN TERRORISM

The United States is not immune to the use of terrorist actions by some of its citizens. We now discuss a history of hate in America. Not the natural discord that characterizes a democracy, but the irrational, murderous hate that has led men and women throughout our history to extremes of violence against others simply because of their race, nationality, religion or lifestyle. Since 1865, the Ku Klux Klan (KKK) has provided a vehicle for this kind of hatred in America, and its members have been responsible for atrocities that are difficult for most people to even imagine. Today, while the traditional Klan has declined, there are many other groups that go by a variety of names and symbols and are at least as dangerous as the KKK.

Some of them are teenagers who shave their heads and wear swastika tattoos and call themselves Skinheads. Some of them are young men who wear camouflage fatigues and practice guerrilla warfare tactics. Some of them are conservatively dressed professionals who publish journals filled with their bizarre beliefs. These ideas range from denying that the Nazi Holocaust ever happened to the conviction that the federal government is an illegal body and that all governing power should rest with county sheriffs. Despite their peculiarities, they all share the deep-seated hatred and resentment that has given life to the Klan and terrorized minorities and Jews in this country for more than a century.

The Klan itself has had three periods of significant strength in American history: in the later nineteenth century, the 1920s, and the 1950s and early 1960s, when the civil rights movement was at its height. The Klan had a resurgence in the 1970s, but did not reach its past level of influence. Since then, the Klan has become just one element in a much broader spectrum of white supremacist activity. It's important to understand, however, that violent prejudice is not limited to the Ku Klux Klan or any other white supremacist organization. Every year, bombings, assaults, murders, and arsons are committed by people who have no ties to an organized group, but who share their extreme hatred.

Knowing the past is critical to making sense of the present. Historical research explains the roots of racism and prejudice which sustain the Ku Klux Klan. As for current events, that is an even easier lesson for most minorities who grew up in the racially torn years of the 1950s. Young civil rights activists working alongside John Lewis, Andrew Young, the late Dr. Martin Luther King, Jr., Julian Bond, and many others, saw the Ku Klux Klan as an all too visible power in many of the places they went to organize voter registration and protest segregation. They knew what the Klan was, and often had a pretty good idea of who the members were. They also knew what the Klan would do to them if they could get away with it.

For many years the KKK quite literally could get away with murder. The Ku Klux Klan was an instrument of fear, and black people, Jews and even white civil rights workers knew that the fear was intended to control them, to keep things as they had been in the South through slavery, and after that ended, through Jim Crow. This fear and terror of the Klan was very real, because for a long time the Klan had the power of Southern society on their side. But in time that changed. It is a tribute to our laws that the Klan gradually was unmasked, and its illegal activities checked.

Now, of course, you can turn on your television set and see people in Klan robes or military uniforms again handing out hate literature on the Town Square. You can read in any newspaper of crosses again burned in folks' yards, and it seems as if we were back in the 1960s. Some say the Klan today should just be ignored. History, however, won't let us ignore current events. Those who would use violence to deny others their rights can't be ignored. The law must be exercised to stay strong. And even racists must learn to respect the law. The knowledge of the background of the KKK and its battle with the law points out the current reasons why hate groups can't be ignored. It is not a pretty part of American history. Some of the things you read here will make you angry or ashamed; some will turn your stomach. But it is important that we try to understand the villains as well as the heroes in our past, if we are to continue building a nation where equality and democracy are preserved.[14]

From Social Clubs the KKK Became a Band of Terrorists

The origin of the Ku Klux Klan was a carefully guarded secret for years, although there were many theories to explain its beginnings. One popular notion held that the Ku Klux Klan was originally a secret order of Chinese opium smugglers. Another claimed Confederate prisoners during the war began it. The most ridiculous theory attributed the name to some ancient Jewish document referring to the Hebrews enslaved by Egyptian pharaohs.

In fact, the beginning of the Klan involved nothing so sinister, subversive or ancient as the theories supposed. It was the boredom of small town life that led six young Confederate veterans to gather around a fireplace on a December evening in 1865 and form a social club. The place was Pulaski, Tennessee, near the Alabama border. When they reassembled a week later, the six young men were full of ideas for their new society. It would be secret, to heighten the amusement of the thing. And the titles for the various offices were to have names as preposterous-sounding as possible, partly for the fun of it and partly to avoid any military or political implications.

Thus the head of the group was called the Grand Cyclops. His assistant was the Grand Magi, there was to be a Grand Turk to greet all candidates for admission, a Grand Scribe to act as secretary, Night Hawks for messengers and a Lictor to be the guard. The members, when the six young men found some to join, would be called Ghouls. But what would be the name for the society itself? The founders were determined to come up with something unusual and mysterious. Being well educated, they turned to Greek. After tossing around a number of ideas, Richard R. Reed suggested the word "kuklos," from which the English words "circle" and "cycle" are derived. Another member, Captain John B. Kennedy, had an ear for alliteration and added the word "clan." After tinkering with the sound for a while they settled on "Ku Klux Klan." The selection of the name, chance though it was, had a great deal to do with the Klan's early success. Something about the sound aroused curiosity and gave the fledgling club an immediate air of mystery, as did the initials KKK., which were soon to take on such terrifying significance.

Soon after the founders named the Klan, they decided to do a bit of showing off. They disguised themselves in sheets and then galloped their horses through the quiet streets of little Pulaski. Their ride created such a stir that the men decided to adopt the sheets as the official regalia of the Ku Klux Klan. And they added to the effect by making grotesque masks and tall pointed hats. The founders also performed elaborate initiation ceremonies for new members. Their ceremony was similar to the hazing popular in college fraternities. It consisted of blindfolding the candidate, subjecting him to a series of silly oaths and rough handling, and finally bringing him before a "royal altar" where he was to be invested with a "royal crown." The altar turned out to be a mirror and the crown two large donkey's ears. Ridiculous though it sounds today, that was the high point of the earliest activities of the Ku Klux Klan.

Had that been all there was to the Ku Klux Klan, it probably would have disappeared as quietly as it was born. But at some point in early 1866 the club, enlarged with new members from nearby towns, began to have a chilling effect on local blacks. The intimidating night rides were soon the centerpiece of the hooded order. Bands of white-sheeted ghouls paid late night visits to black homes, admonishing the terrified occupants to behave themselves and threatening more visits if they didn't. It didn't take long for the threats to be converted into violence against blacks, who insisted on exercising their new rights and freedom. Before its six founders realized what had happened, the Ku Klux Klan had become something they may not have originally intended—something deadly serious.[15]

Victims of the Klan

In the hands of violent men, the Ku Klux Klan has been responsible for some of the worst bloodshed and terrorism in American history. Its weapons have ranged from the whip to dynamite, and down through the years its tactics have included hanging, acid branding, tar-and-feathering, torture, shooting, stabbing, clubbing, firebranding, castration and other forms of mutilation. Its list of victims will never be fully documented because now and in times past many of them were too afraid to report their suffering to the authorities.

The nature of the victims has been as varied as the means of terror the Klan has employed. Blacks were the first targets and have always been and remain today the most likely to be attacked. Carpetbaggers and whites that advocated equality of the races were added to the Klan hate list early in the organization's existence. In the 1920s, Jews, Catholics, labor leaders and strikers, socialists, immigrants and Orientals also felt the sting of Klan whips. By the 1980s, Klan and neo-Nazi criminals had broadened the enemy list to include Asians, Hispanics, Indians, and homosexuals. The most violent of today's neo-Nazis view the federal government as their foremost enemy; some have gone to prison for plotting to kill federal officials and judges. A white civil rights lawyer was named along with prominent Jews on a white supremacist hit list. The man at the top of that list, radio talk show host Alan Berg, was murdered by revolutionary neo-Nazis in Denver. The one thing that the federal officials, civil rights lawyer and talk show host had in common was their vocal opposition to the Klan and its extremist views.

One of the great many Klan crimes documented from the Reconstruction period was the murder of Alexander Boyd in Green County, Alabama, in 1869. Boyd was the prosecuting attorney of the county, which at that time was plagued by Klan activity. He was an unpopular man who had left the South during the war, returned to join the hated Republican Party, and won appointment as solicitor. When three young blacks were arrested on murder charges and subsequently found dead in the countryside, the Ku Klux Klan was immediately suspected and Boyd announced that he knew the names of the guilty parties and would bring them to justice. The following night, a band of more than thirty-five Klansmen rode into Eutaw and to the tavern where Boyd lived. They forced the night clerk to let them into Boyd's room, then riddled him with bullets, including two through the forehead. Then the Klansmen remounted their horses like vigilantes in the West who hanged horse thieves and desperados, circled the town square once for effect, and rode out of town. The epitaph on Boyd's tombstone could have been applied to thousands of blacks and whites over the years. It read: "Murdered by the Ku Klux!"

In the aftermath of the Civil War, lynching came to mean gruesome mob attacks, usually ending in a hanging. Lynching escalated in the late nineteenth century and in 1892 alone, 162 blacks and 69 whites were lynched. The annual death rate for blacks by lynching ranged from 50 to more than a hundred from 1892 until 1925. Although lynching has become rare in the last quarter of this century, it has not disappeared. In 1981, Klansmen in Mobile, Ala., picked a young black student off the street, cut his throat and hung him from a tree limb in a residential neighborhood, for no reason except that they wanted to kill a black person. And lynching is still the symbol of punishment for Klan enemies. Today's most radical racists, who are more frequently seen wearing business suits or camouflage fatigues than Klan robes, refer to the "day of the rope" as the turning point for their white revolution.

The image of a man hanging lifeless by a rope from a tree limb has become a symbol of the worst of Klan violence. Between 1889 and 1941, 3,811 black people were lynched, for "crimes," such as threatening to sue a white man attempting to register to vote, joining labor unions, being "disrespectful" to a white man, or looking at a white woman. During the American Revolution, the term "Lynch Law" described an informal court run by Colonel Charles Lynch of Bedford County, Virginia, who "tried" Tories and criminals in an effort to restore law and order to the frontier.

Lynch's punishments consisted generally of fines or an occasional whipping. In the 1850s, "Lynch Law" was used by the KKK and later as a common phrase, to describe the hanging of one of their objects of hate.[16]

CONTEMPORARY EVENTS: HISTORICAL ROOTS

Is contemporary terrorism different and, if so, then in what ways? One reason for briefly reviewing the historical pattern and roots of terrorism is to be able to discover whether that pattern remains accurate in the contemporary world. If terrorism today is just like the terrorism of previous centuries, then we can use historical patterns to predict behavior and to construct responses based on successful attempts to combat this phenomenon in the past.

If terrorism today is different, however, then historical patterns will be less useful in designing responses, although such patterns may still be of use in understanding the dynamics of the phenomenon. Terrorism has clearly existed before this century. What we need to know as we prepare for yet another century is whether twentieth-century terrorism was significantly different from its historical counterparts.

We have established that prior to the twentieth century, terrorism existed in many forms: political assassins, lethal groups of religious zealots and drug-crazed murderers and dedicated revolutionaries, whose violence is tied to state repression. All of these forms of terrorism still exist in the modern world. But there are important differences. Examination of these differences may help us to understand our contemporary terrorism.

- *Political assassination*: Terrorist acts are no longer directed solely or even primarily at heads of state. Security precautions to guard such persons against attack have made it very difficult for a lone assassin to successfully murder such a person. The assassination in 1995 of Yitzak Rabin, Prime Minister of Israel, demonstrated that it is not, of course, impossible for such an attack to occur with success. However, in the latter part of the twentieth century, attacks have been made with greater frequency on individuals of less significance but who were easier for the assassin to attack. This broadens the range of acceptable victims well beyond the realm justified under the doctrine of tyrannicide.

- *Drugs, religious fanaticism, and political murders*: While this lethal combination still exists in the contemporary world, the relationship between these elements has changed considerably. During the Middle Ages, the caliph rewarded his Assassins with drugs for successfully completed murders of his religious opponents. Today, drugs are used to finance the lethal expeditions of religious zealots, whose targets are not only those of another religion within their community, but include whole nations or groups of nations whose citizens are regarded by the zealots as legitimate targets for murder. Again, this is a drastic broadening of the category of acceptable potential victims.

- *Piracy*: While piracy on the sea has waned somewhat in recent years (although the incident involving the Achille Lauro has reminded us that such piracy still occurs), air piracy has more than taken its place. During the 1970s and 1980s, airline hijacking has become a fairly commonplace occurrence. Whereas pirates of old sought primarily material gain (with political gain a pleasant byproduct for certain governments), modern air pirates have tended to seek political gain first. So although the treatment of victims of piracy has remained essentially the same (pirates throughout the ages have tended to treat their victims as completely expendable), the purpose or goal of the act has changed radically.

- *State-sponsored terrorism*: Modern governments have expanded the concept of "licensed" pirates. Terrorism has, in fact, become an institutionalized form of foreign policy for many nations. Governments privately and sometimes publicly sponsor groups involved in terrorist activities. Moreover, in the latter half of the twentieth century, governments increasingly became involved in revolutionary movements, providing assistance for either the foreign revolutionaries or the foreign regime against which the revolution was fighting. This has blurred the lines between those involved in the fighting of a war, and those who are merely innocent bystanders.[7]

Related to these differences between historical and modern terrorism are important developments in the contemporary world. Modern methods of travel, for example, make it possible to carry out an assassination in the morning in Country X and be halfway around the world from that nation within a matter of hours.

Modern communications, too, have created a "smaller world." Events in places like Nigeria, Cape Town or Sri Lanka, for instance, are immediately transmitted in a dozen ways to New York City, Seattle or Omaha. Such communications, too, have served to expand the theater and enlarge the audience to which the terrorist plays his drama of death and violence. To catch the attention of America, third world terrorists need not travel to New York City with a bomb; they need only plant a bomb in Lagos.

The dramatic increase in the arsenal of weapons available to modern terrorists is also worth consideration. The would-be assassin does not need to rely on a small handgun to eliminate his victim. A **letter bomb** can do the job without endangering the perpetrator, as the Unabomber in the United States has demonstrated.

The potential for destruction through chemical and biological weapons has not yet been fully tapped, although the sarin gas attacks in subways in Japan in 1995 gave ample evidence of the potential for such weapons when used in the very vulnerable mass transit systems of a modern nation. Perhaps, until recently, the consequences of using such weapons were too dramatic for most groups to contemplate. But modern technology has certainly put at the terrorist's disposal a vast array of lethal and largely indiscriminate weapons, of which the **sarin toxin** apparently used in Japan represents only a very simple example. With this arsenal, the selection of victims has become devastatingly indiscriminate. One can be a victim simply by riding a subway train to work—a necessary act for millions of innocent people.

As historical precedents for terrorism grow, it becomes very hard to distinguish between legitimate and illegitimate violence. As the nations born of illegitimate violence, such as Ireland and Israel, become themselves steeped in illegitimate violence, it is increasingly difficult to condemn the terrorist methods employed in the struggles for independence and survival. The longer the history of terrorism grows, the harder it is to make a label of "terrorism" stick to the actions of any group or nation.

SUMMARY

If violence begets terrorism then terrorism is as old as society and began with the first peoples of the earth. This history chapter was not very long. It was done that way to intentionally tweak the curiosity of the student and, hopefully, make them want more. Understanding terrorism without learning something about the history of a terrorist group, individual terrorists and the conditions that spawned them is like eating soup without salt. It feeds the body but is pretty bland and tasteless. Following chapters will involve places, cultures and issues with strange names and exotic locations as well as familiar names and places that have been touched by terrorism. Some will be covered in more depth than others. All of them will tell the student something about the social, religious or economic conditions that allowed the cancer of violence to grow into terrorism, by the state or by groups of people that have gone beyond the pale. The next part will take the student on a trip around the world looking at the most significant terroristic locations. We will start with the "problems" of Northern Ireland and move on to Western Europe and every region of the globe

Terms to Remember

perceived grievance	formation of intent	tunnel vision
assassination	Hur Brotherhood	tyrannicide
divine instruments	State terrorism	selective violence
guerrilla	IMRO	little war
Black Hand	IRA	revolutionary anarchism
Union of Russian Men	Reichswehr	Irgun
sarin toxin	letter bomb	

Review Questions

Describe what violence is and how it differs from terrorism.

Explain the three logical progressions that one must follow in order for a violent act to occur.

Where did the term assassination originate? Expand on that story.

Describe the concept of a "little war" and what it means in comparison with terrorism.

Discuss the differences between state-sponsored terrorism and actions by an individual or group as terrorism against the state.

Endnotes

1. John Lachs, "Violence as Response to Alienation,"*Alienation and Violence* (Science Reviews Ltd., Middlesex, U.K., 1988), pp. 147–160.
2. John Lachs, "Violence as Response to Alienation," p. 155.
3. Cindy C. Combs, *Terrorism in the Twenty-First Century* (Prentice-Hall, Upper Saddle River, NJ, 1997), p. 20.
4. Cindy C. Combs, *Terrorism in the Twenty-First Century*, p. 21 (ibid.).
5. See M. Hodgson, *The Order of the Assassins* (1960); B. Lewis, *The Assassins: A Radical Sect in Islam* (1968).
6. B. Hurwood, *Society and the Assassin: A Background Book on Political Murder* (London: International Institute for Strategic Studies, 1970), p. 29.
7. Carl Sandburg, *Abraham Lincoln: The War Years* (Cambridge: MIT Press, 1939), vol. 4, p. 482.
8. Vidal, *Cours de Droit Criminal et de Science Pententiare*, 5th ed. (Paris: Institute de Paris Press, 1916), pp. 110–112.

9. Political asylum is sanctuary or refuge for a person who has committed such a crime as assassination of a political figure. It is granted by one government against requests by another government for the extradition of that person to be prosecuted for this 'political' crime. *Funk and Wagnall's Standard Dictionary*, Comprehensive International Ed., vol. 1, p. 86, col. 3.

10. F. Venturi, *Roots of Revolution: A History of the Populist and Socialist Movements in Nineteenth Century Russia*, F. Haskell, trans. (London: International Institute for Strategic Studies, 1966), p. 281.

11. F. Venturi, *Roots of Revolution: A History of the Populist and Socialist Movements in Nineteenth Century Russia*, p. 281 (ibid.).

12. Sandra Stencel, "Terrorism: An Idea Whose Time Has Come" in *Skeptic, The Forum for Contemporary History*, no. 11 (January-February 1976), pp. 4–5.

13. Robert Friedlander, *Terrorism: Documents of International and Local Control* (Dobbs Ferry, NY: Oceana, 1979), p. 26.

14. Julian Bond, "Why Study the Klan?" *Special Report. The Ku Klux Klan: A History of Racism and Violence* (Southern Poverty Law Center, Montgomery, AL, 1991) p.5.

15. Editors. "The Terror of The Nightrider" *Special Report. The Ku Klux Klan: A History of racism and Violence.* (Southern Poverty Law Center, Montgomery, AL, 1991), p. 10.

16. Editors, "Victims of the Klan," *Special Report. The Ku Klux Klan: A History of Racism and Violence* (Southern Poverty Law Center, Montgomery, AL, 1991), pp. 25–25.

17. Cindy C. Combs, *Terrorism in the Twenty-First Century*, pp. 31–32.

CHAPTER 3

STATE AND RELIGIOUS SPONSORED TERRORISM

"Traditional state sponsors of terrorism, I believe, will take increasing care to distance themselves from terrorist operations they may sponsor."

–Peter Probst

OVERVIEW

In this chapter the student will examine state terrorism, both internal (against its own people or dissenters) or external (using or funding outside terrorist groups or individuals). Such sponsorship offers a real threat to international stability and security. Internal terrorism can often inspire resistance movements to form and these often resort to terrorist tactics. This cycle of terror-violence can result in a whirlwind that will envelop all within its reach, both innocent and guilty. External terror, as practiced by some states, has resulted in the proliferation of terrorist attacks worldwide. Even states whose official policy specifically rejects the use of terror have been guilty of providing financial and operational aid, often clandestinely, to those who would promote terrorism. With the exception of a few states, such as Iran and Libya, most states have attempted to keep their dealings with terrorists a secret as much as possible.

Few states have been as successful as Syria in placing a foot firmly on both sides of the terrorism issue. President Assad is perhaps the only one with whom the western nations were able to deal in attempting to bring peace to Lebanon. These western states are forced into turning a blind eye to obvious funding, training and equipping of terrorists of many stripes. There is equal reluctance by the western powers to take him to task, as they had Qadhafi of Libya, over the extent to which the Syrian military provided intelligence to terrorist attack teams.

Thus we begin to examine the intricate weave of terrorist activities that are supported by what the U.S. Secretary of State refers to as the "big seven" in providing state sponsorship of terrorism in the 1970s to the end of the century. These are Cuba, Iran, Iraq, Libya, North Korea, Sudan, and Syria. Cuba is on the wane with the collapse of the Soviet Union, the former totalitarian state that perhaps provided the most sponsorship of terrorism in its cold war against the United States. First we examine the pros and cons of state or state-sponsored terrorism as a means to an end in today's world.

STATE TERRORISM AS WARFARE IN THE 21ST CENTURY

For many years, terrorism was perceived as a contest between two sides: on the one hand, a group of people or an organization, and on the other, a sovereign state. However, during the course of the second half of the twentieth century, various countries began to use terrorist organizations to promote state interests in the international domain. In some cases, states have established **"puppet" terrorist organizations**, whose purpose is to act on behalf of the sponsoring state, to further the interests of the state, and to represent its positions on domestic or regional fronts. In other cases, states sponsor existing organizations on the basis of mutual interests.

The Patron State provides its beneficiary terrorist organization with political support, financial assistance, and the sponsorship necessary to maintain and expand its struggle. The patron uses the beneficiary to perpetrate acts of terrorism as a means of spreading the former's ideology throughout the world. In some cases, the patron ultimately expects the beneficiary to gain control of the state in which it resides or to impart its ideology to broad sections of the general public.

State-sponsored terrorism can achieve strategic ends where the use of conventional armed forces is not practical or effective. The high costs of modern warfare, and concern about nonconventional escalation, as well as the danger of defeat and the unwillingness to appear as the aggressor, have turned terrorism into an efficient, convenient, and generally discreet weapon for attaining state interests in the international realm.

Is terrorism to become the preferred method of warfare in the next century? The willingness of nation-states to adopt terrorism and covert insurgency as instruments of foreign policy makes this question essential to answer. Just consider terrorism tactics as an instrument of war:

- Low cost financially: Terrorism offers a relatively inexpensive method of making a point by insurgent groups who lack the finances, personnel or the armament to win against a nation's army on a conventional battlefield. Terrorist tactics also can provide small, non-"superpower" nations a low cost way to wage war, whether overtly or clandestinely, on a hostile state whose resources provide a serious obstacle to waging a full-scale war.

- Low cost politically: For states, particularly those who can successfully provide and hide clandestine support for terrorist groups, the political cost can be quite low, as long as such support remains secret. On the other hand, profit from arms sales might become temptingly high. When such support is not too obvious, as with Libya, other nations have often tended to look the other way.

- High yield financially: States that are arms dealers to terrorists can usually profit quite handsomely, with little or no political, military or economic impact. Sometimes being caught results in the recall of a couple of ambassadors, but seldom has any impact on diplomatic or trade relations.

- High yield politically: For dissenters who decide to use terrorism as a political weapon, the political currency can be very high in value. This is especially true when the targeted government reactions are not supported by the citizen in the middle and could lead to a regime being ousted from power. Major concessions can then be "bought" when a successful terrorist incident shocks the populace too much.

- Low risk politically and financially: Financing of terrorist operations can be much less than for a fully equipped and trained army. And, the individuals carrying out these operations are not subjected to as much risk as they would be in conventional warfare. In a successful terrorist operation, the rewards are often very big. For a failed operation, the losses are generally small, unless the failure can be traced to a state sponsor. Finding these linkages has become very costly in financial and, more importantly, in political terms.[1]

What deters individuals and nations from engaging in this high-profit, low-risk terrorist form of warfare? Nuclear warfare is generally accepted as unthinkable and unconventional or counterinsurgent warfare, as both Vietnam and Afghanistan seem to have illustrated, seems too expensive and often unwinnable today. Is pondering whether or not individuals and nations will turn more and more to terrorism an equally unthinkable alternative?

As noted above, the U.S. Secretary of State and other allies around the world have clearly designated seven governments as supporting state sponsorship of terrorism. These are: Iran, Iraq, Libya, North Korea, Sudan, Syria and Cuba. These governments have and are providing support to international terrorism, either by engaging in terrorist activity themselves or by providing arms, training, **safe havens**, diplomatic facilities, financial backing, logistic and/or other support to terrorists.

The U.S. policy of bringing maximum pressure to bear on state sponsors of terrorism and encouraging other countries to do likewise has paid significant dividends. There has been a marked decline in state-sponsored terrorism in recent years. A broad range of bilateral and multilateral sanctions serves to discourage state sponsors of terrorism from continuing their support for international acts of terrorism, but continued pressure is essential.

Notwithstanding some conciliatory statements in the months after President Khatami's inauguration in August 1997, Iran still remains the most active state sponsor of terrorism. There is little evidence that Iranian policy has changed, and Iran continues both to provide significant support to terrorist organizations and for the assassination of dissidents abroad.

Iraq provides safe havens, weapons and funds to a number of terrorists and terrorist groups. It continues to rebuild its intelligence network, which had been used to support international terrorist activity, but there is no credible evidence to prove active Iraqi participation in terrorist activity in 1997. It seems the presence of U.N. inspectors—although acceptance of them is a political game of "chicken," on again and off again with Saddam Hussein—may be putting a damper on Iraqi support of terrorists.

Libyan intelligence agents Abdel Basset al-Megrahi, right, and Lamen Khalifa Fhimah wanted in connection for the 1988 bombing of Pan Am flight 103. The United States and Britain are considering a trial of the two Libyan suspects in The Netherlands under Scottish law. CP Picture Archive (AP Photo)

Libya also continues to provide safe havens, training sites and funding to actual or accused terrorists. Qadhafi remains obdurate about refusing to hand over the two suspects in the **Pan Am 103** bombing and the six suspects named by French authorities in the attack on UTA 772. Libya also refuses to comply fully with U.N. Security Council sanctions imposed because of Libyan involvement in both bombings. In addition, Libya continues to provide support to a number of Middle Eastern terrorist groups, including the ANO, PU, and the PFLP-GC. Credible evidence indicates Libyan terrorists abducted the prominent dissident and human rights activist Mansur Kikhia, who was a legal permanent resident of the United States in 1993, and executed him in early 1994.

Although North Korea has had terrible hardships imposed on it in recent years, it has not been proven conclusively to have been linked to any acts of international terrorism since the 1987 midair bombing of **KAL 858.** But the North Korean government continues to provide sanctuary for five hijackers of a Japanese airliner.

Sudan has been prominent in the news recently as one of the targets of United States retaliation for the bombings of the embassies in Kenya and Tanzania. The targets were suspected chemical weapons factories supported by Usama bin Ladin. Sudan still denies that this is factual. Prior to this incident, Sudan had taken some positive steps on terrorism. But it still has not complied with U.N. Security Council resolutions that demand an end to Sudanese support for terrorism and Sudanese protection for the three suspects involved with the 1995 assassination attempt against Egyptian President Mubarak in Addis Ababa. Moreover, Sudan continues to allow its territory to be used for safe havens, training and as a transit point by terrorists.

While there has been no conclusive evidence of direct Syrian involvement in acts of international terrorism since 1986, Syria continues to provide sanctuary and support for a number of terrorist groups that seek to disrupt the Middle East Peace Process. In the framework of these changes, it is possible to see significant differences between Syria's use of the "terror weapon" in the 1990s in comparison with the past. The Syrians are now careful to use **"terrorist subcontractors"** and refrain from direct involvement in terrorism as a result of lessons learned in the 1980s. Second, the order of priorities of the targets of terror has changed. Israel has become a preferred target, whereas western countries have ceased to be direct targets of terrorism initiated by the Syrians.

Although there is no evidence to indicate that Cuba has sponsored any international terrorist activity in recent years following the collapse of the Soviet Union and a developing tourist-oriented economy, it still provides sanctuary to terrorists from several different terrorist organizations. Cuba also maintains strong links with other state sponsors of terrorism.

STATE-SPONSORED TERRORISM: THE BIG SEVEN

Iran

This Islamic nation remained the most active state sponsor of terrorism at the end of 1997. Tehran continued to be involved in the planning and execution of terrorist acts by its own agents and by surrogates such as the **Lebanese Hizballah**, and continued to fund and train known terrorist groups throughout 1997. Although the August 1997 accession of President Khatami has resulted in more conciliatory Iranian public statements, such as public condemnations of terrorist attacks by Algerian and Egyptian groups, Iranian support for terrorism remains in place.

Tehran conducted at least thirteen assassinations in 1997, the majority of which were carried out in northern Iraq. Iran's targets normally include, but are not limited to, members of the regime's main opposition groups, including the **Kurdish Democratic Party of Iran (KDPI)** and the Mujahedin-e Khalq (MEK). Elsewhere in Iraq, in January 1997 Iranian agents tried to attack the Baghdad headquarters of the MEK using a "supermortar" of a design similar to that discovered aboard the Iranian ship "Kolahdooz" by Belgian customs authorities in early 1996. The attack was unsuccessful, resulting in the death of one person and some damage to an Iraqi hospital building.

April 1997 witnessed the conclusion of the trial in Germany of an Iranian and four Lebanese for the 1992 killing of Iranian Kurdish dissidents, one of whom was then Secretary General of the KDPI, in Berlin's Mykonos restaurant. A German judge found the Iranian and three of the Lebanese guilty of the murders. Two defendants, Kazem Darabi and Abbas Rhayel, were sentenced to life in prison. Two others, Yousef Amin and Muhammad Atris, received sentences of eleven years and five years and three months, respectively. The fifth defendant, Ayatollah Ayad, was acquitted. The court stated that the Government of Iran had followed a deliberate policy of liquidating the regime's opponents who lived outside Iran, including the opposition KDPI. The judge further stated that the Mykonos murders had been approved at the most senior levels of the Iranian Government by an extra-legal committee whose members included the Minister of Intelligence and Security, the Foreign Minister, the President, and the Supreme Leader. As a result of elections in May, however, individuals other than those who were involved in the **Mykonos murders** now hold the positions of Minister of Intelligence and Security, Foreign Minister, and President. In March 1996, a German court issued an arrest warrant in this case for Ali Fallahian, the former Iranian Minister of Intelligence and Security.

Iran continues to provide support in the form of training, money, and/or weapons to a variety of terrorist groups, such as Lebanese Hizballah, Hamas, and the PIJ. The Iranian Government continues to oppose recognition of Israel and to encourage violent rejection of the Middle East Peace Process. In the fall of 1997, Tehran hosted numerous representatives of terrorist groups, including Hamas, Lebanese Hizballah, the PIJ, and the Egyptian *al-Gama'at al-Islamya* at a conference of "Liberation Movements." Participants reportedly discussed the jihad, establishing greater coordination between certain groups, and an increase in support for some groups. In October, the Algerian Government accused Tehran of training and equipping Algerian terrorists.

Iran still provides safe haven to elements of the **PKK**, a Turkish separatist group that has conducted numerous terrorist attacks in Turkey and on Turkish targets in Europe. Following a late 1997 Turkish incursion into northern Iran in pursuit of PKK cadres, Tehran protested the violation of its territory but in 1997 made no effort to remove the PKK from Iranian territory.

In November, Iran's Minister of Foreign Affairs, Dr. Kamal Kharrazi, publicly condemned the terrorist attack by the Egyptian al-Gama'at al-Islamya on tourists at Luxor, Egypt. Similarly, in early January 1998, the Foreign Ministry's official spokesman, Mahmud Mohammadi, also condemned the vicious attacks on civilians during the Muslim month of Ramadan (late December 1997 to early January 1998) "no matter who was responsible." (President Khatemi, in a January 1998 CNN interview, agreed that terrorist attacks against noncombatants, including Israeli women and children, should be condemned.)

The Palestinian organization most loyal to the Iranian revolutionary ideology is the **Palestinian Islamic Jihad**. In spite of its being a Sunni organization, the Iranian revolution sees in it an example to be followed. After the deportation of its leader, Fathi Shqaqi, from the Gaza Strip, the ties between Iran and the organization have been strengthened, particularly in the field of Iranian military assistance. Instructors of the Guardians of the Revolution give regular military instruction courses to the organization's activists from at home and abroad, as well as in the Hizballah camps in Lebanon and Iran. Iran also provides the organization's activists with logistic support, including Iranian identification papers.

Iranian Terror Against Israel

Since the "Madrid Conference" in October 1991, Iran has been active in attempting to disrupt the peace process in the Middle East, which threatens to increase Iran's political isolation in the region, to limit its influence and interests in Lebanon. This opposition lead Iran to strengthen its ties with those Palestinian organizations that oppose the peace process, such as The Palestinian Islamic Jihad (PIJ), Hamas and the various "fronts." Iran hoped that terrorist attacks carried out by the Palestinian organizations, together with those perpetrated by Hizballah, would hamper the Israeli-Palestinian negotiations and undermine Yasser Arafat's position. This goal concurs with the basic Iranian hostility towards Israel that originates from the regime's Islamic religious ideology. Iran refuses to recognize Israel's existence, and refers to Israel as "the occupation regime of al-Quds," and constantly calls for the destruction of Israel.

Iran does not conceal its ties with the Palestinian organizations that oppose the political process. Furthermore, these organizations make public their connections and cooperation with Iran. Most of the Palestinian organizations that oppose the peace process participated in the "Conferences for the Support of the Uprising" organized by Tehran (4–6 December 1990; 19–22 October 1991).

During these highly publicized conferences, the leaders of the Palestinian organizations met with the top political echelons in Iran. A special committee headed by the Iranian Vice President in charge of Parliamentary and Legal Affairs, Attalla Maharjani, was formed as a result of Tehran's decision to provide the "Palestinian uprising" with financial, military, political and humanitarian support. An Iranian **"Fund for the Martyrs"** gives financial and humanitarian assistance to the Palestinians, in support of the "jihad." Within the framework of Iran's efforts to instill its hostility toward Israel into the rest of the Muslim world, Khomeini declared the last Friday of the month of Ramadan "*al-Quds* Day" to mark the Muslims' aspirations to liberate Jerusalem.

In February 1996 at a meeting in Damascus with the leaders of the ten Palestinian opposition organizations, Iran's Vice President Habibi stressed the need to coordinate the struggle against Israel. Iran also justified the terrorist suicide bombings in Jerusalem and Ashkelon (25 February 1996) and described them as the answer to Israel's "inhumane" policy towards the Palestinians.

IRANIAN ASSISTANCE TO PALESTINIAN TERRORIST ORGANIZATIONS

Palestinian Islamic Jihad

A militant by the name of Khaled Zaqarna of Jenin was given extensive military training in January 1995 at the Hizballah camp in the Baka'a Valley, as well as at the Guardians of the Revolution's camp in Ba'albek, Lebanon. There he underwent advanced training in light weapons, the handling of mines and Lau antitank rockets. He was then infiltrated into the Palestinian territories to establish an extensive network in support of suicide bombings.

Iran also aided the PIJ in laying the groundwork for terrorist attacks abroad. At the beginning of 1996, the organization's representative in Iran visited Turkey to prepare for the training in Iran of several of the organization's activists. These activists were due to infiltrate back into Israel in order to carry out terrorist attacks. The Turkish security authorities arrested some of the PIJ militants and one of them, Khalil Atta, was arrested in Israel. Atta was one of nine PIJ militants who were trained in Iran in the period of July–September 1995.

Hamas

Since 1992, Iran has drawn closer to **Hamas**, which it feels to be the leading Islamic movement. At the foundation of their relationship lies their common interest in the disruption of the political process, and their efforts to undermine the PLO. These common goals transcend the ideological variance between them due to religious differences between the Sunni Hamas and the Shi'ite Iran. These ties are manifest themselves in frequent high-level meetings between the two sides, and the relative importance of the Hamas representative in Tehran. For example, a Hamas delegation headed by two top activists, Imad Alami, Chairman of the Internal Committee, and Mustafa Qanu, the representative in Syria, visited Iran in October 1995 and met with high-ranking Iranian officials.

In addition to political ties, Iran also provides Hamas with military assistance. The movement's activists train on a regular basis at the camps of Hizballah and the Guardians of the Revolution in Lebanon, as well as in Iran. This includes training for suicide attacks. Several Iranian-trained militants succeeded in infiltrating back into the Territories under Palestinian Authority control. Israel has arrested Hamas activists who admitted that they were trained by Iranian instructors in the Baka'a Valley, in Lebanon, and in Iran. The training included the use of light weapons, photography and sabotage.

Iran also gives Hamas financial assistance. In 1992, several million dollars were transferred to Hamas' account, including money originating from the Iranian "Fund for the Martyrs," which grants assistance to victims of the "Palestinian Uprising."

Hizballah

The Hizballah organization is the spearhead for Iran in its use of terrorism in general, and in its fight against Israel in particular. The organization began its large-scale terror acts in 1982, when its militants blew up the American Embassy in Beirut, killing 61 people and wounding more than 120. Later, it was behind a series of terror attacks against western targets, among them the suicide bombing of the Marines Headquarters in Beirut (23 October 1983) and the French Military Headquarters in Beirut, in which 241 Americans and 56 French soldiers were killed. In the 1980s, Hizballah activists were involved in the kidnapping of western citizens in Lebanon whom they held as hostages. In some cases, this was done on Iranian orders, for the purpose of obtaining economic or political concessions from western governments, such as the release of Iranian or Lebanese terrorists imprisoned in western Europe.

Iran provides financial assistance on a large scale to **Hizballah**, reaching, according to some estimates, millions of dollars a year. It also gives tactical assistance in terror attacks against Israel, through the Guardians of the Revolution units posted in the Baka'a Valley. The Hizballah General Secretary, Hassan Nasrallah, made public Iranian support in an interview given to al-Wast (March 1996), where he stated that his organization receives financial and political assistance to continue, in his words, "the legitimate struggle against Israel."

Iran has been Hizballah's main weapons supplier since its establishment. Iranian assistance includes a wide range of weapons and ammunition, such as mortars, Sagger anti-tank rockets, mines, explosives and small arms. As far as is known, the largest arms consignment sent by Iran to Lebanon was in February/March 1992 in the wake of the incidents between Israel and the Hizballah. Since then, there have been no significant arms consignments dispatched by air, probably due to Syrian objection. However, six trucks carrying arms from Iran to Lebanon were apprehended in Turkey in mid-January 1996. Thus it can be assumed that Iran is now making extensive use of the land route to transfer arms to Hizballah.

Iranian assistance to Hizballah in training is mostly advice and supervision of the Hizballah's training program. The organization's militants themselves carry out the basic instruction. The Guardians of the Revolution, the training arm of the al-Quds Forces, provide higher level instruction in Iran, mainly at the al-Quds Force training base, "Imam Ali," in northern Tehran. Training includes courses for officers, company commanders, commandos, and courses in communications and powered-gliders.

Since the Islamic regime came to power in 1979, it has consistently acted to eliminate Iranian opposition activists outside the country and has invested considerable intelligence efforts in surveillance and tracking down of anyone perceived as a threat to the regime. Examples of this activity became glaringly obvious in the wake of the following trials in which Iran was implicated:

- The liquidation of Iran's former Prime Minister, Shahpur Bakhtiar, the leader of one of the main Iranian opposition groups (6 Aug. 91) in France. The investigation of this incident led to the arrest of three Iranians, including a diplomat, who probably belonged to the Iranian Intelligence Ministry. The trial exposed the involvement of various Iranian agencies (the Ministry of Communication, diplomatic representatives, commercial companies, "Iran Air") which assisted in the liquidation. One of the accused was sentenced to life imprisonment, another was given a 10-year prison sentence, and the diplomat was acquitted owing to lack of evidence and returned to Iran.

- The liquidation of high ranking activists belonging to the Iranian Democratic Kurdish Party (17 Sept. 92) at the Mykonos restaurant in Berlin. This operation was carried out by a squad composed of Hizballah and Iranian intelligence operatives, headed by a member of the Islamic Students Association in Germany, Khatem Dara'abi, who apparently was employed by the Iranian Intelligence Ministry as the liaison between the Iranian Consulate in Berlin and the hit team. Dara'abi and four other Shi'ite activists were arrested by the German police. German security officials stressed the involvement of Iranian Intelligence and the Guards of the Islamic Revolution in the affair.

- The German Federal Prosecution issued a warrant for the arrest of the Minister of Iranian Intelligence, Falakhian, who is accused of ordering the liquidation of the opposition members.

Since Rasfanjani's rise to power in 1989, scores of Iranian opposition members have been liquidated worldwide, among them:

- Abdol Rahman Qassemlo, General Secretary of the Kurdish Democratic Party of Iran (13 July 89);
- Kazen Rahavi (in Switzerland, 24 April 90);
- Muhammad Hussein Naghdi, the representative of the National Opposition Council in Italy (the umbrella organization of the Iranian regime's Opposition) (16 March 93).[2]

In 1996, the Iranian regime continued to act against the opposition worldwide, particularly against their main centers in Iraq and Turkey. One example is the assassination (on 20 February 96) in Istanbul of two activists from **Mujahedin-e Khalq** by Iranian intelligence agents and the assassination of another Mujahedin-e Khalq activist in Baghdad (7 March 96). There has been a rise in the volume of Iranian efforts to increase intelligence capabilities in the Kurdish district in Iraq, in order to direct subversive activity, inter alia, against opposition targets there.

Today, Iran seems to be making an effort to improve its relations with the west and to try and appear in a more positive light, and refrains from carrying out terror attacks in western Europe. However, should an occasion present itself, Iran does not hesitate to rise to it. Totally deniable emissaries prevent the attacks from being traced directly to their source, Iran. For proof one need look no farther than the specially built Howitzer mortar intercepted on an Iranian vessel on its way from Iran to Antwerp port (14 March 96). This mortar, addressed to a shop with Iranian intelligence connections in Germany and ready for activation, was probably intended for a future terror attack against Iranian opposition members or Israeli/Jewish targets in Europe.

TERRORISM BRIEF 3–1
THE RUSHDIE AFFAIR

Within the framework of Iranian terror, it is worth mentioning the obsessive and unrelenting pursuit and incitement campaign which Iran was conducting against the writer Salman Rushdie, author of *The Satanic Verses*, whom they perceive to be the symbol of the degradation of Islamic values. Khomeini's "fatwa" or religious ruling (February 1989) permits the shedding of his blood and calls for his liquidation, and also of anyone who knowingly helped to publish his novel. The Iranians are continuing to persecute Rushdie in spite of the strong criticism voiced by the West against them, which continues to overshadow the improvement in relations between the West and Iran. The Iranians have placed a large reward on Rushdie's head and their intelligence apparatus has spared no efforts in trying to locate him, as well as trying to prevent the distribution of his book by eliminating publishers and translators. On 11 July 1993, the Japanese scholar, Hitushi Igarashi, who translated the book into Japanese, was murdered. And in Norway William Nygaard, the local publisher of *The Satanic Verses*, was badly injured in an assassination attempt (11 October 1993). In spite of Iranian pragmatic officials' efforts to find a solution to the Rushdie affair, by giving him a written commitment that he would not be harmed, the religious establishment insists on adhering to Khomeini's ruling and refuses any compromise.

Ayatollah Hassan Sanei offered $2 million for Salman Rushdie's head, and extended the threat of murder to include all supporters of Rushdie, meaning the Rushdie support committees in the west. These groups became increasingly vocal around the February 14 anniversary of the fatwa. One of the latest authoritative pronouncements on the Rushdie affair was that of Mohammad Yazdi, the head of Iran's judiciary, who said (April 1996), "[the fatwa] will finally be carried out someday." Two days later, the Majlis speaker, Ali Akbar Nouri, reaffirmed his support for the fatwa, saying that he "regretted that Rushdie is still alive."

In September 1997, Iran's new leadership affirmed the fatwa on Salman Rushdie, which has been in effect since 1989, stating once again that revocation is impossible since the author of the fatwa is deceased. There is no indication that Tehran is pressuring the Fifteen Khordad Foundation to withdraw the $2.5 million reward it is offering for executing the fatwa on Rushdie. Rushdie's book had so inflamed Muslim anger around the world that an Iranian religious foundation raised its $2.5m bounty on the head of British author Salman Rushdie by $300,000.

The author had been living under police protection since 1989, when Iran's late spiritual leader Ayatollah Khomeini issued a fatwa, a religious edict, calling for him to be killed. Now the more reformist Iranian government has distanced itself from the fatwa and from the $2.5m reward on his head. Iran's Foreign Minister Kamal Kharrazi said his country "dissociates itself from any reward." He said Mr. Rushdie was still guilty of blasphemous abuse of their religion. Iranian officials say they are powerless to lift Khomeini's fatwa, saying it could have been lifted only by the revolutionary leader himself. Rushdie is celebrating the prospect of returning to a relatively normal life following the Iranian government's announcement that it will not support any attempt to kill him. Later, at a news conference, he paid tribute to the book's Japanese translator who was stabbed to death. He also mentioned the Italian translator, who was knifed, and the "distinguished Norwegian publisher who suffered an assassination attempt." He added: "I would like to say that I am sorrowful for all the people who have died in demonstrations against *The Satanic Verses*, particularly in the subcontinent—indeed, I feel in many cases they did not even know what they were demonstrating against."

Mr Rushdie praised the work of the U.K. government and said he had come to learn that freedom of speech is worth fighting for. The author said he had a message for British Muslims: "I'm extremely happy and relieved that almost ten years of trial has come to an end."

"I am very grateful to the British government, which seems to have negotiated very toughly and at great length—I must say I did not know it was going on." But British officials said they did not imagine that the novelist would be walking up and down Oxford Street in central London. The British and Iranian governments have now agreed to re-establish full diplomatic relations. Kofi Annan, Secretary General of the United Nations said he welcomed the announcement, and has been joined in praise for the Iranian government by the French President, Jacques Chirac.

CUBA

Cuba, an island just ninety miles off the tip of Florida, no longer actively supports armed struggle in Latin America and other parts of the world. In the past, the Castro regime provided significant levels of funding, military training, arms, and guidance to various revolutionary groups across the globe. However, with the collapse of its prime sponsor, the Soviet Union in 1989, Cuba has suffered a severe economic decline. Without ready cash, Havana was forced to scale back severely its already waning support to international terrorists. To make up for this economic shortfall, the Castro government's focus in recent years has been on generating revenue through tourism. Cuba's attempts to encourage foreign investment in the hospitality industry have forced it to seek upgraded diplomatic and trade relations with other nations.

Although Cuba is not known to have sponsored any international terrorist incidents through 1997, it continued in past years, and continues today, to give safe havens to terrorists. A number of ETA terrorists who gained sanctuary in Cuba some years ago continue to live on the island. In addition, members of a few Latin America-based international terrorist organizations and U.S. fugitives also reside in Cuba. Castro's government continues to maintain close ties to other state sponsors of terrorism and remains in contact with leftist insurgent groups in Latin America. Colombia's two main terrorist groups, the **FARC** and the ELN, are reported to be maintaining representatives in Havana.

Cuba suffered from a string of small bombings targeted against the island's budding tourism industry in 1997. At least six bombs detonated at Havana hotels and restaurants in April, July, August, and September. An Italian tourist was killed in one blast in early September, the only fatality to date of the bombing campaign. In September, Cuban security forces announced the arrest of a Salvadoran citizen who confessed to planting the bombs. Havana charged that U.S.-based exiled Cuban dissident groups were responsible for directing the bombing campaign, but Cuban officials have repeatedly ignored U.S. requests for evidence to support these charges.

IRAQ

During 1997, Baghdad continued to rebuild its intelligence network, which had been heavily damaged during the Gulf War and which it had previously used to support international terrorism. Press reports citing oppositionist and refugee sources stated that the regime has infiltrated the U.N. refugee camps and Iraqi communities in Europe and the Middle East. Iraqi oppositionists have claimed publicly that the regime intends to silence them and accused Baghdad of planning to assassinate Iraqi exiles. However, there is no credible evidence to indicate that Iraq's agents participated directly in terrorist attacks during 1997. The last known such attack was against former President Bush in 1993.

In October, several gunmen attacked the World Health Organization headquarters in Baghdad with hand grenades, causing property damage but no casualties. The Iraqi government blamed the attack on Iranian agents. Iran denied any involvement. A rocket attack in January 1998 on the headquarters of the United Nations (**UNSCOM**) inspectors in Baghdad did not cause damages because the rocket did not explode. No group claimed responsibility for the attacks.

Iraq continues to provide safe havens to a variety of Palestinian terrorist groups, including the ANO, the Arab Liberation Front (ALF), and the former head of the now defunct 15 May Organization, Abu Ibrahim, who masterminded several bombings of U.S. aircraft. Iraq also provides bases, weapons, and protection to the MEK, a terrorist group that opposes the current Iranian regime.

LIBYA

The end of 1997 marked the sixth year of the Libyan regime's refusal to comply in full with the demands of U.N. Security Council Resolutions (UNSCR) 731, 748, and 883 adopted in response to Tripoli's involvement in the bombings of Pan Am Flight

103 and UTA Flight 772. The bombings claimed a total of 441 lives. UNSCR 731 was adopted following the indictments in November 1991 of two Libyan intelligence agents for the bombing of Pan Am Flight 103 in 1988. The resolution ordered Libya to turn over the two Libyan bombing suspects for trial in the United States or the United Kingdom, pay compensation, cooperate in the ongoing investigations into the Pan Am 103 and UTA 772 bombings, and cease all support for terrorism.

UNSCR 748 was adopted in April 1992 as a result of Libya's refusal to comply with UNSCR 731. UNSCR 748 imposed sanctions that embargoed Libya's civil aviation and military procurement efforts and required all states to reduce Libya's diplomatic presence. UNSCR 883, adopted in November 1993, imposed further sanctions against Libya for its continued refusal to comply with U.N. Security Council demands. UNSCR 883 included a limited assets freeze and an oil technology ban, and it also strengthened existing sanctions.

By the end of 1998, Qadhafi had yet to comply in full with the U.N. Security Council sanctions. Most significantly, he continued to refuse to turn over for trial in the United States or the United Kingdom the two Libyan agents indicted for the Pan Am 103 bombing. (French officials on 29 January 1998 officially completed their investigation into the 1989 bombing of UTA 772. The officials concluded that the Libyan intelligence service was responsible, naming Qadhafi's brother-in-law, Muhammad al-Sanusi, as the mastermind of the attack. A French criminal court in 1998 or 1999 is expected to begin a trial in absentia of the six Libyan suspects, all of whom are intelligence officers and remain at large.)

Despite the ongoing sanctions against Libya for its sponsorship of terrorism, Tripoli continued to harass and intimidate Libyan expatriate dissidents in 1997. Libya is now believed to have abducted prominent Libyan dissident and human rights activist Mansur Kikhia in 1993 and to have executed him in early 1994. Kikhia, a U.S. green card holder, is survived by his wife and children, who are U.S. citizens.

Libya continues to be held responsible for other past terrorist acts that retain current interest. In November 1997, Germany began the trial of five defendants in the 1986 **La Belle discotheque** bombing in Berlin, which killed three persons, including two U.S. servicemen, and wounded more than 200, many of them seriously. In opening remarks, the German prosecutor said the bombing was "definitely an act of assassination commissioned by the Libyan state." German authorities have issued warrants for four other Libyan officials for their role in the case who are believed to be in Libya.

Libya also continued, through 1997, to provide support to a variety of Palestinian terrorist groups, including the **Abu Nidal organization (ANO)**, the PIJ, and the PFLP-GC. The ANO maintains its headquarters in Libya, where the group's leader, Sabri al-Banna (a.k.a. Abu Nidal), resides.

Following the attempted attack at the Nitzanim and Ga'ash beaches in Israel in May 1990, Amnon Shahak, head of the IDF Intelligence Branch, stated that the mother ship had transported the terrorists' boats from the Libyan port of Benghazi to the Israeli coast. The Libyans had assisted in preparations for the attack at all stages. According to Shahak, "The mother ship was Libyan, its crew was Libyan, a Libyan military officer was on board, and the Libyans also helped transport the terrorists from their base to the ship."

U.S. Reaction to Libyan Terrorism

The murderous attacks at the El Al counters at the Vienna and Rome airports in 1985 focused the world's attention on Libya. After a considerable portion of Libya's involvement in international terrorism became public knowledge, U.S. President

TERRORISM BRIEF 3-2
PAN AM FLIGHT 103 (LOCKERBIE)

In December 1988, a Pan American airliner blew up over the Scottish town of Lockerbie. Two hundred and eighty people were killed in the explosion, most of them passengers aboard the plane. Some of the dead were residents of Lockerbie whose homes were struck by falling debris. In November 1991, the Americans and the British announced officially that their investigation indicated the following suspects in the bombing: Abdel Basset al-Meghrahi (former director of security at the Libyan airline and later head of the Center of Strategic Studies in Tripoli) and Lamen Khalifa Fhimah (director of the Libyan airline office in Malta). According to the U.S. spokesman, the two trained for the attack at a military installation in Libya over a period of three years: "They planted the bomb in a Toshiba brand radio-cassette recorder and exploited their aviation connections to ensure that their bag would be on board Pan Am Flight 103, leaving from Frankfurt. When the passengers changed flights in London, the bag followed." The two were indicted and the U.S. demanded their extradition in order to stand trial in the United States and threatened to impose international sanctions upon Libya. Under U.S. and British pressure, the U.N. Security Council adopted Resolution 731, calling upon Libya to extradite the two suspects. At this stage it is unclear how the affair will end. It must be taken into account, however, that in order to prevent the incrimination of senior officials in the Libyan administration, traces of the two suspects in the bombing may disappear.

Reagan, in January 1986, ordered all economic ties with Libya severed and Libyan assets in the U.S. frozen. Reagan also called upon other countries to join the economic boycott against Libya.

The economic sanctions led to fears that Qadhafi would attempt to take revenge on the United States, and Libya did embark upon a campaign of terrorism against the U.S. and western targets in Europe. In March 1986, American targets were struck in Lebanon, Italy and Germany. The most severe was the bombing of a Berlin discotheque, killing two U.S. servicemen and injuring dozens.

In order to put a stop to the wave of terrorism sweeping over Europe, the U.S. concentrated troops from the Sixth Fleet in the Gulf of Sidra opposite Libya. A continuation of the terrorist attacks led the United States to take retaliatory military action. So, in April 1986, American F-111 planes based in England attacked government and military installations in Benghazi and Tripoli, killing thirty Libyans. According to the U.S. State Department annual report on international terrorism published in May 1990, Qadhafi continued to support some thirty terrorist groups, including that of Abu Nidal, with funds, training and other assistance.

In January 1991, President Bush informed the U.S. Congress that he was continuing sanctions against Libya, since the "Libyan government continues to employ international terrorism and to support it, in violation of international law and international rules of conduct."

Senior Libyan officials, both within the political establishment and the upper echelons of the military hierarchy, are engaged in developing and maintaining Libya's ties with terrorist organizations around the world. The scope of the vast aid granted by Libya, both in the past and at present, to international terrorism, varies according to Libya's international standing and its critical interests at any given time. Thus, when the west increases its pressure upon Libya (whether economic, diplomatic or military), it curbs some of its contacts with the various terrorist organizations. However, when Qadhafi feels the economic or military noose loosening, he immediately renews ties with the terrorist organizations, even publicly flaunting those ties.

NORTH KOREA

Iran, Iraq, North Korea and the others of the big seven have been listed many times as countries supporting international terrorist activities. In fact, North Korea has been on this list since 1988. The People's Republic of North Korea (PRNK) has tried to justify terrorism, saying that it is a revolutionary activity contributing to the communization of South Korea and the destruction of the free world. In a North Korean publication dated October 1975 and entitled *The Theory of Revolution in Korea and the Fatherland's Reunification* it says that "decisive victory can be attained only through violent means."

Since the Korean War came to an end with an uneasy truce in 1953, North Korea has committed a total of 420,000 terrorist activities against Korea. Typical examples of such activities include a raid on the presidential residence in Seoul in January 1968, which killed seven Koreans. Another incident was the infiltration of commando troops into the Ulchin-Samchok area of Korea in October 1968, which killed twenty Koreans. There was also a terrorist bombing of a Korean delegation in Myanmar in October 1983, which killed seventeen Koreans.

The best known case of past North Korean involvement in terrorism was the 1987 midair bombing of Korean Airlines Flight 858, which killed all 115 persons aboard. P'yongyang continues to provide sanctuary to five of the nine *Yodo-go* hijackers of a Japan Airlines jet to North Korea in 1970. Of the original nine, two have died of illness, one was arrested in Japan in the mid-1980s, and another was arrested in 1996 by Thai authorities on charges of passing counterfeit U.S. currency.

North Korea also provided terrorist organizations in foreign countries with material support or training: from 1969 to 1971, terrorists in Burundi and Rwanda tried in vain to assassinate VIPs and were later identified as members of dissident guerrilla troops trained and supported by North Korea. In 1982, Israel arrested about eighty terrorists in Lebanon; among them, twenty-four were identified as North Koreans.

North Korea still keeps under its protection Japanese terrorists who hijacked a Japanese civilian airliner to North Korea. It is reported that currently (1997) 175 military instructors are stationed in Tanzania and Uganda to train guerrilla troops there. Since 1974, North Korea's terrorism-oriented operations have been placed under the direct control of Kim Jong-il. Currently, four departments (the Social-Cultural Department, the United Front Department, the External Intelligence Investigation Department, and the Operations Department) in the North Korean Workers Party and the Reconnaissance Bureau of the North Korean Armed Forces Ministry are responsible for carrying out the terrorist operations.

North Korea has not been linked conclusively to any international terrorist attacks since 1987. However, the government in Pyongyang may have ordered and planned the 1997 murder of a North Korean defector in South Korea and the murder of a South Korean official in Vladivostok in 1996.

SUDAN

Sudan at the end of 1997 continued to serve as a safe haven, meeting place, and training hub for a number of international terrorist organizations, primarily of Middle East origin. The Sudanese Government also condoned many of the objectionable activities of Iran, such as funneling assistance to terrorist and radical Islamic groups operating in and transiting through Sudan. The Department of State in November 1997 announced new comprehensive economic sanctions against Sudan. The sanctions convey the gravity of U.S. concerns about Sudan's continued support for international terrorism and regional opposition groups as well as its abysmal human rights record. Hasan Turabi is the leader of the extremist National Islamic Front in Sudan.

Sudan has yet to comply with U.N. Security Council Resolutions 1044, 1054, and 1070, which were passed in 1996. This was the case, despite efforts that year by the regime to distance itself somewhat from terrorism, including ordering the departure of terrorist financier Usama bin Ladin. The Security Council's demands include that Sudan cease its support to terrorists and turn over the three Egyptian al-Gama'at fugitives linked to the 1995 attempted assassination of Egyptian President Mubarak in Ethiopia. President Bashir, in October 1997, consistent with Khartoum's repeated denials that its officials had any foreknowledge of the planning of the event, scoffed at the idea Sudan could be seen to have had anything to do with the attack.

Sudan was placed on the list of state sponsors of terrorism in August 1993, and since that time the Sudanese government has continued to harbor members of several of the most violent international terrorist and radical Islamic groups. These groups include Lebanese Hizballah, the PIJ, the ANO, and Hamas. The Sudanese Government also supports regional Islamic and non-Islamic opposition and insurgent groups in Ethiopia, Eritrea, Uganda, and Tunisia.

Sudan's support to terrorist organizations has included paramilitary training, indoctrination, and money, travel documentation, safe passage, and refuge in Sudan. Most of the organizations present in Sudan maintain offices or other types of representation. They use Sudan as a base to organize some of their operations and to support compatriots elsewhere. Sudan also serves as a transit point and meeting place for several Iranian-backed terrorist groups.

The fundamentalist Muslim ideology which guides the Sudanese regime, as well as Iranian assistance and training have made Sudan a natural base for the activities of many terrorist organizations. There are hundreds of activists in Sudan from the Middle East and Africa. They receive military training in order to return to their countries, carry out attacks, and create anarchy with the intention of taking over their country's institutions and instituting an Islamic regime.

The Sudanese involvement in terrorism manifested itself by involving Iranian activists in the attempted terror attacks in crowded New York centers in the beginning of 1993. Within this framework, it must be pointed out that:

- The head of the terror squad which planned the showcase attack in New York, Sidik Ibrahim Ali, as well as other members of the squad, were Sudanese.

- Several arrested terrorists confessed to their interrogators that Iranian revolutionaries and Hizballah activists from Lebanon trained them at Sudanese terrorist camps.

- It is also possible that the activists who were arrested were supposed to receive operational assistance from Sudanese diplomats at the U.N. building in New York.[3]

Sudan, as a country bordering Egypt, serves as a convenient base for training Egyptian terrorists and as an exit base for attacks in Egypt. Interrogation of Egyptian terrorists returning from Afghanistan revealed that Khartoum is the main link in the planning stage of terror attacks against Egypt. Sudan is an important factor in Iran's strategy and serves as a bridgehead for the penetration of Iranian fundamentalism into Africa. Cooperation between Iran and the regime of Omar el Bashir in Sudan commenced several years ago. The military-political involvement of Teheran in

Sudan became deeply entrenched during 1992. This involvement was noticeable in the signing of military and economic agreements between the two countries and included, inter alia, military and economic assistance within the framework of rehabilitating the Sudanese armed forces.

During 1993, Iran transferred arms to fundamentalist groups in Sudan via the General Secretary of the Iranian-Sudanese Friendship Association, Amin Benani. With Benani's blessing, the Sudanese army was armed and equipped with the sole purpose of strengthening it to deal with the rebels in southern Sudan under the command of John Gering.

The assistance which Sudan gives to the various terror organizations, as well as its possible involvement in the attempted attacks in the U.S. in 1993, has caused the United States to include Sudan in the list of "countries supporting terrorism." As a result, the U.S. has imposed commercial and economic sanctions. This U.S. decision has encouraged a Sudanese effort to improve its international image and, at the same time, to bridge its impaired relations with Egypt and to deny all involvement in terror activity.

It is possible that the assistance given by Sudan to France in the extradition of Carlos the Jackal was intended to score points for the Sudanese in the west and to help them in removing their name from the list of "countries supporting terrorism." A number of publications connect the release of two Iranians from a French prison at the beginning of 1994 to this affair. The two were jailed for murdering a member of the Iranian Opposition residing in Switzerland. It is claimed that their release ensured Iran's tacit assistance in capturing Carlos in Sudan.

Sudan became an independent state in 1956 and considers itself part of the Arab world, whereas the Christian and animistic minority population sees itself as belonging to the black African states bordering Sudan. Even before Sudan attained its independence, there was very little contact between the various divisions of its population. The alienation between the inhabitants of the south and those in the north was due to differences in religion and economic-social levels. Moreover, the geographical barrier (the enormous swamps between the south and the north), as well as the differences in dialect, exaggerated the estrangement.

When Sudan declared its independence, the southerners feared that they would suffer politically and economically with the Arab Muslim majority taking over the reins of government. Against this background, the rebellion of the soldiers in the south against the government in Khartoum broke out in the summer of 1955. This bloody rebellion developed into a civil war which continued for seventeen years.

During the second half of the 1970s, it seemed that all the dissension had been settled between the south and the north, but later on, signs of dissatisfaction began to appear (particularly on the part of the southerners towards Khartoum), against the background of their political-economical-social standing in the country. In the summer of 1977, when President Namiri tried to reconcile with the exiled Muslim opposition by means of the Amnesty Law, the exiled Muslims from the extreme right were able to return home (headed by Zadek el-Mahdi).

SYRIA

While there is no "hard" evidence that Syrian officials have been directly involved in planning or executing international terrorist attacks since 1986, Syria continues to provide safe haven and support for several groups that engage in such attacks. Several radical terrorist groups maintain training camps or other facilities on Syrian territory. Ahmed Jibril, leader of the PFLP-GC, which has its headquarters in

Damascus, is one example. In addition, Syria grants a wide variety of terrorist groups basing privileges or refuge in areas of Lebanon's Beka'a Valley under Syrian control: these include Hamas, the PFLP-GC, and the PIJ. The PKK also continues to train in Syrian-controlled areas of Lebanon, and its leader, Abdullah Ocalan, resides at least part-time in Syria. Another example is Ramadan Shallah, leader of the PIJ, which has headquarters in the Syrian capital.

Although Damascus has stated its commitment to the peace process, it has not acted to stop anti-Israeli attacks by Hizballah and Palestinian rejectionist groups in southern Lebanon. Syria also assists the resupply of Hizballah and Palestinian rejectionist groups operating in Lebanon via Damascus. Nevertheless, the Syrian government continues to restrain the activities of some of these groups and to participate in a multinational monitoring group to prevent attacks against civilian targets in southern Lebanon and northern Israel.

The Assad regime has made systematic use of the "terror weapon" since coming to power in 1970. The basic reason for this is the wide gap between Syria's aspirations to regional hegemony and its desire to play a leading role in the Arab-Israeli conflict, and the objective limitations and weaknesses of Syria from a military, economic and demographic point of view.

From the Syrian perspective, the intensive use of the "terror weapon" allows Syria to advance a range of its interests both domestically and internationally. It guarantees the stability and survival of the regime at home; it enables Syria to apply pressure to its enemies in the Arab world; it strengthens the "Syrian order" in Lebanon. It punishes Western countries and achieves political gains from them; and, above all else, it furthers Syria's strategic interests in the conflict with Israel. A recent example of the importance of the "terror weapon" in Syrian eyes is Syria's strenuous opposition to the implementation of U.N. Security Council Resolution 425, which is based on its fear of losing the use of the "terror weapon" in southern Lebanon.

The manner in which the "terror weapon" is used by the Syrian regime, as well as its targets, changes from time to time in accordance with political developments and changing pressures on Syria. In the past decade, one can perceive changes with regard to the manner in which the "terror weapon" was used when compared with the 1970s and 1980s. The factors underlying these changes were: the elimination of domestic opposition, the downfall of the Soviet Union, Syria's isolation in the Arab arena, Syria's participation in the peace process and its growing need for the United States. All of these factors led the Syrian regime to try and alter its image as a state sponsor of terrorism via tactical changes in the use of the "terror weapon," but without making any strategic concessions concerning its use of terrorism as a weapon for advancing Syrian interests.

Syria's leadership reduced the use of the left-wing Palestinian organizations whose terrorist activities abroad were revealed. They were replaced by a combination of other terror organizations activated by Syria and a joint Syrian-Iranian effort involving the use of Islamic terror organizations within the framework of strategic cooperation between the two sides. In light of these changes, it is possible to characterize the current situation regarding Syrian support and patronage for terrorist organizations as follows:

1. The Syrians provide patronage and political, propaganda and operational support to at least 10 of the 35 terrorist groups (or more than 30%) appearing on the U.S. State Department's list of state sponsors of terrorism (as of April 1998). The ideology of these terrorist organizations calls for the destruction of Israel and they oppose the peace process, the Oslo Accords, the Palestinian Authority and Yasser Arafat.

2. The terrorist groups under Syrian patronage can be divided in to four categories as follows:

   - Hizballah;
   - Palestinian Islamic organizations: Hamas, Palestine Islamic Jihad/Shkaki);
   - Radical left-wing Palestinian organizations: the PFLP-GC/Jibril, the PFLP/Habash, the DFLP/Hawatmeh, The Palestine Liberation Front, the Fatah Revolutionary Council/Abu Nidal, Fatah/Abu Mussa and an extremist faction of the Popular Struggle Front;
   - Other Middle Eastern and International terrorist groups: Kurdistan Workers Party (PKK), Japanese Red Army and other terrorist organizations.

3. Hizballah and other Palestinian terrorist groups' policy of carrying out terrorist attacks is part of Syrian strategy and is influenced by it. However, Syria does not have sole and absolute control over these terrorist groups. Contrary to the 1970s and 1980s, Syria cooperates with its strategic ally Iran, and the terror attacks carried out by Palestinian Islamic organizations serve the joint and shared interests of the two countries. Thus, the Syrians make use of the Islamic organizations, which receive ideological guidance, political and operational instructions as well as military and financial support from Iran.

4. The headquarters, training bases, logistical, political and propaganda offices of these organizations are primarily based in Syria. In this framework, it should be noted that Damascus is the primary center of left-wing Palestinian organizations opposed to the Palestinian Authority and the Oslo Accords. Syria serves as an important arena of activity for Hamas outside of Judea, Samaria and Gaza, and senior Hamas officials carry out operational, political and propaganda activities from Damascus. The infrastructure of the Palestine Islamic Jihad outside of Judea, Samaria and Gaza is primarily located in the vicinity of Damascus, from which its operations and activities in the "territories" are directed.

5. The leaders of most of these terrorist organizations reside in Syria, from where they oversee and direct the military, political and propaganda activities of their organizations against Israel and other Arab states. Among the senior leaders and activists of the terror groups residing in Damascus are: Dr. Ramadan Shalah, Secretary-General of Islamic Jihad and his deputy Ziad Nehaleh; Imad al-Alami, chairman of Hamas' Interior Committee, who is a dominant figure in activating the organizations' military apparatus for carrying out attacks; and Ahmed Jibril, George Habash and Nayef Hawatmeh, leaders of the three main left-wing Palestinian terrorist organizations. Also active in Syria are middle and low ranking military activists of all the above mentioned groups.

6. The Syrians permit these groups to maintain their military and political infrastructure in areas under their control in Lebanon. The most widespread infrastructure belongs to Hezbollah, which is also the leading group which concentrates attacks in southern Lebanon. The Syrians also permit some limited activity by the left-wing Palestinian terrorist groups. With Syrian approval, the Beka'a Valley continues to serve as an organizational and training center for Middle East and international terrorist groups.

7. The Syrians support a number of anti-Turkish terrorist and underground organizations, particularly the Kurdish Workers Party (PKK). They allow the PKK to train in Syria and Lebanon and to use both countries as operational and political propaganda bases against Turkey. The PKK's leader, Abdallah Ocalan, lives in Damascus, and several senior members of the organization also live in Syria. The organization has bases and offices in Damascus, northern Syria, the Baka'a Valley in Lebanon and along the Syrian-Turkish border which are used for operations.

8. Islamic terrorist groups operating in Arab countries against pro-western regimes find sanctuary in Syria and Lebanon and use them as bases for their training activities and logistical infrastructure. The terrorist organizations direct their terrorist and subversive activities against Arab governments from Syria and Lebanon, and the Syrians do not make any serious efforts to prevent it, despite repeated and varied protests by Arab states, including Jordan, Saudi Arabia and Bahrain.

9. The Syrians grant sanctuary to terrorist and criminal industries in Lebanon's Baka'a Valley. Both in areas under Syrian Army control and in those under the control of Hezbollah, there are widespread "industries" for the planting and production of drugs and large-scale currency forgery (especially American currency). The industries' products are marketed in Israel, Arab states and Western countries. There are many indications that the Syrians assist these industries and enable them to exist, since they share in the enormous profits generated, and possibly also because of their interest not to confront Hezbollah and powerful local elements dealing in these "industries."[4]

An analysis of these organizations' terrorist activities in the service of Syrian and Iranian interests in the 1990s shows that the "terror weapon" has caused damage to Israel and the peace process of both a strategic and tactical nature. The use of the "terror weapon" in the era of the peace process has caused casualties in Israel, both among the IDF and the civilian population. Besides this, these organizations' attacks, particularly by the Palestinian Islamic groups, significantly contributed to the disruptions in the peace process, mainly in the Israeli-Palestinian sphere.

It is ironic that Syria is the only member of the "club" of nations supporting terrorism that also participates in the peace process. Syria's participation in the peace process is, in its view, a source of strength, since it gives Syria "immunity" from military retaliation for its anti-Israel terrorist activity. But at the same time it is a source of weakness, since Syria is more vulnerable and exposed than in the past to political pressures from other countries participating in the peace process. Past experience proved that the use of political pressure on Syria, mainly by the United States, brought about restraint and moderation in the use of the "terror weapon," although it did not put an end to the Syrian use of it.

The are some major lessons to be learned from analyzing the phenomenon of Syria's use of terrorism. First, it has been used as an instrument to obtain political gains in the era of the peace process. Second, along with the existence of the process, a determined continuous struggle must also be waged against terrorism and against the countries behind it. Lastly, if over the next several years the use of terrorism is not halted, it will be very difficult, if not impossible, to make progress in the peace process at all levels.

STATE-SANCTIONED AND RELIGIOUS TERRORISM

The Crusades and Genocide

Were the Crusades simply terrorism in the name of religion? One definition of "genocide" is as follows:

> *...a conspiracy aimed at the total destruction of a group and thus requires a concerted plan of action. The instigators and initiators of a genocide are cool-minded theorists first and barbarians only second. The specificity of genocide does not arise from the extent of the killings, nor their savagery or resulting infamy, but solely from the intention: the destruction of a group.*[5]

The Crusades were a series of wars in which Christians and Muslims fought to eradicate each other in the Holy Lands to control the area called the Middle East. Perhaps this effort to destroy the Muslims does fit the definition. So many wars of annihilation seem to fit this category of genocide. Christians considered this area their most holy location and believed that they, not Muslims, should control it. The many wars fought by the Crusaders were ultimately unable to reclaim the region. But there had been an unexpected positive effect: western Europeans had left their homes to fight in a distant war and the stories of the returning soldiers encouraged their countrymen to look beyond their own villages for the first time.

The founder of Islam, the Prophet Mohammad, died in 632 A.D. Abu Bekr became Caliph, or "the one who comes after." Abu Bekr wanted everyone around the world to follow Islam and "to submit to Allah." He then set about to organize the subjugation of the entire world to Allah. A century after Mohammed's death, the lands of Islam under Arab leadership stretched from Spain in the west across North Africa and most of the modern Middle East into Central Asia and northern India. The Arabs were great traders, whose influence reached as far as southwest Asia. The Arabs were interested in learning and in other cultures. Western Europe was mired deep in "the dark ages," so called because the great civilizations of Greece and Rome had fallen. The Arabs, however, had made great advances in mathematics, medicine, and physical science. They provided us with Arabic numerals. Algebra is an Arabic word.

The Turks and the First Crusade

The Turks were not originally from Turkey; they were nomadic people from central Asia known today as Turkmenistan ("land of the Turks"). One Turkish tribe, the Seljuks, began moving into the Anatolian peninsula, or the area we now call Turkey. These Turks were Muslims, but a Christian emperor, Michael VIII, controlled the peninsula. The emperor appealed to Pope Urban II to help him rid Anatolia of "unbelievers." The Pope received Michael's call for assistance, but decided to use the situation to advance a more ambitious plan. Jerusalem is considered Holy Land to Christians, Jews and Muslims, but in 1095, the city was controlled by Muslims. The message from Michael presented Urban II with an opportunity to wage a "War of the Cross," or Crusade, and retake the holy lands and eradicate the unbelievers.

The Pope persuaded the knights of Europe to join the Crusades by appealing to their religious convictions. They were told that Muslim Turks were robbing, raping and killing Christian pilgrims journeying to Jerusalem. The Pope suggested the knights fight Muslims instead of continuing to fight one another. Crusaders left their families for a long journey into the unknown. While they did not succeed in ridding the Holy Lands of nonbelievers, the Crusades had other, more worldly benefits:

- An increase in trade in Europe
- Travels to new lands and learning about new and interesting cultures
- Spices that allowed food to last longer and taste better
- The fine cloths manufactured in the Middle East

The first Crusaders crossed into Anatolia in 1097 A.D. and reached Jerusalem by the summer of 1099 A.D. They conducted pogroms along the way to rid European cities of anyone who appeared to be "Semitic" in appearance. When they finally encountered the Muslims, the fighting was fierce. Bloodthirsty Crusaders killed not only fighting men, but also women and children. The victorious Crusaders quickly established four colonies along the eastern Mediterranean, including one in Jerusalem. A second Crusade was launched when the Muslims recaptured one of the Christian colonies. This time the Muslims were prepared and defeated the Crusaders.

The Christians then recaptured the Holy Lands by the end of the second Crusade, but a Muslim general named Saladin launched a "jihad" (Arabic for an Islamic holy war), and recaptured Jerusalem. Oddly enough, Saladin was neither an Arab nor a Turk. He was Kurdish. The Kurds lived between the Turks and Arabs in the mountainous lands of northern Iraq and eastern Turkey, even to this day. When Saladin recaptured Jerusalem in 1187, the Christians launched a Third Crusade, perhaps the most famous, led by King Richard "the Lion-Hearted" of England. The Christians fought hard in the Third Crusade, but Saladin was able to hold Jerusalem for the Muslims. The two warriors agreed to a truce that left the Muslims controlling the Holy Lands, with Christians free to visit their shrines. Although many other so-called Holy Wars have taken place for countless centuries, the Crusades are considered to be the eight campaigns into the Holy Lands that occurred from 1095 A.D. until 1270 A.D. The following is a listing of those eight major campaigns:

- 1095–1099   The First Crusade
- 1147–1149   The Second Crusade
- 1189–1192   The Third Crusade
- 1202–1204   The Fourth Crusade
- 1218–1221   The Fifth Crusade
- 1228–1229   The Sixth Crusade
- 1248–1254   The Seventh Crusade
- 1270–1291   The Last Crusade

The Muslims controlled all of the Holy Lands by 1291, but the Crusades became a turning point for Western Europe. The next two centuries, what we now know as the Renaissance, would lead to exciting advances in science, technology and the arts.

Hundreds of wars and attempts at extermination of certain groups of people have stemmed from religious, ethnic and tribal differences since the Crusades. Catholics against Protestants, Jews against Arabs, Sheiks against Hindus, Hindus against Muslims, Tutsis against Hutus, communism against democracies, Kosovo against Serbia, Khmer Rouge against republicans, the list goes on and all with the same religious zeal. The main weapon in these latter-day attempts at genocide is terrorism, and the greatest terror of all is genocide. From the Inquisition to ethnic cleansing, the resulting terror has created deep splits among religions, tribes and ideologies around the world.

STATE TERROR AND GENOCIDE

The state-approved use of its power and resources to terrorize and attempt to liquidate a specific group of citizens, immigrants, religious or ethnic groups has some ambiguity. Raphael Lemkin, in his book, *Axis Rule in Occupied Europe* (published in 1944), coined the word "genocide." He constructed it from the Greek word "*genos*" (race or tribe) and the Latin suffix "*cide*"(to kill). At the end of World War II the War Crimes Tribunal was at a loss as to what this crime should be called. History was of little use in finding a proper word to fit the nature of the crimes that Nazi Germany had engaged in at the extermination and concentration camps. "Ethnic cleansing" has been used in recent years to "soften" the eradication of specific groups of people. But hard or soft, the word genocide better describes "the destruction of a nation or of an ethnic group." It implies the existence of a coordinated plan, aimed at total extermination, to be put into effect against individuals chosen as victims purely, simply and exclusively because they are members of the target group.[6]

"Mass murder," the term that was often used at the time, was an inadequate description of the atrocities committed in Nazi-occupied territories. It could not account for the motives, which arose solely from "racial, national or religious" considerations, not the conduct of the war. Genocide required a separate definition as it was clearly not just contrary to the rules of war, but a crime against humanity. Raphael Lemkin was the first person to put forward the theory that genocide is not a war crime and that the *immorality* of genocide should not be confused with the *amorality* of war.[7]

The definition of what constitutes a crime against humanity was established at the Nuremberg Trials. However, despite the significance of this, the jurists at Nuremberg had invented nothing new. They were simply advancing Montesquieu's ideas on international law, which he described as "universal civil law, in the sense that all peoples are citizens of the universe." Killing someone simply because he or she exists is a crime against humanity; it is a crime against the very essence of what it is to be human. This is not an elimination of individuals because they are political adversaries, or because they hold to what are regarded as false beliefs or dangerous theories, but a crime directed against the person as a person, against the very humanity of the individual victim. Thus it cannot be categorized as a war crime. Alain Finkielkraut, the French philosopher, pointed out that it is quite a different thing to be regarded as an enemy than as a particular species of vermin to be systematically wiped out. Genocide is a crime on a different scale from all other crimes against humanity and implies an intention to completely exterminate the chosen group. Genocide is therefore both the gravest and the greatest of the crimes against humanity.

In the same way as in a case of homicide the natural right of the individual to exist is implied, so in the case of genocide as a crime, the principle that any national, racial or religious group has a natural right to exist is clearly evident. Attempts to eliminate such groups violate this right to exist and to develop within the international community.

Lemkin's efforts and his single-minded perseverance brought about the Convention for the Prevention and the Punishment of the Crime of Genocide which

A bulldozer operated by a French soldier shovels bodies into a mass grave at the Kibumba camp near Goma, Zaire, July 31, 1994. CP Picture Archive (AP Photo/Jean Marc Bouju).

was voted into existence by the General Assembly of the United Nations (U.N.) in 1948. After stating in Article 1 that genocide is a crime under international law, the Convention laid down the following definition:

Any of the following acts committed with intent to destroy, in whole or in part, a national, ethnical, racial or religious group, as such:

- Killing members of the group
- Causing serious bodily or mental harm to members of the group
- Deliberately inflicting on the group conditions of life calculated to bring about its physical destruction in whole or in part
- Imposing measures intended to prevent births within the group
- Forcibly transferring children of the group to another group

The final definition as it stands today is based on four constituent factors:

- a criminal act
- with the intention of destroying
- an ethnic, national or religious group
- targeted as such[8]

Consequently the word "genocide" has often been used when making comparisons with later massacres throughout the world in order to attract attention by evoking images of the concentration camps and their victims. The inevitable consequences of such misuse of language are a loss of meaning and a distortion of values.

For example, there is a great danger in the way the media applied the term "holocaust" to the devastation wrought by the cholera epidemic in Goma, which had the largest concentration of Rwandan refugees in the Republic of Congo (formerly Zaire). This puts the medical disaster that resulted from the massive influx of refugees as a consequence of the genocide on the same level as the genocide itself, a premeditated mass crime, systematically planned and executed. This has resulted in a double error with the exaggerated emphasis focused on the cholera victims (catastrophe though that was), deflecting attention from the real crime already committed. The fact that cholera does not hand pick its victims according to their ethnic origin was completely overlooked.

The controversial thousand-plane carpet-bombings that took place over Germany, incendiary and nuclear bombs over Japan, and in more recent times over Vietnam, claimed their victims in a totally haphazard manner. Intrinsic meaning is lost when words like "genocide" or "holocaust" are used loosely to describe any human disaster with a large number of victims, regardless of the cause. As a further problem, we then have a situation where no individuals can be singled out as guilty or responsible because blame is laid at the door of historical fate, "unfortunate circumstances," "the climate of the time," "collateral damage," or just sheer bad luck.

It would be hard to deny that some form of evil has always existed in the world. But if such evil is seen in general, impersonal terms such as barbarism, man's inhumanity to man, chance circumstance or plain hatred, then there are no individual culprits at whom an accusing finger can be pointed. So-called collective blame is just another way of denying the facts. If one uses the definitions above and places them in the context of the larger category of crimes against humanity in general, there have really only been three genuine examples of genocide during the course of the twentieth century: that of the Armenians by the Young Turks in 1915; that of the Jews and gypsies by the Nazis in WW II; and in 1994, that of the Tutsis by the Hutu racists.

SUMMARY

As has been shown above, the death tolls from the acts of antigovernment terrorists are almost insignificant when compared with terrorism and genocide in the name of the state. Throughout history, from the time of the ancient Egyptians, who killed every member of a defeated army, to the "Killing Fields" of Cambodia and Rwanda, this has been true. State terrorism in this century alone has resulted in untold millions of deaths. The human rights movements, such as Amnesty International and others, have begun to shine bright light on the depredations committed by nations against their own people. Power and religious fanaticism have driven the kinds of terrorism that resulted in Hitler's holocaust and the conflicts between the Irish Catholics and Protestants, the Jews and Arabs, the Sh'ites and Sunni and the dozens of other conflicts around the globe. Instantaneous television coverage of these atrocities has begun to make the world aware that the most pernicious forms of terrorism are not single fanatics throwing bombs. The next part will explore the regions of the world to let the student acquire a better understanding of where the causes for terrorism can be found in a large number of nations and cultures.

Terms to Remember

"puppet" terrorist organizations	safe havens	Pan Am 103
KAL 858	terrorist subcontractors	Lebanese Hizballah
KDPI	Mykonos murders	PKK
Palestinian Islamic Jihad	Fund for the Martyrs	Hamas
Hizballah	Mujahedin-e Khalq	FARC
UNSCOM	La Belle discotheque	Abu Nidal organization

Review Questions

Explain why state terrorism has been so pervasive in the history of the world.

What does the use of terrorism offer as advantages in future wars?

List the state-sponsored terrorism states called the "big seven."

Were there any positive results from the Crusades? If so, list them.

What would you respond if you were asked to define "genocide?

Endnotes

1. In the information age, the Internet has become a valuable tool for researchers and authors. Much of the background data contained in this chapter and woven into and throughout this book were extracted from web sites such as: the Amnesty International, The U.S. State Department of State, *1997 Patterns of Global Terror* Report; The U.S. Department of State, *Country Reports on Human Rights Practices*; The U.S. Department of State, *Background Notes: Geographic Entities and International Organizations*; The U.S. Central Intelligence Agency, *World Factbook*; and other government sources. We are grateful for the presence of these modern sources and the information they have provided.

2. U.S. Central Intelligence Agency, *World Factbook*.

3. Ibid.

4. Ibid.

5. U.S. Department of State, *Country Reports on Human Rights Practices*.

6. Raphael Lemkin, *Axis Rule in Occupied Europe* (1944).

7. Ibid.

8. Convention for the Prevention and the Punishment of the Crime of Genocide; General Assembly of the United Nations, 1948.

PART 2

Photogropher's International

TERRORISM AROUND THE WORLD

A survivor of the aGuilford PVB bombings is given assiatance . . . 5 killed, 65 injured

CHAPTER 4

BRITISH ISLES AND WESTERN EUROPE

Its not the bullet with my name on it that worries me.
It's the one that says, "to whom it may concern."

—Anonymous

OVERVIEW

Acts of terrorism in Great Britain proper have been a relatively modern phenomenon for successive prime ministers in the second half of the twentieth century. Only in the last two decades have the British homeland and the U.K. begun to feel the deep resentment of the Irish terrorist. In this chapter we will discuss the rise of Irish terror groups and the rise and fall of the Irish Republican Army. We will also present some of the many other associated terror groups in Northern Ireland and in mainland Britain. We will review the history of Ireland as far back as the sixteenth century and discover how the sectarian/religious factional fighting in modern-day Northern Ireland has evolved. A review of the principal political figures in the "Irish Troubles," from both the terrorist and political viewpoint, will be examined. We will also cover how Britain has combated the escalation of terrorist activities within its shores with "counterterrorism activities." This chapter will show how history continues to repeat itself in the modern political arena of terrorism and how terrorists evolve to become political leaders.

The IRA and, more recently, the Provisional IRA (Provos) is considered to be one of the best-organized terrorist groups in modern times. Other terrorist groups will also be reviewed, including the INLA, the UVF, and little-known groups that prevailed in 1960s Britain such as the Angry Brigade. These will be examined and a chronology of their aims and terrorist activities included. This is a long chapter, as it covers some of areas we need to understand in order to to make sense out of the rest of the world.

The nations of western Europe have all had episodes of terrorism, but to cover them all would render this text unliftable. Instead, we have decided to select those major European countries that have experienced the kinds of terrorists and terrorism groups that represent the clearest picture of this issue in the past and today. At the end of Part II, there are recommended readings that will allow the student to investigate a broad span of countries in the region of the British Isles and western Europe. This chapter is broad and deep, mostly because this region has such a lengthy record of terrorism and conflict, much of it still unresolved. We begin with Ireland, where the fires of modern concepts regarding "terrorism" were lit and fanned into great flames.

IRELAND: A HISTORY OF PAIN AND TERROR

In the early sixteenth century, James I, the King of England, provided land to Scottish settlers in areas of Ireland in hopes of establishing the Protestant church in Ireland, the conversion of the Irish to Protestantism, the forfeiture of their lands, and assuring Protestant ascendancy to the throne of England.

Both William and Mary were staunch Protestants and were "invited" to invade England and seize the throne. In 1688, William, with a predominantly Dutch army, invaded and was rewarded with a bloodless coup. James II fled England for exile in France. By 1689 William and Mary ruled England while James amassed an army in France to oppose them.

In 1690, James II[1] supported by French and Irish armies fought William at the **"Battle of the Boyne."** James was defeated and Protestant rule prevailed throughout Ireland. The Protestants were the landowners of Ireland while the Catholics held onto a tenuous existence and suffered great privations and poverty. Protestants to this day celebrate William's victory over James' Catholic Army. Orange Lodges hold these celebrations in the Protestant regions of Ireland on July 12th annually. The first Orange Lodge was founded in Loughhall, County Armagh, in 1795.

In 1801, the Act of Union resulted in Ireland's becoming part of Great Britain and in 1886, British Prime Minister Gladstone tabled the first Home Rule Bill for Ireland. Irish Protestants opposed the Bill. The second Home Rule Bill was introduced and resulted in street fighting throughout Ulster.

An Irish journalist named Arthur Griffith founded a political organization called **Sinn Fein**, a Gaelic term meaning "we ourselves" in 1905. The aims of the newly formed Sinn Fein were to aggressively seek self-government. The Irish Republican Brotherhood known as the IRB were a secret group that wanted total independence and the formation of an Irish republic. This group was active in Ireland in the early 1900s. In 1912, the Ulster Protestants signed the Ulster Covenant to oppose and resist Home Rule.[2]

In 1914, in spite of strong Protestant opposition, the British Parliament finally passed a **Home Rule Bill**. However, the outbreak of the First World War of 1914–1918 prevented it from taking effect. It would be fair to say that the majority of the Irish people supported the British in the conflict with Germany. The Republican movement in Ireland, led by Patrick Pearse, viewed the war as an opportunity to gain total independence from Britain. In Dublin, on Easter Monday, 1916, fighting broke

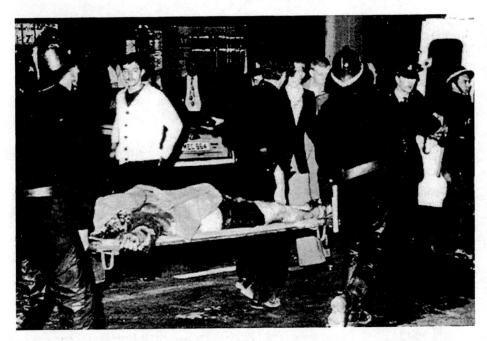

One of the first IRA bombings—in Guilford, Surrey—to target civilians in mainland Britain. *The Surrey Advertiser*

and also set about building his own sophisticated intelligence service for the coming battles. His intelligence network was successful in penetrating the Royal Irish Constabulary and the Secret Service in Dublin. In its efforts to combat Collins' infiltration of the Secret Service, the British put together a counterespionage group called the Cairo Gang to eliminate the IRA volunteers.

Collins' IRA was successful in hitting back and killed fourteen Cairo agents in and around Dublin. The so-called civil war had been going on since 1919, and in July of 1921 a truce was called. Collins was forced by Eammon de Valera to lead the delegation to London for the negotiations. The Irish delegation signed a treaty in December 1921, and Collins commented to Lord Birkenhead at the time that he may have signed his own death warrant. The treaty was to cause a significant rift in the republican ranks and cause bitter infighting. When Collins returned to Ireland, he was ambushed and killed in west Cork on August 22, 1922 at *Beal na Blath* (the mouth of flowers).

SOURCE: IRISH NATIONALIST NETWORK, THE INTERNET

out but was rapidly suppressed by British troops. Fifteen Republicans were executed following the uprising, which came to be known as the "Easter Rebellion." There was little support for the abortive Easter Rebellion, but the execution of the protagonists attracted widespread Irish sympathy.

In the General election of 1918 the Republicans, who had already gained control of Sinn Fein, won 73 of the 105 Irish seats in Britain's Parliament. The Republicans never took their "seats" in London and chose to meet instead in Dublin. They named themselves the House of Deputies (*Dail Eireann*). This body declared publicly that all of Ireland was now independent from Britain on the twenty-first of January, 1919. The British created "The Government of Ireland Act–1920" and officially formed two separate countries. The result was that from 1920 to 1921 wide-scale fighting erupted in Northern Ireland. As a means of combating the troubles in Ireland, the British government hastily assembled a fighting force, known infamously to this day as the **Black and Tans**. The Black and Tans were World War I veterans unsuited to the political and military task of dealing with urban rebels; they were experienced mainly in trench warfare. Their lack of discipline did much to alienate them not only from the Irish, but also from the British. They were officially part of the Royal Irish Constabulary (RIC). By 1921, there were over seven thousand Black and Tans operating in Ireland. Black and Tans burned and rampaged through several Irish villages north of Dublin. This not only shocked the British public, but also brought about their recall from Ireland. The group was disbanded and withdrawn from Ireland in July 1921.

The Act divided Ireland into two separate countries. The six counties of Ulster in the north and the three counties of Ulster in the south were one half, and the remaining twenty-three counties the other. The counties in the north accepted the act and the state of Northern Ireland was formed. The Republicans in the south rejected the act and bitter fighting broke out between the Irish Republican Army (IRA) and British troops.

In 1921, Britain and the Irish Republicans signed a treaty creating the south as a dominion of Great Britain to be called the **"Irish Free State."** There was dis-agreement between the various Republican factions. One group led by Eamon de Valera wanted total separation from Britain and a reunification with Northern Ireland. An opposition group led by Michael Collins[3] and later William Cosgrave was in favor of the treaty.

In 1922, Civil War in Ireland broke out and continued until the fighting ended in 1923. The warring factions then formed opposing political parties within the Irish Free State. Eamon de Valera became leader of Sinn Fein and William Cosgrave led the Cumann na nGaedheal Party. Michael Collins was executed and the **Irish Republican Army (IRA)** was outlawed, but it continued to exist to harass and attack British interests.

Britain's Vietnam?

The 1960s had seen a decade of tremendous worldwide changes, with the British Empire giving up its colonies without a fight. Britain had just quit one of the last remaining colonies, Aden. This was after a total breakdown of law and order, achieved by terrorist violence. The IRA contended that a British government would back down in the face of the kind of violence that had occurred in Aden. Together with the civil rights issues and the perceived U.S. debacle in Vietnam, the Provisionals aimed to make good use of what they considered positive factors. To the Provisionals, Northern Ireland was seen as just another British colony waiting its turn for independence from the mother country. With this and recent history in mind, the terrorists believed that the killing of British soldiers would very quickly influence the decision processes of the British government.

Political Objectives

Before the student can appreciate and understand the terror campaign that has been waged by the IRA against both the Protestant population and the British, it is impor-tant to have a basic understanding of the political goals. The IRA of the 1920s was demanding one united Ireland and total separation from the United Kingdom. In support of this, the nationalists turned to campaigns of terror. As seen earlier the Easter uprising was probably the first in a chain of incidents and acts throughout the twentieth century to emphasize that point. In the early 1920s the bands of IRA men were relentlessly pursued by the Black and Tans.

Cathal Goulding, the Army Council's Chief of Staff for the IRA, had the estab-lished viewpoint of shifting the IRA away from violence as the only means to its ends. His idea was the formation of both a Catholic and Protestant workers group aimed at the overthrow of capitalism, and achieving one united Ireland. As a result, the end of 1969 found a situation of rampant internal disarray and a split developed in the Irish Republican Army ranks. Goulding's ideas offended may Catholics and IRA members who saw themselves as the defenders of the Catholic enclaves of the north. When the renewed fighting broke out in 1969, the IRA's lack of weaponry ren-dered them unable to accomplish their mission and protect the northern Catholics. At a special IRA Convention held in Dublin in August 1969, it was voted, predomi-nantly by the southerners, to adopt a policy of political activism and elect Sinn Fein members to the Dublin and British Parliaments. To the men of the north this was viewed as recognition of partition, "sleeping with the enemy." Led by Sean McStiofain, the Provisional IRA was formed the following month. John Stephenson, Rory O'Brady, Leo Martin, Billy McKee, Francis Card, and Seamus Twomey led the Provisionals of 1969. They believed that physical violence could solve their political problems. Subsequently, splinter terror groups were formed from the original ranks of the IRA. The Provisional Irish Republican Army (PIRA) was formed as a splinter group from the IRA as well as a smaller group, the **Irish National Liberation Army (INLA)**.

Sinn Fein[4], the name used for the political party representing the old IRA, was adopted by the splinter Provisionals and termed as the "political wing." Sinn Fein has risen to prominence over the past three decades as the political party to achieve the goal of separation. Notwithstanding, it must be recognized that the control of the party is exercised through the Army Council of the terrorist group. A sense of fear surrounds this shadowy party, in part because so many of its members have gravitated from the ranks of the PIRA and its Active Service Units.

The PIRA has used terror campaigns to great effect in Northern Ireland against its Protestants neighbors, members of British Army units and the predominantly Protestant **Royal Ulster Constabulary (RUC)**. Indiscriminate attacks on the British mainland took place at a variety of targets. These ranged from military establishments to pubs, shopping centers, business districts and airports, and the seat of British Democracy, No. 10 Downing Street, residence of the British Prime Minister. The object was to successfully attack British military and political targets with the aim of undermining the political will of the government, frightening the citizens and sapping the British economy.

ment tactics over the Dublin lockout of ITGWU members. The Citizens Army was in place as a union protective force. The Army was to play a significant part in the Easter Uprising of 1916 that subsequently led to Connelly's death.

SOURCE: MARIA McGUIRE, *To Take Arms* (LONDON, 1993) PP. 69–70

Provisional Irish Republican Army (PIRA)

It is not surprising the **PIRA** has established itself as one of the most ruthless and well-organized terror groups in the last quarter of the twentieth century. It has achieved success against significant odds. The modern-day "Troubles" have their origins in the working class areas of West Belfast and Londonderry back in 1969.

The success of the PIRA is probably due in great part to its organization. It is generally believed that the operational numbers of the PIRA have not exceeded more than one thousand members since its peak in the early 1970s. Since the mid-1980s, the number of active participants is more likely around 250. There is no doubt

---

⊙ TERRORISM BYTE 4–1

THE RED HAND OF ULSTER (RED HAND COMMANDOS)

Part of Protestant Irish folklore recounts that two captains bringing shiploads of original settlers from Scotland in the early sixteenth century had made a wager that the first to touch the land should own it. As the ships neared the Irish shoreline, the captain that was losing cut off his own hand and threw it onto the land to win the wager. A loyalist paramilitary group called itself "the Red Hand of Ulster." This paramilitary group rose to significance in the 1980s and was believed responsible for numerous sectarian murders

and acts of violence against Catholics. Their leader in the 1970s and early 1980s until his death in 1982 was John Mckeague, a leading Belfast Protestant politician. He is thought to have been the founder of this terror group as well as the Shankill Defence Association. He advocated an Ulster independent of the United Kingdom, and by 1977 was the appointed spokesman for the Ulster Independence Association. Members of the Irish National Liberation Army assassinated McKeague in his Belfast shop in 1982.

widespread support within the Catholic enclaves, which supply and support the terrorists with safe houses, storage and provisions.[5]

The PIRA of the late 60s and early 70s had changed dramatically in its makeup. By the end of the 1960s the Catholic minority was under increasing pressure and assault from Protestant gangs. Catholic enclaves had to be protected against Protestant gangs who were burning and bombing Catholic housing districts. Born out of necessity and the pressure from the authorities, the PIRA evolved from its loosely knit organization to one of a military structure employing geographically-based brigades, battalions and companies. The PIRA reorganized itself to form cells based on the continental structure and better adapted to modern day terrorist activities. Autonomous active service units were formed with these cells and were difficult to penetrate or identify, as each cell had only three to four members. They were given code names and were directed by controllers. It was difficult to operate in the Catholic housing districts of Belfast and Londonderry, as everyone knew everyone else. However, away from Northern Ireland these cells have proved to be successful paramilitary units in operations on mainland Britain. The PIRA owes much of its current success to the effectiveness of the cell system.

The "Troubles"

There is little doubt that in the early days of **the Troubles** (the fighting between Catholics and Protestants), the PIRA was considered to be more of a nuisance than a lasting terrorist threat to the security of a sovereign nation. The current Troubles began with civil rights marches in Northern Ireland. In October 1968, the newly formed Northern Ireland Civil Rights Association organized a march in Londonderry to show its strength and frustration at the discrimination against them by the Protestant majority[6]. The Catholic minority in the north, probably in copycat fashion of the civil rights marches in the U.S. epitomized by Dr Martin Luther King, started marching for better access to jobs, housing and a fairer share of the economy. The marches quickly turned violent. In an attempt to quell the situation, the British government urged the Northern Ireland Prime Minister to make far-reaching reforms to prevent further outbreaks. Without the ability to sway the Unionist politicians, such reforms were doomed. Rioting again broke out in the summer of 1969 and the British government sent troops in to restore order and to protect the Catholic enclaves. By the end of 1970, 153 bombs and incendiary devices had been triggered against Protestant businesses in Northern Ireland.

Turf Wars

Much of the sectarian violence in the early 1970s could be described as turf wars between the warring factions of the IRA, the INLA, the UFF, and the UVF. Revenge killings of both Catholics and Protestants were common, driven by pure hatred. This is epitomized by the infamous Shankhill Butchers, a Protestant gang operating in west Belfast with the purpose of intimidating the community and carrying out merciless killings. It is not a documented fact, but in those early days there was a real struggle for supremacy in the housing districts and ghettos of west Belfast; the feuding was partly ideological and partly material in that they were fighting for control of the rackets in Belfast and Londonderry. Violence within the various terror groups has gone on as a measure of discipline of the membership.

Civil Liberty Issues

Civil rights and civil liberties issues in Northern Ireland have aided, confused and even complicated the processes of both peace and terror. In many instances the British government has conceivably used human rights violations as a tool, both legislatively and as a method of controlling the violence in Ulster.

The Catholic marches of the late 1960s sparked the rioting and bloodshed that led to large troop deployments in Ulster at the outset. This began the modern day Troubles, which were founded on civil rights issues. By the start of the 1970s the British government had made significant moves to curtail the actions of the paramilitary groups with the introduction of internment. This policy had little strategic effect, but gave PIRA members tremendous opportunity to appear as martyrs.

Internment was introduced in August 1971 as a joint decision of the British and Northern Ireland governments; its intention was to confine known or suspected IRA terrorists. By removing the Catholic threat, the action aimed to defuse any Protestant mobilization. In hindsight, internment failed for the government and created a strong recruiting cause for the PIRA.

In the early 1970s there was the serious issue of how the courts could and should deal with terror organizations in Northern Ireland. By nature, the terror campaign also harassed, coerced and intimidated court witnesses, juries, and magistrates. The Diplock Commission[7] was set up to look at ways of dealing with the legal aspects of controlling the terrorist in a free and democratic society. With the aim of insuring control and direction of the PIRA. In looking at the statistics relative to the most recent general election it can been clearly seen that the Social Democratic and Labour Party (SDLP), with its leader, John Hume, won 24 percent of the Catholic vote, compared to only 16 percent for the Sinn Fein Party. Sinn Fein's share of the vote in the 1997 Republic of Ireland elections was only 4 percent. Adams, considered to be a skillful negotiator, does at least provide for the opportunity to begin a peace process.

SOURCE: *PROFILE OF GERRY ADAMS*, SINN FEIN NETWORK, THE INTERNET

⭕ TERRORISM BYTE 4–2

THE IRA IN AMERICA

The IRA had a command structure in the U.S., with a commanding officer to set up and organize procurement on behalf of both Dublin and Belfast. One such commanding officer, Liam Ryan, returned to his home in Tyrone in 1987 to manage the family bar, and was assassinated by a loyalist terror group. Ryan had been responsible for running a courier trail through contacts at John F. Kennedy Airport in New York, and a smuggling operation that involved the movement of both people and money into and out of the U.S. via Canada, through Buffalo. The senior IRA official responsible for the pipeline of weapons from the U.S. was Joe Cahill. He made several trips to the U.S. for the purpose of raising money and purchasing weapons. Old Republican activists, Michael Flannery and George Harrison, ably assisted in the organization of his arms importation.

⭕ TERRORISM BYTE 4–3

A HISTORICAL TURNING POINT

January 30, 1972 is etched in the memories of Catholic Irishmen and is referred to as "Bloody Sunday." The arrival of troops in Northern Ireland in 1969 was, at the outset, seen and welcomed by the Catholic minority as an attempt to protect them from Protestant extremism. As the civil rights movement grew, they continued to march in protest. In Londonderry, the marchers were turned back by soldiers from the elite British Paratroop Regiment, one hundred and eight rounds were discharged by the paratroopers and thirteen Catholic marchers were killed. None were found to be carrying weapons. This singular event had the Catholic youth turn out in large numbers to join the IRA and fight for the 'cause.' The backlash response from the Provisionals was to destroy the Belfast City Center. On July 21, 1972, the PIRA mounted a massive bombing campaign, which culminated with twenty-two explosions inside seventy minutes, killing eleven civilians and injuring more than a hundred.

Source: James Ridgeway and Patrick Farrelly, *The Belfast Connection* (*The Village Voice*, New York, February 8, 1994).

A bullet fired into the back of the knee, which resulted in blowing off the kneecap, was a popular form of meeting out internal justice by the IRA.

the safety and integrity of the security forces and giving them the unfettered ability to bring the terrorists before the courts, the Northern Ireland Emergency Provisions Act was passed in 1973. The measures, seen as Draconian, served the security services well. The Act provided for:

- Terrorist offences to be listed as "scheduled" offenses
- Schedule offenses to be tried by a senior judge sitting alone, with more than the rights of appeal
- Bail was prohibited for schedule offences unless granted by the High Court, with stringent conditions attached
- Person can be held on police arrest without warrant for 72 hours
- Suspects arrested by the military can be held for four hours
- Security forces had extensive powers for search and seizure
- Those arrested for weapons and explosive offences had the onus of proof reversed for them to prove their innocence
- Detention orders could be issued by the Secretary of State from information gathered by the security forces believing it to be valid[8]

Inside the Horse & Groom, the target of the Guilford bombing— 5 dead, 65 injured. *The Surrey Advertiser*

With many convictions for terrorist offences gathered through this sweeping legislation, the PIRA still managed to make both political and publicity gains from their predicament. Once in prison, the terrorist took virtual control of his or her destiny, and intimidated prison officers both inside and outside the confines of jail. Since these laws were adopted in the early 1970s, they have undergone frequent and periodic reviews and amendments. In 1988, fifteen years after it was enacted, the Prevention of Terrorism Act, designed to give sweeping powers to security forces in Britain, was challenged in the International Court. The provision within the Act to detain terrorist suspects for up to seven days violated the European Convention on Human Rights.

OTHER IRISH TERRORIST GROUPS

Irish National Liberation Army (INLA)

This small terror group is an offshoot of the breakup of the IRA in the late sixties, not belonging to the ideology of either the official IRA or the Provisional IRA. INLA is considered more Marxist in orientation than PIRA. Formed in the early seventies with a relatively small membership of about thirty and headquartered in Dublin, its aims and activities on the terrorist front were centered in and around Belfast and Londonderry. The group's political objectives are the formation of a 32-county Socialist Republic in Ireland, the forced removal by any means, including violence, of British troops from Northern Ireland and the overthrow of the elected government of the Republic of Ireland. INLA expresses its solidarity with other national liberation and terrorist organizations around the world. Its leadership consisted of Harry Flynn, Gerard Steenson, Thomas Power and Dominic McGlinchey. McGlinchey, Steenson and Power were all killed in bitter feuding between INLA and the PIRA in the late 1980s.

The INLA's most audacious act of terror was the 1979 assassination of Airey Neeve, the British Conservative Party spokesman on Northern Ireland. Neeve was killed when a powerful bomb destroyed his car as he was leaving the Houses of Parliament in London. This incident marked the first operation outside Ireland by INLA.

The group was decimated in the 1980s as a result of the **"supergrass"** trials. These "supergrasses" were INLA and PIRA militants who inform on their former comrades. By the end of the decade, the problems with admission of supergrass evidence as part of court testimony led to the release of many imprisoned INLA and PIRA members. The result was a bloody feud between INLA and PIRA and many militants were killed. The group still remains a brutal and unpredictable organization.

Ulster Volunteer Force (UVF)

Considered the largest loyalist paramilitary organization. The group is inextricably linked to the Ulster Defense Association and there appears to be no significant ideological difference between them. Over the years it is believed that over 40,000 people were members of this Protestant Loyalist organization. Set up to defend and respond to PIRA violence against Protestants, the UVF was formed in 1912 to respond to the growing demands for Irish independence. When WW1 broke out, many UVF members joined up and served in the 39th (Ulster) Division of the British

Army. After the war, the returning members were a seasoned force to be reckoned with. Their leader in the 1960s was "Gusty" Spence, who was sentenced to life in prison for the murder of a Roman Catholic.

Ulster Democratic Party (UDP)

In 1981, the group spawned a political wing, the New Ulster Political Research Group which in turn became the more formalized, elected Ulster Democratic Party. The **UDP** political aim is the formation of an independent Ulster. There was considerable infighting within this convoluted organization, which led to a new leadership in the early 1990s. The government in 1992 banned UDP membership. Under the terms of Section 30(3) of the Northern Ireland Emergency Provisions Act, 1996, the following loyalist terror groups were proscribed: The Red Hand Commandos, The Ulster Freedom Fighters, The Ulster Volunteer Force and the Ulster Defense Association. Proscribed Republican organizations are: The Irish Republican Army, The Irish National Liberation Army, The Irish People's Liberation Organization, Cumann na mBan, Fianna na hEireann, and Saor Eire.

Ulster Freedom Fighters

Again, there is no defining line between this organization and that of the Protestant paramilitary UDA. It carries out sectarian attacks against pro IRA Catholics in an indiscriminate and particularly violent fashion. The group claims the right to "strike back" at what are termed legitimate Republican targets. At one point, the Provisional IRA claimed that the UFF was in fact an undercover death squad of the British Army.

Loyalist Volunteer Force (LUVF)

Formed in 1996 as a splinter group to the Loyalist Ulster Volunteer Force, it is a violent, sectarian, anti-Catholic terror group, led by Billy Wright, also known as "King Rat." Republican prisoners, who were believed to be members of the INLA, murdered Billy Wright while he was serving a prison term inside Northern Ireland's Maze Prison on December 27, 1997. The aim of the group is to subvert, by violent means, a political settlement with Irish Nationalists in the Northern Ireland peace process.

TERRORISM IN BRITAIN TOO

The Angry Brigade

British politicians and the public have suffered under both the threat and the reality of indiscriminate terror acts by the IRA since the early 1970s. Almost totally forgotten by many, however, is a small terror group that came to life in the 1960s, the decade that saw the Beatles, widespread drug use, and fundamental changes in societal views and values. The Angry Brigade is Britain's only noteworthy homegrown terror group.

One of the earliest workers' movements was the Chartist Movement that started in the 1830s. Prior to this there were other forms of autonomous revolt by workers in the textile mills of the Midlands and the north of England. As a result of threatened job losses due to industrialization, workers formed into armed groups of both employed and unemployed workers. They rioted and caused property damage.

Few may recall the **Angry Brigade**; however, the group was real and did exist. The members of this group were dissimilar in almost every facet to the Irish terrorists and had no clearly defined enemy to focus on other than wealthy middle-class conservatives running business corporations. Unlike the terrorist groups waging war in both Northern Ireland and the mainland, the Angry Brigade was a loosely formed group of communist-style, workers' party members. The philosophy of the Brigade was that of a militant pro-labor, left-wing revolutionary movement.[9]

The Angry Brigade came to some form of prominence in the late 1960s and little has been heard of the group since the main protagonists were jailed in 1971. The group could be termed a copycat, and likened itself to the Weathermen in the United States, and, in a latter period, to the German terrorist group led by Baader and Meinhoff. With no military knowledge or background, the Angry Brigade espoused Marxist theories in the hope that workers would find them acceptable. Britain in the 1960s was a changing society in a great many respects, with a strong Conservative government under Alec Douglas Hume. Modernization and growth in the factories, particularly in the auto industry and the dockyards, was the order of the day. The leaders of the Angry Brigade sought to change government policy and usher in a new era of socialism by murdering politicians and bombing public buildings.

Activists or Terrorists?

As pure activists in a worker's party struggle against the perceived enemy, the state and big business, the Angry Brigade issued communiqués and proclamations stating their cause. The Brigade hoped to gain recognition by professing support for the Irish nationalist movement and such mirror-image "revolutionaries" as the SLA in the United States. Closer to home, the group espoused support for the activities of the Red Brigade in Italy and the German Red Army faction. There is no recorded information that the group received any support, either of a financial or military nature, from either of these terrorist organizations. What is certain is that the Brigade caused explosions aimed primarily at political and business figures. They were hunted down by Britain's Metropolitan Police force and prosecuted for their terrorist and criminal acts. The Angry Brigade's members believed that they were engaged in a workers' struggle that could only come to fruition if the working masses rebelled against their masters. This altruistic goal was never realized, however, possibly due to the atrocious nature of the Brigade's attacks.

Angry Brigade Terrorist Acts

The Angry Brigade is believed to have been involved in a number of bombings in London aimed at banks, corporations and foreign interest businesses such as the Bank of Bilbao, since the group supports Basque separatists in Spain. What this group hoped to achieve by attacks on the homes of the commissioner of the Metropolitan Police, and a member of Parliament is unclear. Certainly these actions demonstrated an ability to coerce and intimidate, but their overall effectiveness can be dismissed as having minimal effect in making any changes in the political arena. Unlike the PIRA, the Brigade had no political machinery, similar to that of Sinn Fein, or any media support. The Angry Brigade was broken up through a series of arrests in 1971. The ringleaders, who became known as the Stoke Newington Eight, were sent to prison for long terms in 1972. The group still remains one of the only examples of home-grown or "internal terrorism" in Great Britain.

Wales and Terror for the Tourists

To a casual observer, the region of the United Kingdom known as Wales seldom conjures up visions of terrorist activity. In fact, Wales is better known for its tourist attractions at Caernavon Castle, the Mountains of Snowdonia, Welsh choirs, famous actors, mining and rugby. So, is Wales a nest of terror groups or a convenient hiding place for the indigenous terrorist? Over the past three decades there have been discussions of an independent Welsh homeland which occasionally have been brought to the attention of Britons by random acts of arson. These acts were usually aimed at unoccupied holiday homes and cottages in the Wales countryside. Claiming responsibility for these acts of arson is a group calling itself the **Miebion Glyndwr**, or "the Sons of Glendower." This group takes its name from Owen Glendower, a Welsh leader from the fifteenth century who vowed to fight the English and their rule over Wales. The arson attacks upon remote cottages resulted in more than one hundred having been destroyed since the first attack in 1979. The group appears disorganized and factional, with no political platform or support. About twenty Welsh activists have been convicted and jailed for some fifteen of the attacks. There appears to be little significance to the arsons and no clear links between them. A group calling itself Cadwyr Cymru (The Defenders of Wales) has claimed responsibility for some of the arsons, but many might well have been committed for insurance purposes.

Scottish Nationalism (APG)

The desire for a separate representation by an assembly different from that at the Palace of Westminster has not been the sole province of Irish nationalism or Welsh nationalism. The 1970s were a period of change in the northern part of the British Isles as well. At that time there was a strong political desire for Scotland to have its own assembly and a measure of autonomy from Westminster. In support of these aims, although fervently denounced by Scottish Nationalist parliamentary candidates, the **APG** was formed. In an attempt to further their cause, the APG planned a series of bank robberies in Scotland and England, and were caught planning to break in to a military arsenal. The group were tried and sentenced on charges of conspiracy in 1975. At the trial it was revealed that some of the APG members had gained their military experience in the service of the British Army and were experienced in counterinsurgency tactics. The official Scottish Nationalist party scorned efforts that they believed could only detract from the legitimacy of the party. Little has been heard from them since that time.

Animal Rights Militia

Animal rights activists have been prevalent in Great Britain for several decades, but this is the only one of their many groups to have moved toward terror tactics and bombings, aimed at companies and research institutes. In 1986, bombs were planted under cars and at the homes of prominent research scientists and animal importers. Although adequate warnings were given, this marked a trend towards violent action by this group. These groups, while perhaps using what could be terrorist tactics, are still considered more like criminals than true terrorists.

Islamic Politics and Terror in the United Kingdom

With a fatwa (religious decree) proclaimed by Usama bin Laden against the United States, one has to question the number of movements based in the capital that give support to terror organizations. A brief look at those groups indicates that London is home to the following organizations with political affiliations to suspect groups and state sponsors of terror:

- *An Islamic Palestine* (Fillisteen al-Muslima); the group is located in London and produces a magazine in support of the Hamas movement.
- *The Emigrants* (al-Muhajiroun), a group led by Syrian supporter of attacks against the U.S.
- *Islamic Liberation Party* (Hizb-ut-Tahir), students' group that has been banned in Arab countries.
- *Islamic Observation* Center; located in the center of London, this group is linked with extremist movements in Egypt.
- *Islamic Salvation Front* (Front Islamique de Salvation), a banned Algerian terror group that publishes a newsletter from a base in the west of London.

There is no doubt that the role played by some of the Islamic front movements in attacks against American interests will lead Britain's Special Branch to consider taking remedial action and investigate these groups and their ties to terrorism. A review of Britain's antiterror laws is currently under way

Britain's Response to Terrorism

As has been shown earlier, judicial processes were already the primary weapon used against the terror groups in Northern Ireland, and Britain's early response in sending troops to protect Catholics from Protestants did not have the desired effect. The PIRA was up against the entire intelligence resources of a major western government, and those resources were significant. The brigade and battalion structures of the PIRA, established at the latter end of the 1960s, became targets for penetration by the RUC (Royal Ulster Constabulary). Informants were placed within the organization and several senior IRA members were arrested. As noted previously, the PIRA remodeled their battalions into smaller cells whereby only a minority of people knew who was who. The British Government was prepared to meet violence head on with their special antiterrorist force, the SAS (covered in Chapter 13).[10]

Countering Irish Terrorism

The advent of terrorism saw the widescale development of antiterror measures being utilized by the British Government against the terror groups in Northern Ireland. Never before in its modern history had a British peacetime government had to deal with internal terrorist activities on the scale that emerged from Northern Ireland. On many occasions Britain has met violence with violence and has had some innovative ideas to counter the terrorists. Among those innovations are its shoot-to-kill policy, internment, removal of a defendant's right of silence during judicial proceedings, and the prohibiting of news media broadcasting statements of PIRA and Sinn Fein. With the "Irish question" still not answered after more than three decades of political and sectarian violence one has to question how effective the countermeasures have really been. The hostility shown by and to Margaret Thatcher helped to feed the terror campaign against British economic, military and political targets. She constantly reiterates that she will "never give in" to the IRA. Each side's inability to achieve military victory should be obvious to the other. The lessons for the rest of the world from Northern Ireland's conflict would seem to be the following:

- Authorities must make every effort to make political compromises with dissidents before violence becomes institutionalized.
- The authorities cannot achieve a military victory over terrorists and still maintain civil liberties and democratic institutions.
- Counterterror techniques by authorities that kill, injure, or frighten noncombatants provide support for terrorist groups. Indeed, revolutionary terrorist groups depend on the authorities to perpetrate provocation and outrages against noncombatants.
- Terrorist groups can be devastatingly effective with very few members, given the worldwide availability of sophisticated weapons and explosives.
- Terrorist groups can sustain community support by using both the latent sympathy of citizens, as well as intimidation.
- Even the most technologically sophisticated, well-organized, well-financed, and highly motivated counterterrorist methods can be frustrated by a small group of terrorists with some community support.[11]

There have been notable successes by Britain's counterterror organizations. The Special Air Service Regiment, which continued to thwart and strike at Republican terrorists through the 1980s and 1990s, was instrumental in preventing terrorist attacks and setting up offensive traps resulting in the capture and often the death of terrorists.

The Peace Process

Peace for Northern Ireland and an agreement that all sides might be able to live with came significantly closer to reality in 1998. The agreement reached at Easter in 1998, and now referred to as the Good Friday Agreement, was seen by many observers of the Troubles as a retreat by the British government. Be that as it may, conditions laid out in the agreement would also require the decommissioning of the paramilitary groups in the province, and that in itself was not an easy prospect for any politician to sell to Sinn Fein or the Republican groups that they represented. Of major importance to the loyalist was the question of the decommissioning by the IRA, a point that the IRA has consistently refused to acknowledge.

The Good Friday accord was to undergo some significant testing over the remainder of 1998 by men of terror who sought to destroy the accord with the use of indiscriminate bombings in Northern Ireland.

To its discredit, the government of Britain made an astonishing political move with respect to a terrorist bombing incident that had taken place in Germany in 1976. Roisin McAliskey, daughter of the former Irish Nationalist Member of Parliament, Bernadette Devlin, was being held pending the outcome of a request by Germany to send her back to face charges in connection with the bombing. The Home Secretary, Jack Straw, turned down the extradition requests on the grounds that McAliskey's poor health made it "unjust and oppressive." The decision was made in March, when Sinn Fein was jeopardizing the all-party talks on Northern Ireland, and the motive

The Grand Hotel, Brighton, UK. Bombing at the conservative party conference, with Prime Minister Margaret Thatcher in attendance. Photographer's International.

for Straw's action was appeasement of Sinn Fein. The Sinn Fein leader, Gerry Adams' demands were seen as extreme; the Republicans demanded that any lasting peace could only be achieved with the disbanding of the Royal Ulster Constabulary, the release of all IRA prisoners and a total withdrawal of all security forces. While the political football match between all the parties and the government went on, the men of terror continued about their business. Revenge killings of Protestants and Catholics continued through the spring. With the approach of the referendum on the Good Friday accord came the Protestant marching season, which in past years had always been a flash point for violence as the Protestant Orange Orders marched down their traditional routes.

Protestant Orangemen have marched through Drumcree and down the now famous Garvachy Road since 1807, to celebrate King William's victory at the Battle of the Boyne. Things would change in 1998, when the marchers were held at bay by a massive contingent of Police and Army personnel. The standoff became increasingly turbulent and violent, as neither side would give way. The Orangemen stood firm. Tensions were eased after a fire bomb attack claimed the lives of three young children. The barricades came down, but a new form of terror was about to surface. At the end of August, a massive car bomb detonated in the Ulster border town of Omagh as Saturday shoppers went about their business. It was the largest bomb of its kind and resulted in twenty-nine deaths. Death is no stranger to the region; however, the people of Omagh understandably thought it was safe to venture into the town center in view of the passing of the historic Good Friday deal. They had neglected to consider the sinister breakaway Republicans who were now calling themselves the "Real IRA." Real IRA is a splinter of disillusioned PIRA members intent on wrecking the status quo. Security sources have identified Michael McKevitt of County Louth as the group's leader and the mastermind behind this bomb attack. All this is taking place at the same time governments of both Britain and Ireland were in the process of releasing more than four hundred prisoners serving prison sentences for terrorist offenses. Included in those released so far are the murderers of

Lord Mountbatten, uncle to the Prince of Wales, and the bombers of the Chelsea Barracks. It is likely that other bombers and murderers will be released by Christmas, including Patrick Magee, the "Brighton Bomber," and Paul Kavanagh, who killed six at the Harrods bombing in London in 1983.[12]

FRANCE

A Long Acquaintance with Terrorism

On the face of it, France has not seen the same levels of terrorist activity as other major European nations. This does not imply that France has been left out of the problems facing other governments in dealing with terrorists. However, Euroterrorists and Middle Eastern terror groups have needed bases, not only safe houses, but also safe countries from which to mount their terror campaigns without too much political and police interference. The country of choice for many groups was France. From a strategic point of view, terror groups have considered France an ideal location from which to strike, then return to hide. It has borders with Spain, Italy, Germany, Switzerland, Belgium and Luxembourg, plus an efficient transportation network of roads, air, sea and rail systems.

France has not been immune to terror, and the history books are full of atrocities perpetrated during the French Revolution. (As noted earlier, the word terrorism was born at that time.) What needs more consideration and discussion is the type of terror groups which utilize France for their base of operations and their reasons for doing so. In this section we will discuss specific groups that have successfully used France as a location to mount terror operations and carry on turf wars outside their own countries.

In Chapter 1, we discussed the difficulty in defining terrorism. Brian Jenkins, Director of Political Science at the Rand Corporation, and Walter Laquer have defined terrorism separately but arrived at the same conclusions. As noted, Jenkins called terrorism the use or threatened use of force designed to bring about a political change. Lacquer concluded that terrorism is a form of political or criminal violence using tactics designed to change behavior through fear. It is clear that both are correct.

Terrorism can and does mean different things to different people. The German Federal Republic used the legal process to combat terrorism, considering terrorism as the use of criminal acts for political purposes. Without laboring again on the topic of definition, the student may want to consider that terrorism can easily be termed an import-export industry.

The PFLP in France

France in the late 1960s and 1970s became a European safe haven for the beleaguered Palestinian terror group the PFLP (Popular Front for the Liberation of Palestine). Controlled as it was by Wadi Haddad from his secure locations inside either Aden or South Yemen, the PFLP set up safe houses and planned operations throughout Europe from Paris. This is true international terrorism at work. In this group is the infamous terror practitioner **Carlos the Jackal**.[13]

The justification for terrorism can be argued vigorously. However, since the end of the Second World War, the use of terror as a means to an end has had several primary benefits: local and, in most cases, worldwide attention for a specific cause or causes; an outlet for political impotence and frustration; and combative measures for countries or states not in the financial position to take direct action themselves. In the political arena, the last would occur where a state did not wish to take direct confrontational action but rather use the cloak of terror, for which it could always deny involvement after the event. The Palestinian cause will be dealt with under a separate chapter; however, many organizations like the PLO and various offshoots used France in the 1960s and 1970s as a base of operations.

Japanese Red Army

Also prominent in France from the field of terrorism in 1970s was the **Japanese Red Army** terror group. The group was pledged to a worldwide Marxist revolution it has actively supported and was very involved in the Middle East struggle for the Palestinians.[14] The group was formed in the early 1970s and is based on feudal Japanese samurai warrior customs as well as Marxism. The group operated throughout the world and has been involved in major international terror attacks in support of the Palestinian cause. The group participated in the ferocious attack on Lod Airport in Israel,[15] killing Puerto Rican pilgrims in the departure lounge. The group also murdered two United States sailors in Italy in 1988. In continuous worldwide support of their Palestinian brethren, they also hijacked an airliner and held the passengers hostage, demanding the sum of $6 million in ransom.

Direct Action (AD)

Having discussed France as a center of operations for international terrorism, we should note that it does have its own brand of internal terrorists. **Direct Action** was a terrorist group unlike many of its other European and Middle Eastern counterparts. It evolved not out of the 1960s but the late 1970s and early 1980s. Considered as a left-wing revolutionary group, it began as a communist revolutionary organization and then restricted, or limited, its focus to virulent anti-American sentiment. With its strong views on American interference in European affairs, it adopted the anti-American sentiments of the Palestinian cause and began to attack Israeli and Zionist targets. Its main European target was NATO (North Atlantic Treaty Organization). France had withdrawn from NATO in 1967. As the group evolved, it began to build a framework of linking up with other left-wing terror groups operating in Europe, particularly Germany, France and Belgium. The Communist Combatant Cells (CCC) in Belgium,[16] the Red Brigade in Italy and the German-based Red Army Faction supported AD's campaign against NATO. Thus, with its original base in Paris, AD also became an international terror organization.

There is some skepticism in official quarters that this group had to feed off and be supported by the other left-wing groups. It must be noted that since the unification of East and West Germany the level of left-wing violence and terror has stopped. This however does not indicate that the group has split up or disintegrated, and AD will most likely continue in some form to espouse and support its philosophical goals.

Alien Invaders

To say that French soil had been invaded from another planet would not be a correct assessment in any shape or form. However, in recent times it has been the breeding ground for unwelcome guests from the European and Middle East theatres of terrorist conflict. On the home front, there has been the FLNC (*Front de la Liberation Nationale de la Corse*), a group of Corsican separatists, as well as the extreme left-wing AD group. Another is the ARB (*Armée Republicaine Bretonne*). The ARB and the FLNC are quite distinct in their aims as compared to the AD. These two, the AB and the FLNC, are purely regional French factions with goals of local autonomy. AD, on the other hand, has somewhat fuzzy international ideological goals. Confusingly to the casual or the informed observer, AD has gone after anti-Jewish interests, which one would normally associate with the extreme right wing as opposed to the extreme left. France's tolerance for the number of groups active within its borders is probably born out of their own realization of how the French Republic was created. This tolerance has led many other groups to use Paris as a primary base for internal and external operations.

With the disintegration of the Empire of the Shah of Iran, students in Paris took control of the Iranian Embassy to show their support for Ayatollah Khomeini. The city was a tolerant host to both sides, with both pro and anti-Khomeini supporters in evidence and making their protests public. Both groups clashed during a street protest. Another region of Europe is also represented in France and that is the group called **ASALA**. This group of exiled Armenians was intent on promoting their cause and airing their grievances against the government of Turkey. Their grievances go back in history to 1915–1922, when over one million Armenians were massacred. Headquartered in the Middle East, believed to be mainly in Beirut, their actions are attention seeking and aimed at securing a homeland of their own. Most Armenians lived within former Soviet bloc countries.

By far the most aggressive group operating out of Paris in the 1960s was the **PLO** (Palestine Liberation Organization). Their headline-catching events included the rocket attack at Orly Airport, when in broad daylight two Lebanese Palestinians calmly parked their car near the runway and, armed with an RPG-7 rocket launcher, fired at an El Al flight taxiing for take off. The rocket missed the El Al aircraft and hit an empty Yugoslav jetliner.[7] The two terrorists escaped capture at the airport. Not to be outdone by the failure, a further attack was again scheduled for Orly Airport six days later. By this time the airport was strongly protected by military security. The group entered the airport with an assembled bazooka, much to the astonishment of the armed police, and a furious gun battle between police and terrorists ensued amid hundreds of passengers and spectators in the airport building.

GERMANY

A History of Fascism, Terrorism and Democracy

Historically, Germany has survived two world wars, been divided into two nations, paid the price of Nazism as well as Communism and come to the end of the twentieth century as a major industrial power and democracy in Europe. The history books clearly define the years between the two world wars as being economically harsh for Germany. This section will deal with the rise of terrorist groups in Germany; however, it is pertinent to look back at some significant periods of the twentieth century affecting the German people as well as their neighboring countries.

Between the two world wars, Germany saw the rise of the Nazi Party and the rise to ultimate power of the Austrian Corporal, Adolf Hitler. Germany was humbled by its reparation payments and, coupled with the devastation of the worldwide Great Depression of 1929, the German populace faced massive unemployment and starvation. The reparation repayment was renegotiated under the terms of the Young Plan. Hitler campaigned long and hard throughout Germany against the Plan. By July of 1932, the Nazi party held 38 percent of the seats in the German Parliament (*Reichstag*).[18]

Hitler's passion was to lead the badly depressed Germany to greatness, rid it of communist and other influences, and purge the society of its ills. To achieve this, he had to have absolute power and control. In 1933 Paul von Hindenburg, the President of Germany, proclaimed Hitler as Chancellor (Prime Minister) of Germany. With total control, he then proclaimed his government the Third Reich. With that, Germany's dictator began his own reign of terror on the German people. By the end of July 1933, through legal process he had destroyed the German constitution and outlawed freedom of the press, unions, and all political parties with the exception of the Nazi Party. His own breed of police, the dreaded Gestapo, hunted down all opponents of the government. Many arrested on suspicion alone were jailed or shot.

The Nazi used terror-like tactics to not only gain, but also to keep, control of the populace. All German children were required to join either the Hitler Youth or the Society of German Maidens. These children of Germany were indoctrinated into the Nazi philosophy and military discipline and were used as spies to inform on family members that did not embrace the Nazi doctrines. A sophisticated network of spies monitored and reported on the German people and fostered an atmosphere of not only physical but also psychological terror.

Germany's New Order

There have been many accounts, books and films about Hitler's Final Solution of the Jewish Problem. His belief was that the German people were a genetically superior race and that his country had to be purged of the impure, non-Aryan peoples. Those groups singled out for special treatment were Jews, Gypsies, Poles and Slavs. The term Holocaust is widely used, which simply means the mass murder of over six million Jewish people. Hitler and his Nazi party members began their reign of terror on the Jews as early as 1933, almost immediately after Hitler came to power. Sometime in early July 1933 (the date has never been precisely confirmed), beginning around the ninth of the month and lasting for about forty-eight hours, Nazi Party members destroyed thousands of Jewish businesses and synagogues throughout Germany, killed dozens of Jews and sent almost 40,000 to concentration camps. The night is referred to as *Kristallnacht* (night of the broken glass). When the German armies rolled across Europe a similar fate awaited Jews in those countries conquered by Germany. Names of camps that today strike fear and loathing and sheer terror for the nature of the atrocities committed are Belsen, Auschwitz, Buchenwald, Dachau and many others. Hitler's unique brand of terror, which accounted for the mass murder of millions of Jews and other persons who failed to fit his Aryan picture of perfection, was a means to an end. The Nazi leadership saw it as the cleansing of a nation and those it conquered. Such use of political terrorism must be considered a weapon of psychological warfare.

Post World War II and Terrorism

After the end of World War II, a long period of rebuilding and healing took place. By the 1960s the Federal German Republic was experiencing three different types of terrorism. The first, left-wing terrorism, came about from the imported views of radical students and their opposition to the U.S. war in Vietnam. This was countered by right-wing terrorists opposed to the left-wing radicals as a continuation of the anti-communist past. Criminals also adopted the terror groups' actions and copied and mimicked their attacks for personal, criminal gain. The 1960s were a period of wide-

BMW FOR BMG

In order to finance their group's operations Andreas Baader insisted on carrying out robberies in the grand style. He instructed his accomplices to steal exotic cars for their getaways. The car of choice was nearly always the BMW. This model of vehicle was so frequently used by the gang that it became nicknamed the Baader Meinhof Wagon (BMW). Their notoriety became a superb marketing tool for the German car manufacturer.

spread student revolt and protest, although in Germany there was no real catalyst to take the protests to the next stage. Student protests were the order of the day on many university campuses in Europe and the United States as a platform for anti-Vietnam protests. Modern terrorism, particularly in Germany's case, has been typified by indiscriminate violence, which is sensationalized by the murder of innocents.

The student body of left wing radicals at the Berlin Free University, in somewhat of a copycat style, protested against American involvement in Vietnam. Although the protests were restricted mainly to marches and the distribution of leaflets, there was not a catalyst in place to take any serious action at a higher level that would involve violence directed at the authoritarian government. Two main protagonists came to the forefront of the student protests, Adreas Baader and Gudrin Enselin.[19] As on many university campuses of the 1960s, both Communism and Marxism were prevalent. This was also the case at the Berlin Free University. Baader, Enselin and later Meinhof were all committed Marxists. Out of the Berlin University was developed the **Red Army Faction**. The RAF was led by Gudrun Ensile and by the freewheeling Andreas Baader, who presented more of a playboy image than that of a terrorist.

Red Army Faction (RAF)

This group of committed Marxists sought to engage the United States in a combative role by extending the Vietnam War to German soil. This they achieved by attacking United States interests in West Germany, and particularly United States servicemen and military bases. Many books describe Andreas Baader as more of a delinquent and a follower than a committed terrorist. He seems in many accounts to draw pleasure from being at the center of an infamous criminal network. To finance their program of violence, the group resorted to a series of bank robberies and other crimes.

The igniting factor in sparking this group into action on the grand scale was in fact an eloquent German lawyer, Horst Mahler, who joined the student movement to give it impetus toward violent action. In 1968, Enselin and her boyfriend Baader attempted to destroy two Frankfurt department stores with fire bombs. They were both captured and sentenced, and a year later temporarily released during an amnesty for political prisoners. When the amnesty was over they fled to France as fugitives. They returned to West Germany to join with Horst Mahler, but Baader was again arrested. At this point in the group's development, Ulrike Meinhof came into the picture. Meinhof was the editor of an underground newspaper called *Konkert*.[20] The paper had been launched in the 1950s, sponsored and supported by communist groups in East Germany. Meinhof is reputed to be a close friend of Gudrun Enselin and it was Enselin who persuaded Meinhof to assist in the break out of prison of Andreas Baader. The jailbreak on May 14, 1970 resulted in changing the name of the group to the Baader-Meinhof Gang. Over the following two years, Meinhof spent time in Jordan not far from the capital Amman being trained in weaponry by the Palestinians. Meinhof and colleagues became skilled in the use of what was to be their favorite weapon, the Kalashnikov, better known as the AK-47 Assault Rifle. Having received their training from the PLO the group went into action and was involved in the attack on the Organization of Oil Exporting Countries (OPEC) headquarters in Vienna, Austria on December 21, 1975. The RAF were at this point joining forces with a group calling themselves the "Arab Revolution" a cover name for the Popular Front for the Liberation of Palestine (PFLP).[21]

Illich Ramirez Sanchez, better known as Carlos the Jackal, led the assault on the OPEC building. This attack, although targeted against the oil-producing countries, was more a case of raising money than having a significant political impact. The Saudi Arabian and Iranian governments are believed to have paid a ransom of $50 million for the safe return of their nationals. Among the five strong groups that attacked the building were two German terrorists, Gabrielle Tiedermann and Hans-Joachim Klein. During a gun battle with Austrian security officers, Klein was seriously injured. No political demands were made other than the Austrians broadcast a political statement for the group. The Austrians allowed the terrorist and a number of the hostages to fly to Algiers and then to Tripoli. The large amount of ransom money was transferred to a bank in Aden to bankroll further terrorism.

The Perpetuation of a Cause

German authorities arrested the principals of the group, which numbered about one hundred active supporters in 1972. Baader, Meinhof and Enselin were all sentenced to long prison terms. The group was housed in the maximum security Stammheim Prison. Over the following years Ulrike Meinhof, suffering from acute depression, hanged herself in her prison cell on May 9, 1976. As for the remainder of the group, it is something of a discussion point as to how they met their ends. On the night of November 18, 1977, several members of the Baader-Meinhof Group died from self-inflicted gunshot wounds in their prison cells.[22] Many questions have been asked about how guns could have been smuggled into a top security prison. The most likely answer to that is that lawyers for the group brought them in to attempt a breakout.

The deaths coincided with news of a dramatic rescue by the anti-terrorist GSG-9 in October 1977. GSG-9 stormed a Lufthansa aircraft at Mogadishu, Somalia, killing three hijackers and rescuing the ninety passengers. It would seem to be entirely logical that the Red Army Faction, or as usually called the **Baader Meinhof Gang**, would cease to exist. However, it exists to this day and its growth has not been stemmed by arrests of prominent members over the past two decades. With arrests of successive leaders and gang members the RAF has continued to rise like a phoenix from its own ashes. It is believed that in both the 1970s and 1980s this was due in part to an elaborate communications system and network setup between the imprisoned terrorists, their lawyers and the activists still working for the cause. Public opinion soured toward the RAF in 1977, an opinion that had generally held them up as romantics fighting for a misunderstood cause. This was naturally embellished by the popular press, which continued to sensationalize the group's criminal activities and misdeeds. However, the previously mentioned hijacking of a Lufthansa airline to

BOLOGNA RAILWAY STATION BOMBING

On August 2, 1982 one of the most catastrophic terror attacks in European history, this century, was carried out at this railway station. The bomb estimated to be about 100 lbs was placed by right-wing Italian extremists and accounted for at least 84 deaths and more than 250 injured. The attack came at 10:25 a.m., a time of day when the station was crowded with tourists and hol-

idaymakers. The bomb devastated the railway station, destroying several rail cars and collapsing the roof of the main station building.

Source: George Rosie, *The Directory of International Terrorism* (Paragon House, New York 1986), Bologna Railway Station Bombing (August 2, 1980), p. 77.

Mogadishu, Somalia, by terrorists supported by the RAF resulted in the murder of the aircraft's pilot, Jurgen Schumann. This single act helped turn public opinion against them.

The RAF probably reached the pinnacle of its terrorist existence toward the end of the 1970s. The group was responsible for the assassination of the West German Attorney General, Seigfred Buback, and Hans-Martin Schleyer. They went so far as to attempt to murder the head of NATO in Europe, U.S. Army General Alexander Haig. The RAF were still active in the 1980s and by now had joined forces with a little known German terror unit called the June Second Movement and another called the Red Cells. Little is known of their members or their numbers; however, it seems likely that the groups continue to operate independently of each other. The significance of the date, June Second, is remembrance of Benno Ohnesorg, who was killed on that date in 1967 during a student protest that turned into a riot. The most notorious act carried out in their name was the abduction of Peter Lorenz, a candidate for the post of Mayor of West Berlin. The ransom paid was the release of four of their compatriots who were then flown to South Yemen. The group was abandoned in the early 1980s, with most of its members joining the RAF.

Reawaking of Germany's Past

Since the collapse of the Berlin Wall and the demise of the Soviet Union, a mood of nationalism and right-wing extremism has returned to some segments of German society, particularly to the German youth and, not least of all, to some senior officers in Germany's military. In echoing Germany's past there have been many instances of anti-Semitic violence and a growing trend in intellectual and university circles to be the breeding grounds for fervent nationalism, anti-Semitism, anti-foreigners and in particular anti-American. What is also being seen is a growing trend in the upper echelons of the German military and also with senior members of the CDU toward Germanizing areas of Eastern Europe. This policy actively supports the propaganda preached by a convicted Nazi terrorist Manfred Roeder. Roeder has even spoken at the elite German Officers Academy. What this web of neo-Nazi activity throughout the German military will mean for one of Europe's strongest nations is as yet unclear. Certainly Jewish groups and other minorities are fearful of history repeating itself with the neo-Nazis. Manfred Roeder's exploits have been well documented in the German press and he is considered a terrorist by German intelligence. Roeder was linked to the bomb attack in 1980 at Oktoberfest in Munich and also the attack on the Bologna Railway station in Italy. He is also believed to have bombed a Paris synagogue. Sentenced to thirteen years in jail for the bombing murder of two Vietnamese immigrants, he was released after eight and returned to his campaign of hate mongering and ultranationalist causes.

Germany Toward the 21st Century

The unification of Germany, which came about as one of the most unexpected of turning points in Germany's history, brought with it doubts about a new Germany's ability to cope with the depression and despair being suffered by its people in the former East Germany. By the end of 1997 there were growing signs in German cities of right-wing neo-Nazi groups in the form of Skinheads fostering hate campaigns against foreign immigrants living in and coming to the new Germany. With most European communities lowering the barriers on movement between countries and with the fall of the Soviet Union, many thousands of ethnic groups surged westward for a "better life" in the West. What they found in Germany was a growing resentment, mainly by extreme right-wing groups, to the rushing tide of outside ethnic groups seeking jobs in an already struggling economy. The Skinheads saw the immigrants as being responsible for the high rate of unemployment and the economic conditions. In many cities extremists took the law into their own hands and, in shows of nationalist strength, set about abusing and intimidating immigrants.

In some cities, by the spring of 1998, immigrants had virtually disappeared from the community, having been frightened away by the blatant onslaughts of neo-Nazism. No specific groups or organized terror campaign is being sustained, although special police units are being utilized to break up obvious gangs of Skinheads. No one can predict how far Germany will regress back towards the Nazi influence, or whether these types of incidents are a mere pothole in the road to unification. What most are watching for from the German government is a signal that it fervently opposes the nationalist movements. However, with a growing number of incidents involving ethnic groups and neo-Nazi influences at various levels inside Germany's military, it is no surprise that there is a feeling of growing terror by those immigrants that can see the unsettling prospect of a rise in the nationalist movement all over again.

SPAIN

Spanish Nationalism and the Basques

The Basque region of Spain spills across the Pyrenees and into southern France. It is estimated that half a million Basques live on French soil and approximately two and a half million live within the borders of Spain. Historical facts about the origins of the Basque people are uncertain. However it is known that they have been in this region since before the Gauls and Iberians settled in Spain and France. The Basques have their own language, which is not derived from any other European language or dialect, called Euskera. With their population size it would be logical to expect that they might be a self-governing principality not dissimilar to Monaco. However, the Basque people do not enjoy their own homeland and, in similar fashion to the Irish Republicans, have been fighting for self-government of their own homeland since the first quarter of the twentieth century. General Francisco Franco came to power during the Spanish Civil War between 1936–1939 and ruled Spain as a Dictator until his death in 1975. In the intervening years Spain has achieved tremendous economic growth.

Basque Separatism

As the century draws to a close there are only two European theatres of nationalist conflict. Of course the most notable and most documented has been the terrorist campaign waged in Northern Ireland; however the Basques of the Pyrenean region of Spain have their own internal struggle for a national identity. The Basques have not had a separate homeland or a separate autonomy since 1035. Surprisingly, they have managed to maintain and protect their own language and culture over the centuries. General Franco's approach to dealing with the Basque nationals was to suppress them at all costs. He incorporated the Basque region into Spain at the end of the Spanish Civil war and outlawed their culture and language. Franco's actions led to a rebirth of Basque nationalist fervor in the late 1950s. Recent elections in Spain have tempered the rage of the Basques and they seem moving toward accommodation.

Euskadi Ta Azkatasuna (ETA)

In 1959, the Basques formed ETA (Basque Fatherland and Freedom) and it was dedicated to promoting Basque independence. The ETA was not originally formed as a terror group but, with Franco's vicious oppression of the Basques, the group was more or less compelled to retaliate with like violence. ETA, like the IRA, gains its membership support predominantly from the working classes. Those members come from regions that identify with the strong ethnic identity of the Basque people. The members are invariably young, frustrated nationalists with a sense of frustration at their lack of autonomy. The majority of Basques favor nationalism but do not support the terrorist's violent "means to an end" approach to reaching a political goal of self-government and determination. The ETA has over the past 25 years been a fragmented organization that has seen several offshoots of the original group being formed.

A political report, commissioned in 1986, describes the Basque region as being susceptible to political solutions. It also described ETA as an " unfortunate child of the Franco dictatorship." Much of the report suggested political solutions such as how to accommodate Basque nationalism within the framework of Spain and the European Economic Community (EEC). One of the recommendations was that Basque terrorists, who under Spanish law were tried in Madrid "special" courts, should in fact be tried in Basque courts. And, policing of terrorists should come under the control of Basque police and not Spain's National Police.[23]

Since its inception in the 1950s, the ETA has been riddled with internal squabbling and bitter dissension. The group split in 1966 into what was known as ETA-Zarra or old ETA, and ETA-Berri or young ETA. ETA-Zarra divided into two subgroups, ETA-5 and ETA-6. The ETA subgroup, ETA-5, sub-divided into ETA-Military and ETA-Politico Military, and the most hardened and seasoned campaigners for armed action come from the sub-group ETA-Military.[24] The splits have caused confusion and consternation among the Basque people as to which of these schisms to support or oppose.

"Actions Unite–Words Divide" is the slogan adopted by ETA-Military, and their terrorist members adopted the same "cell-like" structure adopted by Provisional IRA terrorists on active service unit duties. ETA-Military commandos or "irurko" were made up of three-man cells. "Sleeping commandos" were organized in the late 1970s by the ETA Military commander Miguel Apalategui.[25] The "sleepers" were called from the Basque community to perform one single terrorist act and then returned to their jobs in relative anonymity. To finance their terror campaign the ETA used robbery and extortion as their main means of sustenance.

Development of the ETA Organization

ETA's growth and its youth movement can be traced back to the Basque Nationalist Party (PNV). The party had been an exiled force since Franco's defeat of Spain's Republicans in 1939 civil war. The PNV operated as a government in exile, another group to be based in France. The Basque youth movement determined to ensure that their language and culture did not die. ETA's political standpoint was purely democratic. In 1957 a group of young Basques traveled to France to try to convince the government in exile to resort to an armed struggle against General Franco. The PNV leader Jose Maria Leizaola and his government turned down the idea. The first assembly by ETA came about in May 1962. The small group of university students and activists gathered to discuss how to go forward with their ideals. Much of what they discussed at that first assembly was the example set by other groups struggling for national identity against such regimes as Fidel Castro in Cuba and others struggling against colonial masters in Africa and the Middle East. This became the first steps along the road toward terrorism by the ETA. Determining not to be easily captured by police they set up the three-man cell structure and defined ETA as " a revolutionary movement of national liberation."

The influence of the works and writings of Mao Tse-tung were to play a significant part in the ETA organization. So impressed by Mao, a young Basque named Jose Ortiz studying in Paris, attempted to rouse others in ETA to the same level of influence that he had found in his readings of Mao. Then, the second ETA assembly in 1963 set about attempting to rid itself of Maoist influences. No split occurred as a result of the second assembly. Shortly thereafter, the Maoist militants within the organization produced their own minimanual, *Insurrection in Euskadi*. The tract brought forward the Basque determination to embark on a war of revolution. A third assembly in 1964 broke with the old established and nationalist PNV and, influenced by the Maoists within ETA, redefined the group as being anti-capitalist and anti-imperialist. One of the ETA leaders defined the new direction: "The primacy of the human person and of his rights was the basis for any political action." As the ETA ideology turned to a position veering to the left, the French government took action against ETA founding members on French territory and removed them from the frontier region with Spain.

Eustakio Mendizabel Benito headed the ETA at the start of 1970. This group was known as the military front of ETA. He believed passionately in his homeland and its language and was deeply concerned at what lay in store for the Basques in the future. Benito financed his terror operations, like so many other such groups, by resorting to criminal activities like armed robbery, extortion and kidnappings. The group had no training in the art of weaponry or the use of explosives. They actively purchased arms through the underground arms network and bought their first consignment of 500 Firebird parabellum weapons. They also stole explosives from local factories and quarry operations.

ETA members are known to have received training from the Popular Front for the Liberation of Palestine at the PFLP training base in South Yemen. One of the ETA's most audacious acts was the assassination of Luis Carrero Blanco. Carrero Blanco had been vice-president of Spain under General Franco from 1967 until his assassination on December 20, 1973. When General Franco stepped down from office in June of 1973 Carrero Blanco succeeded him as Prime Minister of Spain.

The resulting carnage blew the chauffeur-driven vehicle more than fifty feet into the air and over the roof of the church, landing in the next street. The chauffeur died immediately and Carrero Blanco shortly after.

SOURCE: WILLIAM GUTTERIDGE, *CONTEMPORARY TERRORISM* (THE INSTITUTE FOR THE STUDY OF CONFLICT), NEW YORK 1986), A CHAPTER BY PETER JANKE, PP. 137–139.

Opposition to ETA

Accion Nacional Espanila (ANE) or Spanish National Action was a right-wing terror movement specifically aimed at Basque separatists. The group was formed in the 1970s and operated against the Basques in the regions of northern Spain. The group is known to be responsible for reprisal killings of ETA terrorists and sympathizers, and has also been active in bombings on both sides of the Spanish border.

Political Movement

By the 1990s the effectiveness of ETA had been dampened by the Spanish government's movement towards devolution for Spanish regions including the Basque region of Spain. It is unlikely that the ETA will stop its acts of terrorism unless it gets its own homeland, however. ETA continues to target politicians in the Basque region that support the Basque region's devolution, which are perceived by ETA as traitors to their cause. This action is alienating the populace of the Basque region and makes ETA's ability to operate somewhat of a difficulty without the local support it has always been accustomed to receiving. ETA continues to target politicians from local parties as well as military and high-ranking officers of the government.

Frente Revolucionario Antifascista y Patriotico (FRAP)[26]

Although little known today, Spain suffered from other terror groups, one of which was the left-wing Maoist group **FRAP**. In an ironic twist, FRAP received worldwide recognition when several of its members were sentenced to death in 1975, for the killing of a Spanish policeman in Madrid. The worldwide outcry led to demands for Spain to be thrown out of the United Nations. Unmoved by these outbursts for clemency the Spanish government followed through with the executions as planned on September 27, 1975.

Grupa de Resistencia Antifascista Primo Octobre[27]

The Anti-Fascist Resistance Group of October First (GRAPO) is another left-wing terror group active in the 1970s at about the same time as FRAP. Four Spanish police officers were killed in a retaliatory action over the execution of five left-wing terrorists. From this action on October 1, 1975 they take their name. GRAPO is also responsible for at least one attempt on the life of King Juan Carlos of Spain. The group was led by Juan Carlos Delgado de Codex, until his death in 1979 while attempting to evade arrest.

Now that we have seen the confusion and problems with terrorism, left and right, in what we consider to be Western Europe, we move on to an examination of the origination and growth of terrorism in Central and Eastern Europe. Much of this area thrived with terrorism as a tactic and spawned the former reign of communist terror known as the Soviet Union.

ITALY

After World War I, Italy under Mussolini had violently suppressed and oppressed the Italian Communists. By 1954 the country was the most likely to turn Communist in the West. With the cessation of hostilities and the formation of democratically elected government in Italy, the opportunity naturally presented itself for the Communists to come to the fore. What the student will learn is that a strong Communist-indoctrinated left-wing group would rise up with some fairly imaginative goals to steer Italy onto a different path than that established by the Allied powers.

The Mafia

Its difficult to discuss Italy without looking at the home-grown criminal organization that flourishes in the southern regions of the country, particularly on the island of Sicily. The word itself is believed to be of Arabic origin, meaning a place to hide or take refuge. Mafia was formed as a secret society in Sicily to challenge their French and Spanish occupiers. Within two centuries they were a leading force covering all aspects of public and political spheres of influence. Mafia members swore an oath of silence not to deal with security forces or police on criminal matters; the silence was part of a code of honor that was called the *omerta*. Those Mafia members that were arrested formed another secret society that was set up in the prisons of Naples and the surrounding areas. This secret society was called the *Camorra*. The Italian Mafia was responsible for the spread of its network to the U.S. through Italian immigrants in the early part of the twentieth century migrating to New York in particular. Catania in Sicily is one particular area where the Mafia has been deeply involved since 1925. Members of the Mafia call themselves Cosa Nostra. The actual word Mafia is not used by the Cosa Nostra, and membership is so secret one member cannot tell anyone that he belongs to it. Cosa Nostra members are always male. Membership can almost be termed as hereditary, as it passes from father down to son. Cosa Nostra members consider themselves men of honor. The weapon of honor used by members of the Sicilian Mafia was the sawn-off shotgun or in local dialect the *lupara*, and a *white lupara* is a bloodless murder in which a victim's body is never found.[28]

The Mafia are embodied in such movie extravaganzas as the Godfather starring Marlon Brando as the Godfather. In most Mafia families depending on size the members elect the godfather or boss of bosses. In the larger families the procedures may vary considerably; with up to 200 members it would not be prudent to have such a large gathering in open view of the security services. Although not directly linked to terrorist actions either at home or abroad the secret nature of the organization and the codes it practiced ensured that measures, particularly violent ones, were used against their enemies to keep the people in line. Blood feuds between crime families was commonplace; extortion, kidnapping and shootings were the norm. During the 1990s the crackdown on the group by the government and special prosecutors did nothing to deter the Mafia from coercing or intimidating witnesses and even assassinating the special prosecutors and judges.

Mafia Trials

The ability of the Mafia to intimidate is legendary, so by the mid-1980s the state had made significant inroads into the organization and setup. The Examining Magistrate of Palermo Giovanni Falcone, for the period 1979–1991, worked tirelessly to bring the Mafia to justice. During his investigations he was able to bring about the first mass trial of Mafia; in total 475 defendants went on trial from 1986. A significant role in the trial was that of the turncoat members of Mafia namely *pentiti*, or collaborators. The foremost collaborator was Tommaso Buscetta, whose arrest in the U.S. and his subsequent extradition played a major role in the trials. Considered by many to be one of the old guard who was less than enamoured at the style and direction of the present Cosa Nostra, he provided significant evidence against the membership and overturned the rule of *omerta*.

Italian Terror Groups

There has only been one notable terrorist group surfacing in Italy since the 1960s, the *Brigate Rosse* (Red Brigade, to give its literal translation). At one end of the revolutionary seesaw is this group and smaller but none the less deadlier and coming from fascist origins the *Ordine Nuove* (New Order), an extreme right-wing organization that was prominent in Italy between 1975 and 1983. The philosophy of the New Order is to intimidate the existing political structure with the aim of procuring a strong Italian state supported with a fascist structure. Like the Red Brigade it has been involved in bombings and assassinations, which on occasion have actually been attributed to the Red Brigade. There is an obvious need for these two groups to discredit each other at every roll of the dice.

The Red Brigade

The **RB** has its fundamental origins, like so many other left-wing movements, on the Italian University campuses in the latter half of the 1960s. The group might be considered as a fledgling of the WWII *Volante Rosse*, formed during the campaign against Nazi Germany as a communist resistance movement. It continued its campaigns until the end of 1949 and had continued links to the Italian Communist Party, no doubt spawning the next generation of left-wing extremists to emerge on the campuses of the 1960s.

Following the end of WWII Italy moved toward a governing style modeled on the political and economic example of the United States. During the years from 1950–62 the industrial growth and success of the Italian government lay in the hands of coalitions of political parties, the Republicans, Liberals, Social Democrats and Christian Democrats, all it would appear trying to remove from its economic systems the Fascist past. While exploiting the need for industrial growth and foreign trade it had neglected the social structure of the country. The bubble burst in 1968 with the cultural-style revolution in the universities and schools, and was quickly followed in 1969 with the worst union unrest in the industrialized north that Italy had experienced. The unions could not be placated and factories were seized and occupied, workers and management were intimidated and attacked. All this became the fertile ground for the emerging Red Brigade.

The founding membership of this organization came from the Sociology Department of Trent University, Renato Curcio and Margherita Cagol.[29] The RB began to target the symbolic nature of the Italian State by attacking senior executives, politicians and parts of Italian society perceived as being repressive by nature. RB did not burst on to the Italian scene but rather confined itself to incubation largely in Milan's industrial heart. It became more active from 1969–1972, as a period of building, training and testing of its avowed objectives. Minor fire bombings and destruction of civil property were the order of the period. The RB support structure outside of Milan at this time was considerably weak. From 1972–1974 the RB entered a new phase where it began to expand to the adjacent areas of Turin and Genoa and experimented in kidnapping and extortion. During this same time frame the Italian

Security forces were able to capture Renato Curcio after a gun battle which accounted for the death of his wife Margherita Cagol. Observers at that time were announcing the imminent demise of the Red Brigade, but their predictions were far from reality. The next generation of RB was on the scene and ready to continue the fight to the Italian Government and society in general. The RB has to some length emulated the tactics laid out by Carlos Marighella in his *Mini-Manual of the Urban Terrorist*, in 1969. Attention to detail and technical knowledge as well as logistical and intelligence information became a hallmark of the BR. Contained in the *Mini-Manual* is Marighellas' definition of assaults:

- Assault is the armed attack which we make to expropriate funds, liberate prisoners, and capture explosives, machine guns, and other types of arms and ammunition.
- Assaults can take place in broad daylight or at night.
- Daytime assaults are made when the objective cannot be achieved at any other hour, as for example, the transport of money by the banks, which is not done at night.
- Night assault is usually the most advantageous to the urban guerrilla. The ideal is for all assaults to take place at night when conditions for a surprise attack are most favorable and the darkness facilitates flight and hides the identity of the participants. The urban guerrilla must prepare himself, nevertheless, to act under all conditions, daytime as well as nighttime.

Kidnapping as a part of the terrorist arsenal is well demonstrated in Italy through the 1970s and perfected by the RB. Mainly symbolic in its action, it did go beyond kidnapping prominent business personages when it kidnapped Genoa's assistant Attorney General Mario Sossi. The RB demanded the release of RB prisoners from jail and in particular Renato Curcio. Sossi was held captive for a month before his release. The concession received from the government was the promised release of RB members. However, the Attorney General would not permit the release, which had been bargained under duress.[30] The RB also believed that the concessions they received had sufficiently undermined the state. On June 8, 1974, the RB struck down Genoa's Attorney General Francesco Coco in an armed ambush, which had a twofold effect. The first was a confirmation of the RB's retaliatory ability against the figure that had blocked their earlier attempts to free their colleagues and secondly their threats to the selected jurors in the Turin trial of Curcio led to the delay in proceeding with the trial. Further attacks by RB on members of the Bar Association had the desired effect of delaying the trial. The intimidatory effect of terrorism was working well.

Structure

As seen with many other urban terrorist organizations the RB based its operating habits on the cell structure to prevent infiltration and detection. Based in large industrial areas it had widespread support among the working classes that provided food and support to the group. Total membership, either active or passive, has been hard to ascertain. It is believed there were active members amounting to over 500 with a support structure possibly in the thousands. It seems likely that by the last decade of the century the RB was reduced to around 50 active members. With its communist Marxist/Leninist ideology its early support would have come from the Soviet Union,

KIDNAPPING AND DEATH OF ALDO MORO

One of the most serious attacks on Italy's constitution was the kidnapping in March 1978 of the former leader of the Christian Democrat Party, Aldo Moro, by the Red Brigade. Careful planning had gone into the operation; however, Moro was a man of regular habits who went to prayers before going to his office. He always traveled the same route at the same time of day to his office. On March 16, 1978, a car forced Moro's vehicle to stop and several others immediately surrounded it. RB terrorists fired their machine guns into the vehicle, killing all five of Moro's bodyguards. They escaped from the scene with Aldo Moro as a hostage.

The RB at first demanded the release of thirteen of their comrades from prison. Like so many other countries, Italy had adopted a "no concession" policy in dealing with terrorists; ironically Moro himself had introduced this policy. Moro pleaded for an exception to be made in his case. The Italian government refused to make any concessions, and fifty-four days later the bullet-riddled body of Aldo Moro was found in the trunk of a car on a Roman street. Moro had been instrumental in bringing the Communist party and the Christian Democrats toward a union the RB was desperate to prevent. The RB kidnapping and killing shocked all of Italy.

BRIGADIER GENERAL JAMES DOZIER

Three years after the Moro kidnapping the RB were to strike again, but this time it was to take on the US. General Dozier was at the time the Deputy Chief of Staff, NATO in southern Europe. On December 18, 1981, two men dressed as plumbers knocked on the apartment door where he and his wife Judy were living. The two young men claimed that they were plumbers and had come to investigate a water leak. General Dozier agreed to let them in to check the apartment. One of the men said something in Italian that Dozier did not understand. While he was attempting to look the phrase or word up they pulled out silenced handguns and pointed them at the General. A fight ensued and was finally

(continued)

which in the Cold War years would have provide succor and support for such organizations operating in the West; after all, any activity likely to disrupt a democracy would be to their advantage.

Kidnapping

Italy has perfected the art of kidnapping and in fact it has been further enhanced with corporations able to get kidnap insurance, making it into a growth industry. This shortsighted provision ensured that kidnappers got their money and those that were kidnapped were released, and everyone went away contented. The RB on the other hand kidnapped for different reasons and rarely for money. Two kidnappings stand out for their sheer audaciousness and the brutality with which they ended.

These two kidnappings were significant watersheds for the RB. The first, which resulted in nothing more than the symbolic execution of the President Elect, was to turn public opinion against the RB. Several communiqués were issued prior to his murder and the RB made every effort to exploit the media coverage of this atrocity. During Moro's captivity the RB showed its strength of purpose and its ability to continue with other operations and carried out two murders and six shootings in Rome, Turin, Milan and Genoa, in spite of the massive police search and crackdown on the RB and any known members.[31] It was a significant demonstration of the RB's ability to conduct several simultaneous operations. The release of General James Dozier was the first successful rescue of a kidnap victim from the RB, by members of the Italian police.

By the mid-1980s, the number of terrorist incidents committed by BR was into single figures following a significant decline in support from the left. By the mid-1990s the group was distributing communiqués to indicate a cessation of all operations. How and what role the RB will continue to play into the next century is at present unclear. However at the latter end of 1998 the group were not functioning.

GAP and NAP

Two other groups were on the fringes of the Italian terrorism scene in the 1970's, and modeled themselves on the same clandestine style activities and systematic violence as the RB.

Partisan Action Group (GAP): The GAP originated in Milan at about the same time (1969) as the RB. Their inception is believed to have involved the wealthy Italian publisher Giangiacomo Feltrinelli, who was the paymaster and group sponsor. Feltrinelli believed that right-wing extremism was on the rise and a return to Fascism a real possibility and he believed that the only way to confront the risk was to form an urban guerilla movement. His approach was to form the GAP into a resistance/partisan movement modeled on the resistance fighters of WWII. This model differed from that of the RB, which probably accounts for the nonmerging of the groups in the early days.[32] In the days of student and union unrest which had also spread to Italy's prison system another movement sprang up. The *NAP*, or *Armed Proletarian Nuclei*, came to life from a left-wing prison movement, the *Movement of Proletarian Prisoners and the Ongoing Struggle (Lotta Continua)*.[33] Unlike the RB they gained little or no public acknowledgement. Coming from the ranks of the Naples prison inmates, the membership immediately began the "armed struggle," financing of which was done primarily by bank robberies. Their main base of operation started in Naples and spread to Rome, using explosives to bomb prisons and also attacking prison officials. Unlike the RB all the members were easily traceable from their criminal records and their *modus operandi*, coupled with their lack of attention to their own security, resulted in numerous arrests of the protagonists. With no ideological base, their recruitment of the criminal elements led to their eventual downfall with the remainder of the membership joining the ranks of the RB. Throughout the terror campaigns, the majority of the targets were either political or paramilitary by nature. Indiscriminate attacks against the Italian populace were uncommon.

The Mancino Law

A decree number 122 issued by the Italian government in 1993 was an emergency measure to control, restrict and limit attacks of a racial nature. Two months later it was transformed into Law No. 205 by the then Interior Minister Nicola Mancino. The law enabled the state to prosecute individuals for "incitement to violence for a broad range of *hate* crimes which included the use of symbol of hate. Hundreds of youths have been charged under this legislation. Two Italian names have become associated with hate crime in Italy: Maurizio Boccacci, a Skinhead organizer, and Dr. Sergio Gozzoli, an outspoken anti-Semite and a Holocaust denier.[34]

Skins Organizations

The Italian Skinheads had by the early 1990s organized themselves under the leadership of the **Movimento Politico Occidentale** (Political Movement of the West), founded by Boccacci and headquartered in Rome. It has links to other far right Skinhead groups in France, Germany and Great Britain. A notable incident that was bound to become a flash point was the painting of yellow stars on over 100 Jewish businesses and shops in Rome. Jews attacked MPO skins as a result. The MPO has been banned by the government but has since renamed itself with the Fascist trappings of *I Camerati*, a term used by Mussolini to address his Fascist followers.[35]

In its effort to become more politically acceptable, at a convention of the neo-Fascist Movimento Sociale Italiano (Italian Social Movement) the delegates voted to move towards the mainstream political parties and to dissolve the MSI. They merged with Alleanza Nazionale (National Alliance), and it was hoped this would make the overall far right movement more respectable. The delegates also agreed on a strong

halted when they threatened to kill Judy Dozier. The General was placed in a trunk and taken to an apartment in Padua. He was kept in a tent, chained to a cot. Due to the high profile nature of their hostage the US FBI were brought in to help with the investigation. Three days after his kidnapping the RB released a communiqué that denounced Dozier as a "Yankee pig" of an "American Occupation Army." However, no specific ransom demands were made for the General. This caused considerable concern, as the default solution was his execution by the RB. The FBI began to profile the kidnappers and eventually information came through that he was being held in an apartment above a grocery store. Following surveillance by the Italians, a crack team of police stormed the building and rescued the General. This was the first occasion whereby a hostage of the RB had been successfully released; it also spelled the beginning of the end for the RB.

position against anti-Semitism. The extremists in the organization, many of them Skinheads, broke away from the Alliance and reestablished a version of the MSI.

Ideology

The Skinhead ideology and that of the far right extremist echo the sentiments of a past generation of neo-Fascists. Their ideology can be loosely based on the following:[36]

- The denial of Nazi genocide against the Jews—"historical revisionism"
- Fear and hatred of foreigners, based on the myths of Aryan purity and supremacy
- The fear and demonization of the Jews in a context of a sinister plot to run the world

The breakdown of the symbolic and all-too-real Berlin Wall and the influx of Russian and eastern nationals to the west, particularly Germany and Italy, has fuelled the far right into action. Sporadic action between Skins of the far right and ethnic and minority groups will continue in Italy into the millennium.

GREECE AND TURKEY

Terrorism is no stranger to these two countries; however, the actions of their respective indigenous terrorist groups is restricted on the most part to actions within the country rather than outside in an international arena.

GREECE

Revolutionary Organization November 17

This group of left-wing extremists to be considered Marxist/Leninist, anti-imperialist and strongly anti-United States. November 17's first action and the first time it came to world attention was the assassination of U.S. diplomat Richard Welsh in 1975.

November 17 Group has operated in Greece with what seems like total immunity. Police and security services have been unable to arrest any members of the organization. The group formed out of the university campuses of Greece much like other left-wing groups of that period. The actual date, November 17, is the commemorative date of the attack on the NTUA students by the military and police under the control of the ruling colonels. On that date, several student activists were killed and many captured and tortured. The military junta of the colonels lasted only a further few months before it was overthrown. The actual membership number is not known but it can be assumed that it is a small group, with approximately twenty to thirty hard-core members. Unlike other groups, it did not take part in low level operations to test its own ability; rather, it burst onto the world stage with a notable terrorist attack on a diplomat from a major foreign power.

Like its Italian counterparts, the November 17 Group is extreme Marxist/Leninist. In its early years, there were relatively few attacks by this group; between 1975–1985 November 17 carried out only six attacks. Perhaps the length of time between operations was relative to the fact that police arrested none. Their failure is a sad reflection on the internal workings of the Greek government and its security services. Over the last twenty years, 61 deaths have occurred, with 250 injured from a total of 345 bombings. Not one terrorist has been arrested and charged with offenses in connection with these incidents.

The group did expand operations after 1985, and by 1990 had carried out about forty attacks including bombing, assassinations and shootings, targeting U.S. military personal based at NATO bases in Greece, Greek industrialists and politicians. The group has been severely critical of the Greek government on its position in respect to U.S./NATO bases in Greece as well as Greece's membership in the EEC (European Economic Community), and therefore the largest number of attacks carried out by the group is directed at internal targets and those foreign targets residing on Greek soil. To ensure that no other group claimed responsibility for their terror acts, a handgun of the same caliber was used in consecutive attacks against Greek targets.

The group views itself as the people's vanguard, there to lead the fight on behalf of the working classes and to take up the armed struggle. It makes its point with ideological communiqués and actions in support of the cause and its attacks appear geared to making the subverted classes more abstractly aware of what is taking place in the political and economic processes in the country. The group also holds the U.S. responsible for complicity with Turkey over the Cyprus crisis, thus making the U.S. a legitimate military target in its relentless war of the oppressed. The group's early attacks were primarily symbolic; the first was against the U.S. and subsequent attacks against the Greek police hierarchy and representatives of the Greek military junta. An example of the hatred towards the U.S. can been seen from the content of one of the November 17 communiqués:

> The American military forces in our country are an occupation force, and we are going to hit anybody who is a member of it or an agent of its secret services. These actions are going to continue and are going to increase until the last Turkish soldier leaves Cyprus and the last American soldier leaves our country.[37]

International Incident

With the outbreak of the Middle East crisis and the invasion of Kuwait by the Iraqi forces of Saddam Hussein in 1991, November 17 went on the offensive against the coalition force countries that were represented in Greece. Between January 25 and February 7, 1991, they carried out eleven attacks against foreign businesses, all originating from coalition countries.[38] November 17 viewed Iraq, through its published communiqués, as an oppressed people fighting against the imperialist forces of the West. Following the capitulation of Iraq to the coalition the group changed back to its internal struggle. It was evident that the group's arsenal was able to mount such an immediate campaign, which indicates considerable efficiency in its internal ability, and makeup. The Greek police and security services have not had much luck in ever capturing members of this violent organization, and to date the group continues sporadic operations with virtual impunity.

Espanastatikos Laikos Agonas (ELA)

The second most destructive group operating on Greek soil is also committed to the overthrow of the Greek system and is a violent Marxist-Leninist organization. That is where the similarity between it and November 17 probably ends. It also grew out of the university campuses of the 1960s and early 1970s. Its fundamental aims and philosophy were directed at the state, imperialism and capitalism; most if not all of its targets for terror were of a symbolic nature. Unlike the secret nature of November 17, which seeks to communicate its position via communiqués, ELA actually utilizes and operates an underground newspaper to forward its aims and political viewpoint. In May 1990, ELA announced that it had merged forces with another left-wing group named the Revolutionary Organization 1 May. Up to this point the strategy of the ELA had been to avoid death and injury to Greeks as well as foreigners on Greek soil. It had conducted a low-level style of campaign and had not ventured into the more glamorous world of remotely detonated bombs. A communiqué to the Greek government in 1993 appeared to be the turning point in its violent methods in its dealings with the state. It perceived all police officers to be the "local representatives of the CIA."[39]

On September 19, 1994 the ELA remotely detonated a bomb beside a police bus killing one and injuring ten others as well as a passerby. No warnings were given by ELA, which had previously been a signature for the group. Detonating the bomb without prior warning signaled a new and more virulent strain in Greek terrorist behavior. Successive and continuous failures by the Greek government to effect any cohesive response to domestic terror has allowed the organizations to continue to operate with impunity. While neighboring countries in Europe, Germany, Italy, France and Belgium had, for the most part, decisively dealt with left-wing violence and terrorist threats with a strong and dedicated response force established by powerful political mandate, it seems to be lacking in 1990s Greece.

Minor Terrorist Groups

An increase was noted in terrorist actions in 1998, not only against the state but also at Jewish and Semitic groups, foreigners as well as politicians. The source of the terror appears to be previously unheard-of organizations operating in Greece. Fire bombing has been the hallmark of the attacks, which have been aimed at vehicles and buildings. Close to the end of 1998, there have been over 160 such firebomb attacks. The government of Greece has indicated that these attacks are coming from various quarters, the New Group of Satanists, the Children of November, the Anarchist Street Patrol, and the Conscientious Arsonists, all unknown before 1998. With the ineptitude of the Greek security services a well-established fact, only time will tell if the newly formed special task force of over 1,000 undercover police officers will be effective. As Greece depends heavily on its tourist trade for much valued foreign currency, this style of attack, which seems so indiscriminate, will do a lot to drive that trade elsewhere.

CYPRUS

Situated in the eastern Mediterranean Sea this small island has a population of some 650,000 people, and consists of 78 percent Greek-Cypriots, 18 percent Turkish-Cypriots and 4 percent Maronite and Latin-Cypriots. The Turks and Greeks have lived together on the island for the last five centuries, and mosques and churches can be found almost side by side in many communities. However, that was about to change.

EOKA

Cyprus had been under the control of the British Empire, which by the 1950s was well into its decline. The majority of the people of Cyprus were of Greek origin and in the 1950s were under the leadership of the Greek Cypriot Archbishop Makarios. Similar to the operations of the Stern Gang in Palestine the **EOKA** terrorist organization began to strike at the occupying influences of Great Britain. By 1955, the British Government had declared a state of emergency on the island and the Archbishop went into exile. Following talks with both Turkey and Greece, the British agreed to grant the island independent status. In 1960 the Republic of Cyprus was born under the leadership of Makarios.

On July 20, 1974 Turkey invaded the island, ostensibly to "protect" the minority Turkish-Cypriot community. The international community condemned the action. The U.N. Resolution 353, adopted on the day of the invasion, called for all states to respect, "the sovereignty, independence and territorial integrity of the Republic of Cyprus." It further demanded an immediate end to foreign military intervention in the Republic of Cyprus. Turkey ignored the U.N. and the International community and seized control of at least one third of the Republic's territory, and since then has engaged in terrorism that we know today as "ethnic cleansing." More than 1600 Greek Cypriots are still unaccounted for following the invasion, and more than 200,000 lost their homes and possessions. This is a festering sore for the November 17 terrorist group that continues to blame the United States for failing to act on behalf of the Greek Cypriots.

TURKEY

The history of the Turkish Ottoman Empire stretches back to when the Ottoman Turks invaded and captured Constantinople in 1453, bringing an end to the Byzantine Empire. The Ottoman Empire stretched across Eastern Europe and into regions of the Middle East as we know it today. It stretched as far south into the western reaches of Saudi Arabia, and to Yemen at the southern end of the Red Sea. Its conquests stretched through North Africa from Cairo in the east and Algiers in the west. By the dawning of the eighteenth century the Turkish Empire was commonly termed "the Sick Man of Europe," and was beginning to lose its huge territorial gains of the previous centuries. The Empire lost Algeria to French rule in 1830 and, by the latter part of 1880, Great Britain had taken control of Cyprus and Egypt. France seized Tunisia in 1881. With a crumbling empire, the Turks had to contend with disruptions on the home front as well, ruled by the dictatorship of Sultan Abdul-Hamid II. His rule was one of fear and violent repression of religious groups, that set up the first covert organization in opposition to the dictator. The Young Turks, as they were known, were dissatisfied students and disaffected military personnel opposed to Hamid. The group staged a successful coup in 1908 with the aim of restoring democracy to Turkey. The replacement for Abdul-Hamid was his brother Mohammad V. The Young Turks had envisioned returning the Ottoman Empire to its former greatness, however the populace were less concerned with aspirations toward empire building and were more concerned with their own democratic rights and freedoms. With the Empire crumbling, Turkey entered World War I on the side of Germany, hoping that it would win back much of its losses of the past half century.

Kemal Ataturk

As witnessed throughout history, many inspirational freedom fighters, military heroes with nationalist aspirations, have risen to take control over and to form popular governments. Mustafa Kemal was one such leader whose origins in the Turkish military and exploits as a natural leader brought him to the forefront of politics in Turkey. He formed the provisional government in 1920, after the invasion of the country by forces from Britain, France and Greece. The Ottoman government was unable to protect the country, so the country turned to its nationalist leader, Kemal. The Sultan's powers weakened and the Nationalists grew stronger and were able to forcibly evict the Greeks from Turkish soil. They then sued for peace with the Allies. Turkey as we know it today was formed around the boundaries outlined in the Treaty of Lausanne signed by the Nationalists in 1923. The word "Ataturk" is the surname given to Kemal and means father of the Turks.[40] Kemal ruled as President of Turkey until his death in 1938. Turkey did not repeat its mistake of joining Germany at the outbreak of WWII and managed to keep out of the war; with Germany's defeat, Turkey joined the United Nations in 1946.

Turkey has witnessed many changes in government since the end of WWII ably assisted by a strong military intent on keeping to the democratic principles established so long ago by Kemal. Turkey has had an uneasy peace with its Greek neighbors, which nearly erupted in an all out war, when Turkey threatened to invade Cyprus in 1964.

Revolutionary Left (*Dev Sol*)

A left wing Marxist group that has its origins in the Turkish Peoples Liberation Army from which it split in the late 1970s to form *Dev Sol.* It's a vehemently anti-NATO as well as anti-United States. The aims of this group are to foster an uprising or popular national revolution amongst the Turkish working classes. The group is financed primarily from criminal activities carried out in Turkey including armed robberies and extortion from businesses. During the 1980s, the group restricted its area of operation to the domestic scene, mainly in Izmir, Istanbul and Ankara. With the Middle East crisis and the Desert Storm operation against Iraq, the group began attacks on United States military personnel. The group launched a rocket attack at the United States Consulate in Istanbul in 1992. Since the early 1980s, the group has suffered from internal factional fighting and has carried out limited operations at home. From the training perspective, it is believed that the membership, which is considered to number several hundred, receives training and indoctrination at Palestinian camps from radical Palestinians. By the end of 1998, this group was not particularly active in Turkey, but indications are that it is beginning to resurface and may threaten U.S. commercial interests as well as Turkish government figures.

Kurdistan Workers Party (PKK)

The leadership and organizer of **PKK** originated from the student movement at Ankara University. Abdullah Ocalan, the leader, set up the organization with the specific aim of liberating the Kurds. Ocalan was considerably brutal in his methods and fostered his version of terrorism on his own followers and fellow Kurds. Any dissent in the group was usually put down by executing the dissenters. It is believed that Ocalan killed more than 10,000 Kurds during the 1980s. His actions had some sobering effects on the Kurdish people. It showed them that PKK was strong and that the people should side with them in the struggle for freedom from Turkey; it also meant that failure to actively support the movement was perceived as being on the side of the Turks. Therefore, violent action will speak louder than words. Operating in southeastern Turkey, this Kurdish terror group seeks to set up a Kurdish state fashioned on Marxist lines. Mainly composed of Turkish Kurds PKK has been in operation since 1974 and has been involved in what would best be described as insurgent activities.

Kurds are not restricted to southeast Turkey. In fact, there are approximately 22 million Kurds scattered throughout Turkey, Syria, Iran, Iraq and Russian states. This ethnic group has a very extensive range of support throughout western Europe, and gets aid from Syria and Iran. In Turkey, the Kurds are more of an urban guerrilla fighting force not dissimilar to the Kosovo Liberation Army. The action being fought in the southeastern part of the country is also tying up about 600,000 Turkish troops. The number of full time guerillas is difficult to determine but estimates put their strength in the 20,000 range, with many more part-time members and ample support from the Kurdish clans. Turkey's response and handling of the whole issue of the "Kurdish problem," which it has been unable to solve for fifteen years, has had some disquieting revelations made about its methods. The question of involvement of the state in criminal activities and the deaths of political dissidents was raised following a car crash in Susurluk in 1996. Those killed in the crash were a Turkish Kurd politician and hitman's girl friend.

The Susurluk Report of Prime Minister Yilmaz's government, as it is named, is an attempt to discredit the former coalition government of the pro-Islamic Welfare Party. It was banned by court order in January 1998, and the conservative True Path Party, led by Tansu Ciller, Mr. Yilmaz's rival for leadership of Turkey's center right. The report blames Mrs. Ciller's government for the worst atrocities and abuses, which involves the use of death squads against the Kurds. A wave of unsolved killings swept Turkey after 1991, when more than 1,500 Kurdish nationalists, politicians, journalists and business people were killed. It seems that this is an example of the state engaging in repression and terrorism to prevent terrorism. The Ciller government's hard line goes beyond any methods employed by most western governments.[41]

Armenian Terrorism

Like the Kurds, the ethnic Armenians of northeastern Turkey have, since 1974, been fighting for their own homeland and autonomy in the region. Two terror groups have come to the forefront, the **Armenian Secret Army** for the Liberation of Armenia and the Justice Commandos of the Armenian Genocide. Both groups have targeted diplomats from Turkey in Europe and the United States as part of their terror campaign. Their attacks became more violent when they started to detonate bombs at airports in the 1980's. They set off a bomb at Orly Airport in France adjacent to the Turkish Airlines check–in counters, killing ten and wounding more than seventy in the process. The leader of ASALA Hagop Hagopian was shot to death on an Athens street in 1988 and since then the group has been a spent force.[42]

The Nationalist Threat

The **Turkish Revenge Brigade** is a previously unknown group that has sprung up in 1998 in opposition to Kurdish movements. Considered to be ultranationalist, its targets have been Kurdish and left-wing journalists, actively supportive to the Kurdish movement. In May 1998, two members of the group attempted to assassinate a leading Turkish Human Rights activist Akin Birdal. The motive for the attack is uncertain, but the head of the Human Rights Association claimed at the time that Birdal had received prior death threats and had asked for protection from the government, but to no avail. How the nationalist movement will develop and who is backing and financing its operations is unclear. No doubt, previous reports of Turkish death squads and their involvement earlier in the decade come back into question.

Belgian Terrorism

Belgium and its involvement with terrorism was of considerable internal concern during the 1980s. A country known for a stable democracy and with a population of only 10 million, political violence had been unheard of in comparison to the troubles besieging its neighbors. Belgium terrorism was not widely publicized by the world press and probably received no mention in the popular U.S. press. Belgium has received little or no mention by experts reviewing European terrorist threats; however, terrorist incidents have taken place on Belgium soil from external terror groups. PLO terrorists from the Black September group hijacked a Belgium state (Sabena) airliner to Israel in 1972, and PLO terrorists also attacked the Iraqi Embassy in Brussels in 1978.

The source for internal troubles appeared to rise from the direction of neo-Fascist terror gangs, who, up until the 1980s, had not been active but had aligned themselves to other terror groups in Europe. Considered to be more of a criminal gang element on the outer fringes of violent political struggle, was the extreme right-wing **DARE**, the New Force Party and the West New Post. All were considered extreme right-wing Fascist movements, but had been nonviolent in comparison to the rest of Europe's experiences.

Belgium is a country unfamiliar with violent armed robberies, so when the outbreak began in 1982, the country was in panic. Terrorism in its ugliest form was on the doorstep. The Belgium press, who nicknamed the group the Mad Killers, sensationalized the first attacks. Most of the early attacks were aimed at a supermarket chain but weapons were used, timing and planning were a hallmark of the operation, and the gang readily killed numerous bystanders. Armed with semiautomatic weapons and wearing bullet-proof vests, they escaped with limited amounts of cash, which gave the authorities grave concern as to the real motive for the attacks and killings. The Belgians were unable to determine where the threat was coming from, the left or the right. Terror was causing a crisis in the government and panic in the country, with innocent bystanders being killed. After all, this was not the U.S. but a hitherto quiet mainstream European country.

FRAP (Revolutionary Front for Proletarian Action)

Another organization with the name FRAP burst onto the scene in 1985 when a bomb went off in the North Atlantic Assembly. It was difficult to ascertain whether this was a right-wing or left-wing organization, but the first response was that it was left wing in make up, so arrests of known leftists were carried out. The investigation of the incident was to reveal some startling facts. The date of the attack, April 20, is commemorated by Nazis throughout Europe, and just happens to be the date of birth of Adolf Hitler. According to information gathered, FRAP could just as easily have been communist or right wing. The circumstances of the attack meant that the left would be held responsible for the attack.[43]

CCC (Fighting Communist Cells)

The **CCC** came into being at about the same time as the so-called Mad Killers. How and where they originated was a mystery, and there was considerable speculation that the membership included members of the Belgium State security and agents of the far right. With no historical traditions for terrorism and violence it seemed strange for this movement to emerge in Belgium so successfully. It was represented as a left-wing organization with affiliations with the other left-wing European groups, Action Directe, and the Red Brigade.

The leader of the CCC was Pierre Carette who had a radical history but was determined to be of no real significance as a leader. Carette and the CCC began their short-lived campaign when in October 1984 they attacked offices belonging to Litton Data Systems and two months later followed with another attack on a NATO oil line near Brussels. Other attacks took place against symbolic property targets in Brussels and Antwerp. Carette was arrested following the death of two fire fighters in a bomb attack in Brussels. Carette's arrest spelled the termination of the CCC. It is still not clear as to who or what was involved in the destabilizing attempt of Belgium. Was it all an attempt by the left, or was it some other form of terrorism with an as yet undefined rationale? Whatever the case, there are some underlying aspects to the Belgium political structure and scene that the student would do well to study. One should not dismiss a theory that an agent provocateur may have been involved in the Belgian experience.

SUMMARY

Terrorism in western Europe, and particularly the region of Northern Ireland, has been an ongoing problem since the beginning of the twentieth century. The rise and continuing clamor for a united Ireland and an equally strong demand from loyalists wanting to remain part of Great Britain has plagued Ulster. The terrorist campaign reached its zenith in the 1970s and 1980s with a shift to attacking soft targets in mainland Britain. As successive governments failed to reach a settlement on the Irish question, the aggression became both sectarian and indiscriminate. As democracy talks began to place when the Labour Government took office in Britain, it seemed that a glimmer of hope for some negotiated settlement was possible. Political posturing and demands invariably brought the talks teetering towards failure on numerous occasions throughout 1997-98. A significant accord was reached with the Good Friday Agreement of 1998. Many of the terms and conditions leaned heavily on commitments from both republicans and loyalists to decommission their weapons. On the other side of the agreement, both the British and Republic of Ireland governments began to release terrorist prisoners before the end of their sentences. Four hundred will likely be released by the middle of the year 2000. Although the prospects for peace and an end to the decades of violence seemed good in comparison to previous years, there is still a long road to travel. The reaction of the mainly Protestant Royal Ulster Constabulary and calls for their disbanding, the reaction of the Protestant loyalists to the release of IRA terrorists and the splinter groups of disaffected IRA members seeking to stall and destroy the peace process have yet to be fully appreciated.

Europe, on the other hand, has seen a decline in major terrorist movements with the end of the Red Brigades and the decimation of the Red Army Faction in Germany. Spain's ETA announced a permanent cease-fire which was still holding at the end of 1998. The terrorist threat to Turkey and the issues surrounding an independent homeland and autonomy for the Kurds continues to occupy the attention of both the military and government of that nation. In the next chapter we shall explore the Central European countries freed from Soviet rule, the Russian Republic and other former Communist states. There we will find that state terrorism has turned into violence; crime and terrorism are perpetrated by the very people who were the state officials before 1991.

Terms to Remember

Battle of the Boyne	Sinn Fein	Home Rule Bill
Black and Tans	Irish Free State	IRA
INLA	RUC	PIRA
the Troubles	Carlos the Jackal	Japanese Red Army
Direct Action	PLO	Red Army Faction
Baader Meinhof Gang	ETA-Military	FRAP
RB	Movimento Politico Occidentale	November 17 Group
ELA	EOKA	Dev Sol
PKK	Armenian Secret Army	Turkish Revenge Brigade
DARE	Kemal Ataturk	CCC

Review Questions

Describe the role of the Provisional Irish Republican Army (PIRA) in the struggle for independence by Northern Ireland.

Discuss the terrorist organizations that are or were in operations in France.

What were then main terrorist actions which made the Baader Meinhof Gang so famous?

Describe the situation with the Kurds in Turkey.

What are some of the potential problems arising out of the neo-nazi movements in western Europe?

Endnotes

1. George Rosie. *The Directory of International Terrorism.* (Paragon House New York 1987.)
2. J.W. Soule. *Terrorism: An International Journal.* (Vol. 12, Number 1, 1989). p. 44
3. The Weekly Telegraph. "28 More Terrorists freed under Good Friday deal," *The Telegraph Group,* London. October 20–26, 1998) p.4 issue 378.
4. *The Weekly Telegraph,* issue #337 p.11
5. "Ulster's Past, Ulster's Future." *The Economist,* January 31, 1998. p. 57.
6. *The World Book Encyclopaedia,* Volume 11, p. 25, World Book Inc.
7. *The World Book Encyclopaedia,* Volume 10, p.427, 428, World Book Inc.
8. Michael Collins. The Irish Nationalist Network, Internet.
9. Introduction to Sinn Fein—Evolution of a Republican Party, Internet.
10. Jonathan R. White. *Terrorism: An Introduction.* Brooks/Cole Publishing. pp. 220,221,
11. *The World Book Encyclopaedia,* Volume 10, p. 427, World Book Inc.
12. *Terrorism An Introduction,* p. 215.
13. David Yallop. *Tracking the Jackal.* Random House Inc. New York 1993.

14. Philip Jackson. "Under two flags: Provocation and Deception in European Terrorism." *Terrorism and International Journal,* Taylor and Francis, New York 1988), p.280 Volume II.

15. Grant Wardlaw. "*Political Terrorism, Theory, tactics and counter-measures,*" (Cambridge University Press, London, 1982) p. 38.

16. Philip Jenkins. "Strategy of Tension: The Belgian Terrorist Crisis 1982–1986", *Terrorism: an International Journal,* Taylor and Francis, New York 1990, p. 299 Volume 13.

17. Yallop. Tracking the Jackal. p. 98

18. *The World Book Encyclopaedia.* World Book Inc. 1990, p. 254, Volume 9.

19. Richard Huffman. *Motivations* from an Internet article Terrorist Motivations 1997.

20. Ibid.

21. George Rosie. *Directory of International Terrorism.* Paragon House, New York, 1986, p. 220.

22. Ibid. p. 65.

23. The Internet. Intel Brief courtesy of U.S. State Department Archives on ETA.

24. William Gutteridge. "Contemporary Terrorism", an article by Peter Janke, The Institute for the Study of Conflict, 1986, p. 152.

25. Rosie. *Directory of International Terrorism,* p. 120.

26. Ibid. p. 135.

27. Pino Arlacchi. *Men of Dishonor,* William Morrow and Co. Inc., New York, p. 27.

28. Gutteridge. Contemporary Terrorism, p. 127, A Challenge to Italian Democracy, Vittorfranco S Pisano.

29. Ibid. p. 176.

30. Ibid. p. 177.

31. Ibid. p. 182.

32. Ibid. p. 184.

33. Ibid. p. 184.

34. The Internet, Anti Defamation League, *The Skinhead International,* a Worldwide Survey of Neo-Nazi Skinheads. New York Anti defamation League 1995.

35. Ibid.

36. Ibid.

37. Andrew Corsun, "Revolutionary Organization November 17 in Greece," *Terrorism: an International Journal,* Taylor and Francis London 1991), volume 14 p. 86.

38. Ibid. p. 97.

39. Gerogr Kassimeris, "Greece: Twenty Years of Political Terrorism", *Terrorism and Political Violence,* Frank Cass, London, 1995) p. 81 Vol. 7.

40. *World Book Encyclopaedia.* World Book Inc. U.S.A 1990 p. 511, vol. 19.

41. Hugh Pope Staff Reporter. *The Wall Street Journal.* January 26, 1998.

42. Ibrahim Cerrah and Robert Peel. "Terrorism in Turkey." *INTERSEC.* England 1997) p. 19 vol. 7.

43. Philip Jenkins. "Strategy of Tension: The Belgian Terrorist Crisis 1982–1986." *Terrorism: an International Journal,* Taylor and Francis, London 1990), p. 304.

44. Paul Wilkinson, Gary Allen & Ullman. *British Perspectives on Terrorism,* p. 83–84.

45. William Gutteridge. "Contemporary Terrorism", (The Institute for the Study of Conflict—Facts on File, New York, 1986).

CHAPTER 5

CENTRAL AND EASTERN EUROPE

*We say outright: These are madmen, yet these madmen have their own logic,
their teaching, their code, their God, and it's as deep set as it could be.*

—Dostoevsky

OVERVIEW

Terrorism in the former Eastern Bloc and in the Soviet Union and Russia is not a new phenomenon in those countries. Its colorful and sad history is depicted in the stories by novelists of the nineteenth century, much as by the novelists of this century under the yoke of the Soviets. Count Leo N. Tolstoy, who wrote *War and Peace* in 1869, captures the fire and horror of the French invasion of Russia in 1812. Reforms made by Czar Alexander II were strongly opposed by his son Alexander III, who succeeded him after his assassination. It was this repressive approach that slowly nurtured the seeds of revolt in Russia, that were at first written about as themes of desperation, discontent and bitterness by the many great novelists and intellectuals of that era.

In this chapter the student will review the early terror theories at work in Russia and the Slavic states and will see the manner in which the Soviet Union fostered state-sponsored terrorism on an international scale. Many of the nineteenth century Russian writers like Maxim Gorki wrote short stories and plays that reflected the theories of a Communist state in Russia. The early seeds of terror grew out of the appalling conditions under which the people of Russia existed under the czars. It grew out of a need for social change and the overwhelming will of the people to see change. We shall start with the most famous and work down to the others in the central and eastern parts of Europe.

RUSSIA AND THE SOVIET UNION

Narodnaya Volya (NV) (1878–1881)[1]

Roughly translated, this term has the meaning **"the people's will."** This highly effective terrorist organization was only in existence for four years. The group grew out of other disaffected Russian movements that were clandestine in nature and formed by the intelligentsia. Hard liners out of several of these groups formed the Narodnaya Volya. As with many current day terrorist organizations, the NV used terrorism as a means to a political end. With the aim of causing distress and turmoil to the ruling Romanovs, they hoped that their actions would shake the Russian Empire's political foundations. Numbering more than 500, with fifty or more extremists drawn from the ruling upper class of Russian society, they set out to overthrow the tyranny of the czars. They sentenced Czar Alexander II to death and made several unsuccessful attempts on his life.

One of the most fanatical members of the organization, twenty-seven year old Sophia Ptrovskaya, succeeded in planting a bomb that killed the Czar in 1881. In addition, the NV was also responsible for the death of General Mezentsev, head of the Third Section of the czarist OKHRNA and also the governor general of Saint Petersburg. The NV were hunted down and arrested by czarist authorities and terrorism in Russia diminished over the next two decades. The NV was to have a profound effect on Russian history. The inspiration for Lenin to form the Social Democratic Labour Party was born out of NV. Lenin's view and appreciation for NV taught him an important lesson: that a revolutionary organization cannot be limited to terrorism, but must seize total autocratic power. The NV symbolized the general social crisis that existed in nineteenth century Russia, and much later during the Bolshevik revolution which replaced the old order in Russia. Terrorism faded with the passing of the NV, until the formation of the Social Revolutionary Party at the turn of the twentieth century. Members of NV took extreme care in planning and carrying out their assassinations in such a manner as not to kill innocents in the process. The targets for retribution were those deemed guilty of acts of corruption and other acts against the people.

Terror and revolution are two words that would be frequently referred to interchangeably for Russians over the first twenty years of the twentieth century. In 1902, the Minister of the Interior was assassinated. The objective for terrorism in early twentieth century Russia was to awaken the masses to the potential for revolution and social change. The philosophy of this approach is seen today in struggles in other regions of nationalist conflict where the intent is to attempt coercion and motivate the masses to revolt and overthrow the existing authority.

ⵔ TERRORISM BYTE 5–1

THE RUSSIAN REVOLUTION

The Revolution of 1917 began in February with the demise of the monarchy and a new provisional government under Kerensky. Vladimir Ilyich Lenin returned from 10 years in exile to lead the Bolshevik takeover. The Bolsheviks moved against the opposition and forcibly stormed the Winter Palace and took control of the new Soviet state. The following year the capital was moved to Moscow. After his death in 1924, the city of Petrograd was renamed Leningrad in his memory.

BLOODY SUNDAY

Czar Nicholas I was to be the last ruling monarch of the Russian Empire. Considered weak and superstitious, he had a total dislike for politicians and the intellectual elite. Following Russia's defeat in the Russo-Japanese war thousands of protesting peasants and workers marched into Palace Square. The event started out peacefully enough. However, the crowd carrying icons of Czar Nicholas had hoped to get his attention. The chief of police ordered his men to open fire on the group, with the resulted in hundreds being massacred. This day, January 9th 1905, is remembered as Bloody Sunday.

Within the Social Revolutionary Party was a sub-terror group that was given autonomy under the Party, **Boevaya Oranisatsia (BO)**, or the Fighting Organization. It can be argued that whereas the NV was more aligned to the educated Russian hierarchy, the BO appealed to a far wider Russian audience. Within the revolutionary movement there continued widespread dissent about the use of terror tactics, and with the emergence of the class struggle, terrorism as a weapon of the period became redundant.

Mikhail Bakunin, the brilliant Russian orator, traveled widely throughout Europe promoting his ideals for revolutionary change. They were based on the destruction of the prevailing social order as it existed in Russia. His approach to anarchy conflicted greatly with that of Marx, and the two were bitter rivals. Bakunin put forward no useful or thoughtful ideas for a future social order and was seen by Marx to be a dangerous fanatic. Bakunin's view was that the state had to be overthrown whereas Marx's contrasted with the view that it was capitalism that had to be purged. Karl Marx's theory and ideology was that violence was necessary to transform the nature of the working class, and that violent insurrection was the only means by which society could be changed.

Opposition to the rule of the Bolsheviks, following their rise to power in 1917, came from the intelligentsia, as well as from opposition newspapers. The Russian republics were basically involved in a civil war between the years 1918–21. In March 1918, Lenin dissolved the Constituent Assembly when it failed to recognize the leadership of the **Bolshevik** government. The protests of the Left Socialist Revolutionary Party went unheeded by Lenin and they withdrew from the coalition. The Bolsheviks began a period of terror and repression against all groups that voiced opposition. Arrests were made of hundreds of artists and intellectuals who were simply aghast at the attitude of the Bolsheviks and had expected a society based on freedom after the overthrow of the czarist government. The Bolsheviks dealt with nationalists, Menscheviks, social revolutionaries as well as members of the intellectual levels of society (professors, writers and artists) in the harshest manner. The Church in Russia also became a target of Communist terror and oppression. A systematic campaign by the Communists to deny the Russian Orthodox Church any voice in the Soviet Union started in the 1920s, and by the year 1939 all the clergy and many of the church's followers had been shot or sent to forced labor camps. Of the 50,000 churches only about 500 remained open.

Josef Stalin

To many, the very name Stalin conjures up scenes of sheer despotic terror. In the early first quarter of the twentieth century, his name was almost synonymous with the word

Josef Stalin, who probably
killed more Russians than
World War II. CP Picture
Archive (AP/Photo File)

terror. This chapter is not designed to teach the student the fundamentals of the Russian Revolution but to explain that the intricate use of terror tactics as practiced by Lenin's Bolsheviks had the unspoken support of the party. Were the Bolsheviks considered terrorists or were they revolutionaries fighting for their political beliefs to achieve a Soviet Republic? As history looks back and such popular movies such as Dr. Zhivago seem to glory in the hostility, as well as man's inhumanity to his fellow man, do we therefore consider the Russian Revolution a result of effective terrorism? In later years and specifically during the Cold War, the USSR is viewed, particularly by the United States and her NATO allies, as the exporter and sponsor of modern-day terrorism. The notorious terrorist Carlos the Jackal is believed to have received his indoctrination, training and funding from the Soviet Union. Although there is evidence that he did indeed receive part of his university education in the USSR, there has been no substantive evidence that the Soviet Union in fact sponsors him.

Josef Vissarionovich Dzhugashvili adopted the name "**Stalin,**" which has the literal translation, "steel". Following the death of Lenin, Stalin became the absolute ruler of the Soviet Union from 1929 until he died in 1953. As a young man, he earned a scholarship to study theology, but was subsequently expelled for preaching Marxist ideals. He was a strong political supporter of Bolshevism throughout Europe, and is credited with being the first editor of *Pravda*, the newspaper voice of the Communist party. Stalin used extreme measures on the Russian population to ensure absolute and blind obedience to his will; any who opposed him were summarily dealt with and either shot or sent to labor camps. This form of state terrorism was carried out under his head of the secret police, Beria, whose very name struck terror in the hearts of the Soviet citizens.

Secret Police

In many states where suppression of the masses by deliberate terror takes place, there is the need for a sanctioned police force or other security network to do the bidding of the dictator. Apart from Adolf Hitler, there can be few other world leaders that have slaughtered and sent to labor camps so many of their own countrymen as Stalin ordered. The Communist regime under Stalin viewed any dissent against Communism as a repudiation of the proletarian struggle, a violation of Marxist-Leninist ideology, and therefore a threat to the very existence of the authority of the state. To this end, the Bolsheviks and then the Communists relied heavily on a strong political secret police to secure and maintain their rule. The original secret police, called the **Cheka**, were formed in 1917 with the intention that they be disbanded after power had been consolidated by the Bolsheviks under Lenin. The first chief of this secret police force was Feliks Dzerzhinskii, who had the power under the Bolsheviks to investigate "counterrevolutionary" crimes.

Much has been written of the Russian Revolution and few would argue that the results of the October Revolution would be felt for decades to come, even though the Soviet Union is no more. The difficulty in defining terrorism again becomes apparent. There is no doubt that the actions of the Social Democrats of the Lenin era were terrorist in attitude and nature. However, when viewed and portrayed as a class struggle or one for worker rights, why are the actions of these fighters now termed revolutionary actions? Is it the popular belief that where a mass or common populace supports the cause, whether it be righteous or not, these activities are no longer referred to as merely terrorist acts but rather a full-blown popular resistance or even revolution?

In the latter part of the twentieth century, Western governments have actively criminalized terrorism and created legislation to deal with specific acts of violence against the state, including the banning of terrorist linked, backed or supported groups. Wouldn't it therefore be correct to rationalize that a popular revolution exists within the borders of Spain (ETA) or in Northern Ireland (IRA)? As we strive to continually master what terrorism means in each specific category and indeed each country, it becomes less and less easy to define. In Afghanistan, following the Soviet "invasion" of that sovereign state, no doubt the rebels fighting for the freedom of their country from the mountains around Kabul would most likely be termed terrorists by the Soviet Union. It is equally fair to believe that to the Afghans these "terrorists" were better described as "freedom fighters."

The Great Terror

Throughout modern history there have been many dictators who have purged their respective societies of all opposition from within their own political structures as well as on the outside. The murder of a senior Politburo member on December 1, 1934, was to set in motion a chain of events that resulted in the Great Terror. Sergei Kirov was leader of the Communist party in Leningrad, and an influential member of the ruling elite. Popular as he was in Leningrad in support of workers' welfare, he disagreed with some of Stalin's policies, and although not thought to be a threat to Stalin, he had been approached by some party members to take over as General Secretary.[2]

Was he possibly perceived as a threat by Stalin, who was having doubts about the loyalty of the Leningrad apparatus? It seems entirely possible that the NKVD could well have planned Kirov's murder on Stalin's instructions. Using the murder of Kirov as the excuse he needed to crack down hard and to purge the Leningrad Party structure, Stalin introduced wide-sweeping laws that resulted in millions of Russians being arrested. This purge lasted for approximately four years and Stalin never again visited Leningrad. This four-year period saw millions sent to Russian labor camps as well as summary executions and show trials. To say the Russian populace was terrified

TERRORISM BRIEF 5-1
RUSSIAN NUCLEAR STOCKPILE A WORRY

The Pentagon maintains that Russia's arsenal of 22,000 nuclear warheads is safe and secure, an island of stability in an increasingly chaotic nation. But experts outside the U.S. government express far more concern.

"We have no reason to believe that there is any problem with Russia's command and control of its nuclear weapons, or the security of its arsenal," said Air Force Lt. Col. Queenie Byars, a Defense Department spokeswoman.

"What do you expect them to say?" responds Robert Norris, a nuclear weapons analyst at the Natural Resources Defense Council, an environmental advocacy group. "It is in both nations' interest to keep a happy face on things—the public position has to be that things are basically in order."

Ralph Peters, a former military intelligence officer who has written extensively on Russian affairs, is even more strident in disagreeing with his old bosses. "Given the disastrous state of things in Russia, we'd be foolish not to worry," he said. "They're sloppy, they're starving, they're stupid, they're mean, and they do maintenance with sledgehammers."

The decade-long effort to control the former Soviet nuclear stockpile hasn't captured many prominent headlines. But experts agree that it probably is one of the great success stories of the post-Cold War era. Since the mid-1980s, the size of the stockpile has been halved, and warhead storage facilities have been streamlined to about 90 sites from about 500.

Partly due to $2.3 billion in U.S. aid since 1991, three states of the former Soviet Union—Kazakhstan, Ukraine and Belarus—have become denuclearized, as warheads on their territories were moved to Russia, where some have been dismantled. The question now is whether that effort to control the stockpile will survive Moscow's new round of political and economic turmoil.

There is general agreement that the strategic nuclear warheads, the crown jewels of the stockpile, are secure. Indeed, in some ways, economic hard times have benefited Russia's strategic nuclear forces: faced with a tight budget, the Yeltsin government has let much of the Russian military waste away, concentrating on just two areas—elite airborne troops and nuclear forces. Nuclear weapons are a relatively inexpensive form of military might. They aren't cheap to build, but simply maintaining an arsenal costs far less than manning, equipping and sustaining dozens of armored divisions.

Earlier this year, Air Force Gen. Eugene Habiger, at the time the chief of the U.S. Strategic Command, reported that "security was excellent" when he visited a base of SS-19 intercontinental ballistic missiles near Moscow. Among other things, the Russians demonstrated how they would use helicopter-borne security forces and armored personnel carriers to repel a terrorist attack.

The problem, private sector analysts say, is that both the U.S. and Russian governments tend to focus too much on the strategic arsenal, and not enough on Russia's 4,000 "tactical" warheads—meant for battlefield use—or the 1,200 tons of fissile material on Russian soil. They also ignore the expertise of scientists who, amid a decaying economy, could be lured to the nuclear programs of Iran or Iraq.

The theft of warheads, the sale of materials that could be used to make weapons, or leakage of expertise all "become more possible as the Russian economy collapses," warned Joseph Cirincione, a nonproliferation expert at the Carnegie Endowment for International Peace, a Washington think tank. If that happens, he said, "You could get a new nuclear power faster than anyone imagines."

"The problem is only likely to worsen if the Russian economy doesn't recover," said Mr. Norris of the Natural Resource Defense Council. "It's going to be a rocky road in Russia for decades, and these weapons aren't going to go away," he said.

But the biggest concern about Russia's nuclear arsenal is political: Government officials and private analysts all worry that Russia could drift into a fearful, insular, hard-line authoritarianism hostile to the West. "If they were in the hands of an unfriendly power," then-Defense Secretary William Perry warned about the Russian nuclear arsenal in 1995, "we would consider them quite threatening."

SOURCE: THOMAS E. RICKS. "RUSSIA'S NUCLEAR STOCKPILE IS SECURE, SAYS U.S., BUT SOME EXPERTS AREN'T SURE" THE WALL STREET JOURNAL, (NEW YORK, WALL STREET JOURNAL PRESS, SEPTEMBER 3, 1998), P. 4A.

would be an understatement. In view of the terror tactics of Stalin, his complete and total domination of the Russian people was further enforced by forcibly resettling over one million people, mainly Muslims, from the Northern Caucasus region and the Crimea. Ethnic Tartars, Chechens, Meskhetians, Kalmyks as well as Bulgarians, Greeks and Armenians from the Black Sea coast were deported.

These deportations took place during and after World War II, with the excuse that they were collaborators with German occupying forces. The forced deportation took place with the use of cattle cars reminiscent of German deportation to forced labor and extermination camps of Jews and Gypsies. The destination for the deportees was Uzbekistan, Siberia and Kazakhstan, names that today have a ring of familiarity to them. By the mid-1950s the forced deportations were denounced by Nikita Khrushchev; however, many were still not permitted to return to their native homeland until after the breakup of the Soviet Union in 1991.

Estonian Guerrilla Movement, 1944–1955

One terror or guerilla group that existed after the collapse of the German Axis was an Estonian movement called the *Metsavennad*, meaning "guerrilla." With the retreat of the German Army, many Estonian soldiers who had been drafted into the German Army attempted to escape the discipline of Stalin, either by leaving the country or fleeing to the forest region of Estonia. These men were known as "brethren." Not only Estonians but deserting Germans also joined the movement. The group was well equipped with an abundance of weapons, and was also supported by those who sought revenge against the Soviet Union for previous forced deportations associated with collectivization in March 1949. The cause was the ultimate independence of Estonia and although this was realized to be a fruitless gesture against the might of the Soviets they had obviously hoped for some relief and withdrawal of the Soviets, possibly with another European theater of war. The movement is sparsely written about and they formed a protective band around Estonians to prevent violence meted out by the Soviets. A post-Stalin amnesty in 1955 saw the movement virtually disappear.

"School for Terrorism"

Also known as **Killer College**,[3] Patrice Lumumba University is located near Moscow and was established in 1961 as the Soviet Union's educational contribution to the Third World countries of Africa and Asia. It was to this university that the infamous terrorist Ilyich Ramirez (Carlos the Jackal) received his post-secondary education. Together with his brother Lenin, the Venezuelan Communist Party had sponsored their admission to the University. Partying seems to have been a big part of their own curriculum while in Moscow, and on several occasions, they went afoul of their Soviet Army and KGB minders. Ilyich was arrested while demonstrating for the cause of thirty Iranian students who had had their passports seized by the Shah's government. Although sponsored by the Venezuelan Communists Iylich and Lenin were not members of the party. Their continuous confrontations with orthodox members of the Venezuelan Communist Youth movement at the University lead to their grants being suspended and subsequent expulsion from the university. Though there have been many books and articles written about Carlos the Jackal, whether the KGB recruited him during the period he spent in Moscow will probably never be known. On his own admission, after leaving the Soviet Union in 1970 his next stop was the melting pot of international terrorism, Beirut.

Bulgaria: State-Sponsored Terrorism

The debate on the level of effort conducted by Moscow in the arena of state-sponsored terrorism can be theorized at length; however, there is considerable belief that its Communist neighbor Bulgaria was active in this area, possibly on its behalf. The extent of Bulgaria's involvement in state-sponsored terrorism is an issue worth discussion. During the period of the cold war Moscow's attempts to destabilize the Western democracies involved the use of terror tactics against not only nations but also symbolic personages. In Rome, Italy, on May 13, 1981, a Turkish Nationalist attempted to assassinate Pope John Paul II in St. Peter's Square. The Pope was shot and his would-be assassin arrested. The ensuing investigation uncovered a link to Bulgaria. The Pope's assailant **Mehmet Ali Agca** is believed to have had an accomplice in place to aid in his escape from Italy. The accomplice, Oral Celik, escaped capture by leaving the country in a Bulgarian Embassy diplomatic truck. The following year, a Bulgarian State Airline official was charged in Rome in connection with the assassination attempt on the Pope.[4] Further evidence of Bulgaria's complicity to export terror is seen in the actions of Sallah Wakkas, a Syrian national operating in Athens. He had purchased over $50 million worth of Soviet made weapons and ammunition from a Bulgarian weapons company, **KINTEX**.[5] Further involvement was uncovered when Greek customs seized a ship en route to North Yemen in 1984. The contents of a consignment of oil tankers revealed huge quantities of weapons and ammunition. The ship's cargo of trucks had been consigned by the Bulgarian state cargo agency, Bulfracht, while the paperwork for the consignment was produced by Inflot, the Bulgarian state shipping agency. It must be assumed that this arms shipment was destined for the Palestine Liberation Organization training camps in North Yemen. One must assume that these were just an example of many other shipments that were not intercepted. In addition Bulgaria's involvement in drug trafficking has been fairly well documented. Drugs of course can be used in the sale or barter for weapons and explosives. KINTEX of Bulgaria has been a supplier of heroin and morphine to Kurdish dissidents in Turkey, and these drugs have been used to trade for weapons.[6]

The Bulgarian tactic of inflicting terror on its own subjects while also being able to strike out at dissidents in European locations came to sudden and painful light with two attacks on Bulgarian dissidents in Paris and London. On August 26, 1978, a Bulgarian defector to the west and a former well-known television personality, Vladimir Kostov, was jabbed with a poison-tipped umbrella, laced with the poison **ricin**. He survived the attack, but an incident in London involving the same method, against outspoken novelist and playwright Georgi Markov, resulted in his death.

Further evidence of the Bulgarian attempts at destabilization revolves around their shadowy involvement in the kidnapping by the Red Brigade of the American NATO General, James Dozier. From evidence deduced by the examining judge at the trial of the Red Brigade ringleader, Antonio Savasta, Bulgaria played a part in the interrogation of the general, as well as offering logistical and training support to the Red Brigade.

Into the Millennium

With the breakup of the Soviet Union, and with many of the Russian republics seeking to go their own way and separate from the Russian Federation, Russia at the end of 1998 found itself in somewhat unfamiliar waters. A country no longer controlled by the Communists, with its people sampling capitalist fare, has seen many of the disaffected youth lean towards right-wing nationalism. In the summer of 1998, Boris Yeltsin was openly commenting in press reports about the right-wing nationalist threat. What was surfacing in Russia, which was now subject to rampant unemployment, had already surfaced in a unified Germany. Russian youth were beginning to blame immigrants and Jews for the lack of jobs and the country's woes. Hate crimes and the like were now commonplace in Russia. Has Russia gone full circle in the last one hundred years? At the turn of the last century, Russia was in turmoil with the uprising of the worker classes; it is possible that this situation may be repeating itself.

The Soviet Union has seen more freedom of the press to report on issues and incidents as they occur in daily everyday life than ever before, and this may become part of the lifeblood of any terrorist group starting out in Russia. Under Communist domination, anti-Soviet acts were rarely reported on by the government-controlled media. Without these restrictions, a key component in any terrorist arsenal is the ability to bring activities to a wide audience. In the democracies of the West, acts of terror and sabotage have received banner headlines. With suppression of the press, there can be little support for any type of terrorist activity.

Russia—Free Market Economy and the Russian Mafia

Russia became a so-called democracy following the breakup of the Soviet Union. What, one must ask, happened to the KGB after the breakup? Organized crime in the Russian Federation was on the rise, with a police force ill equipped to respond. Interpol, on the other hand, was hard at work tracking the exploits of more than 400 Russian international criminals, while the Office of International Criminal Justice estimated at least 4,000 organized crime syndicates operating in the Federation by 1996.

With the breakup of the Soviet Union came the dissolution of the Soviet intelligence service (KGB). Their agents, however, did not fade into oblivion. Scratching the surface of Russian bureaucracy will uncover layers of control dominated by former KGB operatives, many in local government and politics. Organized crime syndicates in the Russian Federation in collaboration with former KGB officers is probably a major factor in a booming trade in Soviet-made weaponry, not the least of which are nuclear capability products. The Russian Mafia's links with former KGB operatives have led to the escalation of weapons sales to terror groups, and the Russian Mafia has moved from purely internal criminal activities to the exporting of terrorist weapons with mass destruction capability. Weapons of mass destruction have been on the market to the highest bidder and some of these sophisticated weapons have reached the hands of third world countries. The potential for global conflict from these sales is yet to be realized and should not be minimized.

At the end of 1998, we find Russia at the crossroads, on the road to reform, or taking the long and winding path to anarchy and corruption. The lawless state of society in Russia has led criminal elements to feed on the possibilities of controlling the state and reaping the rewards from corrupt politicians. With the criminal element playing so large a part in the proceedings of daily life in Russia, it is no wonder that these elements will stop at nothing to achieve their goals. With the economy crumbling, any reform-style politician would be a target in 1998 Russia. On November 22, 1998, the staunch pro-democracy parliamentarian Galina Starovoitova, who was a vocal campaigner for human rights and against political corruption, was murdered in a scene reminiscent of a James Bond movie. She was shot three times in the head at close range as she entered her apartment building. Her campaign was instrumental in exposing corrupt local politicians, and it is believed that this led to her assassination. Starovoitova was well respected, but was by now in a minority of democracy reformers. The killing was done in a very professional manner and had the hallmarks of a gangland-style execution. In a country where few women rise to the heights of local and national politics, her passing is something of a watershed for Russian politics. What the outcome will be is uncertain, but the grip of the underworld on Russia seems to be excruciatingly strong. It was brutally summed up at her graveside by Yevgeny Primakov, the Russian Prime Minister, when he commented that the country was "drifting towards fascism."[7]

CHECHNYA

A Mixed Background

The czars began a three hundred year attempt to subjugate the Northern Caucasus in 1560. By 1585, Chechnya and other areas of the Caucasus had been conquered by the Ottoman Empire and represented its northern reach into what has become modern Russia. Under Ottoman rule, the Chechens adopted Islam. Russia continued its attempt to capture the area and finally forced the retreat of the Ottomans by 1785. After winning the Caucasian war (1817–1864), the Russians deported hundreds of thousands of Chechens. In 1877, 1920, 1929, 1940 and 1943 the Chechens made unsuccessful attempts to rebel against the czars and then the Communists. While most of the Chechen males were fighting against Hitler in the winter of 1943–44, Stalin ordered that Chechnya be obliterated. Villages were burned, 500,000 people were deported to Kazakhstan and Siberia and their land was given to non-Chechens. In 1957, the Chechens were allowed to return to their homeland. Dzhokhar Dudayev seized power in Chechnya in August 1991. After a popular vote elected him president that November, Dudayev declared independence from the Soviet Union, just a month before its collapse.

Another Tar Baby?

In February 1994, Russian President Boris Yeltsin and President of the Republic of Tatarstan, Minitimir Shaimiev, initialed a treaty delineating a division of powers between the Russian national government and the government of Tatarstan. The treaty afforded Tatarstan a considerable amount of autonomy, and was welcomed by Yeltsin's Nationalities Minister, Sergei Shakhrai, as a "breakthrough." Kabardino-Balkaria and Bashkortostan followed in short order. These treaties represented a "fine-tuning" of Russia's evolving federation relations, the basic framework of which had been established by the new Russian Constitution of December 1993. The consolidation of Russia's territorial integrity was essential to prevent another Afghanistan failure to control the huge group of Islamic states within and without the vast Russian borders. Above all, there was the explosive situation in the North Caucasus. There, among other problems, the breakaway republic of Chechnya continued to refuse to consider itself a part of the new **Russian Federation**.

Moscow's previous response to Chechnya's challenge amounted to a policy of benign neglect toward Chechnya and its President, Dzhokhar Dudayev. Moscow allowed the republic to go its own way and even attempted periodically to enter into negotiations with Dudayev. The Russian government repeatedly asserted that under no condition would force be used to resolve their differences with the republic and expressed the hope that these treaties would serve as a model for finding a negotiated solution with Chechnya.

Even as words of encouragement were being spoken, Moscow began stepping up financial and military support for opposition forces to the government in Chechnya. Fighting in the republic intensified over the summer, leading in November to a major attack on Grozny by the combined forces of the Chechen opposition in an effort to overthrow Dudayev. Despite support from helicopters and aircraft with Russian markings, the attack failed. A little more than a week later, President Yeltsin issued a decree authorizing the government, including the military, to take all necessary steps to disarm "illegal armed formations" in the republic. Two days later, 40,000 Russian troops poured into Chechnya. It was a debacle and the Chechen rebels were able to send the demoralized Russian Army home in defeat.[8] In August 1994, the Russian government began military action to stop Chechnya's succession. Russian troops began aerial bombing and attacked the capital of Grozny in December and in February 1995. Subsequently, the rebel Chechen government moved to the hills and Chechnya was put under an armed Russian occupation.

Regardless of whether Russia had a right to use force to defend its territorial integrity against Chechen secession, it is now clear in hindsight that the invasion was a terrible error. The viciousness of the war made it inconceivable that Chechnya will ever become a "normal" member of the Russian Federation, even if it is granted considerable autonomy and a treaty-based relationship with Moscow like Tatarstan's. The hostility of the Chechen people toward Russia, deeply rooted even before the conflict, has been immeasurably intensified by the brutality of the war and will not be ameliorated by Moscow's promises of financial aid to reconstruct the republic, assuming that Moscow is in a position to deliver on these promises, which it is not.

Moscow continues to make the full application of its constitution on Chechen soil as a condition of peaceful existence. With that caveat, the republic will remain a terrible burden on the Russian people, a political nightmare for whatever party is in power in Moscow, and a major and possibly decisive impediment to the preservation of Russian democracy.[9] Chechnya is rapidly deteriorating into a state of civil war. By the latter half of 1998 the beleaguered President, Aslan Maskhadov, had become the target of terrorist attacks by opposition forces. There is some indication that the rebels fighting against him are in fact demanding that the government set up a fundamentalist state and introduce Islamic law or *sharia*.

Current Situation

The Russian army fully withdrew in January 1997, following an August 1996 agreement granting the republic autonomy and establishing it as a free economic zone. Aslan Maskhadov, the Chechen military chief of staff in charge of the war effort, won Chechen presidential elections on January 27th. Over 50,000 civilians died in the war. Six workers from the International Committee of the Red Cross were murdered in their sleep in December 1996, the worst premeditated attack in the history of the organization. Whether one looks at this sad episode as terrorism, rebellion or war, both sides used terror as a weapon and no one seems to have won. The one intriguing question yet to be discussed is the worrisome phenomenon of the Russian nuclear stockpile. There is no sound record of the state and positive location of every type of missile that was under the control of the former Soviet Union. It is highly probable, from newspaper reports, that handheld nuclear missiles are missing or unaccounted for. In either scenario, the threat from their mere existence will have many governments concerned. Many terrorist organizations and not just the Chechens would welcome having this type of capability even only as a threat.

YUGOSLAVIA

World War I to Ethnic Cleansing

Yugoslavia as a nation was established by the League of Nations out of the union of territories dating back to the end of World War I in 1918. Bordered to the east with the Soviet Bloc countries of Romania, Hungary and Bulgaria, the Communist State of Yugoslavia encompassed six separate republics mainly founded on their ethnic or religious background. The area in question has been populated for at least 100,000 years.[10] The first groups of Slavs moved to the area in around the fifth century. They migrated from regions now known as southern Poland and the republics of the Russian Empire. Differing groups of Slavs formed their own enclaves and independent states. Serbians founded Serbia, Croats Croatia; however, from about 1400 onwards the southern Slavs were ruled by foreign powers.

The Turkish Empire controlled Serbian areas, while Hungary and Austria ruled Slovenia and Croatia respectively. As the centuries moved by, the desire for a united region became a goal of Slovenia and Croatia. The movement to unite sparked an incident that was to change the destiny of Europe and the fate of millions. On June 28, 1914, in Sarajevo, a Serbian terrorist named Gavrilo Princip from Bosnia assassinated the **Archduke Franz Ferdinand** of Austria-Hungary. Because of pacts between European nations this single terrorist act fueled the start of the Great War 1914–1918. Yugoslavia was so named by King Alexander I, in 1929. The King ruled briefly as an absolute dictator; he was assassinated by dissident Croat terrorists in 1934.

To say that modern-day terrorism played a part in the structure of a nation such as Yugoslavia would not be far from the mark. Two resistance groups fought against each other as well as the occupying Germans during World War II. The partisans led by Josip Tito and his Communist party, and the Chetniks who supported the monarchy under King Peter. By the end of World War II, the **Partisans** (terrorists?) under Tito established a Communist government and on November 29, 1945 the region became the Federal People's Republic of Yugoslavia, thus abolishing the monarchy and sending King Peter into permanent exile. As will be seen throughout, many dictators have felt the need to dominate and destroy all opponents of the regime. Yugoslavia under Marshal Tito was no different, and opponents of the Communist government were either imprisoned, killed or exiled. Tito declared a one-party Communist state. Although a Communist state in its own right, Yugoslavia was not a puppet of the Soviet Union. In fact, from the late 1940s, Yugoslavia and the Soviet Union severed ties to one another. During the Cold War between East and West, Yugoslavia became a moderate voice.

Modern-Day Problems

The people of Yugoslavia split on ethnic lines into the six republics, with Slovenia in the north, and Croatia on its southern border. To the south of Croatia is the area of Bosnia-Herzegovina. Immediately to the east are Serbia and Montenegro. Civil strife between these ethnic regions has, until recently, not been cause for serious concern. Although nationalist tendencies have been in the forefront of Yugoslavia's political history for the last quarter of this century, they had not erupted into violent conflict until the civil war of the 1990s. Under the rule of Marshal Tito, the country and its republics had been forced to keep their nationalist feelings in check. Tito's aim was to do away with old ethnic divisions and create a social revolution. When Tito died in 1980 all the old nationalist desires of the republics were reborn to a certain extent. Up to this time Serbs, Croats and Muslims had lived side by side in peaceful coexistence.

With tough economic times upon them, the Yugoslavs protested Communist policy and began to demand changes to a political system that had failed to permit other political parties. Nationalism was therefore on the rise for the six republics of Yugoslavia.

Acts of political terrorism in the region have been mostly nonexistent. What has been occurring is a bloody civil war, pitching neighbor against neighbor, almost a Balkan version of Northern Ireland. All sides in this conflict have been using different tactics from those used in the Northern Ireland conflict. Reports out of the various regions cite incidents of "ethnic cleansing," a rather sanitized term for such extreme measures as the extermination of whole villages. This region of nationalist conflict and resulting civil war has not had the hallmark of terrorist activity and such infamous groups as the Stern Gang in Palestine. One event that had the clear markings of terrorist action was the attempted assassination by bombing of Kiro Gligorov, President of Macedonia.

The Yugoslavian government of Slobodan Milosevic had by the end of August, 1998, virtually destroyed all resistance by the KLA with its use of heavy armor and air force against significantly smaller odds. Threats of intervention by the Western alliance under NATO have failed to impress, let alone restrict, the actions of the Serbian-led Yugoslavian government. The slash and burn methods being adopted by Milosevic amount in general terms to a **"scorched earth policy."**[11] The hatred between the Albanians and Serbs is further played out in the reported atrocities by both sides against each other. In all respects this conflict has turned into an all-out war. The lightly armed freedom fighters, as they are now termed (not terrorists), are up against tanks and heavy artillery.[12]

Many unsubstantiated reports of brutal treatment, rape and torture of civilians in the mainly Albanian province of Kosovo continue to emerge. Whatever the eventual outcome, this conflict will likely continue to prompt, from Albanians at the very least, reprisals for years to come. Moderate Albanians in Pristina now fear the emergence of more extremist KLA units. Instead of trying to hold territory, they may launch a campaign of assassinations and car bombs.[13] From this viewpoint, it is likely to become a region masked in death by ethnic genocide. The strong survive and the weak perish.

The representatives of the superpowers, the President of the U.S. and its cross-Atlantic ally, Britain's Prime Minister, have only managed to exert minor pressure on Milosevic to hold back his forces and to encourage both sides to come to the table for meaningful peace talks. It seems highly unlikely that there will be an early end to the misery in the region. All-out war will possibly end soon; however, this could then mark the turn toward a more conventional style of urban terrorism already witnessed in regions of the Gaza Strip and West Bank. The probability that the Yugoslavs will totally overrun the KLA would effect this change in tactics for those remaining committed to the Albanian cause in Kosovo. The actions of the Serbian government almost mirror the Nazi tactics of World War II, with the rounding up and arresting of those who have given any assistance to the so-called rebels. Those arrested have been doctors and aid workers, lawyers and journalists. An end to terrorism in this region is not in the foreseeable future.

SUMMARY

Russia as we know it today has undergone enormous change. No longer is it a Communist-dominated federation; no longer is it the great bear of the east that wielded so much power and influence in the world due to military strength. No longer does it have the respect of its neighbors or its enemies! Russia is at the end of the twentieth century, a country in turmoil. Its social and economic problems are clear for all to see. A monetary system in tatters and an economy in ruins are being bailed out by the International Monetary Fund. The hopes and fears of a nation rest on how the political games are played over the coming months. Many questions are as yet unanswered. What is certain is that Russia is experiencing levels of organized crime with Mafia-style syndicates permeating all levels of the Russian society. Drugs and weapons are freely available, and a dissatisfied and poorly paid military machine has ground to a halt. This military machine, however, has access to weapons of mass destruction. Some are missing; who has them and who controls them is open for discussion. The possibilities are endless for a criminal with access to this kind of weaponry. Chechnya has problems of its own making. This Russian state seems headed towards Islamic Fundamentalism, and with the shadowy terrorist group Hizballah, with sponsorship from Iran, has set up active cells around the world with ruthless efficiency. The early signs are that terrorism is likely to be on the increase as we move to the twenty-first century.[14] The region of Macedonia has been devastated by sporadic wars within its borders; the term ethnic cleansing is now used to describe the mass murder of a particular ethnic group. While the Kosovo Liberation Army lives to fight another day, its Albanian support in the region is strong. In the years to come, if the direct fighting ends and some form of lasting peace can be achieved, there is no doubt that sporadic violence, bombings and assassination will be a pattern of daily life in these areas. Wars fought on ethnic lines, where the wounds run deep, take decades to heal. This particular wound is wide open and bleeding. We now move on to North Africa and the Middle East, a region that often makes Northern Ireland seem peaceful by comparison.

Terms to Remember

The People's Will	Boevaya Oranisatsia	Bolshevik
Stalin	Cheka	Killer College
KGB	Mehmet Ali Agca	KINTEX
ricin	Russian Federation	scorched earth policy
Archduke Franz Ferdinand	Partisans	

Review Questions

The Russian revolution of 1917 installed Communism for three-quarters of a century; why do you think it failed?

Describe how Josef Stalin controlled the Russian people and the military.

What do think is meant by a "scorched earth" policy in the Serbian area of the former Yugoslavia?

How do you think the situation in Chechnya compares to the Vietnam War?

Why do you think so many former KGB are involved in the "Russian Mafia" today?

Endnotes

1. *The New Encyclopaedia Britannica*, volume 8, Encyclopaedia Britannica Inc., 1985.
2. The Internet, Secret Police *Revelations from the Russian Archives*, Library of Congress, 1996.
3. David Yallop, *Tracking the Jackal*, Random House, 1993, p. 20.

4. Claire Sterling, "Bulgaria Hired Agca to Kill Pope," *New York Times*, June 10, 1984.

5. Nathan Adams, "Drugs For Guns," *Reader's Digest*, November 1983.

6. "Bulgarian Connection to Illicit Arms Trade," *Wall Street Journal*, August 10, 1984.

7. "Russia's Criminal Class Delivers a Fatal Blow," *The Vancouver Sun*, November 27, 1998, p. A21.

8. Edward Walker, "The Crisis in Chechnya," *Center for Slavic and Eastern European Studies Newsletter*, Spring, 1995.

9. Edward Walker, "What's Next in Chechnya," *Association for the Study of Nationalities*.

10. Araminta Wordsworth, "Sinking Further in a Morass of Brutality," *National Post*, Thursday, December 10, 1998, p. A15.

11. World Book, "*Yugoslavia*," World Book Inc. USA 1990, p. 579, volume 21.

12. Philip Sherwell, "NATO Planes Strike on Kosovo," *The Weekly Telegraph*, The Telegraph Group Ltd., June 9–15, 1998, p. 19 issue #359.

13. Julius Strauss, "Kosovo Faces All of War as Serbs Attack," *The Weekly Telegraph*, The Telegraph Group Ltd., July 28–August 3, 1998, p. 16 issue #366.

14. "Tattered Army," *The Economist*, August 15, 1998, p. 39.

CHAPTER 6

NORTH AFRICA AND THE MIDDLE EAST

Israel wants peace as soon as possible, but reserves the right to fight terror with terror.

—Yitzak Rabin

We believe that to kill a Jew far away from the battleground has more effect than killing 100 of them in battle; it attracts more attention .

—George Habash

OVERVIEW

This chapter will take the student through the virtual and real minefields of politics surrounding Israel and its foundation as an independent state. We will discuss how the Zionist State was conceived and how it arbitrarily affected the displaced group, the Palestinian Arabs of the region. This chapter will deal with the imperialist influences of the major nations of the time, Britain, France and Russia, and the effect that the two World Wars had on Israel's creation. The chapter will view the warning signs that lead up to terrorist activity and its early beginnings from both the Israeli and Palestinian perspectives. The Palestinian question or Middle East problem has primarily to do with land and terrorism. To the uninitiated, it would appear that the Middle East has been in crisis for the entire twentieth century. It remains to be seen what legacy is carried forward into the twenty-first. This chapter will lead the student through the maze of organizations and persons who are all of a single thought, the elimination of the state of Israel. Thousands of years of conflict and hatred color this strife-torn area of the world. The threads of hatred and envy are woven into a tapestry that is both beautiful and ugly. We start with the early history of this region, the home for several major religions and continuous conflict.

Early History

The Jewish people (Hebrews), settled in the region of Palestine about 1200 years before the birth of Christ. From about 70 A.D. to 700 A.D., the region was under the control of the Romans, who dispersed most of the Hebrews from the region. With the collapse of the Roman Empire, the Ismaelites (Arabs) settled the region and remained resident until the Turkish (Ottoman) Empire subjugated them in 1516.

Political Considerations

In order to fully appreciate the complexities of this unique region, one must first look at what took place due to imperialist influences and designs on this region at the time of World War I. By the latter part of the 1800s, the Ottoman Empire, controlled by Turkey, was in total disarray and internal factional disturbances were continuing within the realm as Turkey's influences waned. The Turkish Empire bordered Persia, which was under the imperialistic controls of the Russians and British. The dwindling Turkish Ottoman Empire comprised a goodly section of the Arab territories of the Middle East and this area was, by the start of World War I, an area ripe for the plucking. Britain most certainly had designs on the Arab lands, as did the French and Russians. As Turkey was fighting on the side of the German Empire against Britain and France, it suited Britain to turn the Arabs against the Turks. In order to sustain the Jews on the side of Britain, the British government issued the **Balfour Declaration**, named for the British Foreign Secretary, Arthur James Balfour. The Declaration read as follows:

> *His Majesty's Government views with favour the establishment in Palestine of a national home for the Jewish people, and will use their best endeavours to facilitate the achievement of this object, it being clearly understood that nothing shall be done which may prejudice the rights of non-Jewish communities in Palestine, or the rights and political status enjoyed by Jews in any other country.*

This Declaration, from the British point of view, was to win support for the war from Jews in Europe and, more particularly, in the wealthy Jewish neighborhoods in the U.S. The Jews viewed this as tacit agreement for their own homeland in Palestine, while the Arabs read a different meaning in to the wording. The Arabs believed that they had to agree to any terms put forward before an agreement on self-determination of lands for the Jews was realized. The Arabs fought in the belief that they were assured independence; the Jews in Palestine had offered to raise troops to fight on the side of the British.

With the promise of independence to both Zionists and Arabs alike, the British government had unwittingly sowed the seeds for an almost ceaseless succession of wars. In the decades to come the Jews and Arabs would fight conventional wars that would then turn into what is now modern-day terrorism that would last for the remainder of the twentieth century. With the two groups now focused on fighting the Turks, Britain had achieved its immediate aim of control of the region and was assured support from both. It was a shortsighted political decision which, it will be seen, left the Middle East with the distinction of being a home base and fertile breeding ground for future generations of terrorists. To many people, the very name "Palestinian" is synonymous with terrorism, and often the words "terrorist" and "Palestinian" are used in the same sentence. This adequately portrays the immense problem that beset this area of the Middle East. British strategic aims at the end of World War I were to solidify a friendly presence in Palestine to insure protection of its routes into Africa and to the East into India. Of major importance would be the Suez Canal and the major shipping route from the Indian Ocean to the Mediterranean. The British set up Arab kingdoms after the war, and in such a fashion that they were controlled by strong traditional family groups. Emerging were the states of Saudi Arabia, Iraq and Syria.

The Palestinian Question remains unanswered to this day. There were political machinations by the League of Nations, forerunner of the United Nations, and Britain wished to leave behind the problems it had created with the Balfour Declaration. In 1922, with the consent of the League of Nations, Britain created the Protectorate of Trans Jordan.[1] This gave Britain control of Palestine, placing it squarely in the middle of the Mideast conflict between Jew and Arab. The Arabs believed they had been given a false promise, while the Jews demanded their own homeland. Britain appointed Herbert Samuel as its High Commissioner to Palestine. Samuel, as a Jew, was only too pleased to oblige the Zionists and initiated the influx of Jews to Palestine.

Between 1920 and 1936, there were periods of sporadic violence by both Jews and Arabs directed against each other, and from both sides against the British in Palestine. In 1918, the number of Jews residing in Palestine was 58,000; this number increased from 1939-1945 to 92,000 and from 1946-1948 to 161,000. By 1992 the figure was 4.2 million. The Jews foresaw the collapse of the British Empire after WWII and began to align with the United States. Britain wanted no interference from the U.S. in Palestinian issues in the Middle East and referred the issue to the Security Council of the United Nations. So on May 8, 1948, the General Assembly of the International Security Council recognized the state of Israel, established on Palestinian land. From this point forward the Arabs and the Israelis would fight short conventional-style wars up to the Six Day War of 1967.

Early Terrorism Acts, 1930-1947

The convoluted study of terrorism in the Middle East takes the student back to the years preceding the formation of the state of Israel. During the warring years of the 1930s the terrorist groups and organizations developed. On the Jewish (Israeli) side was a group named the Stern Gang. This group's ideology was the preservation and protection of Jewish interests in Palestine. To assist the Jews in handling the Arabs was a British Army officer by the name of Orde Wingate.

Wingate's extraordinary talents lay in the field of commando raids and actions against the Arabs. With resident Arabs in Palestine in open revolt at the mass infusion of migrant Jews to the region, the Stern Gang kept themselves busy with the internal defense of Palestine. The terror tactics employed by the Stern Gang became

TERRORISM PLAYER 6-2

BRIGADIER ORDE CHARLES WINGATE

Orde Wingate was a British Army officer who taught guerilla tactics to the Jews in Palestine in the latter half of the 1930s. He is more famous for exploits in the Far East during WW II. Wingate's Raiders, as they became known, were a group of allied servicemen who fought behind enemy lines against the Japanese. Wingate trained Burmese and Nepalese troops in jungle warfare in 1942. They became known as the Chindits. Wingate was killed in a plane crash in 1944. Wingate's Raiders were the forerunners of commando-style operations and an early version of behind the line actions by specialist teams such as the Special Air Service Regiment.

SOURCE: GEORGE ROSIE, "*THE DIRECTORY OF INTERNATIONAL TERRORISM*" (PARAGON HOUSE, NEW YORK, 1987), P. 164.

known as Night Squads, and by the end of 1948, over 150,000 Palestinians had fled the region. With these numbers, its no wonder the area became a terrorist cauldron with displaced Palestinians seeking to regain their traditional homeland. The Stern Gang's leader and founder was Avraham Stern and its operations commander in 1942 was Yitzak Shamir, later to become Prime Minister. Very little is on record in Israel about this movement, probably with good reason. In his account, *Tracking the Jackal*, David Yallop[2] details how the Stern Gang attacked British interests in the region. The gang assassinated Lord Moyne, the British Minister resident in the Middle East, on November 6, 1944 and Count Folke Bernadotte, the U.N. special mediator to Palestine, on September 17, 1948. What is most remarkable is the fact, discussed by Yallop, of the Stern Gang's involvement with the Nazis, who are, no doubt, a horrifying memory for the Israelis. At the time, the only real enemy in the eyes of Stern and his group were the British and its occupying presence in Palestine. Yallop details how the Stern Gang drew up an agreement with an Italian agent in Jerusalem through which Mussolini would recognize a Zionist State in return for Stern group collaboration with the Italian Army when it invaded Palestine. It is hardly surprising that Israel chose to expunge from its records the fact that Stern had sought alliances with Hitler's Third Reich to eliminate the British occupation of Palestine. A copy of an agreement, dated January 11, 1941, between the Stern Gang and the Third Reich, was discovered after the war in files found in the German Embassy in Turkey. Stern and his gang claimed the name National Military Organization. Stern's pact with the Third Reich was aimed solely at solving the Jewish problem over Palestine. The content of the proposal between Germany and Stern went as follows:

- Common interests could exist between the establishment of a New Order in Europe in conformity with the German concept, and the true national aspirations of the Jewish people as they are embodied by the NMO.
- Cooperation between the new Germany and a renewed volkish-national Hebrium would be possible and
- The establishment of the historical Jewish state on a national and totalitarian basis, and bound by a treaty with the German Reich, would be in the interest of a maintained and strengthened future German position of power in the Near East.

Proceeding from these considerations, NMO in Palestine, under the condition the above-mentioned national aspirations of the Israeli freedom movement are recognized by the German Reich, offers to actively take part in the war on Germany's side.[3]

Irgun Zvaileumi (National Military Organization)

The **NMO** was an umbrella organization, and Stern's group came within its sphere of influence. Over the years of the mid 1940s Stern broke away almost completely, and the Night Squads were under the control of a terrorist, in the view of the British, named Menachem Begin. Irgun operated exclusively in Palestine as a Jewish group for the establishment of a modern-day Israel. Their main targets were the resident Arab Palestinians and the occupying British Army in Palestine. Bombings were the order of the day and the two-pronged attacks were designed to have two legitimate aims for the Jews. The first was to destabilize the British presence in the region and make it costly for the British to retain a presence. As seen above, the effect on the demoralized Palestinians was to produce a mass exodus from the area. Several notable members of Irgun played an important role over the following years in the development and political status of Israel. These included Menachem Begin, who would one day become Israeli Prime Minister, the charismatic Moshe Dyan, later to become Chief of Staff, and Ariel Sharon. The second, more obvious reason, was to make life in Palestine extremely unpalatable for the Palestinians. With the agreement on partition by the United Nations, the terrorists of the Irgun began to immediately attack and kill Arab families and individuals that remained in the Jewish sector.

The State of Israel Is Born

By 1947, the British had no power and very little desire to continue to hold a mandate over Palestine. Referring the issue of Palestine to the United Nations was the easy way to disentangle itself from the growing problems of the region. With the referral to the U.N., the state of Israel was created by agreement of the General Assembly on November 29, 1947. The agreement was to divide Palestine into two states, one for the Jews and one for the Arabs. Jerusalem, however, would come under international control. Accepted by the Jews in Palestine and roundly rejected by the Arabs, fighting broke out immediately. Israel came into full existence on May 14, 1948. The following day, the Arab states of Lebanon, Syria, Transjordan, and Egypt declared war on the new state, hoping to win back by force the lands handed to the Jews by the U.N. and to destroy the infant state of Israel in the process. The Arabs were soundly defeated by Israel, and, adding insult to that already suffered, the Israelis gained land that had been destined for Arab control under the U.N. agreement. The remainder of Palestine not controlled by Israel was occupied and controlled by Egypt and Jordan with the Israelis controlling the western half of Jerusalem. Israel held its first elections in January 1949 and elected Chaim Weizmann as President. He appointed Ben-Gurion as Israel's first Prime Minister.[4] Sporadic fighting continued over the next decade.

The Palestinian people remain to this day a dispossessed people, scattered among neighboring Arab nations in the Middle East and still demanding a return of their homeland. The Suez crisis of the late fifties, which saw the British and French invade Egypt to restore control of the Suez Canal, and the Six Day War of 1967 did nothing to improve the lot of the Palestinians. It is not surprising that so many years of forced exile gave rise to a new form of terrorism with the creation of the Palestine Liberation Organization.

TERRORISM PLAYER 6–3

MENACHEM BEGIN (1913–1992)

Menachem Begin, former Prime Minister of Israel, remained on the Interpol wanted list until his death! "An unrepentant terrorist who won the Nobel Peace Prize...and then launched another war" quotes from one of his obituaries. Begin was an organizer and founding member of Irgun and masterminded the attack on the British at the King David Hotel in Jerusalem in 1946. That bomb attack left ninety-one people dead. Begin served in the Knesset from 1949–1984.

SOURCE: GEORGE ROSIE, *THE DIRECTORY OF INTERNATIONAL TERRORISM* (PARAGON HOUSE, NEW YORK, 1987), P. 39.

ⓞ TERRORISM BYTE 6–1

THE ATTACK ON THE KING DAVID HOTEL IN JERUSALEM

As part of its terror campaign to remove the British from Palestine, the Irgun, the Jewish terrorist organization, led at the time by the future prime minister of Israel Menachem Begin, planted a bomb in the south wing of the hotel. The King David Hotel was the military government headquarters of the British in Palestine. Irgun notified the hotel that a bomb had been planted; however, the warnings were ignored by the British, with the resulting death toll of ninety-one.

Source: George Rosie, *The Directory of International Terrorism* (Paragon House, New York, 1987), p. 164.

TERRORIST ORGANIZATIONS

Palestine Liberation Organization (PLO)

In May 1964 , 422 Palestinian national figures met in Jerusalem under the chairmanship of Ahmad Shuqeiri and, following an Arab League decision, founded the Palestinian Liberation Organization (PLO). It laid down the foundations and structure of the **PLO** and in the early years followed pan-Arabism ideology. The PLO was set up as an umbrella movement for a large number of varied interest groups of the Palestinian people. This organization was regarded by many, the Israelis in particular, as a terrorist organization. The early PLO was not cohesive and contained a broad spectrum of moderate to extremely radical political viewpoints. The militant members of PLO were known as **fedayeen**, warriors prepared to die for Allah. With such diverse opinions, the PLO soon became splintered and factional. This internecine struggle was much like the many Republican factions to be found in Northern Ireland.

The PLO's driving philosophy was the restoration of Palestine, the destruction of Israel as a nation state and the recreation of an Arab state in former Palestine. The PLO is loosely organized under three headings: the Executive Committee, the Central Committee and the Palestine National Council. The Executive Committee houses the major terror activities while the Central Committee acts as an advisory structure to the Executive Committee. During the 1960s, PLO guerilla groups carried out sporadic attacks against Israel. However, the organization lacked a strong leader for its political and operational activities. During this period, the PLO operated from bases inside the **Hashemite kingdom** of Jordan, ruled by British-educated King Hussein. There, Yasir Arafat lay the groundwork for his operations among the Palestinians in Kuwait. In 1964, Arafat began to take control of the PLO and turn it from a weak political movement to one that would be recognized as the one true body to represent all the Palestinian people. By 1974, the Arab nations had recognized the PLO as "the sole, legitimate representative of the Palestinian people." In the same year, the United Nations similarly recognized the PLO, with Israel being the exception.

Like all good political and terrorist organizations, Arafat's PLO had a senior security advisor, Ali Hassan Salameh (a.k.a. Abu Hassan), the "Red Prince." The Israeli intelligence agency believed him to be the PLO member responsible for planning the Munich Olympic Games massacre. Then Prime Minister of Israel, Golda Meir, set Mossad the task of tracking down the man responsible for the attack, wherever he might hide. The search lasted seven years. In their attempt to assassinate Salameh, the trackers killed an innocent Moroccan bartender in Lillehammer; such was their fervor to exact retribution on the PLO. Salameh met his end dying as he had lived, when a remote controlled bomb detonated in a stationary vehicle as he drove by with his bodyguards. The attack took place in Beirut on January 23, 1979.

Arafat worked tirelessly toward steering the PLO towards legitimacy as a political organization. In 1988 he took a monumental step in announcing the right of Israel to exist and renouncing the further use of PLO terrorism. This commitment from the man that spoke for the displaced Palestinians moved Israel toward discussions on Palestinian self-rule. Young Palestinians, frustrated with the slow progress toward self-rule in a homeland of their own, have increasingly turned to Hamas or Hizballah for leadership.

On September 13, 1993, the **Declaration of Principles** between the Israelis and the Palestinians was signed in Washington D.C. Palestinian groups formerly

---

CP Picture Archive
(AP Photo/Joe
Marquette)

**TERRORISM
PLAYER 6–4**

YASIR ARAFAT

His real name is Abdel-Rahman Abdel-Raouf Arafat al-Qudwa al-Hussein, born into a Sunni Muslim family in1929. His actual birthplace is something of a mystery and is possibly either Egypt or Jerusalem. He studied engineering at the University of Cairo and while there met Palestinian activists Salah Khalaf and Khalil Wazir. With these young activists, he co-founded the terrorist/guerilla movement **FATAH** in October 1959. Following the humiliation of the 1967 Six Day War, there was little military left with which to attack Israel. Arafat's fedayeen set up bases in Jordan from which they continued to attack Israel. There were few options open to the PLO other than terrorist-style hit and run tactics. Today Arafat remains chairman of the PLO, a widely accepted political force in Mideast politics.

On October 7, 1985, four Syrian-backed members of the Palestine Liberation Front hijacked the Italian cruise ship, Achille Lauro. The hijack coincided with joint Palestinian /Jordanian talks in London formulated by the then British Prime Minister Margaret Thatcher. Abul Abbas masterminded the hijacking. It took place in the Mediterranean shortly after 8:00 a.m. when four young Palestinians burst into the cruise ship's dining area firing automatic weapons. Their demands were simple; the release of fifty captive Palestinians for the release of the ship, its crew, and over 400 passengers. When negotiations began to turn sour they executed an elderly American Jew. Leon Klinghoffer and his wheelchair were tossed overboard. The ship attempted to dock at the Syrian port of Tartus but was turned away. It came to Port Said, Egypt, on October 10, where the hijackers agreed to surrender to Egyptian authorities. The four hijackers plus Abul Abbas, the leader of the PLF, were flown to Tunisia. In a show of strength F-14 fighters from the USS Saratoga intercepted the aircraft over the Mediterranean and forced the Egyptian aircraft to land at a NATO air base in Sicily. They were arrested by Italian police but not before diplomatic wrangling between the U.S. and Italians was eventually resolved by the intervention of President Reagan. It is believed the intended target was not the cruise liner. In fact, the terrorists were planning a raid in Egypt when they were discovered on the Achille Lauro with weapons and explosives.

In August 1997, the family of Leon Klinghoffer reached a legal settlement with the PLO for damages. The family of Klinghoffer and the travel agents that had booked the cruise liner sued Arafat and the PLO for damages. Although it is not known what that settlement was, it appears that restitution has been paid for the family's suffering, as a result of Klinghoffer's murder.

SOURCE: GEORGE ROSIE, *THE DIRECTORY OF INTERNATIONAL TERRORISM* (PARAGON HOUSE, NEW YORK, 1987), P. 39.

under the umbrella of the PLO, such as the Popular Front for the Liberation of Palestine (PFLP) and the Democratic Front for the Liberation of Palestine-Hawatmeh (DFLPH), suspended their participation in the PLO in protest and continued their campaigns of violence not only against the Israelis but also Americans and members of Arafat's PLO. As a political figure, Arafat continues to talk with the Israeli government to reduce tensions and stabilize the situation and to eventually come to an agreeable solution to this decades-old problem.

Al-Fatah (or Al-Asifa)

Al-Fatah is the fighting machine within the PLO, which actually predates the PLO by some six years. Under the leadership of Yasir Arafat it took total control of the PLO after the debacle of the 1967 Six Day War. It is considered the largest terrorist group under the PLO banner. It is estimated to have up to 15,000 fedayeen, financed mostly from the support to the Palestinian coffers by wealthy Arab states. **Al-Fatah**, however, has never managed to prove itself as a military machine against the Israelis in spite of its size and support structure, not even in the occupied territories of the Gaza Strip and the West Bank region of Jordan. It was not able to prevent the Jordanian army from forcibly removing the PLO from its Jordanian training camps around Ajlun and Jerash in 1970, nor could it prevent a repetition in Lebanon, when the PLO were swept out by an Israeli invasion force in 1982.

An Al-Fatah terror wing calling itself **Black September** commemorated the eviction from Jordan in its name. They were to become legendary for their vicious attack at the Munich Olympic Games village and the massacre of Israeli athletes. Black September is an operational military arm of Fatah. As a result of the Munich

Masterminded by the Palestinian Abu Iyad, the head of the Palestinian intelligence network, the attack on Israeli athletes in the Olympic Village shocked and outraged the world. The attack was carried out by Black September terrorists. The terrorists broke into the village and during the initial attack two members of the Israeli team were shot dead. All the Black September terrorists carried AK-47 assault weapons. Their demands were for the release of 234 Palestinians held in Israeli jails and also members of the Baader Meinhof Gang, Red Army Faction and specifically Kozo Okomato from the Lod Airport massacre in May 1972.

The Israeli government refused to negotiate with the terrorists. After long hours of negotiations the terrorists and their remaining hostages were flown by helicopter to Furstenfeldbruk Airport where an aircraft was being readied to fly them to Cairo. What happened next caused a major turnaround in how hostage-taking would be handled in the years ahead. The Bavarian Police opened fire on the terrorists while they still controlled the hostages; the resulting bloodbath left all the hostages dead. So appalling was the carnage from this

CP Picture Archive, AP Laserphoto

failed police operation that radical changes would take place, stressing significant emphasis on special forces to handle any future incidents.

Source: Richard Clutterbuck, *Guerrillas and Terrorists* (Ohio

Olympics massacre the prominent members of the squad involved were hunted by Mossad all across Europe and "disposed of" by assassination.

In spite of the extensive Mossad operation in Europe, Black September rebounded to flourish as the defense arm of Al-Fatah, protecting it and Arafat from extremist groups sponsored by Syria and Iraq, who were funding Adu Nidal's Black June.

During the sixties and the seventies, Al-Fatah offered training facilities to a wide range of Middle Eastern, European, Asian and African terrorist organizations as well as insurgent groups. In David Yallop's account, *Tracking the Jackal*, he confirms that one such terrorist movement of the early seventies included the notorious West German Baader-Meinhof Gang.[5] Reciprocal arrangements within these groups allowed for terror operations to be carried out in each other's names throughout the world. It also helped with the financial support required to maintain operations. It is estimated that Al-Fatah numbers about 7,000–8,000 trained members. Like the Palestinian people as whole, Al-Fatah is spread throughout the Middle East, but is headquartered in Tunisia. Al-Fatah has been provided with aid from Saudi Arabia, Kuwait and some of the other Arab states in the Persian Gulf region. Al-Fatah members have likewise received training from the former U.S.SR as well as former Communist Eastern Bloc countries.

The tangled web of Middle East terrorism does not start and finish with the PLO. As time goes on and attitudes change, either they soften or harden in their fundamental approach to Israel and its supporters. The PLO, like most organizations that are divided over a wide area, will have many different points of political view to contend with. Sabri al-Banna was extreme in his belief that the enemy must be attacked on all fronts, the enemy being Israel, and wavering from that belief was contemptible in his eyes. al-Banna and his supporters split from Fatah and he moved to Iraq in the early seventies.

Abu Nidal Organization

Abu Nidal is the cover name for Sabri al-Banna. The group also uses the following names:

- Fatah Revolutionary Council
- Arab Revolutionary Council
- Arab Revolutionary Brigades
- Black September
- Revolutionary Organization of Socialist Muslims

Similar to the splits in the Irish Nationalist movement, the ANO split from the Al-Fatah organization of the PLO as al-Banna believed Arafat's approach to dealing with Israel was softening and Arafat tending to become more moderate in his approach to Israel. This was most definitely not to al-Bana's liking and in 1974 he and his supporters left Al-Fatah and set up headquarters in Baghdad, Iraq. The Abu Nidal organization is now recognized as one of the bloodiest terror groups operating in the Middle East. It became a true international terror operation by expanding its horizons to strike at its enemies wherever they might be throughout the globe.

Easily recruited, al-Bana was drawn to Baghdad most likely because of what is termed its rejectionist approach to those Middle East countries that favored a peace deal with Israel. Rejectionism is a Middle Eastern political term meaning unilateral refusal of any peaceful settlement with Israel. Iraq would be considered one of the most extreme rejectionist states and one that would not sanction any such action. This also had the effect of alienating those states in favor of moderation, such as Jordan and Egypt. al-Bana's goals can be simply summarized: first and foremost, the destruction of Israel, and secondly, control of the PLO with the support of the rejectionist Iraqi government. It seemed to suit Iraq to have a terrorist group within its boundaries that would do its bidding in return for bases and logistical support. al-Bana, under the protection and watchful eye of the Iraqis, trained about 200 fighters for the cause.

To accomplish his goals, al-Bana believed that, by creating terror on a world stage rather than just a Middle East one, he could meet his goals. His ruthless approach to terrorist actions and atrocities focused the world media and political attention firmly on the regional problems. Abu Nidal has carried out attacks in at least twenty countries and is responsible for the deaths of over 900 people. The group has not just targeted Israel. The United Kingdom, the United States, France and those moderate Palestinians with the temerity to seek a peaceful settlement with Israel have been hit as well. Many of Abu Nidal's attacks were spectacular in their audaciousness. The Abu Nidal group credits itself with the assassination attempt on the Israeli Ambassador outside the Dorchester Hotel in London, in June 1982. In broad daylight, a young Arab later identified as the nephew of Sabri al-Bana walked up to the ambassador and shot him in the head at point blank range. The ambassador, Shlomo Argov, was seriously injured. His assailant was also injured by members of the Metropolitan Police Diplomatic Protection Group. This single terrorist attack precipitated an "eye for an eye" response from the Israelis.

However, the PLO, under Yasser Arafat, denied any involvement in the attack. But this was insufficient from the Israeli viewpoint. Terrorism begets terrorism. Israel's response was a military hard line. The Israeli air force mounted a bombing raid on Palestinian camps in Beirut, Lebanon with a death toll of some fifty persons and 200 injured. It has been speculated that this same act provided the Israelis with the excuse to conduct a full-scale invasion of southern Lebanon to purge the region of PLO fighters. The invasion commenced two days after the attack on Argov, and was termed "Operation Peace for Galilee." The action was to destabilize Lebanon and force the PLO to flee the country to Syria, Tunisia and Iraq. Comparisons can easily be drawn to other assassinations which precipitated a war or invasion, notably the death of the Archduke Franz Ferdinand, which started World War I. As the strength and notoriety of Abu Nidal increased, so too did the international flavor of the training camps in and around Baghdad. These training centers attracted the radical European elements wishing to learn the trade of murder and mayhem.

Some Significant Incidents

Abu Nidal carried out numerous attacks on innocent people and one was a coordinated attack at two major international airports, Rome and Vienna, over the Christmas holiday, 1985:

December 27—Rome Airport 08:15

Leonardo Da Vinci Airport is situated on the outskirts of Rome and is the principal international airport in Italy. At 08:15 four young Arabs threw hand grenades at a line of passengers waiting in the check in line for the El Al flight. El Al's check-in desks are flanked by those of TWA. The four Arabs then opened fire with Kalashnikov AK-47 assault rifles on the American and Israeli passengers waiting in line. Other passengers, including Greeks, Mexicans and two Arabs, were killed in the attack. El Al has a record of being proactive in aviation security, and at Rome airport their armed security staff returned fire, along with Italian police, and killed three and injured one of the terrorists. Fifteen passengers were killed and seventy injured.

In view of the fact that the terrorists were Arabs, the PLO was immediately denounced as having orchestrated the attack. In this instance Abu Nidal was the likely culprit; however, the incidents in Rome and Vienna were most likely aimed at discrediting Arafat and the PLO. Both Austria and Italy were well disposed to the Palestinian cause and this action would have been designed to turn those countries against Arafat.

December 27—Vienna Airport 08:15

Timed to coincide with the Rome attack, the injuries were less in Vienna than in Rome with two dead and forty-six injured. The terrorists used the same modus operandi as their colleagues in Rome. However they were able to fight their way out of the airport and escape temporarily by car, pursued by Austrian police. A gun battle followed and one of the terrorists was killed and the remaining two surrendered. Again informed experts put this attack down to Abu Nidal and his attempt to discredit Arafat.[6]

The **Abu Nidal** group has now shifted bases periodically from Iraq to Syria and has also had bases in Lebanon and Tripoli. Its presence has also been noted in the Sudan. Its support network and financial aid comes primarily from Iraq and Syria, and more recently from Libya. During the 1990s al-Bana was reputed to either be dead or near death. None of these are confirmed reports and the Abu Nidal group is still operational and active. Neither the United States nor the government of Egypt has confirmed reports in the American press that Abu Nidal was captured entering Egypt in August 1998. Reprisals for such an arrest would surely result in retribution toward Egypt.

Popular Front for the Liberation of Palestine (PFLP)

The **PFLP** was founded under the umbrella of the PLO in 1967. Its co-founders and leaders were George Habash and Wadi Haddad. George Habash was born in Lydda, Palestine in 1925, of a wealthy family that followed the teachings of the Greek Orthodox Church. When the British Mandate on Palestine ended in 1948, he was studying medicine at the American University in West Beirut. He and his family became refugees overnight and fled to Jordan. Wadi Haddad was born in Safad, Galilee in 1939.[7]

After completing his studies, Habash set up a clinic with another Palestinian from the Greek Orthodox Church, Wadi Haddad, in Amman. It might seem strange to the casual observer that two committed doctors trained to save lives should organize a terrorist group destined to take them. They were both committed to the belief in the 1950s that Gamal Abdel Nasser was the best hope for the liberation of Palestine. Both were extreme left-wing Marxists. In 1957, Nasser's supporters came close to toppling the Hashemite monarchy in Jordan; however, King Hussein was able to defeat the uprising. Habash and Haddad fled and relocated their base of operations to Syria. The PFLP grew out of the Arab Nationalist Movement that the two men had set up. Both viewed Yasir Arafat with total disdain and loathing for his involvement with the imperialist United States and for his efforts at appeasement of the Israelis. Their philosophy espoused pure terror and was born of the rationale that since Israel won its prize by terror, Arabs should gain Palestine back with similar terror tactics.

JORDAN

Jordan became safe haven for the Palestinians after the creation of Israel, but problems would arise with so many extreme elements actively embroiled in terrorist campaigns against Israel. The PFLP had training camps within striking distance of

---

⊙ TERRORISM BYTE 6-2

ATTEMPT TO KILL WADI HADDAD & LEILA KHALED

On July 11, 1970 an Israeli commando unit successfully launched an attack against Haddad in his Beirut apartment. At around 2:00 A.M. six Katyusha rockets were fired by timing devices from a rented apartment across the street from his apartment on Muhiedden Elchayat Street. Four of the six detonated and two failed to explode. His wife and son were injured but miraculously no one was killed.

Source: David Yallop, *Tracking the Jackal* (Random House, New York 1993), p. 40.

Jordan, and for the leadership of the PFLP the King of Jordan himself became a target. There were open confrontations in the streets of Amman between fedayeen members and King Hussein's troops. Haddad and Habash were desperate to get the Palestinian question into the focus of world attention. Terror on a grand scale would do that for them. It is not certain whether the two men were actually in concert over the operation, but in July 1970, Haddad was in Beirut with Leila Khaled, a committed member of PFLP, planning what has been recorded as one of the most spectacular hijacking events of this century. The hijacking of international airliners to Dawson's Field in Jordan provoked a reaction around the world, and the travelling public still has to contend with the daily disruption of airport security checks.

Hijacking of Airliners: A New Tactic

Over the last forty-five years of this century there have been so many attacks of a terrorist nature that it is hard to recall them. The spectacular ones seem to be held in our minds: the Munich Olympic games massacre, the Iranian Embassy siege in London, the destruction of the U.S. Marine barracks in Beirut, the Oklahoma bombing, Pan Am 103 over Lockerbie, and the Air India bombing off the coast of Ireland. Hijacking of airliners and the taking of hostages have the immediate ability to focus world attention through media coverage.

The actions of the PFLP almost led to a civil war in their adopted base of Jordan, and certainly led King Hussein to forcibly remove the PLO from its territory. The hijackings were audacious for their sheer nerve, daring and lack of any respect for international convention. The first hijacking took place on a TWA Boeing 707 at 11:50 A.M. on September 6, 1970, en route from Frankfurt, West Germany to New York. The airliner had a full complement of crew and 145 passengers when it was seized in the skies above Belgium and the pilot ordered to fly to Jordan. At about the same time a Swissair DC-8 with a similar number of passengers and crew was also seized over France and flown to the same location, Dawson Field, Jordan, as the

An armed terrorist holds a gun on Trans World Airlines pilot John Testrake during an interview from the hijacked plane at the Beirut airport. *Photos courtesy of ABC News.*

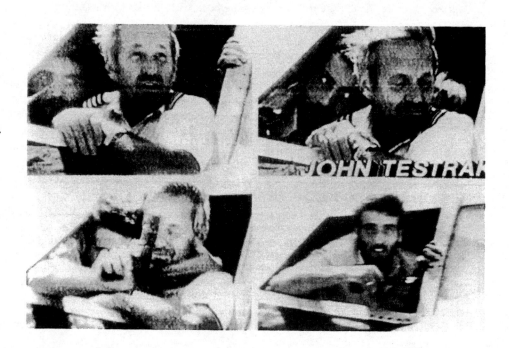

TWA airliner. At about 2:00 P.M. an attempt was made to hijack a third airliner belonging to El Al en route from Tel Aviv to Amsterdam. Due to confusion at check-in, the hijack team was reduced to three members, including Leila Khaled, Patrick Arguello and a third Arab. When the pilot refused to obey the instructions, a violent fight ensued, a flight attendant was shot, and an Israeli sky marshal killed one of the hijackers. Khaled and Arguello were overpowered and the aircraft landed at London's Heathrow Airport. Arguello and Khaled were arrested and taken to a secure metropolitan police station in South London. The remaining members of Khaled's group failed to make the flight, then hijacked a Boeing 747 operated by Pan American Airlines. The airliner flew to Beirut, where it refueled and went on to Cairo. The PFLP blew the aircraft up on the ground at Cairo airport after the crew and passengers were taken off. This action by the PFLP, though aimed at the international arena, was a statement to the Egyptian government about its acceptance of the Middle East peace agreement. With hostages numbering about 300 being held in Jordan, the PFLP laid out their demands to the international community.

The hijackers demanded the release of the three members of the PFLP who had been jailed for the attack on Zurich Airport and were presently languishing in a Swiss jail. They also demanded the same for terrorists being held in West Germany for the Munich Airport attack. Their third demand involved Leila Khaled's release from police custody for attempting to hijack an El Al airliner over Europe. Edward Heath's government was in utter turmoil over how to deal with this problem, so the PFLP gave them another nudge by hijacking a BOAC VC-10 and adding 110 British passengers to their hostage list. After heavy pressure and diplomatic talks, the PFLP moved the hostages to the comfort of Amman, Jordan. Over the next two weeks, the hostages were moved around Amman in small groups before all were released on September 30, 1970. The PFLP had previously destroyed the British, Swiss and American Airliners at Dawson Field before the watchful lenses of the world's media.[8] Aerial terrorism had been born and imprinted on the air traveler's psyche ever since.

The last British hostages were released on the same day that Leila Khaled was flown out of the United Kingdom and back to the Middle East. Israel has always steadfastly refused to negotiate with terrorists, and they strongly criticized the western powers for giving in. Britain never made that mistake again. These events pushed the Middle East to the brink of war and a confrontation between the two superpowers. The Bonn Summit conference of major western powers met in 1978 and agreed to sanctions against states which aided and abetted the hijacking of aircraft. The countries agreeing were the United States, United Kingdom, Canada, France, Italy, Japan, and West Germany.

The Gaza Strip

The Gaza Strip[9] is an area of 140 square miles. It is home to over 830,000 Palestinians and between 4,000 and 5,000 Israeli settlers. The Palestinian population is concentrated in four cities and eight refugee camps. Ninety-nine percent of the population is Sunni Muslim. Although Gaza City is one of the oldest cities in the world, the borders of the area we know as the Gaza Strip were only created in 1949. With the end of the British mandate in Palestine and the resulting Arab-Israeli battles, eventually two-thirds of this area were claimed by Israel. The remaining third was claimed by Egypt. After the creation of the Gaza Strip, over 250,000 Palestinians escaped from the fighting in other areas of the Middle East, and came to settle there. Since that time, Israel has refused to allow those Palestinians to return home, in defiance of U.N. Resolution 141. Most of the inhabitants of the Gaza Strip today are descendants of this group.

So many Palestinians now live in the Strip that 99 percent of the population lives on land that is almost 40 percent controlled by the Israelis. It is not surprising that attacks against Jews by Palestinians are commonplace. Al-Fatah has now found a political rival in the Palestinians of Gaza. The Islamic Resistance Movement or Hamas has grass roots support in the Gaza Strip and the West Bank areas.

Hamas

Ahmad Rashad, a Research Associate at the United Association for Studies and Research, puts the **Hamas** popularity down to several factors:[10]

- Hamas calls for the liberation of all Palestine
- Its reputation as an efficient organization
- Its honesty and lack of corruption
- Hamas has been resilient to Israeli crackdowns
- Daring and successful attacks at Israeli military targets
- Home-based leadership within the occupied territories, as opposed to the PLO's expatriate direction

Organization and Structure

Israel portrays Hamas to western nations and the United States in particular as a determined terrorist organization eager to raise funds with the aim of striking down America. This does not seem to be borne out by terror tactics against the United States by this group. Headquartered mainly in the Gaza Strip, it is composed of administrative, charitable, political and military elements. The military wing is most active in the occupied territories, as its main goal is battling Israeli occupation.

Hamas has been heavily involved in the local political scene in Gaza by putting up candidates in local elections for union representatives and the board of trade. Its political opponent is the PLO. Hamas dates back to the mid-1980s, when it identified itself as a wing of the Palestinian Muslim Brotherhood. The Brotherhood had been seeking to establish a political wing for its organization, and in 1985 and 1986 it issued leaflets in Gaza to encourage a policy of civil disobedience. The leaflets were issued under names such as Harakat al-Kifah al-Musallah (Armed Struggle Movement), al-Murabitoon ala Ard al-Isra' (The Steadfast on the Land of al-Isra'), and Harakat al-Muqawama al-Islamiyya (Islamic Resistance Movement, IRM). As the tensions grew in the mid 1980s these communiqués became more and more politicized, and by 1988 the name Hamas began to appear.

The founders of Hamas were members of the Brotherhood, and the structure of Hamas reflects this. The military and intelligence wings of Hamas function independently. The intelligence wing gathers information and carries out surveillance operations on collaborators, drug dealers and other antisocial activities and metes out punishment ranging from warnings to executions. It also distributes literature about Israeli recruitment policy and methods of collaboration and warns the populace about complicity. The intelligence wing also monitors crime in the region.

The military wing has different but well-defined goals and objectives:

a. establish usar (families) and underground cells
b. gather information on Israeli Defense Force activities for use in planned operations

c. carry out training programs in hand-to-hand combat

d. carry out military-style operations against the IDF

Hamas military strikes have continued predominantly against Israeli settlers in the territories and in Israel. Tactics are of a hit and run nature, planting a bomb or a suicide bomb in populated areas of Jerusalem for example. Despite the PLO agreements with Israel, the Hamas movement declares Arafat as a traitor for his agreement with the Zionist enemy.

Hamas' response to these agreements is likely to result in an increase in disputes with the PLO. Hamas receives support from other Muslim countries, including Turkey, Iran, Afghanistan, Saudi Arabia and the Gulf States, Yemen and even Malaysia.

Hamas, although similar to the PLO, is willing to settle for a peace agreement with Israel, but has firm objectives which must be met before agreement can be reached. In 1994, Hamas proclaimed that it was not opposed to peace; however, for it to "...cease military operations in Gaza and the West Bank...," the following conditions would have to be met:

1. complete Israeli withdrawal from the occupied territories

2. disarming the settlers and dismantling the settlements

3. placing international forces on the "green line" established in the occupied territories during the '48 and '67 wars

4. free and general elections to determine true representation of the Palestinian people

5. the Council, which will be composed of electoral victors, shall represent the Palestinians in any negotiations that determine their future and that of the occupied territories

Many Palestinians lauded the Gaza-Jericho agreement of 1993, as they saw the prospect of establishing their own legitimate homeland. However, the slow progress since the agreement was reached and the continued development of the occupied territories by Israeli settlers has led to disillusionment by many Palestinians. This is leading to internal strife between PLO and Hamas, with pro-Arafat supporters being assassinated. While Israel continues to wrangle over interpretation of sections in the agreement with the PLO, sporadic acts of terror continue on the West Bank, Gaza Strip and in the occupied territories. To date, no final accord has been achieved.

Palestine Liberation Front (PLF)

The PLF terror group split from the PFLP General Command in the mid 1970s and then again into pro-Syrian, pro-Libyan and pro-PLO factions. Its membership cadre is estimated to be between fifty and one hundred.[11]

The PLF's operations are now based in Iraq, having moved there from Tunisia after the attack on the cruise liner Achille Lauro and the murder of an infirm U.S. citizen, Leon Klinghoffer. A longtime supporter of Yasir Arafat leads the PLF. Renounced terrorist Abu Abbas, born in a refugee camp in Syria in 1948, is a longtime Palestinian activist and terrorist. With a price on his head for his involvement in the Achille Lauro incident, he is wanted by the U.S. for the murder of Leon Klinghoffer. Abas rose to prominence in the PLO and was elected to the powerful and influential Executive Committee of the PLO in 1982. Until 1985 he operated from Tunisia. After the Achille Lauro the Italian authorities briefly detained him until he was flown to the Yemen. He is now headquartered in Iraq and was an outspoken supporter of Saddam Hussein during the Gulf War.

Democratic Front for the Liberation of Palestine (DFLP)

A strong and vocal opponent to the Israeli peace accord with the PLO, this Marxist group split from the PFLP in 1969.[12] **DFLP** believes the Palestinians can only achieve their goals by mass uprising. Its political position in the early years of the 1980s was somewhere between Arafat and the rejectionists. It again split into two more factions in 1991, one pro-Arafat and one hard line group headed by Nayif Hawatmah. This group has suspended its membership in the PLO as it opposes the Declaration of Principles signed in 1993.

The DFLP is estimated to have a membership totaling about 500 activists across both groups and has carried out its terror campaign mostly in Israel and the occupied territories. Since 1988 the DFLP has only been involved in cross border raids in Israeli areas. It receives its funding and logistical support from Libya and Syria.

Palestinian Islamic Jihad (PIJ)

PIJ has its roots among the Palestinian fundamentalists in the Gaza Strip dating back to the 1970s. Its goals differ from the PLO and its aim is to achieve an Islamic Palestinian state through a holy war and the destruction of Israel. This group strikes at Arab and Jew alike. It has not limited its area of operation to the territories and the Gaza Strip like Hamas. It ranks the United States alongside Israel as one of its prime targets. Its acts of terror have been brutal and efficient. In 1991, PIJ attacked a tourist bus in Egypt, killing eleven passengers, nine of them Israelis. Its method of attack in Israel and the occupied territories has been suicide bombings of bus stations and markets.[13]

Kach and Kahane Chai

This organization was declared a terrorist organization by the Israeli government under the 1948 Terrorism Law, in 1994.[14] Binyamin Kahane, the son of an Israeli-American rabbi who was assassinated in the U.S., leads this group. The aim of the group is to restore the biblical state of Israel. The **Kach and Kahane** were outspoken supporters for the terrorist attack on the al-Ibrahimi Mosque by Dr. Baruch Goldstein in February 1994. The group has threatened and attacked Palestinians and Arabs in Hebron and the West Bank and is an embarrassment to the Israeli government.

On September 13, 1993, a major breakthrough took place in the relationship between Israel and the Palestinians. In Washington, D.C., Shimon Peres, representing Israel, and Mahmoud Abbass, representing the PLO, U.S. Secretary of State Warren Christopher and Anatole Kozyrev from the Russian Federation penned their signatures to an historic document. The key paragraphs are shown below:

DECLARATION OF PRINCIPLES

ARTICLE VI: PREPARATORY TRANSFER OF POWERS AND RESPONSIBILITIES

1. Upon entry into force of this Declaration of Principles and the withdrawal from the Gaza Strip and the Jericho area, a transfer of authority from the Israeli military government and its Civil Administration to the authorized

Palestinians for this task, as detailed herein, will commence. This transfer of authority will be of a preparatory nature until the inauguration of the Council.

2. Immediately after the entry into force of this Declaration of Principles and the withdrawal from the Gaza Strip and the Jericho area, with the view to promoting economic development in the West Bank and Gaza Strip, authority will be transferred to the Palestinians on the following spheres: education and culture, health, social welfare, direct taxation, and tourism. The Palestinian side will commence in building the Palestinian Police Force, as agreed upon. Pending the inauguration of the Council, the two parties may negotiate the transfer of additional powers and responsibilities, as agreed upon.[15]

The above signaled a major breakthrough and a new hope for a definitive solution to the Palestinian question, even peace in the area. The full text of the Declaration of Principles is not included in this chapter; however, its contents form the basis and fabric for both the Israelis and Palestinians to move toward the goal of a homeland for the displaced Palestinians. It has been a very bumpy road since 1993, and whether the two sides are able to fulfill the Declaration and meet all that is stipulated remains to be seen. There is considerable resentment in the territories and Gaza Strip of the slow pace toward meeting the goals of the Principles. This has led to a rise in terror attacks, by members of Hamas in particular, and by dissident PLO member groups operating without the sanction of Yasir Arafat's council.

Indoctrination into the terrorist cause is believed to continue unabated in the Gaza Strip as the next generation of terrorists are groomed and schooled in hatred aimed purely at their Israeli neighbors. Children as young as seven are seen parading with automatic assault weapons and singing patriotic Palestinian songs that glory in the destruction of Israel.[16] This is hardly a harbinger of a peaceful settlement in the years to come. The core of mistrust between the Palestinians and the Israelis, in both words and deeds, runs deep in the occupied territories.

LEBANON

A Melting Pot of Hatred

Lebanon has been in existence for centuries and is occupied by both Christians and Muslims. The Christians settled mainly in the mountainous regions while the Muslims inhabited the coastal region. Like most of the Middle East, the area was under the rule of the Turkish Ottoman Empire until the end of World War I. After the war, the French began to prepare the region for independent status. The French assisted in the creation and writing of the Lebanese constitution. Lebanon gained its full independence in 1943 and, like its population, the government was designed to reflect the two majority religions, Christian and Muslim. From its very early days as an independent state, Lebanon had close links to the western powers. In the 1950s and 1960s, Beirut was affectionately termed the "Riviera of the Middle East." Its hotels and restaurants and vibrant market scene made it a popular spot for tourists and the wealthy. Its situation on the Mediterranean helped it flourish as a port as well as a business center.

Significant incidents brought about drastic changes in the Lebanese way of life, beginning with what must be termed an uprising. The first signs of trouble surfaced in 1958, when dissatisfied Muslims violently opposed the government strengthening its ties to the west. The uprising was tempered when U.S. forces were sent to the aid of Lebanon, and all seemed to return to relative tranquility in very short order.

Palestinians Come to Lebanon

With the reversal in the fortunes of the PLO in 1969, which saw them being evicted by King Hussein of Jordan's troops, its members spilled into Lebanon in dramatic numbers. King Hussein's actions were in response to the rapidly growing number of confrontations between the PLO and Hussein's military. Support for the embattled king came by way of monetary contributions from the U.S. on a regular basis. Pressure was applied to the Jordanian king with the tightening of the purse strings, and the eviction of the PLO was imminent. The PLO were expelled from Jordan and moved primarily to Lebanon. This move, which took place in September, gave rise to the Black September terrorist group (which reached worldwide notoriety at the Munich Olympic Games in 1974). The Arab Muslim population of Lebanon swelled, and they were treated, at best, as fourth class citizens. Many lived in the refugee camps around Beirut International Airport and in areas of southern Lebanon that were in easy striking distance of Israel. Terror campaigns of the PLO continued with strikes against Israel from these havens of south Lebanon. These actions further destabilized not only the government of Lebanon, but the country as a whole.

By 1975, the constant warring from incursions by the PLO into Israel and the retaliatory strikes by the Israeli air force against Palestinian camps brought the country to civil war. The PLO in Lebanon was widely supported by the predominantly Muslim Arabs, but were opposed by the Lebanese Christians. To the casual observer, Beirut and Lebanon have seen a never-ending cycle of violence perpetrated by warring factions from within its borders and unsympathetic neighbors such as Syria, Iran, Iraq and Israel. What for many was an "Orchid in the Mediterranean" turned rapidly into a patch of thistles and thorns, a lawless society with a feeble government unable to restore order or control internal and external elements bent on its destruction.

The style and structure of terrorism to be played out in this theater of conflict can be viewed as political in nature. It is considered to be the oldest technique of psychological warfare. Political terrorism may be simply defined as coercive intimidation. It is the systemic use of murder and destruction, or the threat of murder and destruction, in order to terrorize individuals, groups, communities or governments into conceding to the terrorists' political demands.[7] While Syria had its own agenda and a desire to include Lebanon as a part of Greater Syria, far more sinister notions were spreading from the Persian state of Iran.

Islam

Before we proceed to discuss the bloodbath which Beirut became, the student should understand some fundamental philosophies about the world of Islam. Islam is a religious faith much like any other. However, it is actually divided into two separate spheres of influence, the **Sunni** sect and the **Shi'a**. There are Five Pillars of Islam:

- *Shehada*, the statement in Arabic which says "There is no god but Allah and Mohammed is Prophet"
- *Salah*–prayer five times a day. Prayer in Islam is praise of God

- *Zakat*–the paying of alms to the poor. This is traditionally calculated at 2.5 percent. Different Muslim countries have differing views on Zakat, now that income tax is a reality for many
- *Ramadan*–the month of holy fasting. During Ramadan, Muslims must not eat, drink or make love from sunrise to sunset
- *Hajj*–pilgrimage to Mecca. This is an obligation of all Muslims who can afford it to make the trek to Mecca in Saudi Arabia once in their lifetime[18]

Sunni Muslims account for about 90 percent of the world's Muslim population with the remaining 10 percent being the Shi'a Muslims. Struggles between the two groups date back as far as the seventh century. Both hold the Quran as their sacred text and Mohammed as the Last Prophet. The Shiites have and believe in their own version of Islamic Law and their own theology. The Shiites believe in a chain of leaders, or imams, who came after Mohammed, and in a structure of spiritual authority through mullahs and a religious establishment.[19] Iran has the largest population of Shi'a Muslims in the world.

So, with an unstable government and warring factions fighting openly in the streets of Beirut, the country was ripe for the fundamentalists to move in. With the Shah of Iran deposed and an Islamic Revolution underway, the actions of fundamentalists spread to the Middle East.

The Shi'a Sect in Lebanon

Imam Mousa el-Sadr, an Iranian-born cleric, was by the end of the 1960s the undisputed leader of the Shi'a community in Lebanon.[20] The Shi'a was not at this point involved in any type of terrorist activity. They were, however, aligned to politically

---

TERRORISM BRIEF 6–3
A FIRST PERSON ACCOUNT OF BEIRUT

In 1981, Beirut was a divided city, Muslim East and Christian West. The two areas of the city were separated near the Museum District along a tentatively unmarked border called "the green line." During the day, life went on along almost normal lines (normal for Beirut, that is). Traveling from the International Airport down to the city, one's first impression of the region and its people is their remarkable resilience in the face of a battle/civil war. On most street corners, children as young as nine or ten are armed with the traditional fighting machine of the Middle East, the Kalashnikov assault weapon (AK-47). The wartorn streets bear the scars of years of fighting; small stones laid in a line across a street quickly indicate to a passerby that a sniper is active in the area. Check points controlled by the Syrian army appear as one approaches the once affluent West Beirut waterfront or Corniche area. One such check point is located opposite the Iraqi Embassy, which was soon to be destroyed by a massive underground bomb explosion. The reality of Beirut life is that anything can happen to anyone at any time. Ask the British cleric Terry Waite or the World War II fighter pilot Jackie Mann, who ran a popular pub for expatriate British and Australians in Beirut. West Beirut was considered safer than East Beirut. Antiaircraft guns were still situated at street corners and most of the citizens carried guns. The occasional Israeli fighter would overfly the city and anyone with a weapon aimed it skyward and opened fire. The risk to life in Beirut for a foreigner was not considered serious enough in early 1981 to warrant evacuation; this, however, would change with the Israeli invasion of southern Lebanon and the semi-expulsion of the PLO from Lebanon. Arafat and his fighters dispersed to bases in Tunis and set up operations there.

SOURCE: JEREMY SPINDLOVE (CO-AUTHOR), *PERSONAL EXPERIENCES IN BEIRUT*, 1981.

---

defend and represent the poor of Lebanon. Together with Gregoire Haddad, a Catholic archbishop, they set up Haraket el-Mahroumeen, or Movement of the Deprived. Its stated intention was to work within the Lebanese political system to achieve its political objectives. With the passing of time the Imam found it no easy task to reach his goals for the poor and oppressed, so he changed his doctrine and approach to the government. His party would become rejectionist and take up the sword to fight the injustices. The group was known by the acronym Amal. In stark contrast to its near neighbors in Iran, the Shi'a sectarian movement continued to operate within the political system after the civil war of 1975. The Lebanese Shi'a community saw a significant ray of sunshine with the formation of a government out of the Iranian Revolution, particularly given the background and birthplace of the Imam. His contacts and involvement with the Iranian movement, as well as the leadership of Amal, was to end with his abduction and disappearance in 1978. A natural vacuum now ensued and the Amal became the Islamic Amal, with headquarters in the Beka'a Valley of Lebanon under the new auspices of Hussein el-Musawi. Islamic Amal was now foundering and Musawi joined forces to bring Amal under the umbrella of Hizballah.

Hizballah

The origins and development of the **Hizballah** movement in Lebanon represent the most important and successful example of Islamic Iran's efforts to export its pan-Islamic brand of revolution beyond its border.[21] Hizballah is also known as:

- Islamic Jihad
- Ansarollah
- Organization of the Oppressed
- Party of God
- Revolutionary Justice Organization

Mousa Abu Marzook, the political leader of Hamas, responds to a question during an interview in a visitation room at New York's Manhattan Correctional Center. CP Picture Archive (A/P Photo/ Richard Drew)

The goal of Hizballah was and is to establish an Islamic state in Lebanon.[22] The establishment of the Hizballah in Lebanon was supported and financed by the revolutionary government of Iran, to the point where members of the Revolutionary Guard were sent to the Beka'a Valley to join with the training cadres. Its is widely known that the Hizballah is controlled and directed by radical Shiite clerics under the more central control of Iran through contacts in the Syrian capital of Damascus. Up until his death in 1989, the supreme guardian of revolutionary causes was the Ayatollah Khomeini, who called on "all oppressed Muslims to replace their governments with Islamic fundamentalist ones." His brand of terror stretched far and wide and with sweeping ferocity he used terror as his instrument of punishment. His continued diatribes against the Great Satan,[23] his term for the United States, and his religious Fatwa (death sentence) against British author Salman Rushdie for writing a novel called *The Satanic Verses* constantly stirred the boiling pot of the Middle East.

With their rise to prominence in 1982, they became a further embarrassment to the Lebanese Government. Prior to the Israeli invasion of Southern Lebanon, which led to the PLO retreating to Tunis, the streets of Beirut were governed by warring militia groups. These included the indigenous Druze populace of the hills around Beirut Airport. It was not uncommon for rockets and mortars to be fired over the airport at the Palestinian positions nearby. The damage and destruction this caused was tremendous.

Hizballah's main targets are the Israeli Jews. Not restricted to hitting Israel, they have also targeted non-Islamic influences in Europe, the U.S. and Latin America. The U.S. is considered a legitimate target, as are other western powers with alliances to the U.S. and its Middle East policies. Internally, it targets the South Lebanese Army and also the Israeli Defense Force operating in the secure buffer zone of Southern Lebanon.[24]

Kidnapping

This is not a new tactic in the terrorist's arsenal, but the speed and efficiency with which Hizballah executed kidnappings and executions in Beirut took the western world completely by surprise. The audacious kidnapping of the Archbishop of Canterbury's special envoy to the Middle East was remarkable in that it was carried live on the major news networks. Hizballah believed that the envoy, Terry Waite, was working for the CIA. This of course was never proven. However, news bulletins which showed Waite leaving an aircraft in Cyprus several steps ahead of Colonel Oliver North provided ample excuse for the kidnappers to justify their actions. Both British and U.S. positions of not dealing with terrorists or acquiescing to their demands resulted in Terry Waite and others being incarcerated for several years in the suburbs of Beirut before their eventual release.

Structure and Development

From its original inception, it operated like a "halfway house" for terrorists. It appears that Hizballah received its direction from three different people within its hierarchy! Abu Musawi, Hassan Nasrallah and Sheik Mohammed Hussein Fadollah, the last being the Hizballah's spiritual leader. As a former fighter with the Islamic Amal Nasrallah's role was to format a terrorist force for the Southern Lebanon region.[25] As has been noted earlier, the Hizballah were intent on establishing an Islamic state in Lebanon. This would undoubtedly not be welcomed by the confessionalist style of government that had been established with the creation of Lebanon in the first quarter of the century, which assured that government would predominantly be in the hands of the Maronite Christian majority. As no census had been taken in the country for decades, it was probable that the Maronite Christians were no longer in the majority, a fact not lost on the Beirut militia commanders. With so many different groups fighting for control of the streets and the government, the Hizballah were not content to act like the PLO as an umbrella for other groups. With the death of Musawi, Nasrallah tuned his terrorist forces toward the same style of revolution as had occurred in Iran and effectively created a regional militia movement. The many other groups had, by 1991, laid down their arms and signed a peace accord. Hizballah, on the other hand, remained the one major force against the Israelis in Southern Lebanon and have been waging a terrorist campaign ever since.

Hizballah used the human bomb to great effect, as did the Islamic Jihad. The Hizballah are blamed for the suicide bomb attack on the U.S. Marine Barracks in West Beirut in October 1983. The suicide bomber drove a truck loaded with explosives and detonated it as he crashed into the camp. The impact was devastating, taking the lives of 241 U.S. Marines. The outcry in the United States was loud and clear: What are our boys doing over there? In spite of the carnage and outrage, the suicide attacks continued with spontaneous irregularity and with the same devastating results. Intelligence was scant at best on the group, and bringing any culprit to trial was almost impossible.

The terror tactics employed in Beirut significantly changed when, on March 28, 1986, two British teachers were kidnapped in what until this time had been considered the "safe" area of West Beirut. The following month, Brian Keenan, a British national with dual nationality in the Republic of Ireland, was abducted, and the following week one of the Muslim militia groups operating in West Beirut announced that they had executed a British journalist, Peter Collett. The following day the three bodies of Americans Peter Kilburn, Leigh Douglas and Philip Padfield were discovered, and another journalist, John McCarthy, was kidnapped. Beirut had become an extremely hostile place for westerners. Hizballah does not confine its attacks against the state of Lebanon exclusively to the Middle East theater; it is in fact a true international terrorist group with the ability to strike at Jewish targets throughout the world. Through local cell structures in South America it is believed to have been responsible for several large bomb attacks in Buenos Aires in 1994, as well as a car bombing in London.

Islamic Jihad

Not to be confused with the Palestinian Jihad, the Islamic Jihad is believed to be based in the Beka'a Valley of Lebanon and was an offshoot of the Muslim Brotherhood within Iranian influences. It is a shadowy organization believed to be under the control of the Syrians from Damascus. Much of its success is due to the inability of western intelligence to accurately target the group. Its secrecy and very tight cell structure makes it difficult to infiltrate. Formed in 1981 under the leadership of Fathi Shekaki, it came under the umbrella of Hizballah. It seems the Islamic Jihad tactics are to split and split again, in order to form impenetrable cells. Through this, they believe, a new form of terrorism will be born. The world of intelligence gathering and security is aimed at detection and prevention, provided it knows where to look and who and what to look for. Islamic Jihad chose a new weapon for its terror attacks against the Israelis and the west, the suicide or kamikaze bomber. The human bomb was a new phenomenon for the intelligence communities and the results of human bomb attacks are invariably devastating and on target.

By the spring of 1986 the world was well accustomed to the specter of airport delays caused by security checks. Heathrow is no exception. The travelling public was subjected to monotonous lines waiting for hand luggage to be searched, blissfully ignorant that the suicide or mule bomber even existed. There had, at this juncture, been no recorded attempts to destroy an aircraft by suicide bombing. This was to change dramatically on April 17, 1986. Terminal One at Heathrow International was the hub for the British Airways European and domestic arrivals and departures. However, on several days of the week it was also the terminal used by Israel's El Al Airlines for their Boeing 747 flight to Israel. At mid-morning, with the El Al 747 on the jetty at Gate 23, passengers for that flight and also the BA flight to Tel Aviv, coincidentally being checked in and boarded at the adjacent departure gate 21, were coming through the preboarding security checks. All passengers leaving the U.K. in 1986, and specifically those with checked baggage, were asked a series of questions:

- Is this your baggage?
- Did you pack it yourself and are you taking any packages for somebody else?
- Have you left your baggage unattended at any time?

After the questions, the passengers would proceed to an immigration desk for passport inspection, not far from the watching eye of Metropolitan Police Special Branch officers. On this particular day a young girl from the Republic of Ireland had answered all the questions had had her passport checked and her hand luggage and hold baggage screened by x-ray. The girl unwittingly proceeded to the El Al boarding gate with her single piece of carry-on baggage. The bag was of nylon construction with an expanding compartment at the base, a type used by millions of travelers. El Al airline prides itself on being one of the most secure airlines in the world, with good reason, and conducts a secondary manual security check and questioning of every passenger. This is conducted by El Al's own security team. The young lady who was pregnant with her boyfriend's baby was apparently going to visit his family in the Middle East; he, however, was not traveling. The security staff thought this a strange story, and while doing the physical check on the bag noticed that even when it was empty it seemed overly heavy for its construction. At that point, a police explosive search dog passed by, and immediately reacted to the bag. Further inspection revealed several sheets of plastic explosive wired to a calculator and battery. The bomb was in a false bottom of the bag. The boyfriend, Nazer Hindawi, had befriended the girl, gotten her pregnant and was sending her to her death. A Jordanian Palestinian sponsored by Syria, he had gone to remarkable lengths and considerable planning to pull this attack off. He was sentenced to forty-five years in prison.

SOURCE: JEREMY SPINDLOVE (CO-AUTHOR), *PERSONAL EXPERIENCES AT HEATHROW*, LONDON 1986.

SYRIA

Though not really a North African nation, Syria is such a major player in the issues involving Israeli/Palestinian problems that we discuss it here in that context. Syria is a Muslim country with a population which is 90 percent Sunni Muslim. The country gained independence from France in 1946, and by the mid-1960s, the Ba'ath party rose to power with Hafez al-Assad as its president. Syria had for years been dominated by a succession of military governments. Assad, a former air force colonel, is still in power and controls Syria with an iron fist today. Syria is a longtime supporter of the Palestinian cause and an sworn enemy of Israel. It has fought two unsuccessful campaigns against Israel and lost control of the Golan Heights on its southern border.

Although Syria is a sponsor and harborer of terrorists, it is likely that any terrorist acts perpetrated on its soil would quickly be suppressed. Assad himself shies away from the public and international eye and quietly assists groups such as Islamic Jihad and Hizballah by allowing Iran to resupply them through Damascus. Assad's government has been in open conflict with U.S. forces stationed in Lebanon and in 1983 shot down an unarmed U.S. reconnaissance flight.

There is no direct or hard evidence to connect Syria to any terrorist attacks since 1986. Meanwhile, the Damascus government continues to push forward to a peace settlement with Israel. It tries to maintain some measure of control over Hizballah and its actions. Syria continues to hedge its bets and maintains a thriving business in its support of training camps for expatriate terror groups such as the PFLP-GC, led by Ahmad Jibril, the Palestine Islamic Jihad and the Japanese Red Army. Not far away in the Beka'a valley are members of the PKK, the Kurdish Workers Party, led by the university-educated Abdullah Ocalan, who spends part of his time in Syria.

Syria does not permit homegrown terrorists to perpetrate actions against the state, and Assad's government violently suppresses any attempts, particularly by Islamic fundamentalists, to disrupt the workings of the state. Not only terrorist and fundamentalist but other political factions are suppressed in the one-party state of Syria. This is not to say there have not been attempts by the Muslim Brotherhood to raise their banner in Syria. In 1982 an open revolt in the city of Hama by Islamic fundamentalist resulted in the Syrian Army taking immediate and decisive action to crush the uprising, the result being many deaths and casualties. Syria has not declared and there is no positive indication to suggest otherwise its involvement in sponsoring terror on an international basis. Syria does however continue to provide a safe haven for terrorist groups that are currently active. Among those groups that have headquarters and training camps in Syria are the Popular Front for the Liberation of Palestine General Command (PFLP-GC) under Ahmad Jibril, and Palestinian Islamic Jihad (PIJ). In addition to bases in Syria, areas under its influence and military control in the Beka'a Valley of Lebanon also have camps for the Hamas, PIJ, PFLP-GC and the Turkish PKK.

Now that we have examined the core of the terrorism problems in the Middle East, we will continue with the next ring of terror in North Africa with Algeria, Morocco, Libya, Egypt and others. The prospects for peace in the Middle East which at one time looked promising have, since 1993, turned rather cloudy. Cooperation between the Israelis and the Palestinian Police of Yasir Arafat, under the provision of the Declaration of Principles, has led to the death of Hamas members in the Gaza Strip. Success for the Israelis came when their forces killed two senior members of Hamas on September 11, 1998. What effect this will have on relations between occupying Israelis and Arafat is yet to be determined, but indications are that another round of indiscriminate bombings will likely follow. If a lasting peace can be sustained, there must be a definite sign of support for such from the Israeli government. To date, that sign appears to be missing or perhaps misplaced. Terrorism will continue in Gaza and the West Bank for the foreseeable future and into the millennium.

MOROCCO

This North African country, neatly sandwiched between the Atlantic Ocean and Algeria, has been remarkably adept at keeping terrorism at bay. The government has rigorously investigated all terrorist acts and threats and has been successful in countering any Islamic fundamentalist unrest within its borders. Morocco also arrested a member of the Algerian Islamic Salvation Front in December 1997.[26] Morocco gained its independence from French rule in 1955, after rioting broke out when the French sent the Sultan into exile. The uprising resulted in the Sultan being returned to his native Morocco. Sultan Mohammad V changed his title to that of king and established a constitutional monarchy to oversee and control all aspects of governing the country. On his death in 1961, his son Hassan assumed the mantle of king and also prime minister. Since its independence, Morocco has laid claims to regions of the Saharan desert under Spanish mandate. Morocco and Mauritania both had claims on the region and had to contend with the Polisario Front, an indigenous group operating in the Sahara region. The Polisario Front wanted self-determination and was not likely to accept being consumed by either Mauritania or Morocco. Mauritania dropped its claim to the desert region, and in its place Morocco claimed the whole area. In its efforts to stave off Morocco, the Polisario Front received military support from Libya and Algeria.

EGYPT

The history of Egyptian contributions to modern society has been fascinating. Their feats of civil engineering, craftsmanship and overall attention to detail in developing a dynasty before most of the world became civilized is a matter of historic record. The influences of the Egyptian people and the Pharaohs swept through Africa, the Middle East and Mesopotamia and dominated societies for centuries. Even now, the study of ancient Egyptian writings and stegonography occupies countless professors and universities. It is believed that the first Egyptian pyramid was built 2500 years before the birth of Christ. Egypt became a part of the Roman Empire in 31 B.C., and Roman rule dominated Egypt until approximately 395 A.D., when the country was overrun and ruled by Muslims from the Arabian peninsula.

TWENTIETH-CENTURY POLITICS

History sometimes repeats itself and that is the case with Egypt, which had been a country within the the Ottoman Empire. The Muslim Brotherhood, which comprises a large percentage of native Egyptians, was to play a part in the assassination of President Anwar Sadat. Sadat's readiness to make a peace deal with the Israeli government was as much about economics as anything else. Egypt was suffering from excessive military spending and Sadat had promised that this would be lessened with the signing of a peace treaty with the Israelis. At the latter part of the 1970s, Egypt was considered by Israel to be its most powerful enemy as well as its next door neighbor. A deal between the two countries was being brokered under the influence of U.S. President Jimmy Carter and on March 29, 1979 in Washington D.C., Menachem Begin and Anwar Sadat signed a peace accord. In hindsight, this may have been the significant political action which was to lead to Saddat's untimely death. Immediately after the signing of the historic treaty, a summit of Arab League nations was held in Baghdad, with the result that Egypt was ostracized, both economically and politically, from the Arab world. Under the terms of the treaty, the Israelis gave up the Sinai in return for a peace deal and financial support from the U.S. Similarly, Egypt was now an outcast Arab state that was dependent on the U.S. for its aid. A large majority of Egyptians welcomed the accord.

The Muslim Brotherhood

Christians and Muslims have occupied Egypt for centuries. Egyptians who are born Christians are referred to as *Copts*, and number about 5 to 6 million. Formed in 1922 by Sheik al-Banna, the Brotherhood had stood as President Nasser's most vitriolic opponents in Egypt. There had been an attempt on his life by a member of the Brotherhood, which gave Nasser the excuse he needed to round up and jail the membership and proclaim a ban on the movement. The Brotherhood would see an about-face by the presidential office with the arrival of Sadat, and those factions of the Brotherhood willing to support Sadat against the extreme left opponents of his regime were themselves supported with large donations. The Brotherhood would eventually bite the hand that fed it, with considerable ferocity.

ANWAR SADAT, 1919–1981

Sadat's style of government became increasingly autocratic and though he had suggested that the country would benefit economically, there was no immediate change regarding military spending. In fact, spending in this area increased. Sadat was not gaining any allies among his Arab neighbors as he continued to attempt to keep the peace accord with Israel alive. Israel's attentions by 1981 were diverted to the northeast and Lebanon. When the Israeli invasion of southern Lebanon began in 1982, the peace process with Egypt became mired in the sand. On the home front in 1981, Sadat was now facing increasing hostilities from the Muslim Fundamentalists of the Brotherhood. Far from supporting Sadat, the Brotherhood was now actively challenging his rule. In June 1981, fighting erupted between Muslims and Christians in Cairo, which resulted in massive property damage and a large number of deaths. Sadat began to suppress the Brotherhood and arrested 1500 members, including many of the organization's leaders.[27] Clearly out in the cold, Sadat's only close ally was the United States. This alliance fuelled the hatred of Sadat by the Muslim Brotherhood, and it was not aimed at the government but at Sadat himself. President Nasser was, by all accounts, mourned by an entire nation; not so with the passing of Sadat. The Sadat government was seen as increasingly corrupt, with the ordinary Egyptians suffering food shortages. Sadat's promise of a better life for Egyptians never seemed to materialize. At a military review on October 6, 1981, Sadat was taking the salute when he was cut down by a burst of machine gunfire from his own troops in a bloody twenty-five second rampage. The planning was meticulous and

Terrorist fires submachine gun at point blank range into presidential reviewing stand where President Anwar Sadat and at least six others were killed. CP Picture Archive (AP Wirephoto)

allowed the assassins to reach the dais. A three-ton military transport stopped in front of the grandstand and Lieutenant El-Sambouli and his co-conspirators opened fire on Sadat, killing him and six others on the grandstand instantly. Thirty others received injuries. There was no spontaneous eruption of violence, no revolution to carry the Muslim Brotherhood forward in Egypt, which had been the intention of the Muslim cell involved in the attack. Although the western world leaders and governments mourned his passing, Egyptians seemed to breathe a collective sigh of relief and, to some extent, regarded Lt. El-Sambouli as a hero! With Islamic fundamentalism on the rise throughout the Muslim world, it seemed probable that a revolt should occur, but this did not happen in Egypt. In elections in 1987, the Muslim Brotherhood, allied with two political parties, won 17 percent of the vote, which translated into 56 seats in the Egyptian National Assembly.[28] In April 1982, El-Sambouli and his five co-conspirators were found guilty and executed for their crimes.

EGYPT'S ISLAMIC FUNDAMENTALISTS

A continuation of the threat posed by the Muslim Brotherhood has been realized with the appearance of al-Gama'at al-Islamiyya (Islamic Group IG).This fundamentalist group is violently opposed to the Egyptian government's ties and peace treaty with Israel. It targets government members, police and Coptic Christians in southern Egypt. The government of President Hosni Mubarak has been embroiled in a six-year battle to crush the life out of these extremists, who have a base in Assuit, halfway between Cairo and Luxor. Foreign tourists have suffered the brunt of the attacks, for which the group makes no apology. In September of 1997, an assault on a tour bus left nine German tourists and their Egyptian driver dead outside the National Museum in Cairo. On November 17, 1997, IG carried out an attack at the temple in Luxor which left fifty-eight European tourists dead, including women and children. This attack was by far the most devastating and took aim at Egypt's flourishing tourist industry. Announcements from the group indicated that the original plan had been to take hostages to bargain for the release of Sheik al-Rahman, currently serving a life sentence for terrorist conspiracy in the U.S. This theory has been refuted by eye-witness accounts from survivors, who say the gunmen ruthlessly and methodically executed those trapped inside the temple and that there was no attempt to take hostages.

With unemployment running at over 40 percent, any diminution in Egypt's tourist traffic, which accounts for about 6 percent of the country's economy and is second only to the oil industry for foreign revenue, is catastrophic. Those involved in the massacre were shot and killed by police at the scene. The philosophy of the fundamentalists is to overthrow the government and to replace it with a radical and extreme Islamic government similar to the Taliban movement in Afghanistan. Over the last six years, the Mubarak government's crackdown on the IG has seen many militants either jailed or executed under military tribunals. Those in jail are believed to number more than 14,000.

CONCLUSION

The hard line response to terrorism taken by Egypt has been somewhat successful in slowing the tide of terror, but it has not damaged the ability of the group to continue to strike at the government. With Islamic fundamentalism increasing throughout Asia and Africa, the scenes being played out in the latter half of the 1990s are expected to continue. If the government is able to contain the terrorist movement and make economic progress, the fundamentalists will likely become a less potent influence. However, if the reverse occurs, we should expect to see a rise in popularity for the fundamentalist movements.[29]

LIBYA

Overview

Libya is situated at the northern tip of Africa and has a northern border on the Mediterranean Sea. Its near neighbors to the east are Egypt and the Sudan, with Chad and Niger to the south and Algeria and Tunisia to the west and northwest, respectively. The country is made up of 97 percent Sunni Muslims or Arabian Berber tribesmen. In the 1930s, under Italian dominance, there was discrimination against Libyan Jews, who have been persecuted in Libya ever since. The Jewish sector of Benghazi was attacked by Libyans during WWII and about 2,000 Jews were deported. By the time Libya had achieved independence in 1951 nearly all the remaining Libyan Jews had migrated either to Israel or Europe.[30]

Colonel Muammar Qaddafi

Muammar Qaddafi is a man driven by hatred for the state of Israel and any foreign power that supports it. The U.S. is second on the Libyan leader's hate list, with the United Kingdom not far behind. Libya does not limit itself to attacking the foreign governments, but also seeks out and kills opponents of Qaddafi.

Qaddafi came to power following a military coup that deposed King Idris in 1969, and has now achieved dictatorial status as leader of the Libyan people. His views are anti-Israeli, anti-Zionist and anti-Jew, although in his public statements he makes no distinction between them. As a mark of his hatred for the Jewish people, he seized all Jewish-owned properties and businesses in 1971. He rules with an autocratic style and ruthlessly "removes" all dissenters. His control of the government is absolute through the setup of peoples' committees. As a former military student and officer, he had never been cast in the secular role which he seems to have adopted in the 1990s. Reports out of Libya indicate that several attempts on his life have taken place, by a group calling itself the Libyan Militant Islamic Group.

Support for Terror

The relatively modern phenomenon of state-sponsored terrorism applies most specifically to Libya, Iran and Syria. By far the most outspoken of the Arab world leaders, Qaddafi has embarked on what may be described as a reign of external terror against the U.S. and its citizens, specifically in Europe. The Libyans have supported other terror groups in Europe and have allowed them to train on Libyan soil. Libya has also provided weapons to such groups as the Provisional Irish Republican Army. In one notable incident, the Libyans supplied several tons of explosives and automatic weapons, which were seized by security forces in the Irish Republic. To Qaddafi, the PIRA are fighting a guerrilla war of independence from the dominance of an imperialist power. Such actions have not been taken lightly by U.K. security experts. Libya has been a home and training ground for more than thirty terrorist organizations.

TERRORISM PLAYER 6-5

MUAMMAR QADDAFI

Born in Libya in 1941, he is a devout Muslim and follower of Islam and comes from a family of Bedouins. He trained as an officer at the Libyan Military Academy in Benghazi and also at the Royal Military Academy, Sandhurst, Berkshire, England. Denounced by many western countries, but has been strongly supported with military aid and hardware from the former Soviet Union, which supplied his air force with MIG fighter aircraft and tanks. Attempts have been made on his life from different quarters. At home he has been the target of several military coups by his own officers. In 1985, fifteen army officers were executed for attempting to assassinate him. On the international front, the United States government under the Reagan administration has attempted, albeit unsuccessfully, to target him with attacks by aircraft from the U.S. Navy in the Mediterranean. He survives to this day as a continued sponsor of international terrorism.

There was sufficient opposition to the Qaddafi regime to prompt him to unleash internal assassins to track down and coerce the dissidents into returning to Libya. Failure to return left only the option of death. In 1984 alone more than thirty terrorist attacks by representatives of Libyan Revolutionary Committees on Libyans residing in Europe and the Middle East were carried out.[31] Not only did Qaddafi focus on dissidents in Europe and the Middle East, he also sought them out in neighboring Chad and the sub-Saharan African states that were vociferously against his government.

Diplomatic Immunity

To circumvent the interference of foreign customs officials, Qaddafi used diplomatic privileges to move weapons into and out of diplomatic missions in Europe. By the 1980s, Qaddafi had renamed the Libyan embassies and was now referring to them as the Libyan People's Bureaus. The problems faced by the British government of Margaret Thatcher and public protests outside the Libyan People's Bureau in St James's Park, London would result in the severing of diplomatic ties between the two countries.

The following are extracts from the Vienna Convention on Diplomatic Relations:

Article 22

1. The premises of the mission shall be inviolable. The agents of the receiving state may not enter them, except with the consent of the head of the mission.

2. The receiving State is under a special duty to take all appropriate steps to protect the premises of the mission against any intrusion or damage and to prevent any disturbances of the peace of the mission or impairment of its dignity.

3. The premises of the mission, their furnishings and other property thereon and the means of transport of the mission shall be immune from search, requisition, attachment or execution.

Article 29

The person of a diplomatic agent shall be inviolable. He shall not be liable to any form of arrest or detention. The receiving State shall treat him with due respect and shall take all appropriate steps to prevent any attacks on his person, freedom or dignity.

Comment: *It is possible that a request made to the British authorities about the peaceful but vociferous protest outside the Libyan Peoples Bureau in April 1984 would have been covered by this section of the Vienna Convention.*

Article 31

1. A diplomatic agent shall enjoy immunity from the criminal jurisdiction of the receiving State. He shall also enjoy immunity from its civil and administrative jurisdiction.

2. A diplomatic agent is not obliged to give evidence as a witness.

Comment: *The actions occurring inside the Libyan People's Bureau as a result of gunfire from within the diplomatic mission would have been covered by this article.*

If diplomatic relations are broken off between two States, or if a mission is permanently or temporarily recalled:

a. the receiving State must, even in case of armed conflict, respect and protect the premises of the mission, together with its property and archives;

b. the sending State may entrust the custody of the premises of the mission, together with its property and archives, to a third State acceptable to the receiving State;

c. the sending State may entrust the protection of its interests and those of its nationals to a third State acceptable to the receiving State.

The siege of the Libyan People's Bureau, which was being covered by both the major news networks in London, the BBC and ITN, showed the dramatic turn of events when gunfire erupted from the bureau into the crowd in the street. The demonstrators were mainly exiled Libyan students protesting against Qaddafi. The gunfire killed a Metropolitan Policewoman, Yvonne Fletcher. The incident, which took place in the heart of the diplomatic center of London on April 17, 1984 and accounted for a dozen injuries to the demonstrators, was not a random maniacal act, but a deliberate attack on the demonstrators. Intelligence intercepts of messages between Tripoli and the London Libyan People's Bureau revealed that those inside were ordered to fire on the demonstrators. On the home front, the Libyan-controlled press released a different story about the incident, stating that police had stormed the building and describing the episode as a barbarous outrage. The standoff at the Libyan People's Bureau ended on April 27, when the occupants agreed to be taken to the Civil Services College in Berkshire to be interviewed by police. Under diplomatic privileges to which they were entitled, they refused to help in the investigation and were returned to Libya. The events at St. James's Square were the culmination of a series of bombings and attacks against dissident Libyans in London and the northwest of England.

Qaddafi and the U.S.

Qadaffi sees himself as a latter-day Abdel Nasser, with the ideology of leading and uniting the Arab nations. Fanatical and fundamentalist, he has targeted U.S. interests and personnel in Europe. Its is believed the attack on the La Belle discotheque in Berlin on April 5, 1986, which claimed the life of one U.S. serviceman and injured scores of others, was the work of Libyan agents. This incident did not have a particularly high body count, but the U.S. was in no mood to trifle with the Libyan government of Colonel Qaddafi. This death of U.S. personnel was either the trigger or the excuse the Reagan administration was searching for to launch a military response against Libya. U.S. intelligence indicated that the disco bombing was planned and directed by "diplomats" from the East Berlin Libyan People's Bureau.

Operation El Dorado Canyon

International relations between the U.S. and Libya were at an all time low by the middle of the 1980s. Behind the scenes at this time was the Soviet Union, which had been supplying weapons and aircraft to Libya. In a blatant effort to make the Libyans lose face, the U.S. began maneuvers with its Sixth Fleet in the Mediterranean off the north coast of Libya, in an area proclaimed by Libya as an exclusion zone. The area in question was the Gulf of Sirte. These exercises began on March 24, 1986, and were calculated to intimidate the Libyan leader. Far from intimidation, the result was the detonation of two bombs in Europe. The first, on April 2, 1986, exploded in the cabin of a TWA passenger jet in Greek airspace. Four Americans were killed in the blast; however, the aircraft landed without further incident.

Four days later a powerful explosion ripped through La Belle discotheque in West Berlin, killing an American serviceman. These two actions appear to have triggered a previously planned strike at Libya by U.S. forces. On April 14, 1986, aircraft from U.S. bases in the United Kingdom and from the U.S. Navy carriers in the Mediterranean attacked and bombed targets inside Libya. One could argue that the U.S. had violated the U.N. Charter and international laws with a preemptive strike against a sovereign state. Over one hundred aircraft took part in the raid in and around Tripoli and Benghazi, causing heavy damage and loss of life. It is believed that Colonel Qaddafi's adopted daughter was one of the fatalities. In all, more than one hundred lives were claimed. The U.S. actions can be viewed in many different ways with analysis. Was the attack sending a message to other state sponsors of terrorism or was this strike designed to help topple or kill the Libyan leader and allow a more moderate government to be formed in its place? This was the first time such stringent military action had been aimed at a specific country in retaliation for terrorist attacks. Would other terrorist groups heed the example of the Libya attack and cease activities against the U.S.? On the political front, the U.S. was condemned by members of the U.N., including France and Italy, two countries which had refused overflight clearances for strike aircraft from U.K. bases. Did the French and Italian governments fear some form of reprisal from the Libyan leader? The U.K. government on the other hand, America's strongest ally at the time, had already severed diplomatic ties with Libya. Whatever analysts may think, a far more serious terrorist attack was not far away, proving that preemptive military actions would not be successful against determined and fanatical terrorist movements. However, thirteen years later, under a different U.S. administration, spy satellites and long-range smart bombs would again target terrorist sites in the Sudan and Afghanistan.

PAN AM 103

With the Christmas holidays approaching in the winter of 1988, a major terrorist attack was being planned. It is generally believed, though evidence has yet to be heard, that the perpetrators were from Libya, supported by Colonel Qaddafi.

On December 21, 1988 a Pan Am Boeing 747-121 was destroyed over the border counties of Scotland by a bomb in the cargo container of the aircraft. The belief that the incident is the responsibility of Libyan agents is a result of the painstaking investigation conducted by the Dumfries and Galloway police. The Pan Am flight departed from London's Heathrow International Airport at 6:04 pm, and was headed for New York's John F. Kennedy Airport. As with many flights, this one had passengers from prior flights on board, their baggage having been transferred directly to the cargo containers of Pan Am 103. The aircraft headed north over England before beginning its route over the Atlantic to New York. At about 7:01 PM, on December 21, an explosion in the cargo hold ripped the aircraft apart at a height of nearly 30,000 feet, scattering debris down onto the Scottish border town of Lockerbie. The impact and damage on the ground destroyed twenty-one homes and claimed the lives of eleven residents. Those on the aircraft numbered 243 passengers and sixteen crewmembers. The wreckage of the aircraft was strewn over an area of about a hundred square kilometers and as far east as the North Sea. Among the victims was Charles McKee, the head of a U.S. intelligence team, and Mathew Gannon, the CIA's deputy station chief in Beirut. One passenger, Pik Botha, of South Africa, had arrived late at the airport and had been booked on an alternate flight.

The Evidence

Painstaking investigation and a thorough search of the wreckage, which was spread over a wide area, identified items from a baggage container as exhibiting damage likely to have been caused by an explosion. Further forensic evidence deduced that the explosion had taken place in baggage container AVE 4041 PA. A piece of the skin of the metal container was found by an Accident Investigations Inspector to contain, trapped within its folds, an item which was subsequently identified by forensic scientists at the Royal Armaments Research and Development Establishment (RARDE) as belonging to a specific type of radio-cassette player and that this had been fitted with an improvised explosive device (IED).[32]

The hunt was now on to establish who owned the suitcase and the materials inside. Evaluation and forensic analysis found that a piece of the clothing came from a bolt of material that could be traced to only two locations, Ireland and Malta. The inquiry and investigation focused in on a small clothing store in Malta, where the owner was able to recall the purchaser due to the fact that he picked clothes at random, with no concern for their size. The male was identified as being of Libyan origin. It became apparent that Libya may well have had a hand in this atrocity, and subsequently two Libyan Nationals, Abdel Baset Ali Mohamed al-Megrahi and Lamen Khalifa Fhimah were charged with the terrorist bombing of flight 103.

The two men charged with the bombing have returned to Libya, and the Libyan government has refused to hand them over either to British authorities or the United States. It took until November 1991 for the charges against them to be filed.

TERRORISM BRIEF 6–5

The following notice was posted on boards in the U.S. Embassy, Moscow and was provided to students, businessmen and journalists of American origin in Moscow.

ADMINISTRATIVE NOTICE

American Embassy, Moscow
December 13th 1988

To: All Embassy Employees
Subject: Threat to Civil Aviation

Post has been notified by the Federal Aviation Administration that on December 5, 1988, an unidentified individual telephoned a U.S. diplomatic facility in Europe and stated that sometime within the next two weeks there would be a bombing attempt against a Pan American aircraft flying from Frankfurt to the United States.

The FAA reports that the reliability of the information cannot be assessed at this point, but the appropriate police authorities have been notified and are pursuing the matter. Pan Am has also been notified.

In view of the lack of confirmation of this information, post leaves to the discretion of individual travelers any decisions on altering personal travel plans or changing to another American carrier. This does not absolve the traveler from flying an American carrier.

(signed) William C. Kelly, Administrative Counselor.

Political posturing between the U.S., U.K. and Libya has lasted up to this time on a location and jurisdiction for any court proceedings. In 1994, the U.K. government rejected an offer from Libya to have the two stand trial under the auspices of a Muslim court anywhere in the world. Abdel Baset, aged forty-six, is alleged to have been a senior officer of the Libyan intelligence service and the head of Libyan Arab Airlines security in Malta in 1988, and to have purchased the clothes that were placed in the suitcase with the bomb. Khalifa Fahima, aged forty-two, is alleged to be a member of the Libyan intelligence organization and been a station officer for Libyan Arab Airlines in Malta.[33]

U.N. Sanctions

In an unprecedented action, the United Nations approved sanctions against Libya for failing to surrender the two men charged in connection with the bombing of flight 103. These economic sanctions have been in place for most of the last decade of the twentieth century. United Nations Security Council Resolutions (UNSCR) 731, 748 and 883 were adopted in response. What effect this is having on the people of Libya one can only guess; however, the U.N. sanctions on Iraq following the Gulf War have taken a harsh toll on the Iraqi people, with food and medical supplies shortages. Whether this tactic of punishing a nation for the actions of its government is an effective method of limiting terrorism is a moot point. The two suspects charged with the bombing of Pan Am 103 have not been brought to trial almost eleven years after the event. There was indication in October of 1998 that the Libyan Government would agree to a trial being held at the Soestterberg air base near The Hague, Holland. The United Nations has agreed to lift the sanctions on Libya once the two suspects arrive in Holland.

SUDAN

Sudan has been fighting an almost endless civil war between Muslims in the north and Christians in the south. Its government appears to have been devastated by the famine and poverty that has wrecked the nation. Sudan has, however, been on the U.S. State Department's list of countries which sponsor and support international terror groups. Safe haven and training grounds have been available to the Abu Nidal Organization, Hizballah, Hamas and the PIJ. The U.N. Security Council passed several resolutions concerning the role of Sudan in sponsoring terror groups; not all have been complied with. One name stands apart from all others at the end of this decade: Usama bin Ladin was ordered to leave the Sudan in 1997, but his legacy was to cause a military confrontation with the U.S. some twelve months later. Following the massive bombings of the U.S. embassies in the Kenyan and Tanzanian capitals which claimed hundreds of lives, the U.S. struck back. In a reaction similar to that of Ronald Reagan, the Clinton administration retaliated during the night of August 20, 1998. In his address to the nation on August 20, Bill Clinton stated, "Today I ordered our armed forces to strike at terrorist related facilities in Afghanistan and Sudan because of the imminent threat they presented to our national security...In recent history they killed American, Belgian and Pakistani peacekeepers in Somalia. They plotted to assassinate the Pope and the President of Egypt. They planned to bomb six United States 747's over the Pacific...their (terrorist) mission is murder and their history is bloody. The most recent terrorist events are fresh in our memory. Two weeks ago, twelve Americans and 300 Kenyans and Tanzanians lost their lives. Another 5,000 were wounded when our embassies in Nairobi and Dar es Salaam were bombed." The attack against a factory believed to be developing chemical weapons was carried out by a sea-launched missile attack from U.S. naval ships in the Red Sea. The exact details of the strike were not confirmed; however, news reports seen on television indicate massive damage to the Al-Shifa Pharmaceutical Factory in Khartoum.

This attack will, in all likelihood, only harden the fundamentalists' resolve to continue the fight. Throughout the Middle East and Asia, there were spontaneous demonstrations against the U.S., and the action has probably given significant impetus to the Islamic fundamentalist movement in Afghanistan. As in the 1986 strike against Libya, this kind of response is not seen as an effective deterrent; to many analysts it is seen as having precisely the opposite effect.

SUMMARY

Marked changes have taken place in the Middle East and North Africa over the last seventy-five years of this century. Israel's statehood became a reality, and displaced Palestinians, who are now seen as a sort of indigenous terrorist movement seeking their own nationhood within the Gaza Strip. A peace settlement for the region, brokered by the United States and signed by both Israel and Palestinian representatives, has not resolved longstanding hatreds and the demand by Palestinians for land. We have reviewed in this chapter the many different faces of terrorism as it applies to this area of the world. The countries involved in issues surrounding major terror attacks (Libya and Pan Am 103) continue to resist international pressure to bring those responsible to justice. Islamic fundamentalism and fatwas against a common enemy of the Islamic fundamentalists, the U.S., have shown that terror comes in many forms and has the ability to strike at perceived "soft targets" in U.S.-friendly states. The multimillionaire Saudi dissident, Usama bin Laden, has brought a new meaning to global terrorism, as he sits and prepares for his next strike against the West. In the next chapter, the student will review the methods which countries dealt with, and continue countering incipient terrorism, and also some major anti-terror strategies in the Persian Gulf.

Terms to Remember

Balfour Declaration	NMO	PLO
Fedayeen	Hashemite Kingdom	Declaration of Principles
Al-Fatah	Black September	Abu Nidal
PFLP	Hamas	PLF
DFLP	PIJ	Kach and Kahane
Sunni	Shi'a	Hizballah

Review Questions

Discuss the importance of the Balfour Declaration and its influence on terrorism.

Describe the genesis of the PLO and what has been their role in the Middle East.

What role has Hamas had in the stability of Palestine and peace in the Middle East?

Explain the role of the extreme right-wing orthodox Jews in the peace process.

Why do you think that the Libyan president has kept such a low profile?

Endnotes

1. Jonathan R. White, *Terrorism an Introduction*, Brooks Cole Publishing 1991, p. 92.

2. David Yallop, *Tracking the Jackal*, Random House, New York 1993, p. 250.

3. David Yallop, *Tracking the Jackal*, p. 251, 252.

4. World Book Inc., *World Book Encyclopaedia*, World Book U.S.A. 1990, p. 487, 488.

5. David Yallop, *Tracking the Jackal*, p. 335.

6. George Rosie, *The Directory of International Terrorism*, Paragon House, New York, 1987, p. 290.

7. David Yallop, *Tracking the Jackal*, p. 36.

8. Richard Clutterbuck, *Guerrillas and Terrorists*, Ohio University Press, 1980, p. 80.

9. Union of Palestine Relief Committees, " An Overview of the Gaza Strip", p. 3 issue # 25, March 1997.

10. This material was drawn from an article by Ahhmad Rashad, "The Truth about Hamas" on the Internet September 6, 1998.

11. This material was drawn from MILNET articles maintained by George Goncalves, "Patterns of Global Terrorism," United States Department of State Publication 10321, 1997.

12. Ibid.

13. Ibid.

14. Ibid.

15. David Yallop, *Tracking the Jackal*, p. 601.

16. Tom Gross, "Children are Indoctrinated into Terrorism," *The Weekly Telegraph* (London, Telegraph Group Inc. September 1, 1998), p. 20, Issue No. 371.

17. Paul Wilkinson, *Terrorism and the Liberal State*, New York University Press, 1979 p. 49.

18. The Internet, "The Five Pillars of Islam," *Political Islam Glossary*.

19. The Internet, "Sunnis and Shiites, the Great Schism," *Political Islam Glossary*.

20. Ayala Hammond Schbley, "A Study of Some of the Lebanese Shi'a Contemporary Terrorism," *Terrorism, an International Journal*, Taylor & Francis 1989, p. 220, Vol. 12, No. 4.

21. Magnus Ranstorp, "Hizballah's Command Leadership," *Terrorism and Political Violence*, Frank Cass, London, 1994, p. 304, Vol. 6, No. 3.

22. Yonah Alexander, "Hizballah: The Most Dangerous Terrorist Movement," *Intersec*, Three Bridges Publishing Ltd., October 1994, p. 393, Vol. 4, Issue 10.

23. Edgar O'Balance, "Islamic Fundamentalist Terrorism," *Intersec*, Three Bridges Publishing Ltd., January 1995, p. 14, Vol. 5, Issue 1.

24. Yonah Alexander, "Hizballah: The Most Dangerous Terrorist Movement," p. 394.

25. Jonathan R. White, *Terrorism, an Introduction*, Wadsworth Publishing Co., Second Edition, 1997, p. 141.

26. Patterns of Global Terrorism: 1997 U.S. State Department, Hellenic Resources Network.

27. Heather Blearney and Richard Lawless, *The Middle East Since 1945*, B.T. Batsford Ltd., London, 1989, p. 37.

28. Ibid., p. 60.

29. Middle East Overview, *Patterns of Global Terrorism, 1997,* U.S. State Department, Hellenic Resources Network.

30. Libya, *Anti-Semitism World Report 1997*, The Internet.

31. *Patterns of Global Terrorism: 1984*, Terrorism, an International Journal, Crane Russak & Company, Inc. 1987, p. 419, Vol. 9, No. 3.

32. Air Accident Investigations Branch, Aircraft Accident Report No 2/90 (EW/C1094).

33. Fast Facts on Lockerbie, BBC News August 24, 1998: BBC Online Network.

CHAPTER 7

THE PERSIAN GULF

If we suppose that humans are by nature wicked, then kindness and love need special explanation. If, on the other hand, we think that the depth of our soul knows only good we must provide and account for wickedness and violence.

–John Lachs

OVERVIEW

Because of recent historical events, the Persian Gulf, a body of water surrounded by a number of Arab and Islamic states, is well known to most students. The oil crises, the exile of the Shah of Iran, the Iraq-Iran war, the Gulf War and its continuing aftermath and other headline events have made the Persian Gulf a household term. But little is really known about this faraway area and why it is the way it is today. Perhaps the most important area of the world when considering terrorism, the Persian Gulf is surrounded by some of the biggest players in that arena. The student will be given a history of the political and religious events in this fascinating region. How these countries are molding the future of this region and how their past has influenced the present will be discussed. The oil-rich countries have the power to bring modern technological societies to their knees by cutting off the supply of that most critical commodity. We begin our visit to the Arabian nights with the largest oil producer, Saudi Arabia.[1]

SAUDI ARABIA

The Kingdom of Saudi Arabia borders the Persian Gulf and the Red Sea, north of Yemen. The kingdom is slightly more than one-fifth the size of the United States, with only two percent of its land arable. Bordering countries are Iraq, Jordan, Kuwait,

Oman, Qatar, United Arab Emirates and Yemen. Most of the country is a harsh, dry, largely uninhabited desert, with great extremes of temperature. Despite these conditions, petroleum, natural gas, iron ore, gold and copper make Saudi Arabia very rich. The country's long coastlines on the Persian Gulf and Red Sea provide extensive shipping capabilities, especially for crude oil, through the Gulf and Suez Canal. With a population of twenty million, which includes five million nonnationals, the infrastructure for the kingdom is maintained in grand style. Ethnic groups are limited, with 90 percent being Arab and the remainder Afro-Asian. One hundred percent are Muslim and the official language is Arabic. As an Islamic monarchy, there is no constitution; government is according to Shari'a (Islamic law), as is the legal system.

King Fahd bin Abdul al-Aziz Al-Saud (since 13 June 1982) is both the chief of state and head of government. No political parties are allowed. Saudi Arabia has an oil-based economy with firm government controls over major economic activities. Economic and political ties with the U.S. are especially strong. The petroleum sector accounts for roughly 75 percent of budget revenues, 35 percent of GDP, and 90 percent of export earnings. Saudi Arabia has the largest reserves of petroleum in the world (26 percent of the proven total), and ranks as the largest exporter of petroleum. It plays a major role in the Organization of Petroleum Exporting Countries (OPEC).

In the 1990s, the government is bringing its budget, which has been in deficit since 1983, back into balance, and is encouraging more private economic activity. Roughly four million foreign workers play an important role in the oil and service sectors. For over a decade, Saudi Arabia's domestic and international outlays outstripped its income. The government cut its foreign assistance and is beginning to rein in domestic programs. A substantial drop in oil prices has had an impact on all oil-producing countries in 1998. The Kuwaiti ownership of Qaruh and Umm al Maradim islands is disputed by Saudi Arabia but, in 1996, they agreed with Qatar to demarcate borders per 1992 accords. Consumption and trafficking in narcotics is a problem in the kingdom, and the death penalty is imposed on traffickers, but the consumption of heroin and cocaine is still increasing.

King Abdul Aziz

The history of modern Saudi Arabia begins in the year 1902, when Abdul al-Aziz Al-Saud and a band of his followers captured the city of Riyadh, returning it to the control of his family. **Abdul Aziz** was born about 1880 and spent the early years of his life with his father, who was exiled in Kuwait. After the capture of Riyadh, he spent the next twelve years consolidating his conquests in the area around Riyadh and the eastern part of the country, from which the Turks had been expelled. The Arab tribes had never liked the Turks, and were only too willing to listen to a new ruler whose ambitions were aided considerably by the troubles of the Ottoman Empire. In 1933, the lands under the control of Abdul Aziz were renamed the Kingdom of Saudi Arabia and in 1936 a treaty was signed with Yemen marking the southern borders of the Kingdom.

The main preoccupations of Abdul Aziz were the consolidation of his power and the restoration of law and order to all parts of his recently created kingdom. To these ends, he developed a system whereby every sheikh was responsible for his own tribe under the authority of the king, who was empowered to intervene to impose law and order. It was clearly understood that internal anarchy within the kingdom could quickly lead to foreign intervention. All were agreed that this was unacceptable. King Abdul Aziz died in 1953, after more than half a century as leader and king. Saud bin Abdul Aziz, his eldest son, succeeded him.

British soldiers in rescue operation at the site of the bomb-wrecked U.S. Marine command center at Beirut Airport. CP Picture Archive (AP Wirephoto)

A Long Line of Kings

The new king then devoted a great deal of time to fostering the kingdom's relations with its neighbors. His reign saw solid achievements in the field of education, and social services as well as the expansion of the Holy Places in **Mecca and Medina**. After eleven years, King Saud abdicated in favor of his brother Faisal, the Crown Prince. In March 1975, King Faisal was assassinated in Riyadh by one of his nephews. The transfer of power, however, went smoothly and King Khalid bin Abdul Aziz took power, with Fahad bin Abdul Aziz being made Crown Prince. King Khalid continued most of King Faisal's popular policies. It was during King Khalid's reign that Saudi Arabia enjoyed the enormous prosperity of the so-called "petro-dollar boom years."

In November 1979, several hundred armed radicals seized control of the **Grand Mosque** in Mecca and used the public address system to denounce the royal family and the country's rush to modernization. The people of the kingdom, however, failed to support them and government troops were involved in a ten-day operation to regain control of the mosque. At the end of the operation, 117 of the radicals had died and 63 were captured by government troops. Six weeks later, they were executed in various cities throughout the kingdom.

King Khalid died in June 1982 and was succeeded by Crown Prince Fahad bin Abdul Aziz. King Fahad was well versed in the art of government, as he had served as the country's first minister of education. King Khalid had been in poor health for much of his reign, so Fahad had been ruling in all but title. Continuing development within the country and the infrastructure marked King Fahad's reign. On the political front, the open hostility from Iran toward Saudi Arabia led the government to strengthen its ties of defense with the United States, Britain and France.

Within days of Iraq's invasion of Kuwait in 1990, King Fahad allowed U.S. troops into the kingdom to help defend the country. In November 1990, King Fahad announced that plans were being made for the formation of a Consultative Council; there was some feeling that this was done in response to criticism that he had not consulted widely enough before allowing foreign troops into the kingdom. In any case, in March 1992, the king announced that the Consultative Council would be appointed by year's end and he also made its duties clear. Like other such creations in the Gulf States, the Council is a purely consultative body with no legislative powers whatever. Its formation, however, simply puts an official stamp on the longstanding system of consultation in Arab politics and society.

KUWAIT

The State of Kuwait, a nominal constitutional monarchy, is slightly smaller than New Jersey, and lies between Iraq and Saudi Arabia, bordering the Persian Gulf. While its primary natural resource is petroleum, fish, shrimp and natural gas are also plentiful. It is another Persian Gulf country with no arable land and no permanent crops, because approximately 75 percent of its potable water must be distilled or imported. Kuwait has strategic value due to its location at the head of the Persian Gulf. The small population of only 1,834,269 includes 1,381,063 nonnationals. The ethnic mix is as follows: Kuwaiti 45 percent, other Arab 35 percent, South Asian 9 percent, Iranian 4 percent and others 7 percent. Muslims make up 85 percent of the religious followers, but are split, (Shi'a 30 percent, Sunni 45 percent, other 10 percent). Christians, Hindus, Parsi and others make up the remaining 5 percent. While the official language is Arabic, English is widely spoken, as Kuwait only gained independence in 1961 from the United Kingdom.

The chief of state since December 31, 1993 is Amir Jabir al-Ahmad al-Jabir Al Sabah, and the head of government is a prime minister. While there are no official political parties and leaders, several political groups act as de facto parties (i.e., Bedouins, merchants, Sunni and Shi'a activists, and secular leftists and nationalists).

Kuwait has a small and relatively open economy with proven crude oil reserves of about 94 billion barrels, or 10 percent of world reserves. Kuwait has rebuilt its war-ravaged petroleum sector; its crude oil production averaged 2 million barrels per day in 1996. Petroleum accounts for nearly half of GDP, 90 percent of export revenues, and 75 percent of government income. Kuwait lacks water and has practically no arable land, thus preventing development of agriculture. With the exception of fish, it depends almost wholly on food imports.

Because of its high per capita income, comparable to western European incomes, Kuwait provides its citizens with extensive health, educational, and retirement benefits. The bulk of the workforce is non-Kuwaiti, living at a considerably lower level. Per capita military expenditures are among the highest in the world. The economy improved moderately in 1994–1996, with the growth in industry and finance. The World Bank has urged Kuwait to push ahead with privatization, including in the oil industry, but the government will move slowly on opening the petroleum sector. Current low petroleum prices will have a serious impact on the Kuwaiti economy. The civil telephone network suffered some damage as a result of the Gulf war, but most of the telephone exchanges were left intact and, by the end of 1994, domestic and international telecommunications had been restored to normal operation; the quality of service is excellent

In November 1994, Iraq formally accepted the U.N.-demarcated border with Kuwait, which had been spelled out in Security Council Resolutions 687 (1991), 773 (1993), and 883 (1993). This formally ends Iraq's earlier claims to Kuwait and to Bubiyan and Warbah islands. Saudi Arabia disputes ownership of Qaruh and Umm al Maradim islands.

The present **Al-Sabah dynasty** was established in Kuwait in the mid-eighteenth century, about 1760. Kuwait was nominally a province of the Ottoman Empire, ruled from Constantinople. This was observed on paper but seldom in fact. In 1899 when the Turks threatened to take actual control of the country, the ruling sheikh sought and received British protection.

The Kuwait Oil Company discovered oil in Kuwait in 1938 but, because of World War II, it was not exported until 1946, after which time Kuwait's economy flourished. Kuwait remained a British protectorate until 1961, when it became independent under Sheikh Abdullah Al-Salem Al-Sabah. However, when Iraq claimed the emirate in the early 1960s, it once again received British protection. In July 1961, Kuwait joined the Arab League and in 1963 became a member of the United Nations. Also in 1963, the first legislative elections were held and Sheikh Abdullah, the Emir of Kuwait, inaugurated the first National Assembly in February.

Kuwait, or officially the State of Kuwait, was referred to by the name **Qurain** (or Grane) in the early seventeenth century. The names Qurain or Kuwait are diminutive of the Arabic words "qarn" and "kout." Qarn is a high hill, and kout is a fortress. In the dialect of southern Iraq and the neighboring countries, kout means a house built in the form of a fortress adjacent to water. The plural of kout is akwat, as used by the Arabian Peninsula's historians when they referred to a number of castles in towns with forts and walls. Some historians believe that Barrak, Sheikh of the Bani Khalid tribe, built Kuwait City in Grane, and that since then the city has been mostly referred to by the name Kuwait. This agrees with the local traditional story that Sheikh Barrak Ibn Ghurair Al-Hamid, who ruled the Bani Khalid tribe from 1669 to 1682, built Kuwait before the beginning of the eighteenth century (AD)/the twelfth century (AH).

The geographic location of Kuwait made it a meeting point for the civilizations of the Old World. Stands and sacrifices to safeguard territory and tradition despite all obstacles and difficulties marked Kuwait's long, eventful history. The people of Kuwait displayed heroism that was famous in the Gulf, transmitted from generation to generation, and told in tales and songs. It was a heroism that stemmed from diving and its hardships, from surviving the harsh conditions of life in the desert and from bravely and steadfastly warding off any invaders who threatened Kuwait's independence.

Kuwaitis earned a living from the sea through patience, perseverance, and struggle. When the oil industry was developed, the resources were used to tame the desert through construction and the planting of greenery. The oil resources were also used for the good of the Kuwaiti people and their brothers and sisters in developing countries around the world. Rather than befriend a tyrant or surrender to Saddam Hussein in the Gulf War, Kuwait stood firm in the heart of all battles. The resistance against aggression was followed by the struggle to extinguish the oil fires and rebuild a ravaged nation. During the period of the Iraqi occupation, from August 2, 1990, to the liberation on February 26, 1991, the inhabitants of Kuwait once again gave evidence of their unwavering strength and determination.

During the 1980s, Kuwait experienced several terrorist attacks by Shiite Muslim extremists, including one in 1985 that attempted to assassinate the emir. Kuwait, like most Arab states, supported Iraq in the Iran-Iraq War (1980–1988). Kuwait played a major role in establishing the **Gulf Cooperation Council (GCC),** consisting of Saudi Arabia, Kuwait, Bahrain, Qatar, the United Arab Emirates and the Sultanate of Oman in 1981. The Council held a firm position during Iraq's invasion of Kuwait on 2 August 1990, and its seven-month occupation of the emirate.

IRAQ

The Republic of Iraq, which is slightly more than twice the size of Idaho, borders the Persian Gulf between Iran and Kuwait. Iraq gained independence from a League of Nations mandate under British administration in 1932. Iraq has rich natural resources of petroleum, natural gas, phosphates and sulfur. Its population of a little over twenty-two million is 75–80 percent Arab and 15–20 percent Kurdish, with the remainder Turkoman, Assyrian or other. Iraq is 97 percent Muslim (Shi'a 60–65 percent, Sunni 32–37 percent) and 3 percent Christian or other. The official languages are Arabic and Kurdish. The chief of state and head of government is President Saddam Hussein. Political parties and activity are severely restricted.

The **Ba'thist regime** engages in extensive central planning and management of industrial production and foreign trade, while leaving some small-scale industry and services and most agriculture to private enterprise. The economy has been dominated by the oil sector, which has traditionally provided about 95 percent of foreign exchange earnings. In the 1980s, financial problems were caused by massive expenditures in the eight-year war with Iran and damage to oil export facilities by Iran. This led the government to implement austerity measures and to borrow heavily and later reschedule foreign debt payments. Iraq suffered economic losses of at least $100 billion from the war. After the end of hostilities in 1988, oil exports gradually increased with the construction of new pipelines and restoration of damaged facilities. Seizure of Kuwait in 1990, subsequent international economic embargoes, and military action by an international coalition beginning in January 1991 drastically changed the economic picture. Industrial and transportation facilities, which suffered severe damage, have been partially restored. Oil exports are at only 25 percent of the prewar level because of implementation of U.N. **Security Council Resolution 986** in December 1996. The U.N.-sponsored economic embargo has reduced exports and imports and has contributed to a sharp rise in prices. The Iraqi government has been unwilling to abide by U.N. resolutions so that the economic embargo could be removed. The government's policies of supporting large military and internal security forces and of allocating resources to key supporters of the regime have exacerbated shortages. In accord with a U.N. resolution, Iraq agreed to an oil-for-food deal in 1996, under which it would export $2 billion worth of oil in exchange for badly needed food and medicine. The first oil was pumped in December 1996, and the first supplies of food and medicine arrived in 1997.

Iran and Iraq restored diplomatic relations in 1990 but are still trying to work out written agreements settling outstanding disputes from their eight-year war concerning border demarcation, prisoners of war, and freedom of navigation and sovereignty over the Shatt al Arab waterway. In November 1994, Iraq formally accepted the U.N.-demarcated border with Kuwait that had been spelled out in Security Council resolutions. This formally ended earlier claims to Kuwait and to Bubiyan and Warbah islands. There is still dispute over water development plans by Turkey for the Tigris and Euphrates rivers. Ironically, the area of the Middle East we now call Iraq, which we have seen in recent decades as a major source for state sponsored terrorism and constant wars, was also where many scholars agree recorded history, as we know it, began.

In ancient times, the land area now known as modern Iraq was almost equivalent to Mesopotamia, the land between the two rivers (Tigris and Euphrates). The Mesopotamian plain was called the **Fertile Crescent**. This region was the birthplace of the varied civilizations that moved us from prehistory to history. An advanced civilization flourished in this region long before that of Egypt, Greece and Rome, for it was here, in about 4000 B.C., that the Sumerian culture flourished.

Land was cultivated for the first time in this area, early calendars were first used and the first written alphabet was invented. Its bountiful land, fresh waters, and varying climate contributed to the creation of a deep-rooted civilization that fostered humanity. Mesopotamia is suspected as the location of the Garden of Eden.

Hammurabi was the king and a great lawgiver of the Old Babylonian (Amorite) dynasty. His law code was produced in the second year of his reign. Many new legal concepts were introduced by the Babylonians, and many have been adopted by other civilizations. These concepts included:

- Legal protection should be provided to lower classes
- The state is the authority responsible for enforcing the law
- Social justice should be guaranteed
- The punishment should fit the crime

A copy of the code is engraved on a block of black diorite nearly eight feet high. A team of French archaeologists at Susa, Iraq, formerly ancient Elam, unearthed this block during the winter of 1901–1902. The block, broken in three pieces, has been restored and is now in the Louvre Museum in Paris.

Abu Ja'far Muhammad ibn Musa al-Khawarizmi (680–750 A.D.), a great scholar and mathematician, originated algebraic equations. And some credit him with the invention of concept of "zero." Al-Khawarizmi wrote ten math textbooks, which have survived the test of time. His "Kitab hisab al'adad al-hindi" was an arithmetic textbook which introduced Hindu numbers to the Arab world. Now they are generally known as "Arabic numbers." Christian Europeans at first rejected the Arabic numbers and declared them the work of Satan! His major work is entitled "Kitab [al-jabr] w'al-muqabalah," from which the word "algebra" is derived.

With a long and important history, Iraq developed into a major country on the Persian Gulf. In 1936, King Ghazi I formed the Pan Arab movement with the other Arab states, promising kinship and nonaggression. The first coup d'etat in the modern Arab world came in 1936 as well, led by General Baks Sidqi. This marked a major turning point in Iraq's long history, opening the door for further military involvement in politics. In 1945, Iraq became a founding member of the Arab League and joined the United Nations.

Iraq joined in the war with Israel in 1948, allied with Jordan in accordance with a treaty signed by the two countries during the previous year. The war had a negative impact on the Iraqi economy. Oil royalties paid to Iraq were halved when the pipeline to Haifa was cut off. The war and the hanging of a Jewish businessman led, moreover, to the departure of most of Iraq's prosperous Jewish community, and about 120,000 Iraqi Jews emigrated to Israel between 1948 and 1952.

Inspired by the example of Gamal Abdel Nasser in Egypt, the Hashemite monarchy was overthrown on July 14, 1958, in a swift, predawn coup by Brigadier General Abdul-Karim Qassim and Colonel Abdul Salam Arif. King Faisal II and Abd al Ilah were executed and hung by their feet outside the palace, as were many others in the royal family. Nuri as-Said escaped capture for one day, but was then caught and put to death, his body tied to the back of a car and dragged through the streets until there was nothing left but half a leg. Iraq was then proclaimed a republic.

Later the same year, on two occasions, Arif attempted to assassinate the new prime minister, Qassim, but failed. In 1959, the Mosul garrison, disillusioned with the new government, organized a revolt against Qassim. The revolt was ruthlessly suppressed, with the massacre of many hundreds of disaffected Arab nationalists and Ba'athists. Another assassination attempt against Qassim, this time organized by the Ba'ath Party, failed. Ironically, among the unsuccessful assassination squad was a young officer named Saddam Hussein.

In 1961, Kuwait gained its independence from Britain and Abdul-Karim Qassim immediately claimed the emirate as originally part of the Ottoman province of Basrah. Britain reacted strongly by dispatching a brigade to the country to deter Iraq. Qassim backed down. In 1963, Iraq finally recognized the sovereignty and borders of Kuwait. But this was not to be the last page of that story. One military coup after another marked the 1960s and early 1970s. Qassim was assassinated in February 1963, and Ba'ath Arab Socialist Party members seized power. Hasan al-Bakr became Prime Minister with Colonel Abdul Salam Arif as president. Nine months later, President Arif led a successful coup against the Ba'athists, ousting the Ba'ath government. In 1966, President Abdul Salam Arif died in a suspicious helicopter crash and was succeeded by his brother, General Abdul Rahman Arif. Following the **Six Day War** of 1967, the Ba'ath Party felt strong enough to overthrow Arif and regained power in a coup on July 17, 1968.

In 1979, Ahmed Hasan Al-Bakr was replaced by Saddam Hussein, who then assumed both of the vacated offices. Saddam then purged political rivals in order to assure his position. Once more the political situation flared into hostilities with Iran. The Iran-Iraq War, which began in 1980, lasted for eight years and had a crippling effect on the economy of both countries. It was a monumental disaster and neither side gained any territory. But an estimated total of one million lives were lost. In July 1988, Iran accepted the terms of U.N. Resolution 598, and the cease-fire came about. Before Iraq had a chance to recover economically, Saddam once more plunged into war, by the invasion of Kuwait in 1990.

The invasion was the result of a longstanding territorial conflict. Iraq accused Kuwait of violating the Iraqi border to secure oil resources from a disputed supply, the **Rumaila oil field**. Direct negotiations were begun in July 1990, but failed. This was the go-ahead that Hussein needed. Iraqi troops overran the country in August. The United States became involved and declared interest in keeping Saudi Arabia safe. In the ensuing months, the United Nations Security Council passed a series of resolutions condemning the Iraqi occupation of Kuwait, and applied total, mandatory economic sanctions against Iraq. A coalition of NATO nations as well as Arab States subsequently provided support for Operation Desert Shield. In November, the U.N. Security Council adopted Resolution 678, permitting member states to use all necessary means, authorizing military action against the Iraqi forces occupying Kuwait, and demanding a complete withdrawal by January 1991.

Saddam Hussein failed to comply with this demand, and the Gulf War, **Operation Desert Storm**, began on January 17, 1991, with alliance troops from twenty-eight countries. The combined air forces of Great Britain and the United States launched an aerial bombardment on Baghdad to start it. The war, which proved disastrous for Iraq, lasted only six weeks, but one hundred and forty thousand tons of munitions were dropped on the country and as many as 100,000 Iraqi soldiers were killed. Coalition air raids destroyed roads, bridges, factories, and oil industry facilities and disrupted electric, telephone, and water service. Finally, a cease-fire was announced on February 28, 1991. Iraq agreed to U.N. terms for a permanent cease-fire in April of that year, and strict conditions were imposed, demanding the disclosure and destruction of all stockpiles of weapons, including weapons of mass destruction (WMD).

Insurrections quickly broke out in southern Iraq and in Kurdistan in the north, where rebels took control of most of the region's towns. Units of Saddam's elite Republican Guard that had survived the conflict suppressed protest with extreme brutality to gain control in the Basrah, Najaf and Karbala regions. In the southern cities, rebels killed Ba'thist officials, members of the security service and other supporters of the Saddam regime. In **Kurdistan**, Iraqi helicopters and troops regained control of the cities taken by the rebels and there was a mass exodus of Kurds to the Turkish and Iranian borders, fleeing from a possible repeat of the 1988 deadly chemical attacks. By the end of April, 2.5 million refugees had left Iraq.

The United States, attempting to prevent the genocide of the Marsh Arabs in southern Iraq and the Kurds to the north, established air exclusion zones north of the 36th parallel and south of the 32nd parallel. The attempted assassination of former President George Bush while in Kuwait prompted a swift military response on June 27, 1993. The Iraqi Intelligence Headquarters in Baghdad was targeted by twenty-three Tomahawk cruise missiles, launched from U.S. warships in the Red Sea and Persian Gulf.

In October 1994, Iraq again moved some Republican Guard units toward Kuwait, an act that provoked a large-scale United States troops deployment to deter an Iraqi attack. The move was interpreted as a sign of Saddam's frustration with the continuation of stiff U.N. sanctions, but he backed down, establishing a pattern of behavior he is still using, and agreed to recognize the existence of and borders of Kuwait. In the months that followed, his position appeared to become more precarious as dissatisfaction with his rule spread in the army and among the tribes and clans at the core of his regime.

In 1995, Saddam fired his half-brother, Wathban, as interior minister, and in July demoted his notorious and powerful Defense Minister, Ali Hassan al-Majid, to give more power to his two sons, Udai and Qusai. It became clear that Saddam felt more secure when protected by his immediate family members. Major General Hussein Kamil Hassan al-Majid, his Minister of Military Industries and a key henchman, defected to Jordan, together with his wife (one of Saddam's daughters) and his brother, Saddam (also married to one of the president's daughters), and called for the overthrow of the regime. In response, Saddam promised full cooperation with the U.N. commission disarming Iraq (U.N.SCOM) in order to pre-empt any revelations from the defectors. Not surprisingly, when the defectors were "forgiven" by Saddam and returned to Iraq, they were both murdered, apparently by other clan members, after they crossed the border.

The weakening of the internal position of the regime occurred at a time when the external opposition forces were as weak as ever, too divided among themselves to take any effective action. At the same time, France and Russia have pushed for an easing of sanctions. The United States and Britain's determination to keep up the pressure on Iraq has prevailed, however. In any case, the apparent weakening of the regime was illusory. In fact, during 1996, the regime's grip on power seemed to have significantly strengthened despite Saddam's inability to end the U.N. sanctions against it. Even as this is being written, there is now another major buildup of U.S. forces in the Gulf, as a result of Saddam's refusal to allow unrestricted inspections of suspected sites for storing weapons of mass destruction. It is clear that Saddam will continue to play his unique game of cat and mouse with the world until he is eliminated.

IRAN

The Islamic Republic of Iran borders the Gulf of Oman, the Persian Gulf, and the Caspian Sea, between Iraq and Pakistan. Iran is slightly larger than Alaska with large resources of petroleum, natural gas, coal, chromium, copper, iron ore, lead, manganese, zinc, and sulfur. Its estimated population of 67,540,000 includes 917,078 nonnationals with a broad base of ethnic groups (Persian 51 percent, Azerbaijani 24 percent, Gilaki and Mazandarani 8 percent, Kurd 7 percent, Arab 3 percent, Lur 2 percent, Baloch 2 percent, Turkomen 2 percent, other 1 percent) and religious affiliations (Shi'a Muslim 89 percent, Sunni Muslim 10 percent, Zoroastrian, Jewish, Christian, and Baha'i 1 percent). This broad spectrum is reflected in languages as well (Persian and Persian dialects 58 percent, Turkic and Turkic dialects 26 percent, Kurdish 9 percent, Luri 2 percent, Balochi 1 percent, Arabic 1 percent, Turkish 1 percent, other 2 percent). Iran is a theocratic republic and the constitution codifies Islamic principles of government.

Political pressure groups that generally support the Islamic Republic include Ansar-e Hizballah, Mojahedin of the Islamic Revolution, Muslim Students Following the Line of the Imam and the Islamic Coalition Association. Opposition groups include the Liberation Movement of Iran and the Nation of Iran party. Armed political groups that have been almost completely repressed by the government include **Mojahedin-e Khalq Organization (MEK)**, People's Fedayeen, Democratic Party of Iranian Kurdistan and the Society for the Defense of Freedom.

Iran's economy is a mixture of central planning, state ownership of oil and other large enterprises, village agriculture, and small-scale private trading and service

---

TERRORISM BRIEF 7–1
MOJAHEDIN-E KHALQ ORGANIZATION (MEK)

Also known as the National Liberation Army of Iran (NLA, the militant wing of the MEK), The People's Mojahedin of Iran (PMOI) Muslim Iranian Student's Society, the MEK was formed in the 1960s by the college-educated children of Iranian merchants. The MEK sought to counter what is perceived as excessive Western influence in the Shah's regime. In the 1970s, the MEK concluded that violence was the only way to bring about change in Iran. Since then, the MEK—following a philosophy that mixes Marxism and Islam—has developed into the largest and most active armed Iranian dissident group. Its history is studded with anti-Western activity, and, most recently, attacks on the interests of the clerical regime in Iran and abroad.

The MEK directs a worldwide campaign against the Iranian Government that stresses propaganda and occasionally uses terrorist violence. During the 1970s, the MEK staged terrorist attacks inside Iran to destabilize and embarrass the Shah's regime; the group killed several U.S. military personnel and civilians working on defense projects in Tehran. The group also supported the takeover in 1979 of the U.S. Embassy in Tehran. In April 1992 the MEK carried out attacks on Iranian embassies in 13 different countries, demonstrating the group's ability to mount large-scale operations overseas. Several thousand fighters are based in Iraq with an extensive overseas support structure. Most of the fighters are organized in the MEK's National Liberation Army (NLA).

In the 1980s, the MEK's leaders were forced by Iranian security forces to flee to France. Most resettled in Iraq by 1987. Since the mid-1980s, the MEK has not mounted terrorist operations in Iran at a level similar to its activities in the 1970s. Aside from the attacks into Iran toward the end of the Iran-Iraq war, and occasional NLA cross-border incursions since, the MEK's attacks on Iran have amounted to little more than harassment. The MEK has had more success in confronting Iranian representatives overseas through propaganda and street demonstrations. Beyond support from Iraq, the MEK uses front organizations to solicit contributions from expatriate Iranian communities.

SOURCE: PATTERNS OF GLOBAL TERRORISM, 1997. UNITED STATES DEPARTMENT OF STATE, APRIL 1998.

ventures. Under President Rafsanjani, the government adopted a number of market reforms to reduce the state's role in the economy, but most of these changes have moved slowly or have been reversed because of political opposition. In the early 1990s, Iran experienced a financial crisis caused by an import surge that began in 1989 and general financial mismanagement. In 1993–1994, Iran rescheduled $15 billion in debt, with the bulk of payments due in 1996–97. The strong oil market in 1996 helped ease financial pressures, however, and Tehran has so far made timely debt service payments. In 1996, Iran's oil earnings–which account for 85 percent of total export revenues–climbed 20 percent from the previous year. Iran's financial situation will remain tight through the end of the decade, and continued timely debt service payments depended, in part, on persistent strong oil prices during the following years, a prediction that has failed badly as petroleum prices plummeted in 1998.

Iran and Iraq restored diplomatic relations in 1990 but are still trying to work out written agreements settling outstanding disputes from their eight-year war concerning border demarcation, prisoners-of-war, and freedom of navigation and sovereignty over the Shatt al-Arab waterway. Iran is an illicit producer of opium poppy for the domestic and international drug trade, but is a net opiate importer and acts as a key transshipment point for Southwest Asian heroin to Europe

The 1979 Islamic revolution and the war with Iraq transformed Iran's class structure politically, socially, and economically. In general, however, Iranian society remains divided into urban, market town, village, and tribal groups. Clerics, called mullahs, dominate politics and nearly all aspects of Iranian life, both urban and rural. After the fall of Shah Pahlavi's regime in 1979, much of the urban upper class of prominent merchants, industrialists, and professionals, favored by the former Shah, lost standing and influence to the senior clergy and their supporters. Bazaar merchants, who were allied with the clergy against the Pahlavi Shahs, have also gained political and economic power since the revolution. The urban working class has enjoyed somewhat enhanced status and economic mobility, spurred in part by opportunities provided by revolutionary organizations and the government bureaucracy.

Unemployment has many different causes, including population growth, the war with Iraq, and shortages of raw materials and trained managers. Farmers and peasants received a psychological boost from the attention given them by the Islamic regime but appear to be hardly better off in economic terms. The government has made progress on rural development, including electrification and road building, but has not yet made a commitment to land redistribution.

Modern Iranian history began with a nationalist uprising against the Shah (who remained in power) in 1905, the granting of a limited constitution in 1906, and the discovery of oil in 1908. In 1921, Reza Khan, an Iranian officer of the Persian Cossack Brigade, seized control of the government. In 1925, he made himself Shah, ruling as Reza Shah Pahlavi for almost 16 years and installing the new Pahlavi dynasty. Under his reign, Iran began to modernize and to secularize politics, and the central government reasserted its authority over the tribes and provinces. In September 1941, following the Allies' (U.K.-Soviet Union) occupation of western Iran, Reza Shah was forced to abdicate. His son, Mohammad Reza Pahlavi, became Shah and ruled until the revolution in 1979.

During World War II, Iran was a vital link in the Allied supply line for lend-lease supplies to the Soviet Union. After the war, Soviet troops stationed in northwestern Iran not only refused to withdraw but backed revolts that established short-lived, pro-Soviet separatist regimes in the northern regions of Azerbaijan and Kurdistan. These were ended in 1946. The Azerbaijan revolt crumbled after U.S. and U.N. pressure forced a Soviet withdrawal and Iranian forces suppressed the Kurdish revolt.

Outside U.S. Embassy in Tehran shortly after it was occupied by Iranian militants. CP Picture Archive (CP Laserphoto)

In 1951, Premier Mohammed Mossadeq, a militant nationalist, forced the parliament to nationalize the British-owned oil industry. The Shah opposed Mossadeq and he was removed, but he quickly returned to power. The Shah fled Iran but returned when supporters staged a coup against Mossadeq in 1953.

In 1961, Iran initiated a series of economic, social, and administrative reforms that became known as the Shah's White Revolution. The core of this program was land reform. Modernization and economic growth proceeded at an unprecedented rate, fueled by Iran's vast petroleum reserves, the third largest in the world. Domestic turmoil swept the country as a result of religious and political opposition to the Shah's rule and programs, especially SAVAK, the hated internal security and intelligence service. In January 1979, the Shah left Iran and died in exile several years after.

On February 1, 1979, exiled religious leader Ayatollah Ruhollah Khomeini returned from France to direct a revolution resulting in a new, theocratic republic guided by Islamic principles. Back in Iran after 15 years in exile in Turkey, Iraq, and France, he became Iran's national religious leader. Following Khomeini's death on June 3, 1989, the Assembly of Experts, an elected body of senior clerics, chose the outgoing president of the republic, Ali Khamenei, to be his successor as national religious leader in what proved to be a smooth transition. In 1989, an overwhelming majority elected Ali Akbar Hashemi-Rafsanjani the speaker of the National Assembly, President. He was re-elected June 11, 1993, with a more modest majority of about 63 percent; some Western observers attributed the reduced voter turnout to disenchantment with the deteriorating economy.

Iran's post-revolution difficulties have included an eight-year war with Iraq, internal political struggles and unrest, and economic disorder. The early days of the regime were characterized by severe human rights violations and political turmoil, including the seizure of the United States Embassy compound and its occupants on November 4, 1979, by Iranian militants. By mid-1982, a succession of power struggles eliminated first the center of the political spectrum and then the leftists, leaving only the clergy. There has been some moderation of excesses both internally and internationally, although Iran remains a significant sponsor of terrorism.

TERRORISM BRIEF 7-2
MINISTRY OF SECURITY (SAVAK)

Shah-an-Shah [King of Kings] Mohammad Reza Pahlavi was restored to the Peacock Throne of Iran with the assistance of the Central Intelligence Agency in 1953. The CIA assisted in a coup against the left-leaning government of Dr. Mohammad Mossadeq, which had planned to nationalize Iran's oil industry. The CIA also provided organizational and training assistance for an intelligence organization for the Shah. With training focused on domestic security and interrogation, the intelligence unit was given the mission to eliminate threats to Shah.

Formed under efforts of United States and Israeli intelligence officers in 1957, SAVAK became an effective secret agency. General Bakhtiar was appointed its first director, only to be dismissed in 1961. He was assassinated in 1970. His successor, General Pakravan, was dismissed in 1966, failing to crush the opposition from the clerics in the early 1960s. The Shah then turned to his childhood friend and classmate, General Nassiri, to rebuild SAVAK to properly serve the monarchy. Mansur Rafizadeh, the SAVAK director in the United States throughout the 1970s, claimed that General Nassiri's telephone was tapped by SAVAK agents reporting directly to the Shah, an example of the level of mistrust pervading on the eve of the Revolution. SAVAK increasingly symbolized the Shah's rule from 1963–79, a period of corruption in the royal family, one-party rule, the torture and execution of thousands of political prisoners, suppression of dissent, and alienation of the religious masses. The United States reinforced its position as the Shah's protector and supporter, sowing the seeds of the anti-Americanism that later manifested itself in the revolution against the monarchy.

Accurate information concerning SAVAK is not publicly unavailable. Pamphlets issued by the revolutionary regime after 1979 indicated that SAVAK had been a full-scale intelligence agency with more than 15,000 full-time personnel and thousands of part-time informants. SAVAK was attached to the Office of the Prime Minister, and its director assumed the title of Deputy to the Prime Minister for national security affairs. Although officially a civilian agency, SAVAK had close ties to the military and many of its officers served simultaneously in branches of the armed forces.

Another childhood friend and close confidant of the Shah, Major General Hosain Fardust, was deputy director of SAVAK until the early 1970s, when the Shah promoted him to the directorship of the "Special Intelligence Bureau," which operated inside Niavaran Palace, independently of SAVAK.

Originally formed to round up members of the outlawed Tudeh, SAVAK expanded its activities to include gathering intelligence and neutralizing the regime's opponents. An elaborate system was created to monitor all facets of political life. A censorship office was established to monitor journalists, literary figures, and aca-demics throughout the country; it took appropriate measures against those who fell out of line. Universities, labor unions, and peasant organizations, among others, were all subjected to intense surveillance by SAVAK agents and paid informants. The agency was also active abroad, especially in monitoring Iranian students who opposed Pahlavi rule.

SAVAK contracted Rockwell International to develop a large communications monitoring system called IBEX. The Stanford Technology Corp. [STC, owned by Hakim] had a $5.5 million contract to supply the CIA-promoted IBEX project. STC had another $7.5 million contract with Iran's air force for a telephone monitoring system, operated by SAVAK, to enable the Shah to track his top commanders' communications.

Over the years, SAVAK became a law unto itself, having legal authority to arrest and detain suspected persons indefinitely. SAVAK operated its own prisons in Tehran (the Komiteh and Evin facilities) and others throughout the country. SAVAK's torture methods included electric shock, whipping, beating, inserting broken glass and pouring boiling water into the rectum, tying weights to the testicles, and the extraction of teeth and nails. Many of these activities were carried out without oversight. At the peak of its influence under the Shah, SAVAK had at least 13 full-time case officers running a network of informers and infiltration covering 30,000 Iranian students on United States college campuses. The head of the SAVAK agents in the United States operated under the cover of an attaché at the Iranian mission, with the FBI, CIA, and State Department fully aware of these activities.

In 1978 the deepening opposition to the Shah erupted in widespread demonstrations and rioting. SAVAK and the military responded with widespread repression that killed twelve to fifteen thousand people and seriously injured another fifty thousand. Recognizing that even this level of state terrorism and violence had failed to crush the rebellion, the Shah abdicated the Peacock Throne and departed Iran in 1979. Despite decades of pervasive surveillance by SAVAK, working closely with CIA, the extent of public opposition to the Shah and his sudden departure came as a considerable surprise to the U.S. intelligence community and national leadership.

The SAVAK organization was officially dissolved by Khomeini shortly after he came to power in 1979. However, it was no surprise that SAVAK was singled out as a primary target for reprisals, its headquarters overrun and prominent leaders tried and executed by Khomeini representatives. High-ranking SAVAK agents were purged and 61 SAVAK officials were among 248 military personnel executed between February and September 1979.

SOURCE: THE FEDERATION OF AMERICAN SCIENTISTS WEBSITE, A PRIVATELY-FUNDED NONPROFIT POLICY ORGANIZATION 1998.

The **Islamic Republican Party (IRP)** was Iran's dominant political party until its dissolution in 1987; Iran now has no functioning political parties. The Iranian Government is opposed by a few armed political groups including the Mojahedin-e-Khalq (People's Mojahedin of Iran), the People's Fedayeen, and the Kurdish Democratic Party.

Khomeini's revolutionary regime initiated sharp changes from the foreign policy pursued by the Shah, particularly in reversing the country's orientation toward the West. In the Middle East, Iran's only significant ally has been Syria. Iran's regional goals are dominated by wanting to establish a leadership role, curtail the presence of the U.S. and other outside powers, and build trade ties. In broad terms, Iran's "Islamic foreign policy" emphasizes:

- Vehement anti-U.S. and anti-Israel stances
- Eliminating outside influence in the region
- Exporting the Islamic revolution
- Support for Muslim political movements abroad and
- A great increase in diplomatic contacts with developing countries

Despite these guidelines, however, bilateral relations are frequently confused and contradictory due to Iran's oscillation between pragmatic and ideological concerns.

Iran's relations with many of its Arab neighbors have been strained by Iranian attempts to spread its Islamic revolution. In 1981, Iran supported a plot to overthrow the Bahrain Government. In 1983, Iran expressed support for Shi'ites who bombed Western embassies in Kuwait, and in 1987, Iranian pilgrims rioted during the **Hajj** (pilgrimage) in Mecca in Saudi Arabia. Nations with strong fundamentalist movements, such as Egypt and Algeria, also mistrust Iran. Iran backs Hizballah, Hamas, the Palestinian Islamic Jihad, and the Popular Front for the Liberation of Palestine-General Command, all groups violently opposed to the Arab-Israeli peace process.

Relations with western European nations have alternated between improvements and setbacks. French-Iranian relations were badly strained by the sale of French arms to Iraq. Since the war, relations have improved commercially but periodically are worsened by Iranian-sponsored terrorist acts committed in France.

Another source of tension has been Ayatollah Khomeini's 1989 call for all Muslims to kill Salman Rushdie, (see Chapter 3, Terrorism Brief 3–2), British author of *The Satanic Verses*. This is a novel many Muslims consider blasphemous to their Holy Scriptures. The United Kingdom has sheltered Rushdie, and strains over this issue persist. There are serious obstacles to improved relations between the two countries. The United States Government defines five areas of objectionable Iranian behavior:

- Iranian efforts to acquire nuclear weapons and other weapons of mass destruction
- Its involvement in international terrorism
- Its support for violent opposition to the Arab-Israeli peace process
- Its threats and subversive activities against its neighbors
- Its dismal human rights record.

The United States believes that normal relations are impossible until Iran's behavior changes. However, the United States has offered to enter into dialogue with authorized representatives of the Iranian Government without preconditions. The Iranian Government has not accepted this offer. The United States has made clear that it does not seek to overthrow the Iranian Government but will continue to pressure Iran to change its behavior. The continuing support by Iran of terrorists and terrorism creates continuing danger for Americans in Iran because of the generally anti-American atmosphere and Iranian Government hostility to the U.S. Government. U.S. citizens traveling to Iran have been detained without charge, arrested, and harassed by Iranian authorities.[2]

OMAN

The Sultanate of Oman borders the Arabian Sea, Gulf of Oman, and Persian Gulf, between Yemen and United Arab Emirate. It is a country slightly smaller than Kansas with dry desert; is hot and humid along the coastal region. Although small, its natural resources include petroleum, copper, asbestos, some marble, limestone, chromium, gypsum and natural gas. This parched nation has no arable land and no permanent crops. Oman is strategically located on the Usandam Peninsula controlling the Strait of Hormuz, a vital transit point for world crude oil. The population of Oman, 2,264,590, is 75 percent Sunni Muslim, with the remainder Shi'a Muslim and Hindu. Oman is a Sultanate, a monarchy which has been independent since 1650, when they expelled the Portuguese.

On November 6, 1996, Sultan Qaboos issued a royal decree promulgating a new basic law. Among other things, it clarified the royal succession, provided for a prime minister, barred ministers from holding interests in companies doing business with the government, established a bicameral Omani council, and guaranteed basic civil liberties for Omani citizens. The sultan is the chief of state, the head of government and a hereditary monarch. Oman's economic performance is closely tied to the fortunes of the oil industry. Petroleum accounts for 75 percent of export earnings and government revenues and for roughly 40 percent of GDP. Oman has proven oil reserves of 4 billion barrels, equivalent to about 20 years' supply at the current rate of extraction. Agriculture is carried on at a subsistence level and the general population depends on imported food.

The earliest settlements in Oman, as in the Arabian Peninsula generally, date from some time in the 3rd millenium B.C.. Though at that time and for some hundreds of years more, Oman was on the edge of the trade routes linking ancient Mesopotamia to the Indus Valley, it does not appear to have profited a great deal from its location. Some centuries later, however, an area of what is now Oman became of paramount importance to the ancient world.

The southernmost region of Oman, modern Dhofar, was responsible for the area's importance. It is one of the few spots in the world where frankincense trees grow. Frankincense is an aromatic gum from certain species of trees that grow only in southern Oman, the Wadi Hadhramaut in Yemen, and Somalia.

The incense burns well because of its natural oil content. And in addition, it has medicinal uses. These two factors plus its relative scarcity made it an extremely sought-after substance in the ancient world. (The gifts of the Magi to the Christ Child were gold, **frankincense** and myrrh. At the time, gold was far less valuable than the other two.)

Frankincense was vital to the religious rites of almost every civilization in the ancient world. The great temples of Egypt, the Near East and Rome itself were all major consumers of the scarce commodity, not to mention the thousands of other temples found in every city, town and village. It was also used by medical practitioners. Indeed, the writer Pliny in the first century A.D. claimed that control of the frankincense trade had made the south Arabians the richest people on earth.

In the second century A.D. at the height of the trade, some 3,000 tons of frankincense were transported each year by ship from south Arabia to Greece, Rome and the Mediterranean world. The center of the trade was in a place now called Khor Rouri which the Greeks called Moscha. Though the trade went into a decline after the third century A.D., it still managed to keep south Arabia relatively wealthy for another three centuries.

The tribes in the northern part of Oman were converted to Islam during the first generation of the Islamic era, the middle of the seventh century A.D. and shortly after, and came under the rule of the Umayyads, whose center was in Damascus. About a century later, the Omanis revolted against the Umayyads and expelled them from their country. The Umayyads had only a short time remaining as the leaders of the Muslim world, for the Abbasids, whose capital was in Baghdad, soon overthrew them.

Oman managed to remain free of the Abbasids and continued its adherence to Ibadi Islam, which is still dominant in the country today. Because of Oman's remoteness from other Muslims, the Ibadis survived as a group long after they had vanished from other parts of the Muslim world

By the end of the eighteenth century, the Omanis were in control of an extensive empire. At its height in the nineteenth century, the empire ruled both Mombasa and Zanzibar and had trading posts much further down the African coast. Oman's last colonial outpost, Gwadar, on what is now the coast of Pakistan, was not surrendered until September 1958, when Sultan Said bin Taimur allowed it to be re-integrated into Pakistan in return for a payment of £ 3 million. In 1749, the first ruler of the present dynasty, Al-Busaid, gained power, and in 1786 the capital was formally moved from the interior to Muscat. About this same time, Al-Busaid adopted the title of Sultan that continues to this day.

The heyday of the Omani Empire occurred in the midnineteenth century under Sultan Said bin Sultan, who ruled from 1804–1856. He was responsible for bringing Dhofar under the Omani flag and he also extended Omani influence and control quite a way down the East African coast. He had an army of 6,500 men and a navy consisting of fifteen ships.

When he died, the empire split in two: one son became the Sultan of Zanzibar and the other the Sultan of Muscat and Oman. In the very name of the latter, the perceived difference between the interests of the coast and those of the interior was acknowledged. In fact, they were regarded as two entities ruled by the same monarch, though the writ of the ruler in Muscat sometimes did not extend very far into the interior. Muscat's control depended very much upon the regard for the Sultan held by the tribes of the interior. In the early twentieth century, the sultan's power to control the interior of the country was felt to have decreased.

In February 1932, Sultan Said bin Taimur, father of the present ruler, came to power. When he tried to exercise his nominal control in the interior of the country in the early 1950's, the British who felt that there was oil there, backed him. And in order to look for it, they needed the Sultan to have actual control of the area and for Oman's indefinite borders with Saudi Arabia and Abu Dhabi to be clearly defined and drawn. The ultimate result of this was a territorial dispute over the Buraimi oasis involving Oman, Saudi Arabia and Abu Dhabi. With British help and his own bravado, Sultan Said in the end was the winner and the Buraimi oasis is today firmly within the borders of Oman.

Sultan Said bin Taimur was, in the words of one British writer, "an arch-reactionary of great personal charm." He wanted no change of any sort in Oman and did all that he could to isolate his country from the world. All visas were issued personally by him. He forbade travel to the interior by coastal residents and vice versa. Believing education was a threat to his power, he opposed it.

In general, Omanis were not allowed to leave the country and those who did were seldom allowed to return. The Sultan's only contact with the outside world was through his British advisers and Muscat's merchant families. He allowed these last to establish enormously lucrative monopolies for the import of goods, which he saw as crucial to his survival. In exchange, the merchants stayed out of politics and imported nothing which Sultan Said felt reeked of progress or the West (radios, books, eyeglasses). Through their customs receipts, the merchants provided the Sultan with most of the country's income. Aside from a few rich merchants, most of the population relied upon agriculture and fishing.

Oman has been Islamic since the seventh century. In about 1507, the city of Muscat and its hinterland came under Portuguese control. The Portuguese maintained their control until 1650 when the Omanis revolted and extended their influence as far south as the island of Zanzibar, off the African coast. The country was under Persian control for a short time (1741–1749) and then in 1798, a treaty of friendship was signed with Great Britain though Oman retained its independence.

From 1932 to 1970 Oman was controlled by Sultan Said bin Taimur, a reclusive and repressive ruler whose policies finally resulted in revolt in Dhofar in 1965. In 1970 his son, the British-educated Qaboos bin Said, overthrew him and embarked upon an ambitious modernization program. This small and tightly controlled country has been bypassed by most of the terrorism and violence in the region and is almost totally unknown in the rest of the world.

BAHRAIN

The State of Bahrain is on a scattered archipelago in the Persian Gulf, east of Saudi Arabia. These landmasses are small, totaling only 3.5 times the size of Washington, D.C. Bahrain has resources of oil, associated and nonassociated natural gas and fish.

It is close to primary Middle Eastern petroleum sources, in a strategic location in the Persian Gulf that much of Western world's petroleum must transit to reach. It has a very small population of 603,318 (including 221,182 nonnationals). Bahrain gained independence in 1971, from the U.K.

The chief of state is Amir Isa bin Salman Al Khalifa (since 1961), the head of government: Prime Minister Khalifi bin Salman Al Khalifa (since 1970). The Amir appoints the cabinet. The Amir is a traditional Arab monarch, and political parties are prohibited.

Political pressure groups and leaders include several small, clandestine leftist and Islamic fundamentalist groups which are active. Following the arrest of a popular Shi'a cleric, Shi'a activists have fomented unrest sporadically since late 1994, demanding the return of an elected National Assembly and an end to unemployment.

In Bahrain, petroleum production and processing account for about 60 percent of export receipts, 60 percent of government revenues, and 30 percent of GDP. Economic conditions have fluctuated with the changing fortunes of oil since 1985, for example, during and following the Gulf crisis of 1990–91. With its highly developed communication and transport facilities, Bahrain is home to numerous multinational firms with business in the Gulf. A large share of exports consists of petroleum products made from imported crude. Construction proceeds on several major industrial projects. Unemployment, especially among the young, and the depletion of both oil and underground water resources are major long-term economic problems.

Bahrain has an international territorial dispute with Qatar over the Hawar Islands and the maritime boundary with Qatar. The Sultanate continued to be plagued by arson attacks and other minor security incidents throughout 1997, most perpetrated by domestic dissidents. The most serious incident was an arson attack on a commercial establishment on 13 June that resulted in the death of four South Asian expatriates. One day later an abandoned vehicle detonated outside the passport directorate of Bahrain's Interior Ministry with no injuries. Bahraini courts in March convicted and sentenced to jail 36 individuals for being members of **Bahraini Hizballah**, an Iranian-backed organization that sought the overthrow of the island's government. The jail sentences range from five to fifteen years. Some Bahraini Hizballah members reportedly underwent terrorist training in camps in Iran and Lebanon.

In November, the government convicted eight individuals in absentia for orchestrating and funding from abroad a campaign aimed at disrupting the security of Bahrain. Several of the defendants were charged with sending propaganda to Bahrain inciting violence and destruction, which led to damage to public property, such as electricity and water installations. In addition to jail sentences, six of the defendants, along with others previously convicted, were ordered to pay compensation totaling over $15 million for damage to public property.

YEMEN

The Republic of Yemen was established on May 22, 1990 with the merger of the Yemen Arab Republic (Yemen Sanaa or North Yemen) and the Marxist-dominated People's Democratic Republic of Yemen (Yemen Aden or South Yemen). The newly formed republic borders the Arabian Sea, the Gulf of Aden and the Red Sea, between Oman and Saudi Arabia. Yemen is slightly larger than twice the size of Wyoming, with borders to Oman and Saudi Arabia. There is an extraordinarily hot, dry, harsh desert in eastern Yemen. Yemen has potential control of **Bab el Mandeb**, the strait linking the Red Sea and the Gulf of Aden, one of world's most active shipping lanes. Its population estimates run from 13.9 million to as high as 16.6 million people of Arab, Afro-Arab concentrations in western coastal locations, South Asians in the southern regions and small European communities in the major metropolitan areas. Muslims, including Sha'fi (Sunni) and Zaydi (Shi'a), and a small numbers of Jews, Christians, and Hindus practice their religions.

The former Aden (South Yemen) gained independence from the United Kingdom in 1967. North Yemen had become independent in 1918 from the Ottoman Empire. The northern city Sanaa became the political capital of a united Yemen. The southern city Aden, with its refinery and port facilities, is the economic and commercial capital. Future economic development depends heavily on western-assisted development of the country's moderate oil resources. Former South Yemen's willingness to merge stemmed partly from the steady decline in economic support after the demise of the Soviet Union. The low level of domestic industry and agriculture has made northern Yemen dependent on imports for practically all its essential needs. Once self-sufficient in food production, northern Yemen has become a major importer. Land once used for export crops such as cotton, fruit, and vegetables, has been turned over to growing a shrub called qat, the leaves of which are chewed for their stimulant effect by Yemenis. Qat has no significant export market.

A Long History of Strife

The history of Yemen, like much of the Persian Gulf, stretches back over 3,000 years, and its unique culture is still in evidence in the architecture of its towns and villages. From about 1000 B.C. three successive civilizations–Minean, Sabaean and Himyarite–ruled this region of the Southern Arabian Peninsula. These three kingdoms all depended on the spice trade. Aromatics such as myrrh and frankincense were greatly prized in the ancient civilized world and were used as part of various rituals in many cultures, including Egyptian, Greek and Roman.

In the eleventh century BC, land routes through Arabia were greatly improved by using the camel as a beast of burden, and frankincense was carried from its production center at Qana (now known as Bir 'Ali) to Gaza in Egypt. The camel caravans also carried gold and other precious goods that arrived in Qana by sea from India. The chief incense traders were the Minaeans, who established their capital at Karna (now known as Sadah), before they were superseded by the Sabaeans in 950 B.C. The Sabaean capital was Ma'rib, where a large temple was built. The mighty Sabaean civilization endured for about fourteen centuries and was based not only on the spice trade, but also on agriculture. An impressive dam, built at Ma'rib in the 8th century, provided irrigation for farmland and stood for over a millennium. Some Sabaean carved inscriptions from this period are still in existence.

The Himyarites established their capital at Dhafar (now just a small village in the Ibb region) and gradually absorbed the Sabaean kingdom. They were culturally inferior to the Sabaeans and traded from the port of al-Muza on the Red Sea. By the first century B.C., the Romans had conquered the area.

British and Turkish Domination

The British conquered Aden (Southern Yemen) in 1839 and it became known as the **Aden Protectorate**. The British also made a series of treaties with local tribal rulers, in a move to colonize the entire area of Southern Yemen. British influence extended to Hadhramawt by the 1950s and a boundary line, known as the "violet line," was drawn between Turkish Arabia in the north and the South Arabian Protectorate of Great Britain, as it was then known. (This line later formed the boundary between northern and southern Yemeni states in the 1960s.)

In 1849 the Turks returned to Yemen and their power extended throughout all of that region not under British rule. Local insurrection against the Turks followed and autonomy was finally granted to the Zaydi imam in 1911. By 1919 the Turks had retreated from Yemen for the last time and the country was left in the hands of Imam Yayha, who became the country's king. Britain recognized Yemen's independence in 1925.

Civil War

Imam Yayha ruled the Yemen until his assassination in 1948, and was succeeded by his son Ahmad (1896–1962). Clashes with the British over Aden were characteristic of Ahmad's rule, and he sought protection from Cairo, resulting in a short-lived pact between Yemen, Egypt and Syria. On his father's death in 1962, Ahmad's son, Muhammed al-Badr, ruled for only a week before a military coup led by Colonel Abdullah al-Sallal proclaimed a republic. Backed by the United Arab Republic, this new regime was known as the **Yemen Arab Republic (YAR)**.

The deposed Imam fled to the mountains of the north, and his royalist forces, backed by Saudi Arabia, waged a civil war against the YAR that lasted for eight years. Egypt gave aid to the Republican army and a meeting between Egyptian President Gamal Abdel Nasser and King Faisal of Saudi Arabia in 1965 led to an agreement to end the involvement of both these countries in the civil war. Arrangements were made to hold a plebiscite to allow the people of YAR to choose their own form of government, but this never happened and fighting was resumed in 1966.

Egyptian troops withdrew from the region in 1967, and President al-Sallal was overthrown. He was sent into exile in Iraq and replaced by Abdul Rahman al-Iryani. The war continued until 1970, when the YAR was finally recognized by Saudi Arabia.

Separate States and Unification

In the late 1960s, the British presence in southern Yemen was minimal outside of Aden itself. Intense guerrilla fighting throughout the mid-sixties resulted in a British withdrawal from Aden in 1967. With the closure of the Suez Canal, Yemen's economy was on the verge of ruin, and the new People's Republic of South Yemen, which came into being in 1967, relied heavily on economic support from Communist countries. It became, in effect, the first and only Arab Marxist state. In 1970 the republic's name was changed to the People's Democratic Republic of Yemen, or PDRY.

Mutual distrust between the two Yemens characterized the seventies, and tensions flared into a series of short border wars in 1972, 1978 and 1979. Two presidents of the YAR were assassinated during this period. But under the presidency of Ali Abdullah Salah of the Hashid tribe, in the late seventies/early eighties, the stability of the YAR steadily improved. By the end of 1981 a constitution had been drafted in order to implement a merger between the two states. Attempts to consolidate this, however, were delayed by political instability in the PDRY and it was not until 1990 that the merger was made official.

The new country was named the Republic of Yemen. The border was opened and demilitarized, and currencies were declared valid in both of the former countries. A referendum sealed the unification of the Yemen, and today's Yemen is probably more accessible than it has been throughout its history. Although there is no major tourist industry, visitors are now welcomed on a modest scale, and Yemeni society is fast becoming modernized.

Sanaa took major steps during 1997 to improve control of its borders, territory, and travel documents. It continued to deport foreign nationals residing illegally, including Islamic extremists identified as posing a security risk to Yemen and several other Arab countries. The Interior Ministry issued new, reportedly tamper-resistant, passports and began to computerize port-of-entry information. Nonetheless, lax implementation of security measures and poor central government control over remote areas continued to make Yemen an attractive safe haven for terrorists. Moreover, Hamas and the PIJ maintain offices in Yemen.

A series of bombings in Aden in July, October, and November of 1997 caused material damage but no injuries. No group claimed responsibility. The Yemeni Government blamed the attacks on Yemeni opposition elements that had been trained by foreign extremists and supported from abroad. A principal suspect confessed in court he was recruited and paid by Saudi intelligence, but this could not be independently verified. Yemeni tribesmen kidnapped about forty foreign nationals, including two U.S. citizens, and held them for periods ranging up to one month. Yemeni Government officials frequently asserted that foreign powers instigated some kidnappings, but no corroborating evidence was provided. All were treated well and released unharmed, but one Italian was injured when resisting a kidnap attempt in August. The motivation for the kidnappings generally appeared to be tribal grievances against the central government. The government did not prosecute any of the kidnappers.

Economic growth in former South Yemen has been constrained by a lack of incentives, partly stemming from centralized control over production decisions, investment allocation, and import choices. Yemen's finances had been supplemented by remittances from Yemenis working abroad and by foreign aid. Since the Gulf crisis, however, remittances have dropped substantially. Floods in June 1996 caused the loss of much valuable topsoil in the agricultural sector, increasing the need for imports of foodstuffs. Oil production and GDP as a whole increased moderately in 1997. A large section of boundary with Saudi Arabia is not defined; a dispute with Eritrea over sovereignty of the Hanish Islands in the southern Red Sea has been submitted to arbitration of the International Court of Justice.

SUMMARY

If there are any students who had never heard of the Persian Gulf, they have now. This extremely vital area, which supplies much of the world's oil, is constantly in turmoil over religious and power issues. Most of these nations were not even nations at the turn of the twentieth century. As we approach the twenty-first century, these oil-rich countries seem to be calling the shots with the EEC, Japan and the United States. Still, Iraq's attempt to take over Kuwait's oil fields reflects the concern shared by all these states, except Saudi Arabia, that one day the oil gauge will plunge to "empty." Few of the rich citizens of the region would desire a return to riding camels instead of driving Mercedes.

Many of these Persian Gulf states are actively sponsoring terrorists around the world, but they are united when it comes to terrorism against Israel and lately, the United States. The peace process between Israel and the PLO may result in a differferent arrangement of players in the Persian Gulf. Religious hatred in places like Iran and Iraq runs deep; however, an incredibly frightening scenario would be those two countries combining their efforts against the rest of the Persian Gulf states. Saddam Hussein continues to play cat and mouse with the rest of the world because he knows oil is so important to the industrial economies. Perhaps there will be a new source of energy discovered in the next millennium, but for now, the Persian Gulf is probably the most valuable land on earth. In the next chapter, the student will explore the central and southern areas of Africa, an area rife with racial and tribal divisions that have led to terrorism and genocide.

Terms to Remember

Abdul Aziz	Mecca and Medina	Grand Mosque
Al-Sabah dynasty	Qurain	Gulf Cooperation Council
Ba'thist regime	Security Council Resolution 986	Fertile Crescent
al-jabr	Six Day War	Operation Desert Storm
Kurdistan	MEK	IRP
Hajj	*The Satanic Verses*	frankincense
Bahraini Hizballah	Babel Mandeb	YAR
Aden Protectorate	Rumaila oil field	

Review Questions

Why is there such hatred and a split between the Shi'a and Sunni Muslims sects?

Which of the Persian Gulf states has the most oil reserves and what kind of governmental system?

How was the present state of Yemen assembled and how is it ruled?

The Gulf War was fought over what issue?

Describe the way the state of Oman is ruled and its importance in the Gulf.

Endnotes

1. Most of the background data contained in this chapter, and woven into and throughout this book, were extracted from web sites such as: The U.S. Department of State. *1997 Patterns of Global Terror* Report; The U.S. Department of State *Country Reports on Human Rights Practices*; The U.S. Department of State *Background Notes: Geographic Entities and International Organizations*; The U.S. Central Intelligence Agency *World Factbook* and other government sources. We remain grateful for the presence of these sources and the information they have provided.

2. U.S. Department of State, Public Affairs, Washington, D.C., July 1994.

CHAPTER 8

CENTRAL AND SOUTHERN AFRICA

Political power grows out of the barrel of a gun.

—Chairman Mao's Little Red Book

OVERVIEW

In this chapter the student will review a different source of terror, that of the state against ethnic, religious and tribal enemies. In the central and southern regions of Africa, power allows the ruler to effect measures of **genocide** as he sees fit. This chapter discusses terror methods used by that despicable modern day tactician, Field Marshall, President for Life, Idi Amin Dada. We shall examine the histories of Rhodesia and South Africa, each with significant and uniquely different issues which require evaluation. We start with a little-known country located on the horn of Africa that has suffered tragic wars, famines and terrorism for decades, Ethiopia.

ETHIOPIA

Ethiopia has undergone some dramatic changes since the overthrow of the **Emperor Haile Selassie** in 1974. In 1935, the country became the object of Italian colonialism, and the emperor fled the country to live in exile in England. During WW II, the British, with the help of the Ethiopians, evicted the Italians from the country and returned Haile Selassie to the throne.

Eritrea, a region that lies to the north of the country along the Red Sea coast, had been under Italian control and influence since the 1880s. The Ethiopian government took over control of Eritrea in 1961, and ever since has been fighting a battle with Eritrean Nationalists seeking independence from Ethiopia. Poor living conditions coupled with resentment of Selassie's autocratic methods and corrupt regime gave rise to a military coup led by Lt. Colonel Mengistu in 1974. Trouble also flared in a southern region known as the **Ogaden**, which was claimed by neighboring Somalia. Many of the inhabitants of that region were Somali, and the resulting invasion of the region by Somalia in 1977 has been an ongoing problem between the two nations. By the latter half of the 1980s, the military rulers were moving toward an elected, civil government under a new constitution. Although elections were held the military continued to control the country. On May 28, 1991 the **Ethiopian People's Revolutionary Democratic Front (EPRDF)** toppled the authoritarian government of Mengitsu Haile-Mariam and took control in Addis Ababa; a new constitution was promulgated in December 1994, and national and regional elections were held in May and June of 1995. The main issues facing Ethiopia at the end of the decade are that of rebuilding a crumbling infrastructure following years of civil war. Ethiopia and Somalia continue to squabble over the Ogaden region. The country is also an interchange for the shipment of illicit drugs from Asia destined for Europe and North America, as well as cocaine for the markets of South Africa.

SOMALIA

Much interclan fighting and a weakened military left the country in desperate straits. In 1969, the clans within Somalia felt that the distribution of wealth only benefited a small number of people. The control of Somalia reverted to military rule under the **Somali Revolutionary Socialist Party**, led by Major General Said Barre. The economy, banks, schools, and land came under the direct control of the military government. This action coincided with one of the major famines of the latter half of this century. The effect on the region was disastrous, increasing the suffering of the sick, starving and dying population of Somalia.

Resistance eventually came in the form of the United Somali Congress (USC), which ousted **Said Barre** on January 27, 1991. Since that date, the country has deteriorated, and has no viable government. Anarchy has taken over, marked by brutal interclan fighting and banditry. One of the poorest countries in Africa, Somalia now stumbles forward blindly with no functioning administration and clans vying for power. Widespread civil war in Somalia is likely.

UGANDA

Located in Central East Africa and bordering on Lake Victoria in the south, Uganda as we know it today has gone through much upheaval in recent history. For Ugandans, the 1970s were turbulent indeed, a time when the President for Life gave a new meaning to the modern phrase **ethnic cleansing**.

Uganda gained its independence in the 1962 from Britain, and elected **Milton Obote** as its first prime minister. The country's president, **Sir Edward Mutesa II** and Obote were at odds with each other on political issues, and so in 1966, Obote overthrew Mutesa, who was exiled to Britain. Obote established a new constitution which would encompass all the regions in the area including Buganda and assumed the role of President of Uganda. Political stability was not longlasting in that turbulent African state, and by 1971, the Ugandan Army, under the control of General **Idi Amin**, led an overthrow of the government of Milton Obote, sending *him* into exile.

Idi Amin Dada

The sheer scope of the terror this man perpetrated on his own people, during very dark days from 1972–1979, is almost inconceivable. His praise of Adolph Hitler for attempting to exterminate the Jews, and his open demands for the destruction of Israel, seemed to come from the mind of a psychopath. To try and understand any ideology that Amin may have had is a difficult task. He was highly temperamental and prone to changing his mind frequently. What cannot be questioned are his excesses in purging Uganda of all his opponents, political and social. His first move was to "cleanse" the country of foreign influence and return its wealth to native Ugandans. This meant the expulsion of over 60,000 Africans of Asian decent. As Uganda was part of the Commonwealth, those 60,000 moved mainly to the United Kingdom, where their passports permitted them to relocate. The son of a witchdoctor, Amin's appetite for wealth knew no bounds.[1] To achieve it he engaged in smuggling and murder, "*rape, plunder and pillage.*"

A Regime of Terror

One of the first actions Amin took in terrorizing his own nation was the creation of a bureaucracy to carry out his bizarre wishes. His Presidential Palace was linked by a series of tunnels to the Bureau of State Research in an adjoining building in the capital city of Kampala. Amin surrounded himself with a team of specially trained Palestinian bodyguards. He established two secret state police organizations, the **Public Safety Unit** and the **Bureau of State Research**. The Public Safety Unit was empowered to shoot to kill on mere suspicion, while the Bureau of State Research carried out interrogations and torture, usually resulting in the death of the hapless prisoner. The actual number of Ugandans killed during Amin's reign is not known, but is believed to be as high as *half a million.* As in other regions of Africa, tribal rivalries and old hatreds have a great part to play in selective genocide. Amin, a member of the **Lugbara** tribe, set in motion the calculated elimination of all of the Lugabaras' historical tribal enemies. The Acholi and Langi tribes were the primary victims of Amin's wholesale slaughter. Handpicked secret police and interrogation units from the Lugbara tribe were eager participants in this state-sponsored genocide. To say that Amin relished his work would be an understatement. On many occasions, he would observe or conduct torture personally. One particularly sadistic method of execution was to provide a hammer to a prisoner who was then commanded, at gunpoint, to hammer the skull in of the prisoner next to him. This gruesome procedure repeated until the last prisoner was dispatched with a gunshot. Many executed prisoners were returned in mutilated condition to their families. Others were dumped in rivers or in forests to be ravaged by predators. Among other atrocities practiced by Amin and his tribesmen was **cannibalism.**

Amin and International Terrorism

The Palestinian hijacking of an Air France airliner after takeoff from Athens, Greece, allowed a first clear glimpse into the world of madness that Idi Amin had created.

Idi Amin, self-styled
president for life of
Uganda. CP Picture
Archive (AP/
WideWorld Photos)

Palestinians and German terrorists from the Red Army Faction had hijacked the airliner on June 27, 1976 and flown south to Benghazi in Libya. There it was refueled and continued south to land at Uganda's Entebbe International Airport on June 28. The terrorists were demanding the release from prisons in West Germany, France, Switzerland, Israel and Kenya of about fifty of their comrades. After a period of negotiations, the release of some of the passengers was achieved, all of whom were of non-Jewish birth and origin. They were immediately flown to Orly Airport in France, where they were debriefed by undercover operatives from Israel, who were able to ascertain how well armed, organized, and competent the hijackers appeared to the hostages. One of the hijackers was identified as **Wilfred Bose** from Germany's Red Army Faction (**RAF**). The Palestinians were hardcore members of the **PFLP**. Terrorist operations of this nature were not uncommon in the 1970s. What was to make this hostage-taking different from others was the response planned by the Israeli government and military. Once it was known that the hijackers had separated Jews from others on the aircraft, their intent to coerce and intimidate Israel became readily apparent. The subsequent events at Entebbe showed the terrorists that a coordinated military response to hijackings was feasible for states with the technical expertise to carry out such an operation. Israel's meticulous planning and intelligence work were to produce memorable results.

Ironically, Israeli military personnel had earlier been involved in some of the training for the Ugandan military forces. Those Israeli trainers provided invaluable logistical data about the layout of the airport and its buildings, as well as the level of training and competency of the Ugandan army and air force personnel. A daring plan to release the hostages was designed by **Major-General Dan Shomron**, the Israeli Director of Infantry and Paratroopers. It was reviewed and fully authorized by the Israeli cabinet. Finally, Israeli Defense Force troopers flew out of the Ophira Air Force base on July 3, in four Hercules transport aircraft, toward Entebbe. Up until this time, intense negotiations for the release of the hostages had been underway with the Ugandan government, but to no avail. Idi Amin himself had even visited the airport to talk to the captives. But this had been clearly a public relations ploy, and no support was expected from Amin or his government.

Operation Thunderball

The effort to release the hostages, dubbed **Operation Thunderball**, started when the aircraft landed safely and taxied to a remote area of the Entebbe Airport. The Israeli Defense Force (IDF) troopers approached the terminal building riding in a convoy preceded by a big Mercedes limousine. It was hoped that this vehicle would fool the Ugandan soldiers into thinking that Amin was coming to the airport unexpectedly. The ruse worked perfectly and the troopers stormed the building and rescued the hostages. Other IDF troopers secured the airfield to prevent any intervention from Ugandan forces. The assault on the terminal building resulted in the deaths of six of the terrorists, including Wilfred Bose and Gabriele Krocher-Tiedemann, both members of the German Baader Meinhof Gang. Three of the hostages were killed, two during the rescue and a third, an elderly British woman named Dora Block, who was murdered in a Ugandan hospital in retaliation for the attack by the IDF. The entire operation was completed when the IDF ground forces destroyed the MIG fighters of the Ugandan Air Force on the ground. It had taken only three minutes to secure the terminal and rescue the hostages.[2] The only casualty on the Israeli side was the team's leader, Colonel Jonathan Netanyahu, who was shot in the back by a Ugandan soldier outside the terminal building. The daring and successful raid was subsequently renamed **Operation Jonathan** in his memory. The IDF raid on Entebbe went a long way in showing the world that terrorism could be met and defeated by the clinical application of controlled force.

Milton Obote

After almost a decade of brutality and depravity by Idi Amin and his followers, Milton Obote and his supporters overthrew the Amin Government in 1979, forcing Amin into exile. His first port of call was Libya, but shortly after that he went quietly into permanent exile in Saudi Arabia. Obote's return to power signaled vicious reprisals against his former oppressors. His own human rights record of torture and killing of his opponents was not as horrific as Amin's; however, he did reorganize and rename the two state instruments of Amin's terror and called the unit the National Security Agency. A Human Rights Commission of inquiry into atrocities in Uganda under the reign of Milton Obote concluded that over *150,000* Ugandans had been systematically killed since his return to power. The country did not fare well under the rule of Obote, and he continued with human rights abuses against Ugandans. Obote was ousted from power by a military coup led by Lt. Col. Basilio Olara-Okello, in July 1985, proclaiming a military government. Since 1980, an urban guerilla movement, the National Resistance Army (NRA), had been operating in the countryside to the north of Kampala, and had been working to overthrow Obote. The new government in power in Kampala immediately began to open up a dialogue with the NRA to cease hostilities. The Okello government had made pledges to the NRA to reduce the human rights abuses and to hold free and democratic elections. However, the Okello government, while negotiating, was also busy murdering supporters of the NRA, and in doing so continued with human rights abuses. The NRA continued to have widespread support, and by 1986 was fighting in the streets of the capital. Under the leadership of Yoweri Museveni, the NRA forced Okello to flee north to the Sudan. To a large extent, the NRA government has restored some semblance of normalcy to Uganda; however, Okello and his supporters still pose a threat as do the supporters of Milton Obote in the eastern region.

RHODESIA—ZIMBABWE

Many black African states were looking to shed the yoke of the British Empire in the 1960s and 1970s. White rule in Rhodesia under Ian Smith ended in 1980 when the country gained its independence and Robert Mugabe became the country's first prime minister. The idyll so longed for by the black Africans was not immediately achieved, however, and Mugabe and his government faced violent opposition, mainly from the region of Matabeleland. Mugabe's ruling party, the **Zimbabwe African National Union (ZANU)**, was also strongly opposed by the **Zimbabwe People's Revolutionary Army (ZIPRA)** and the Zimbabwe African People's Union (ZANPU). Mugabe used what can be termed state terror on the peoples of Matabeleland to ensure his own position in Zimbabwe. To do this he used the Zimbabwe Army Fifth Brigade as a vehicle to control, repress, restrict, torture, interrogate and execute all armed opponents in Matabeleland.

The UDI

November 11, 1965 is the date when Ian Smith declared a **Unilateral Declaration of Independence (UDI)** for Rhodesia. If one were to look to the north about this time, the scenes being played out in the name of independence were far from gratifying. Millions were dead in Nigeria and the Congo, more than 500,000 in the Sudan and over 200,000 in Rwanda and Burundi. In nearly all instances it was black man killing black man, and the countries were in the hands of blood-crazed dictators.[3] Is it hardly surprising that the people of the former Rhodesia did not want this same ravening form of liberation? Unfortunately for the Ian Smith rebel government, the rest of the world, including Britain and the United Nations, would not recognize the new breakaway state and instead enforced strong economic sanctions on the country. In the years preceding the UDI, most forms of terrorism and similarly violent criminal action were well under control of the authorities. However, with UDI, the country was being denounced from all quarters of the globe. In that era, when there was a perception of weakness and an opportunity arose to destabilize a region in Africa, the possibility of communist involvement was never far away.

So, too, it was with Rhodesia. Many of the young blacks were lured out of the country on promise of "scholarships" in Zambia and Tanganyika. In fact, these young men were being sent for communist indoctrination and weapons training to camps in North Korea and the former U.S.S.R. They were returned via such ports as Dar es Salaam, on the coast of Africa, and then infiltrated back into Rhodesia to fight against the Smith government. With so many ways to define terrorism, would these men be viewed as terrorist, insurgents, freedom fighters or just violent criminals? The answer is not easy to settle upon. From the Rhodesian standpoint, they were certainly seen as terrorists, so the Smith Government used the Rhodesian Special Air Service Regiment to good effect in destroying them. The task from the military standpoint was almost hopeless, given the makeup of the borders that surrounded the country. The only friendly region lay to the south with the South African government. The numbers of terrorists and insurgents continued to grow in a situation similar to that faced by the United States as its forces fought an impossible war in Vietnam.

The politics of the day did nothing to inhibit the violence in Rhodesia; on the contrary, to most people in Rhodesia, both black and white, it seemed that the terrorist forces had the tacit support of the British government in the name of African Nationalism. The two leaders of the terror groups, **Joshua Nkomo** and **Ndabaningi**

REWARD NOTICE

Substantial rewards will be paid by Government to any person who volunteers information, to the Security Forces, which leads to the death or capture of terrorists or their supporters, or to the recovery of terrorist weapons. This information will be kept secret.

Rewards can be paid in cash, or into a Post Office savings account, bank savings account, or building society savings account. The payment of such reward money will be kept secret by Government.

LISTED BELOW ARE THE REWARDS:

$5 000   Not less than $5 000 FOR INFORMATION LEADING TO THE DEATH OR CAPTURE OF A SENIOR TERRORIST LEADER.

$2 500   Not less than $2 500 FOR INFORMATION LEADING TO THE DEATH OR CAPTURE OF A TERRORIST GROUP LEADER.

$1 000   Not less than £1 000 FOR INFORMATION LEADING TO THE DEATH OR CAPTURE OF ANY TRAINED TERRORIST.

$500   Not less than $500 for EACH anti-vehicle mine, heavy weapon of war.

$300   Not less than $300 for EACH full box of small arms ammunition, grenades, anti-personnel mines.
OR
EACH light personal weapon.

A substantial reward will be paid for INFORMATION LEADING TO THE ARREST of any person who voluntarily houses, feeds, associates with or helps terrorists.

These rewards will not be payable to a civil servant who is engaged on duties concerned with anti-terrorist activities or to a member of the Security Forces, unless he obtained the information while he was off-duty.

BY ORDER OF THE GOVERNMENT OF RHODESIA

Reward poster dropped
by air in Rhodesia.
*Personal collection of
J. Spindlove.*

Sithole, were openly supported in Britain, even though they were leaders of the two parties banned by the Smith Government. The black nationalists, Robert Mugabe being one of them, formed ZANU as a result of a split with the Nkomo leadership. Nkomo formed the opposing ZAPU movement. Formed along tribal lines, Nkomo's support came principally from the Ndebele tribes of Matabeleland in the west, while Mugabe's support lay in the tribes of Mashonaland in the east of the country.

Rhodesian Special Air Service

Rhodesia did not boast of an official army of white combatants, although it did have staff instructors for the black regulars. The formation of the Rhodesian Special Air Service began in the early days of the 1960s and was composed of members of the old C Squadron that had been in operations in Malaysia. The Royal Rhodesian Air Force, with South Africans and Britons, trained in Great Britain and was attached to Britain's elite 22nd SAS Regiment.

SOUTH AFRICA

For the past half of the century, South Africa operated under a white government using apartheid as the official method of controlling the actions, activities and opportunities of native blacks, and African Asians in the Republic of South Africa. The

Antiterrorism troops
search for guerrillas
in Rhodesia.

main political party set up to fight apartheid was the **African National Congress (ANC)**. Strangely, the party started on a political platform and moved toward armed confrontation with the South African Government.

Color alone, however, by no means carries with it a unity of belief, purpose or ambition. The most virulent and persistent of hatreds in Africa exists between people of the same color. The black population of South Africa is divided into at least seven distinct ethnic and tribal groups, each with its own written language and home area, and each resolved to retain its own identity. That is a way to "develop separately" to stay apart. The South African governments of the forty years preceding the early 1990s set out to regulate this problem by the establishment of separate, self-governing "homelands" for each group.[4] To most people on the outside looking in, apartheid has always had an evil connotation. Although this text is not intended to be a forum for debating the pros and cons of segregation of ethnic groups in South Africa, it is relevant to the South African experience with terrorism.

Britain's involvement in the Cape Colony dates back three centuries, when the region along the Cape was important as a refueling and trading post for shipping to and from the Orient and India. The Cape Colony was also home to Dutch migrants from Europe who had settled the colony in 1652. From the middle of the sixteenth century, the Dutch East India Company had had executive powers over the colony and all its inhabitants, but was allowing Dutch settlers to leave the "company" and start their own farms. These people became known as Boers. With the migration inland, the white farmers fought the tiny San tribespeople (bushmen) and either killed or enslaved them for work on the farms.

The Dutch Government formally turned the Colony over to Britain in 1834. The first British settlers had arrived in the Cape in 1820, and so with control going to Britain, the unpopular decision was made to end slavery. Britain established English as the official language of the Cape, to the extreme resentment of the Boers in the colony. Unhappy with British rule, the Boers began to move north and settle in regions farther away in the Transvaal, the Orange Free State and Natal. The move north became an historic event for the Boers and is generally referred to as the **Great Trek**.

With the discovery of diamonds in the Kimberley region and gold in the Johannesburg areas, Anglos and Boers would fight the first Anglo-Boer war. Overwhelming force of arms allowed the British to defeat the Boers by 1902, thus bringing the Orange Free State, Transvaal and Natal under British rule. This rule, not surprisingly, included all the black tribes, most of which submitted peacefully to their new masters. As in most matters, there is an exception to a rule; the South African exception was the Zulus. A warlike tribe, they would submit to no one, and in 1879 defeated and destroyed a well trained British regiment at Isandhlwana. Overwhelming superiority of forces and firepower would defeat the Zulus, and by 1888, none of the black African tribes retained their independence.

Afrikaner Nationalism

Two famous Boer generals, Louis Botha and Jan Smuts, had a great part to play in the rise of Afrikaner nationalism in South Africa. General J. Hertzog formed the Nationalist Party, which had the ideology that the Boers had a right to rule South Africa and to unite the Anglos and Afrikaners. When a nationalist government came into power in South Africa for the first time in 1922, it began the changes to shape a united South Africa. This included the recognition of Afrikaans alongside English as the official language and also the development of industry less dependent on Great Britain. With the outbreak of WWII and South Africa already an independent nation within the British Commonwealth, there was considerable debate as to which side, if any, to support. Hertzog favored neutrality while the Boer General Smuts sided with the British against Germany.

Apartheid

During the war years, the Nationalist Party underwent a rebirth and change of direction under the inspiration of D.F.D. Malan, a strong supporter of the Nationalist South African cause. Under his guidance, the adoption of segregation along racial lines (**apartheid**) was developed and instituted as part of government policy with sweeping police powers of enforcement. The government had the power to direct the masses on where to live and where to work. The struggle against apartheid, or racism as some observers prefer to call it, became a part of the South African struggle for fifty years.

Extreme Right-Wing Afrikaner Movement

Extremism in South African politics emerged at the end of the 1960s groups that had split from the National Party and called themselves the Herstige Nasionale Party (HNP). By 1971, all the hard-liners of Afrikaner Nationalism had been forced out of the National Party and formed the **Afrikaner Weerstandsbeweging–The Afrikaner Resistance Movement.** The AWB became known principally for its menacing but flamboyant leader Eugene Terre'Blanche. Likened to Adolph Hitler, his speechmaking skills were legendary. This ability allowed him to attract large crowds of supporters to his meetings. He was not only a consummate politician and orator but an accomplished sportsman. He served in the South African Police Service as a warrant officer. After leaving the police service, he went on to form the AWB in July 1973 with another former police colleague, Jan Groenewald. The early movement was extremely small and the meetings were secret, for fear of drawing the attention of the **Bureau of State Security (B.O.S.S.).** When the group first became public, it adopted the same trappings and uniform, complete with swastika, as the German Nazi movement. Albert Hertzog, a former cabinet member of the National Party and founder of the HNP, was at this time outside the party hierarchy following

Sometimes civilians are hit by landmines set by terrorists. Courtesy of "Spike Ross" – Private Collection

the party's disastrous showing in the general election, and was looking for a cause to support. That support, together with his business acumen, went to Terre'Blanche and the AWB. Although the 1970s were the formative years for the AWB, no specific acts of terror can be attributed to the organization. With the dismantling of the apartheid system in South Africa, that would change over the next seventeen years.

AWB became labeled by many observers as a neo-Nazi organization. Although the leadership of the AWB vehemently denied the label, their uniforms did not easily dispel this viewpoint. Still searching for its true identity, the AWB went through several different scenarios, usually linked to storm trooper and motorcycle gang images with fearsome-sounding names like the Lightning Falcons and the Storm Falcons. Most members were burly men outfitted with jackboots and helmets.

The first signs of violence came in 1985, when Terre'Blanche proclaimed that the AWB would form units of guards. These groups were called the Sentinels or **Brandwag** and were formed mainly along the Northern Transvaal border with Zimbabwe. The white farmers in this area formed Brandwags to protect against border incursions from Zimbabwe. The AWB equipped itself with "heavies" to "control" and monitor meetings. Most of the white farmers in the remote regions of the Transvaal were also local commando (army) members, so it was not surprising that they would be armed with sophisticated weapons. With the extreme right-wing sympathy and weaponry now in their hands, the AWB was ready to make black groups and political organizations targets for action. What made the AWB so popular was their belief in preserving their claims to land and their demands for an Afrikaner nation formed out of the former Boer Republics.

By the end of the 1980s it became clear that the enemies of the AWB were both left-wing politicians and the African National Congress (ANC). Over the years that led up to the first ANC-elected government and the ending of the apartheid system in South Africa, AWB members and supporters carried out various terrorist acts to destabilize the ANC and the elected government. The AWB had hoped to escalate the violence into a full-scale civil war. As we now know, that was not to be the case. However, bomb attacks were directed mainly at black civilian targets in the major cities. The bombing campaign would result in many AWB arrests and convictions, and in 1996 the AWB, still under the control of Terre'Blanche, announced that the movement would henceforth operate underground.

The AWB symbol is the eagle, the meaning of which it details in its official guidebook. "This emblem enables the AWB to give its full acknowledgement to the symbolism of the eagle which epitomizes the protection of the Lord: Like an eagle that stirs up its nest, that flutters over its young, spreading out its wings, catching them, bearing them on its pinions" (Deuteronomy 32:11).

The Future

With the general acceptance of the new government, South Africa's recognition once again by the U.N., and the rapid lifting of international sanctions, it is difficult to imagine the AWB or any similar nationalist movement figuring prominently in the country's near future. As long as Afrikaner nationhood is alive and well, however, there will always be the opportunity and threat for a new generation to take up where Terre'Blanche left off.

The African National Congress (ANC)

This quasi-political movement dates as far back as 1912 and has consistently, along with other liberal groups, opposed the Nationalists and their apartheid policies. Garnering support for any action, given the overwhelming numbers (75 percent of the population is black and 14 percent white, the balance Asian), would not be difficult. Probably the most famous name connected to the movement is that of the current president of South Africa, **Nelson Rolihlahala Mandela**. Born in 1918, the son of a tribal chief, he received an excellent education, became a lawyer, and toward the end of WW II joined the African National Congress.

An outspoken opponent of apartheid, Mandela led protests and demonstrations against apartheid and police brutality during the 1950s, for which he was charged with treason. The charge was not proven, however, and he was acquitted. He was arrested again in 1962, charged with terrorist offenses, and sentenced to life in prison. His release some thirty-two years later would become the harbinger of the new South Africa and a black majority government. The role of the ANC and various acts of terrorism in South Africa are intertwined. The ANC contention is that they had been driven to acts of criminal violence, bombings, shootings and murder because they lacked any political alternative. With the apartheid firmly in place and their leader in jail, the ANC embarked on a terror campaign aimed at the state, the white minority and their own black brothers who failed to support them. Intertribal fighting has been a hallmark of fighting in the south; however, some of the brutalities used are particularly gruesome. One favored most of all in killing recalcitrant blacks was the "**necklace**," with a victim beaten and then placed in a stack of used car tires and set on fire.

The ANC received support from communist sources outside the South African borders. This led to the government reducing the effects of apartheid on the black and colored communities. The ANC has a military wing that advocates revolutionary violence. It further advocated the kind of communist revolution that swept into Russia at the start of the century. In 1987, **Winnie Mandela**, wife of the imprisoned Nelson Mandela, clearly defined the communist goals of the ANC: "The Soviet Union is the torchbearer for all our hopes and aspirations. In Soviet Russia, genuine power of the people has been transformed from dreams into reality." Since the middle of the 1980s, the Republic of South Africa has undergone drastic political changes. Dreams of the overthrow of the regime and the system of apartheid have been realized. Banned since 1961, the ANC had been headquartered outside the country in neighboring Zambia. One may assume material support was given by the Zambians to ANC terrorists crossing into South Africa. The South African police and military were very effective in patrolling and controlling border incursions from neighboring African countries hostile to the apartheid regime. Lesotho, Mozambique and Botswana have been, at varying times, locations for terrorist training bases for the ANC which were supported by Russian technicians. The external location did not prevent the South African security forces from taking preemptive actions in those countries against the training bases. The ANC also aided in defining the term terrorism by declaring in the 1980s that the South African government was a terrorist government and that the ANC was acting in self defense.

Robben Island (Isle of Purgatory)

Many historic landmarks are centerpoints for penal servitude around the world. Well known among those landmarks are Wormwood Scrubs in London, England, the Island of Elba, Devil's Island and Alcatraz. Not so well known to the world is Robben Island, situated off the southern coast of Africa, at Capetown, with a splendid view of Table Mountain. This island served as a port for Cape traders in the sixteenth century. It has also been a leper colony, a hospital for the insane, an army garrison and, more recently, the longtime residence of Nelson Mandela and other banned and convicted members of the ANC. Today, it is a national monument and tourist attraction. The island was turned over to the South African Department of Prisons when the South African Artillery School vacated it in 1959. The first African political prisoners arrived there to serve sentences in 1962, along with Pan-African Congress activists and soldiers from an armed group called Poqo. Members of the ANC, including Nelson Mandela, arrived soon after. Many arrived in a state of general illiteracy; however, B Section, which housed Mandela and his cohorts, became known as **Robben University**. Many were able, through learning, to further articulate their political beliefs. A prison code was observed by the ANC "students," which required that they maintain their commitment to changing South African society and finding positive development through their term of imprisonment. The code also required that none were to leave the prison without education. The last prisoners left the island in 1991, after the ANC had finally received political recognition.

Winnie Madikizela-Mandela

The former wife of the now current president of South Africa, Winnie Mandela has been described as the Mugger of the Nation by *Time Magazine*. During the political buildup to her husband's dramatic release from his life sentence on Robben Island, in true charismatic fashion, Winnie surrounded herself with a phalanx of bodyguards. As the ex-wife of the president, her actions and those of her bodyguards have been questioned. The depth of their involvement in any specific crimes or terrorist activities committed is still in question. Known as the **Mandela United Football Club**, they have been involved in beatings of blacks in the townships. Mandela herself was convicted of kidnapping in 1991.[5] The "football team" was made up of a group of tough youths from the Soweto Township and was led by the coach Jerry Richardson, who was convicted of murder.

Is South Africa out of the shadow of terrorism? Presumably not, with the 1998 bombing of Planet Hollywood in Cape Town. The passage of time and the removal of the white-dominated South African government have not resulted in any marked improvement in everyday living conditions hoped for by millions of South African blacks. Questions are now coming to the table about corruption and incompetence of the highest order under the government of Nelson Mandela. What this will mean, in terms of terrorist activity, is that the borders will no longer be strictly controlled and external influences and tensions will be brought into play. Weak governments in the African continent have often been susceptible to terrorism. However, until recently South Africa had a strong democratic system of government, control of its borders and an effective security force. It seems probable that South Africa and it's neighbors may have serious problems with refugees and lack of jobs. As whites leave the country in ever-increasing numbers for a safer life outside the Republic, the fabric and wealth of South Africa may suffer instability.

KENYA

Myriad tribal groups, spread throughout the land, have populated Kenya for centuries. The Kikuyu, one of the largest tribes of the region, work the land alongside the Kamba, Masai, and Luo tribes. The beginnings of colonialism in the nineteenth century saw the erosion of the tribal rights in Kenya and Britain was granted title over what is now called Uganda and Kenya. Uganda became a British Protectorate in 1893, and Kenya followed shortly after in 1895. Britain in those days was interested primarily in the rich natural resources of Uganda and constructed a railway system between Kampala and Mombassa. Much of the construction was done by imported labor from the Indian subcontinent. Most of the merchants of Kenya and Uganda are the descendants of these railway workers. By 1915, British settlers had claimed the fertile highland regions for growing crops for export, and displaced the tribes. African and Asians were prohibited from being landowners.[6] The British, unprepared to deal with the native issues in Kenya, permitted the growth of black nationalist movements, and in 1929, one of the most prominent African leaders of this century, Jomo Kenyatta, went to England to negotiate for land rights on behalf of the Kikuyu Central Association. With the onset of WW II, Africans were conscripted, and their subsequent training became the foundation for the Mau Mau.

In relation to its neighbors, Kenya has been relatively untroubled by terrorist activity and atrocities. But insurrections and uprisings in Kenya have been perpetrated by what is still considered one of the most shadowy organizations to gain a foothold on the African subcontinent, the Mau Mau. This almost mythical, mysterious organization came to prominence again as a result of what may be construed as a colonial land-grab. In fact, the tribes of Kenya were farmers and cattle herders who considered the land "everyone's land." But much of their area was now "owned" by white families. Kenya became part of Britain's far-flung empire, bringing taxation as well as education to the natives of the region. Britain and the settlers were of an unshakable belief that the land was the sole property of the colonial government. Naturally such an assumption did not sit well with the tribes of Kenya. The land grab gave rise to a resurgence of the Mau Mau. Although the specific aims of the organization have never been specifically detailed, the group flourished in the tribal lands of Kenya.

One of the best educated tribes of the region was the Kikuyu, and it was in this environment that the Mau Mau found its roots. The Kikuyu, like the other tribes, had been reduced to third-class citizens, serfs in their own country. In a region of the world where superstitions and magic have a considerable foothold, the groundswell of support for a secret society to fight for them quickly became apparent. The **Mau Mau** had sworn an oath, an act taken extremely seriously by the Kikuyu, for the total removal of all whites and those who supported the colonial British government. In the early 1950s, the Mau Mau began attacking white settlers on their farms in Kenya. In 1956, the attacks became to a full-scale rebellion, which was crushed by the British. Many tribesmen were sent to detention camps or were hunted and killed. The Mau Mau leader at the time was Dedan Kimathi, who was executed for leading the uprising.

The Mau Mau campaign had a softening effect on the British and sincere efforts were made to stabilize the country. However, from 1956–1960, Kenya was under a state of emergency. **The Kenyan African Union (KANU)**, which was led by Jomo Kenyatta, sought independence. In 1963, Britain granted full independence to Kenya and Kenyatta became the country's first president.

International Terrorism in Central Africa

With the emergence and spread of Islamic fundamentalism throughout the Middle East and into regions of northern and southern Africa, it is not surprising that a "soft" target, such as an embassy of a foreign superpower, would suffer a terrorist attack. Such was the case in Nairobi, in early August 1998. The U.S. embassy in Nairobi certainly did not have the levels of protection afforded other U.S. legations, particularly those in the Middle East. Security was considered below the acceptable standards, particularly after the bombing of the U.S. Marine Corps Barracks in Beirut in 1984, which claimed the lives of 242 U.S. Marines. Recommendations to beef up security had not included Kenya, presumably because the threat assessment was considered low for this region of the world. With lax security and a location in the center of Nairobi, it became a prime target for the determined terrorist. A massive car bomb decimated the embassy building and caused extensive damage to the surrounding buildings. The bomb claimed 170 lives, mostly Africans, and wounded several thousand. The object of the attack was the U.S. administration, not Kenya. The incident demonstrates how a terror unit can strike without warning to press home its vengeful message to a nation. The suspect in this case is **Usama bin Laden**, a Saudi Arabian dissident with operational training bases believed to be in Pakistan (see Chapter 7).

Politically Expedient Response

This incident will be viewed as history repeating itself, as it is similar to many other catastrophic terror events. The terrorists had caught President Clinton unprepared for a problem of such magnitude, at a time when he was facing serious personal and legal problems of his own. The outrage at the loss of life prompted the same kind political and military response as the attack on U.S. servicemen in Germany. That incident resulted in President Reagan's reprisal against Libya, though there was no confirmed evidence that the Libyans were in fact responsible.

If retaliation is to be undertaken (and it seems to have been in this case), governments must be cautious about the level of violence and the message they are sending, not only to a small group of terrorists, but nations that have become targets for retribution. At this writing, the effects of retaliatory attacks against the Sudan and

Pakistan have yet to be determined. Do these counterattacks result in a diminished number of terror attacks against the U.S. and other western governments? The answer to this question is not simple nor is it easy to quantify. The police crackdown after IRA bombings on the British mainland in the early 1970s and the supposed apprehension and trial of those accused in the Guildford Pub bombings did little to deter further terrorist activities, both on the mainland and in Northern Ireland. In a similar vein, the attacks against Libya did not prevent the bombing of a TWA airliner over Lockerbie, Scotland, in 1988. The suicide attack against the U.S. Marines in Beirut did not deter President Reagan from ordering the Marines to invade Granada shortly afterward, in response to fears of a Cuban takeover of the island.

ANGOLA

Angola has been Portugal's prize in Africa for more than 500 years. The land was first claimed for Portugal by the navigator Diego Cam, who landed in 1482 and left his mark in the traditional Portuguese shape of the Cross. Over the centuries, the Portuguese failed to exploit the natural wealth of the country, which was rich in mineral deposits. With colonial development all around, Angola continued in its quiet slumber. All this was to change on March 15, 1961, when gangs of guerillas loyal to Holden Roberto crossed the border and raided villages in northern Angola, killed the inhabitants and committed atrocities on both the living and the dead. At one location, the victims still alive were fed through a sawmill.[7] Men, women and children were attacked with axes, limbs and heads severed from their bodies. This invasion was, over the next decade, to spur Angolan economic development to fever pitch. It also brought communist factions bent on controlling the country and removing Portuguese influence.

Popular Movement for the Liberation of Angola (MPLA)

This popular movement started in the late 1950s in the Angolan capital of Luanda, and by 1961 had begun to fester into a civil war. In the northern region of Angola, the Front for the Liberation of Angola (FNLA) was formed, and in 1966, the National Union for the Total Independence of Angola (UNITA). Sporadic fighting continued for years; however, the 1974 military overthrow of the Portuguese government in Lisbon led to Angola's independence a year later. With the guerilla armies throughout the country, none of the factions could agree as to who would lead the new government, and fighting resumed. The **MPLA** was receiving considerable aid from both the U.S.S.R. and Cuba. The Soviets supplied weapons, training and support and Cuba supplied fighters to help with the guerilla war. By 1976, the battles were over and Marxists dominated and influenced MPLA. With a Marxist government so close to the northern border of Namibia, formerly South West Africa, the South African government continued to provide support and weapons to the UNITA rebels fighting against the Marxist forces of the MPLA. Many of those fighting with the UNITA were South African mercenaries and former British soldiers. A cease-fire eventually was established in May 1991 and lasted until October 1992, when UNITA refused to accept the election results and fighting resumed between UNITA and the MPLA government. Sporadic fighting continued over the next two years and finally, in 1994, it was agreed that UNITA guerillas would merge with the Angolan army. All this took place under the watchful eye of United Nations Peacekeepers, and although the transition was slow the new Government of National Unity came into office in April 1979. Since then, U.N. forces have begun to pull out of Angola.

MOZAMBIQUE

Sandwiched between Tanzania and South Africa, this legacy of Portuguese colonialism bears the ravages of civil war and is today one of the poorest nations in Africa. Many of Mozambique's problems originate with its near neighbors in South Africa and the former Rhodesia. The current government progressed from a guerrilla/terrorist organization to a political party. In the early 1960s, many inhabitants were becoming increasingly frustrated with the Portuguese rule and the **Front for the Liberation of Mozambique (FRELIMO)** was formed. The movement carried out operations against the Portuguese until 1974, when the country was granted independence. FRELIMO is a strong Marxist regime opposed to the white minority rule of South Africa in the 1980s and the Ian Smith minority independence government of Rhodesia. When UDI was declared, FRELIMO closed its western border with Rhodesia and many dissidents from Rhodesia set up bases in Mozambique to attack the Smith government, ably assisted by the Russian-supported FRELIMO. As the ideological focuses of the surrounding states changed, so to did Mozambique. The

Samora Machel government in Maputo supported the banned ANC movement in South Africa, and supplied weapons, training and support to terrorists fighting cross-border battles with the South African security forces.

Mozambique also had its own internal strife at this time and South Africa supported the Mozambique National Resistance (RENAMO) movement in its guerilla war with the Marxist government. By 1984, agreement had been reached between South Africa and Mozambique to stop supporting terrorists and guerillas in each other's countries. However, this did not stop the RENAMO from continuing its war against apartheid with the FRELIMO. The RENAMO aim was to totally destabilize the country, and it began to destroy schools and medical institutions. Over 1,800 schools were destroyed, and 500 health centers. Added to that total are nearly 100,000 people killed in the countryside villages. By 1992, an uneasy peace was reached between the two sides and called for an election process that would include RENAMO on the ballot. When voting took place in 1994 FRELIMO had 44 percent of the vote and RENAMO 33 percent.

Death of Samora Machel

President Samora Machel met his untimely death when his Russian-made Tupolev aircraft and its Russian crew crashed into a hillside on the South African side of the border. There has been speculation since the crash, in 1986, that there was a high-level South African plot to remove Machel. Evidence from the crash suggests that there may have been tampering with the directional systems of the Tupolev 134A-3 aircraft. It was so wildly off course, it is suspected that a decoy navigational beacon had been activated to redirect the aircraft onto a crash course. South Africa covertly supported the increasing number of RENAMO raids into Mozambique and had angered Machel. Whether South Africa was involved or not, tensions were raised in the weeks preceding the crash, as there were threatening signals from the South African Defense Ministry.

RWANDA

A small, landlocked African state, Rwanda became infamous as the country where Diane Fossey, the naturalist of silver-backed gorilla fame, was murdered. In the sixties, its fabulous pictorial postage stamps had graced many a philatelist's collection. But, in 1994, it became a killing ground for the native Hutus, who massacred well over 500,000 Tutsi.

Rwanda has for centuries been a land of farmers, occupied by the Hutu tribesmen and Pygmy hunters. In the thirteenth century, the warrior Tutsis invaded and took control of the Hutus. To the casual onlooker, it might seem logical to assume that the Hutu and Tutsi were sworn enemies. That, in fact, could not be farther from the truth. Hutu and Tutsi have lived side by side and intermarried. There is no perceptible difference in the physical characteristics of the two tribes. They look the same, pray to the same gods and have peacefully coexisted for centuries. What happened to cause the genocide that took place in 1994? One must first look at the role played by the colonial forces of Belgium, which ruled up to the early 1960s. The Belgian authoritarian control in Rwanda decided to organize and institutionalize the ethnic stereotypes in the country. As it was impossible to physically distinguish between Hutu and Tutsi, the Belgians decreed a system, which sounds as though it came out of the dark ages, to define which ethnic group a person belonged to. If a farmer owned nine cows or less he was issued an identity card stating he was a Hutu; if he owned ten or more cows he was a Tutsi. The Belgians had, overnight, created a class structure dependent on the details of an identity card, and this has been the basis for division of the two tribes since the 1930s.

Now that the Belgians had created a minority elite, they gave them privileges and positions on the Belgian colonial administration structure. The Belgians ruled by the grace of the Tutsi minority in Rwanda, whom they had schooled and educated. As they grew more powerful, they sought to throw off the mantle of colonialism and demanded independence for the country. To counter the Tutsi demands, the Belgians began to switch their allegiance to the Hutu majority, producing enough hatred for the Tutsi to start a popular uprising. The uprising brought the Hutu into government, and over 100,000 Tutsi were killed. A similar number, fearing further atrocities, fled north to neighboring Uganda where they remained in exile. It was this exiled group and their descendents that returned to begin the civil war in 1990. The group had formed, in exile, the Rwandan Patriotic Front (RPF), which was made up of displaced Tutsis and Hutus dissatisfied with the Hutu government. The aims of the RPF were to replace the repressive government with a new democratic order.

The Hutu-dominated government of President Habyarimana was determined not to be removed from power, and they planned to eradicate the Tutsi in methods not dissimilar to the Nazi genocide perpetrated against the Jews in Germany. The tool of choice in this instance was propaganda. As most of the Hutus were illiterate farmers, the government began to systematically bombard the population with radio announcements that were deliberately and openly anti-Tutsi. It went beyond just denouncements of the Tutsi and actively demanded that the civilian Hutus kill any Tutsi they came across. The words "terror" and "threat" were repeated incessantly in an effort to sow the seeds of death for the Tutsi. In a format reminiscent of South American death squads, the Hutu government set up a civilian militia and trained them in weaponry, hand-to-hand combat and methods of quickly killing the enemy. This organization was called the *Interahamwe*, which, simply translated, means "those who attack together." The militias began killing Tutsi wherever they found them and it became apparent that this was not considered a crime. When the civil war had gone on for almost three years, a cease-fire was reached between the two sides in 1993; under the auspices of the United Nations in 1994, the country prepared to set up some form of transitional government. But the Hutu continued to arm and train their civilian militia openly and under the noses of the U.N. observers. It is still unclear to the international community why the U.N. made no effort to either report these facts or seek any clarification on how to handle the issues.

Death of a President

Uprisings sometimes have need of a trigger mechanism to set them off. In April 1994, the plane carrying President Habyarimana was shot down as it approached Kigali, the Rwandan capital. President Habyarimana died, and this incident was the green light for the genocide to begin. Within hours of his death, killings of Tutsi began anew, and within a month, nearly half a million lay dead throughout the country. Those who were able escaped to neighboring countries. The U.S. stood by while all this went on and has been criticized for its failure to intervene to stop the massacres.

With the death of the president, the world came to hear about the genocide being perpetrated on the Tutsi with graphic and horrifying pictures and accounts in daily newspapers. Two months into the killings, the U.N. finally passed a resolution to send in a peacekeeping force of around 5,000 troops. With the slaughter nearly over and the RPF advancing from the north, many of the Hutu militia escaped to Tanzania to refugee camps set up inside the border. The point may have been missed in newspaper articles about the need for urgent humanitarian aid, but most of the refugee camps held only murderous members of the Hutu, as nearly all the Tutsi had been caught and killed in the preceding six week period. A long rebuilding process has begun, but how long the scars will take to heal is anyone's guess.

Unique in world history is the country's demand that the Hutu and Tutsi reintegrate within Rwanda. Genocide, civil war, refugee flight, abundant hate propaganda, a culture of impunity and ongoing insurgency and atrocities are items of daily note in Rwanda. The most telling and difficult question is whether the people of Rwanda can rewrite the social contract intrinsic to any functioning society. Can they overcome their mutual suspicion and live as neighbors again? The Hutu returning to Rwanda fear the same actions as those they perpetrated on the Tutsi in 1994. Such reintegration has never happened; it certainly did not take place in the similar circumstances of post-WW II Germany, and the international community created a sovereign Jewish state, Israel. Survivors of the killing fields of Cambodia resettled in other countries. Following the Armenian genocide early this century, a separate nation was carved out for them. Rwanda today is still a dangerous place; atrocities continue to take place, as old and not-so-old scores are settled.

ZAIRE (DEMOCRATIC REPUBLIC OF CONGO)

Located in the center of Africa and straddling both the equator and the mighty River Congo, with a population of around 40 million, Zaire is rich in mineral resources of gold, copper, zinc and diamonds, to name but a few. Zaire was discovered by Henry Stanley in the 1870s, after he was asked to set up Belgian trading posts along the Congo River in 1878 by King Leopold of Belgium. The King ruled this African country as his own private fiefdom, and it only came under the control of the Belgian government in 1908. At that time it was called the Congo Free State. By the end of the 1950s, the colonial Belgian rule was coming to an end and on June 30, 1960, the Belgian Congo became the independent Republic of Congo. The first president of the new central African republic was Joseph Kasavubu, and the legendary Patrice Lumumba as the prime minister. Unluckily for the young, communist-inspired Lumumba, his position was extremely tenuous in the eyes of the West and particularly the U.S. At the height of the cold war, intent on reducing and eliminating any Soviet involvement in mineral-rich central Africa, the CIA conspired with factions that were anti-Communist to overthrow the Lumumba government and install a pro-West regime. This was achieved by infiltrating mercenary elements into the country. The CIA had worked out a plan to poison Lumumba; however, prior to his assassination, the army mutinied in July 1960. In September of the same year, Desire Mobutu, a colonel in the army, announced the suspension of all political parties and took control of the country. In November 1960, Lumumba was arrested and handed over to rebel forces, who executed him on January 17, 1961. For the next four years the government was in turmoil, until the military coup of Mobutu. For the next thirty-two years, Mobutu Sese Seko ruled the country with an iron fist. This leader was violently anti-Communist and strongly pro-West, which suited the U.S. in the Cold War years.

Mobutu Sese Seko

Mobutu's tyrannical reign was characterized by pillage and plunder. He was estimated to be one of the five richest men in the world and was president of one of the poorest nations in the world. In a country of such enormous mineral wealth, it is not difficult to determine where the wealth had gone. Mobutu lived a lavish lifestyle, and had expensive villas throughout Europe. One of the earliest uprisings against the Mobutu regime came in 1964 in the area of the eastern Congo. It was led by a young rebel of Marxist trappings, Laurent-Desire Kabila, who would later return to lead the civil war against the Mobutu regime. Much of what took place in the Congo was a result of outside influences and internal disputes between the many ethnically diverse tribes that had settled in the region or were forced in from the actions and atrocities in neighboring countries.

Hutu and Tutsi hostilities after the genocide in Rwanda played a significant part in the eventual rebellion and civil war that overtook Zaire. Insurgent rebellion has been prevalent throughout the dictatorial reign of Mobutu, but he had always managed to put down the uprisings either by force or by proclaiming presidential or legislative reforms. The country existed as a one-party state under Mobutu, so challenges to his rule were frequent. Citizenship issues and land rights have also added to the tensions of Zaire. The complications of the various regions of Zaire are interwoven with the ethnic groups that vie for power amongst themselves. The principal groups are located in the province of Kivu, which has a long history of ethnic violence; these groups are the Hunde, Nande and Banyarwanda people.

Banyarwandans are a collection of displaced Rwandans who were brought into the region by their colonial Belgian masters to work the land, and included both Hutu and Tutsi. They were not considered citizens of Zaire under Mobutu's rule, and that did not change with the establishment of Kabila's government in 1997. Most of the land occupied by the Banyarwandans had been rented to them by the local chiefs in northern Kivu province. The Banyarwandans, by 1993, were pushing for reforms and an end to injustices against them. What was to complicate the situation in Zaire was the sudden mass exodus of Hutus from Rwanda. Many had been members of the militia *Interahamwe*, which had been responsible for the genocide in Rwanda following the death of the Rwandan president.

An uprising in 1993 escalated into a full-scale ethnic battle. Most of those killed were Banyarwandan. The situation was not improved by the arrival of the Hutu refugees. The uprising spread and soon became a national movement to overthrow Mobutu. The rebel forces consisted mainly of Tutsi warriors, and soon Laurent Kabila became their revolutionary leader.

Widespread disillusionment in the Zaire army led to the eventual capitulation of the Mobutu government. On May 16, 1997, with only his personal bodyguard remaining in Kinshasa and the rebel forces on the doorstep, Mobutu left quietly for the safety of Morocco, where he lived in exile until his death in September 1997 from prostate cancer. However, since Kabila came to power the ethnic violence has not ceased, and Zaire has seen an increase in rebel attacks from outside its unprotected borders. From within, the fighting and massacres have continued, particularly in the North and South Kivu provinces. Hutu and Tutsi continue to kill each other. An end to the carnage is not expected any time soon. Much of Kabila's support comes from the army that has been dominated by Rwandan Tutsis.

SUMMARY

The turbulent passage to independence in many central and southern African countries has led to widespread violence that is often termed ethnic cleansing. The establishment of an apartheid-free South African nation under the presidency of Nelson Mandela had its fair share of violence perpetrated by both sides. South Africa is still considered one of the most powerful nations in Africa, and its influence on its neighbors over the coming years will be of considerable interest to students. The troubles plaguing the regime of Robert Mugabe and the struggle that brought him to power were all characteristics of nationhood in southern Africa. Many of the fledgling countries that fought for independence have suffered under the tyrannical dictators whose only real interest was using capital and foreign investment in their respective countries to bankroll their personal lifestyles. The influence of communist involvement in the region over the past forty years has been considerable and destabilization seems to continue in one form or another. In the following chapter we will chart the rise of terrorism on the Indian subcontinent and beyond.

Terms to remember

genocide	Emperor Haile Selassie	Ogaden
EPRDF	Somali Revolutionary	Said Barre
ethnic cleansing	Socialist Party	Milton Obote
Sir Edward Mutesa II	Idi Amin	Public Safety Unit and the
Lugbara	cannibalism	Bureau of State Research
Wilfred Bose	PFLP	Major-General Dan
Operation Thunderball	Operation Jonathan	Shomron
ZANU	ZIPRA	Unilateral Declaration of
Joshua Nkomo	Ndabaningi Sithole	Independence
African National Congress	Great Trek	apartheid
(ANC)	Afrikaner	Bureau of State Security
Brandwag	Weerstandsbeweging–The	(B.O.S.S.)
necklace	Afrikaner Resistance	Nelson Rolihlahala
Winnie Mandela	Movement	Mandela
Robben University	Mandela United Football	Mau Mau
Kenyan African Union	Club	Usama bin Laden
(KANU)	MPLA	FRELIMO

Review Questions

What was so important about the fact the Nelson Mandella became the first black man to become president of South Africa?

Describe the reign of Idi Amin Dada and tribal rivalries in Uganda.

Explain the manner in which Cecil Rhodes influenced the development of terrorism in Rhodesia.

Discuss why it was that apartheid could be maintained for so long in South Africa.

Present an argument as to whether you think there will be peace in that region in the near future.

Endnotes

1. Bruce Quarrie, *The World's Secret Police* (Octopus Books Ltd., London 1986), p. 104.
2. Major Louis Williams, "Thunderball at Entebbe" (*Israeli Defense Force Journal*, May 1985).
3. Douglas Reed, *The Siege of Southern Africa* (Macmillan South Africa, 1974) p. 45.
4. Ibid., p. 95.
5. Peter Hawthorn, "Mugger of the Nation," (*Time Canada Limited*, December 8, 1997), p. 37.
6. Kenya, Capsule history. Africanet, the Internet.
7. Douglas Reed, *The Siege of Southern Africa* (Macmillan South Africa, 1974), p. 25.

CHAPTER 9

SOUTHERN AND SOUTHEAST ASIA

...regional instability is exacerbated not by a general sort of "ethnic conflict," as many claim, but rather by a number of intertwined issues relating to ethnicity, nationalism, religion, economic inequality, environment degradation and popular belief.

—Richard H. Shultz and J. Marlow Schmauder

OVERVIEW

Nowhere outside the Middle East are the words quoted above more appropriate than in South Asia. In that part of the world, the splits between religions and factions within the same religion are longstanding and deep. To add to that delicate situation, two of the major powers are known to have nuclear weapons. This is one of the most misunderstood parts of the world to Westerners. The region is continuously faced with terrorism and violence. This chapter will acquaint the student with some of the major problem areas in the most troubled countries, from enormous India to tiny Sri Lanka. The student will become aware of ongoing battles for autonomy and freedom fought largely by terrorism and insurrection. It will be shown how difficult it is to separate the problems of this vast region into neatly defined categories. In addition, we will take a critical look at the potential threat of Islamic efforts to unite into a global power stretching from the Persian Gulf to the eastern parts of the Russian republic. We will start with South Asia and examine the history of ancient, mysterious India.[1]

SOUTH ASIA

India

It is important for the student to have some historical background on the Indian subcontinent and its bordering states, which have long been the crossroads of Southern Asia. In some ways this area is like the Balkans, with many cultures passing through on the way east and west. The Indian subcontinent has had a civilization since 2500 B.C., when the inhabitants of the Indus River Valley developed a culture based on commerce and sustained by agricultural trade. During the second millennium B.C., pastoral Aryan-speaking tribes migrated from the northwest into the subcontinent and settled in the middle Ganges River Valley. A brief history of this region is essential to understanding its development on many levels, to include religious discord, violence and terrorism. The map of ancient and medieval India was made up of many kingdoms with fluctuating boundaries. In the fourth and fifth centuries A.D., northern India was unified under the Gupta Dynasty. During this period, known as India's Golden Age, Hindu culture reached new heights.

Islamic influences spread across the subcontinent over a period of 500 years. Starting in the tenth and eleventh centuries, Turks and Afghans invaded India and established sultanates in the areas around Delhi. Descendants of Genghis Khan swept across the Khyber Pass in the eleventh century and established the Mogul Dynasty, which lasted from the eleventh to the fifteenth centuries. During this period, there were two major cultural and religious systems, those of the Hindus and Muslims. These cultures had centuries of mutual contact and lasting influences upon each other.

The British appeared on the subcontinent in 1619, and by the middle 1800s controlled most of present-day India, Pakistan and Bangladesh. In 1857, a bloody rebellion in north India led by mutinous Indian soldiers resulted in the transfer of all political power to the British Crown, which began administering most of India directly and controlling the rest through treaties with local rulers.

By the late 1800s, the first steps had been taken toward self-government. The British viceroy established provisional councils comprised of Indian members to advise the Crown. The British subsequently widened Indian participation in such legislative councils. By 1920, the Indian leader Mahatma Gandhi had transformed the **Indian National Congress** political party into a powerful movement against British colonial rule. Following Gandhi's concepts of nonviolent resistance, the party used both parliamentary means and noncooperation to compel the British to give India its independence. In 1947, India was awarded Commonwealth status and Jawaharlal Nehru became the first prime minister. A period of continuing and escalating bloody conflicts between Hindus and Muslims led to the British partition of India. This division, created on the basis of religion, resulted in forming East and West Pakistan, where there were Muslim majorities. These groups were forcibly moved, Muslims north and Hindus south, creating animosity that continues to the present. After partition, India became a republic and a full member of the Commonwealth on January 26, 1950.

Always volatile, present-day relations between India and Pakistan took a downward plunge when both acquired nuclear weapons capability. Recent tests seem more calculated to divert attention from economic and international issues than to "rattle nuclear sabers." India has long complained about continuing foreign interference from Afghanistan and Pakistan, with the menace of escalating terrorism in the region. For years, the most ruthless Islamic and other terrorist organizations have been known to use Afghanistan as a base for recruiting, training and harboring terrorists to carry out operations abroad. On many occasions, India has drawn attention to the presence of training camps in neighboring **Kashmir** and **Afghanistan**. There, terrorists are trained and equipped to carry out operations in India. Many hundreds of thousands of refugees from the war in Afghanistan are easily recruited by their protectors in Pakistan and are used to foment terrorism and to pressure India to grant even more territory in the Kashmir.

America has followed India's concern over Pakistan-sponsored cross-border terrorism in Jammu and Kashmir carefully. The U.S. government has expressed continuing concern over the fate of the four remaining western hostages kidnapped in Kashmir in 1995. Of the six original hostages, one managed to escape and another was killed in captivity. But the fates of the remaining four, Keith Mangan and Paul Wells (U.K.), Donald Hutchings (U.S.) and Dirk Hasert (Germany) remain unknown. The kidnappings did, however, reveal and highlight the involvement of the Pakistan-sponsored Harkat-ul-Ansar (**HUA**), which was branded a terrorist organization by the U.S. Government in 1997 under the Anti-Terrorism and Effective Death Penalty Act of 1996. It is difficult to separate issues of internal terrorism within India from external terrorism by surrounding Muslim states. Therefore, we shall examine the most prevalent of these not-so-friendly neighbors as collateral to the issues inside India.

In November 1997, their Pakistani driver and four U.S. employees of Union Texas Petroleum were murdered in Karachi when the vehicle in which they were traveling was attacked near the United States Consulate. Shortly after the incident, two separate claims of responsibility for the killings were made, one by the Aimal Khufia Action Committee, a previously unknown group, and one by the **Islami Inqilabi Mahaz**, a Lahore-based group of Afghan veterans. Both groups cited as the motive for the attack the conviction of Mir Aimal Kansi, a Pakistani national who was tried in the United States for the murder of two CIA employees and the wounding of three others in 1993. Kansi was found guilty and sentenced to death. Ramzi Ahmed Yousef, who was extradited from Pakistan to the United States in 1995, was also convicted in New York in November for his role in the 1993 World Trade Center bombing in New York City.

Deadly incidents of sectarian violence, particularly in Punjab Province, surged in 1997. According to press reports, 200 people died during that year. In addition, five Iranian air force technicians were killed in Rawalpindi. *Lashkar i-Jhangvi*, a violent offshoot of the anti-Shiite, Sunni group called *Sipah i Shahaba Pakistan*, claimed responsibility. In Iran, the government-controlled press held Pakistan responsible for failing to stop the attack and accused the United States of conspiring in the murders.

Security problems persist in India as a result of insurgencies in Kashmir and in the northeast. The violence has also has spread to New Delhi, where there were more than 25 bombings in 1997, mainly in the marketplaces and on the public buses of old Delhi, leaving 10 killed and more than 200 injured. These attacks appeared to be designed to spread terror among the public rather than cause casualties. Nearly 100 bombings with similar characteristics took place elsewhere in India, most with no claims of responsibility. Although foreigners were not the primary targets of these attacks, foreign tourists were injured in a train bombing outside Delhi.

Pakistan, Afghanistan and Islam

As can be seen above, religious differences and a long history of violence and hatred among former brothers separate India and Pakistan. Sponsoring international terror-

TERRORISM BRIEF 9–1
INDIA'S NUCLEAR EXPLOSIONS

India's nuclear weapon test explosions have rocked Washington as few other events have in recent years. Among senior officials, there is a palpable sense of outrage at having been deceived by the new BJP-led government. "We were told privately and publicly that India would continue to show restraint in the nonproliferation field, and would do nothing to surprise us," Assistant Secretary for South Asian Affairs Rick Inderfurth told a Senate committee on May 13.

This time around, it is still by no means clear that India now knows what it wants to achieve with nuclear weapons, or how it is going to get there. But the world in the meantime has changed a great deal. The idea that a more convincing demonstration of India's nuclear weapon capabilities will somehow boost India's international standing is so out of step with the times that it could almost be considered quaint if it were not also so damaging to the very cause of disarmament that India professes to support. The Cold War ideological rivalries that spawned the nuclear arms race are gone, nuclear arsenals are in steep decline, and something of a global consensus has emerged that the interests of international security are best served by halting the proliferation of nuclear weapons while reducing existing arsenals and building the international norms and institutions that can eventually displace the role of nuclear deterrence in the international system.

While American policymakers have long understood that India does not accept this framework for coping with the nuclear danger, the Clinton administration thought it was working toward a new understanding with India. India's stealthy preparation and conduct of the recent test series has wiped out what was to have been a cooperative effort at mutual accommodation, and it has sowed seeds of distrust that may continue to sprout for years to come.

As for the nuclear threat from Pakistan, exactly how does detonating five nuclear explosives control, reduce, or in any way mitigate this threat? Think about it. Pakistan does not pose a conventionally superior military threat to India, so Indian nuclear weapons are not "needed" for this purpose. And it is absurd to think that Pakistani leaders must be actively "deterred" from deliberately launching a "bolt out of the blue" nuclear attack for the unprovoked and purely genocidal purpose of killing millions of Indians, including millions of fellow Muslims.

Today the Cuban missile crisis is widely acknowledged as involving supremely irresponsible risk-taking by both national leaderships. Without either leadership actually willing it, the crisis could well have culminated in inadvertent nuclear war. Reducing but by no means eliminating this risk—through robust nuclear command and control systems, survivable basing, and nuclear options short of immediate Armageddon—while still seeking the deterrent benefit of nuclear weapons in conventional military confrontations with another nuclear weapon state, requires the expenditure of billions of dollars. Is India really prepared to go down this road? If not, India may wind up with the worst of both worlds—a nuclear "deterrent" that emboldens and then ensnares the national leadership in crisis situations, but ultimately provokes rather than deters nuclear attack.

If the CTBT ultimately unravels as a result of India's ill-considered actions, and nuclear explosions once again rock the earth in the five declared weapons states and other states as well, I doubt the rest of the world will find much consolation in the notion that India was ostensibly acting in accordance with its "principled" stand against "nuclear discrimination." And in favor of a "timebound disarmament." The international community will remember a nation whose long delayed and now utterly improbable nuclear ambitions came cloaked in the rhetoric of disarmament, and it won't be fooled again.

SOURCE: EXTRACTED FROM AN ARTICLE BY CHRISTOPHER E. PAINE, SENIOR RESEARCHER AND CO-DIRECTOR, NRDC NUCLEAR PROGRAM, MAY 18, 1998.

ism, separatist subversion and insurgency is not new to Pakistan. Since the 1970s, Pakistan has also trained rebel Sikh and other Indian separatist movements. Such efforts are seen as a part of Pakistan's strategy of revenge for India's support of an independent Bangladesh. The **Shironami Gurudwara Prabandhak Committee (SGPC)** is the major Sikh terrorist organization in India. It began to establish tight control over the culture and economy of the Indian State of Punjab in the early 1980s. The SGPC forced Sikh traditionalism and conservatism on Punjabi society. Pakistan was quick to recognize this as an opportunity to exploit any further divisions in India.

The Sikh struggle for an independent state attracted Pakistan's attention. Pakistan had long held claims to Kashmir and saw possible benefit from encouraging the formation of a Sikh state, **Khalistan**, in the Punjab, as this would weaken India's defense of the remaining portion of Kashmir. Pakistan looked to exploit the tensions in Kashmir in order to destabilize India. Pakistan began to provide training and military assistance, and terrorist actions of the Sikh militants increased. The Sikhs began to represent such a potential threat that India launched an assault on the Golden Temple at Amritsar, one of the holiest places for Sikhs, in July 1984. That event started an unprecedented bloodletting between Sikhs and Punjabis, with casualties far exceeding all Sikh terrorism efforts combined to that point. Ultimately, the escalation of Sikh separatist terrorism resulted in the shocking assassination of Indira Gandhi, the prime minister. The Gandhi assassination was proof, from Pakistan's viewpoint, of the strategic value of exporting subversion and terror. The Sikhs' armed insurrection escalated, as high-quality weapons became available. The arsenal included sophisticated bomb-making techniques and better training for Sikh terrorists of the Dal Khalsa separatist movement in the **Afghanistan Mujahidden** camps.

A corresponding ideological development in Indian Kashmir occurred. Almost overnight, the prevailing popular sentiment in Indian Kashmir was the belief that Islam was in danger. This had a galvanizing effect on the youth of the Kashmir region, and they formed new cadres of terrorists. The extent of Pakistani and Afghan influence on the Islamist transformation of the Kashmir insurgency was profound and deadly.

The **ISI** (Pakistan Intelligence) then assumed quite a different role from its behind the scenes maneuvers. It began to take over direct control of the Sikh movement. The ISI made the city of Darra, in Pakistan, the primary source of weapons for the Sikh, Tamil and Kashmiri liberation movements. The escalation of terrorism by the Karachi-based organizations rejuvenated the domestic Darran market and the Pushtan population in Karachi became the storefront for the regional arms market.

The availability of weapons, primarily from supplies to the Afghan resistance, turned Karachi into a center for Islamic international terrorism involving Palestinians and people from Bangladesh, India, Nepal, Afghanistan, Burma, Thailand, Sri Lanka, the Philippines, and Africa. These were Muslims who lived in Karachi, providing manpower for the development of terrorist operations. Having witnessed the initial impact of the Islamist message in Indian Kashmir, Pakistan began to broaden its horizons and set it sights higher. In 1986, with growing experience in training, organizing and operations with Afghan Mujahideen, and with military supplies available, Pakistan began expanding its operation to sponsor and promote separatism and terrorism, primarily in Kashmir, as a strategic long-term program. Among the most crucial activities of the ISI were the following:

- Religious fundamentalism was propagated in small but lethal doses to promote separatism and communal outlook.

- Training and indoctrination of selected leaders from the Kashmir Valley was arranged to create militant cadres.

- A large number of youths from the Kashmir Valley and Poonch Sector was given extensive training in the use of automatic weapons, sabotage and attacks on security forces. Automatic weapons and explosives were now issued to these people.

- Special teams were trained to organize disruption and engineer incidents to damage the democratic and secular image of India.

SIKH TERRORISM

Sikh terrorism is sponsored by expatriate and Indian Sikh groups who want to carve out an independent Sikh state called Khalistan (Land of the Pure) from Indian territory. Active groups include Babbar Khalsa, International Sikh Youth Federation, Dal Khalsa, Bhinderanwala Tiger Force. A previously unknown group, the Saheed Khalsa Force, claimed credit for the marketplace bombings in New Delhi in 1997.

Sikh attacks in India are usually against Indian officials and facilities, other Sikhs, and Hindus. They include assassinations, bombings, and kidnappings. These attacks have dropped markedly since 1992. Indian security forces killed or captured many of the senior Sikh militant leaders and extremist groups. Many low-intensity bombings that might have been due to Sikh extremists occur without subsequent claims of credit. Sikh militant cells are active internationally and extremists gather funds from overseas Sikh communities. Sikh expatriates have formed a variety of international organizations that lobby for the Sikh cause overseas. Most prominent are the World Sikh Organization and the International Sikh Youth Federation.

Source: Patterns of Global Terrorism, 1997. United States Department of State, April 1998.

The head of the ISI Political Section developed a long-term program called K-2, aimed at unifying the Kashmiri and Sikhs subversion efforts by bringing under one umbrella Sikh and Kashmiri extremists and Muslim fundamentalists. This would then intensify acts of violence in Punjab, Jammu and Kashmir, and the Terai region of Uttar Pradesh. Escalation of terrorism and subversion since the early 1990s is widely believed to have been a direct outgrowth of the ISI's implementation of the K-2 program.

After their revolution, Iran had a special commitment to the Islamist struggle in Kashmir. The maternal branch of the family of the Ayatollah Khomeini had lived in Kashmir since the eighteenth century. The Khomeini-based branch of the family had continued to maintain relations with their relatives in Kashmir, and in the twentieth century, the Persian Khomeinis have cared for children of Kashmiris sent for higher religious learning in Qom and Najaf. Ayatollah Khomeini still retained contacts with the main branch of his Kashmiri family and had emotional ties to its cause.

Sikh terrorists were increasingly smuggling their weapons from the Jammu and Kashmir area and from Ganganagar in Rajasthan, where the ISI had its own bases. Clandestine ISI support for the Sikh rebels continued to improve. Eventually, Sikh terrorists in Punjab were receiving instructions from Pakistan-based leaders for an intensification of terrorist operations. Sikh terrorists received additional explosives and small arms from Pakistani stockpiles, as well as antiaircraft guns and recoilless rifles, sniper rifles and "the latest weapons" for special operations. These weapons now dominate the insurgency in the Rajasthan area. By 1992, the ISI was operating 13 permanent, 18 temporary and 8 joint training camps for Kashmiris in Pakistan and Kashmir alone. Thus, while these Kashmiri terrorists failed to incite a popular war, they did establish wide and solid enough popular backing to embark on the second phase, namely a direct and violent confrontation with the Indian security forces. That would not have been possible without Pakistani and other Islamist support.

Many of the factions involved in the Afghanistan civil war included large numbers of Egyptians, Algerians, Palestinians, and Saudis. Many of these continue to provide haven to terrorists by facilitating the operation of training camps in areas under their control. The factions remain engaged in a struggle for political and military supremacy over India. The Indian and Pakistani governments each claim that the intelligence service of the other country sponsors bombings on its territory. The government of Pakistan acknowledges that it continues to provide moral, political, and diplomatic support to Kashmiri militants but denies allegations of other assistance. Reports continued in 1997 of official Pakistani support to militants fighting in Kashmir. In Pakistan, deadly incidents of sectarian violence, particularly in the Sindh and Punjab provinces, continued throughout 1997. There continue to be credible reports of official Pakistani support for Kashmiri militant groups that engage in terrorism, such as the HUA.[2]

SRI LANKA

The Democratic Socialist Republic of Sri Lanka (Sri Lanka) is an island in the Indian Ocean, south of India, which is slightly larger than West Virginia and was known as Ceylon until 1972. It was the center of Buddhist civilization in the third century B.C. and remains a strong Buddhist majority at 69 percent, with minority representation by Hindu 15 percent, Christian 8 percent and Muslim 8 percent among an estimated population of over 18,700,000. The Portuguese first settled it in 1505, followed by the Dutch in 1658. The British arrived in 1796 and it was made a colony in 1853. It was finally granted independence in 1948. The Ceylonese government resisted an insurrection by terrorists attempting its overthrow in 1971. It commands a strategic location near major Indian Ocean sea lanes.

There have been hostilities between the Sri Lankan government by armed **Liberation Tigers of Tamil Elam (LTTE)** and other smaller Tamil separatist groups since the mid-1980s. Several hundred thousand Tamil civilians have fled the island, and as of late 1996, 63,068 were housed in refugee camps in south India. Another 30,000–40,000 lived outside the Indian camps, and more than 200,000 Tamils have sought political asylum in the west.

Drought, slow economic reform, and civil war, in 1996, exacted a heavy economic toll. Insufficient monsoon rains caused power cuts that hurt industrial and agricultural production, and the stepped-up LTTE insurgency reduced foreign investment and tourism, Sri Lanka's two key sources of foreign exchange. Meanwhile, the government counterinsurgency efforts caused defense expenditures to overrun budget targets by 42 percent. In 1997 and 1998, agricultural production should improve, but industry will still be hampered by high real interest rates, slow improvement in foreign investment inflows, and stalled progress on privatization. The government's main challenge will be to curb defense and social welfare spending to cut the budget deficit as a percentage of GDP in half by yearend 1998, as stipulated in its deficit reduction program.

The LTTE continued its terrorist activities in 1997, attacking government troops, economic infrastructure targets, and assassinating political opponents. The LTTE's most spectacular terrorist attack in 1997 was a truck bombing directed at the newly opened **Colombo World Trade Center** on October 15. The explosion injured more than 100 persons, including many foreigners, and caused significant collateral damage to nearby buildings. Eighteen persons–including LTTE suicide bombers, hotel security guards, and Sri Lankan security forces–died in the explosion and aftermath. Sri Lankan authorities shot two of the terrorists as they tried to escape, and another three killed themselves to avoid capture. One of the bombers lobbed a grenade into a monastery as he fled the scene, killing one monk. In two separate incidents in June in the Tricomalee area, the LTTE assassinated two legislators and nine other civilians.

During the summer months, naval elements of the LTTE conducted several attacks on commercial shipping, including numerous foreign vessels. In July LTTE rebels abducted the crew of an empty passenger ferry and set fire to the vessel. The captain and a crewmember—both Indonesian—were released after three days. The LTTE stormed a North Korean cargo ship after it delivered a shipment of food and other goods for civilians on the Jaffna Peninsula, killing one of the vessel's 38 North Korean crewmembers in the process. The Tigers freed its North Korean captives five days later and eventually returned the vessel. Sri Lankan authorities charged the LTTE with the July hijacking of a shipment of more than 32,000 mortar rounds bound for the Sri Lankan military. In September the LTTE used rocket-propelled grenades to attack a Panamanian-flagged Chinese-owned merchant ship chartered by a U.S. chemical company to load minerals for export. As many as 20 persons, including five Chinese crewmembers, were reported killed, wounded, or missing from the attack.

In August, a strange group calling itself the Internet Black Tigers (IBT) claimed responsibility for e-mail harassment of several Sri Lankan missions around the world. The group claimed in Internet postings to be an elite department of the LTTE specializing in "suicide e-mail bombings" with the goal of countering Sri Lankan Government propaganda disseminated electronically. The IBT stated that the attacks were only warnings.

The Sri Lankan Government strongly supports international efforts to address the problem of terrorism. It was the first to sign the International Convention for the Suppression of Terrorist Bombings in January 1998. Colombo was quick to condemn terrorist attacks in other countries and raised terrorism issues in several international venues, including the U.N. General Assembly and the Commonwealth heads of government meeting in Edinburgh. No confirmed cases of LTTE or other terrorist groups targeting U.S. citizens in Sri Lanka occurred in 1997.

In Sri Lanka, the LTTE showed no signs of abandoning their campaign to cripple the Sri Lankan economy and target government officials. The group retains its ability to strike in the heart of Colombo, as demonstrated by an October bomb attack on the World Trade Center in the financial district that was reminiscent of the January 1996 truck bomb attack that destroyed the Central Bank. The LTTE was designated a foreign terrorist organization in October pursuant to the Antiterrorism and Effective Death Penalty Act of 1996.[3]

Other known terrorist front organizations:

- The Liberation Tigers of Tamil Eelam (LTTE)
- World Tamil Association (WTA)
- World Tamil Movement (WTM)
- Federation of Associations of Canadian Tamils (FACT)
- The Ellalan Force
- The Internet Black Tigers (IBT)[4]

Of all these organizations, the LTTE is the most powerful Tamil group in Sri Lanka and uses covert and illegal methods to raise funds, acquire weapons, and publicize its cause of establishing an independent Tamil state. Founded in 1976, the LTTE began its armed conflict with the Sri Lankan government in 1983 and relies on a guerrilla strategy that includes the use of terrorist tactics. The group's elite Black Tiger squad conducts suicide bombings against important targets, and all rank-and-file members carry a cyanide capsule to kill themselves rather than allow themselves to be caught. The LTTE is very insular and highly organized, with its own intelligence service, naval element (the Sea Tigers), and women's political and military wings.

The LTTE has integrated a battlefield insurgent strategy with a terrorist program that targets key government and military personnel, the economy, and public infrastructure. Political assassinations include the suicide bomber attacks against Sri Lankan President Ranasinghe Premadasa, in 1993, and Indian Prime Minister Rajiv Gandhi, in 1991 (the group's only known act outside Sri Lanka). The LTTE has detonated two massive truck bombs directed against the Sri Lankan economy, one at the Central Bank in January 1996, and another at the Colombo World Trade Center in October 1997. The LTTE also has attacked infrastructure targets such as commuter trains, buses, oil tanks, and power stations. They prefer to attack vulnerable government facilities then withdraw before reinforcements arrive, or to time its attacks to take advantage of security lapses on holidays, at night, or in the early morning. The LTTE has recruited approximately 10,000 armed combatants in Sri Lanka, with about 3,000 to 6,000 forming a trained cadre of fighters. The LTTE also has a significant overseas support structure for fundraising, weapons procurement, and propaganda activities.

The Tamil Tigers control most of the northern and eastern coastal areas of Sri Lanka but have conducted operations throughout the island. Headquartered in the Wanni region, LTTE leader Velupillai Prabhakaran has established an extensive network of checkpoints and informants to keep track of any outsiders who enter the group's area of control. The LTTE's overt organizations support Tamil separatism by lobbying foreign governments and the United Nations. They also use its international contacts to procure weapons, communications, and bomb-making equipment. The LTTE exploits large Tamil communities in North America, Europe, and Asia to obtain funds and supplies for its fighters in Sri Lanka. Information obtained since the mid-1980s indicates that some Tamil communities in Europe are also involved in narcotics smuggling. It should be obvious to the student that the LTTE has learned well from the tactics employed by the IRA in Northern Ireland.

AFGHANISTAN

Islamic extremists from around the world—including large numbers of Egyptians, Algerians, Palestinians, and Saudis—continued to use Afghanistan as a training ground and home base from which to operate in 1997. The Taliban, as well as many of the other combatants in the Afghan civil war, facilitated the operation of training and indoctrination facilities for non-Afghans in the territories they controlled. Several Afghani factions also provided logistic support, free passage, and sometimes passports to the members of various terrorist organizations. These individuals, in turn, were involved in fighting in Bosnia and Herzegovina, Chechnya, Tajikistan, Kashmir, the Philippines, and parts of the Middle East.

Saudi-born terrorist financier Usama Bin Ladin relocated from Jalalabad to the Taliban's capital of Qandahar in early 1997 and established a new base of operations. He continued to incite violence against the United States, particularly against U.S. forces in Saudi Arabia. Bin Ladin called on Muslims to retaliate against the U.S. prosecutor in the Mir Aimal Kansi trial for disparaging comments he made about Pakistanis and praised the Pakistan-based Kashmiri group HUA in the wake of its formal designation as a foreign terrorist organization by the United States. According to the Pakistani press, following Kansi's rendition to the United States, Bin Ladin warned the United States that, if it attempted his capture, he would "teach them a lesson similar to the lesson they were taught in Somalia."

BURMA

Burma is a faraway Southeast Asian land about which most people know very little. Veterans of World War II may recall the Burma Road or the Flying Tigers, but probably know nothing of the Burma of today. Images of shining pagodas, elephants, and flying fish at play along the mighty Irrawaddy River and Rudyard Kipling's famous "Road to Mandalay" may come to mind. But Burma's reality today has little in common with romantic legends. For most of its modern history following independence from Britain in 1948, in classic state terrorism style, Burma has been run by an army-controlled socialist regime that isolated the country, wrecked its economy, and repressed its diverse ethnic populations.

A massive and peaceful "people power" movement demanded an end to dictatorship in 1988. The army reacted violently and quickly to repress this movement and maintain the status quo. A new junta, the **State Law and Order Restoration Council (SLORC)**, seized direct power to quell any movement toward democracy. Crowds of peaceful protesters were machine-gunned by troops and thousands died. For a few days, events in Burma captured world headlines, but were soon replaced by other world events in more familiar locales. Global attention briefly picked up again in December 1991, when Daw Aung San Suu Kyi, the detained democracy advocate and leader, was awarded the Nobel Peace Prize.

Still, to most of the world, Burma remains mysterious and unknown. To further confuse the situation, the SLORC generals changed the country's official name in English to "**Myanmar**," a transliteration of the country's Burmese language name. This change, done by decree and without public consultation, was rejected and has not been recognized by Burma's democratic opposition. More confusion came when, in November 1997, the generals renamed their own junta the **State Peace and Development Council (SPDC)**, in hopes of improving their international image.

The people of Burma suffer under one of the world's most brutal and repressive regimes. The United Nations, world religious leaders from Pope John Paul to the Dalai Lama of Tibet, many governments, and human rights groups have urged an end to human rights violations in Burma. The military regime's response so far has been intensified abuse, such as murder, torture, rape, political imprisonment, and forced labor. There is no free expression or freedom of association in Burma, and the junta does not allow Burmese citizens a voice in the shaping of their own future.

The military regime allows and perhaps participates in an explosion of heroin production. Cease-fires with several ethnic opposition armies that have long traded drugs have allowed an estimated increase of nearly 400 percent in Burma's heroin production since the junta took power in 1988. Around the world, this flood of cheaper and purer heroin is causing a vast new wave of addiction. In recent years, approximately 60 percent of the heroin reaching the United States has been of Burmese origin. And in Burma itself, an estimated half million addicts are spreading an AIDS epidemic at a rate equaling the areas in Central Africa.

Burma plays a pivotal role in Asia's security, due to its strategic position linking South and Southeast Asia and bordering the continent's two most populous countries, China and India. Independent Burma had long pursued a policy of neutrality. To the alarm of many countries, the military regime is now increasingly dependent on China as a political ally and arms supplier. Fear of Chinese military influence in Burma is helping to spur a costly regional arms race, which diverts funds desperately needed for human development.

Pressing for increased international involvement with the military regime are people who argue that trade and tourism can promote respect for human rights.

Some claim that "constructive engagement" could convince the junta to fight drug trafficking and to reduce their reliance on China. A few declare simply that business and human rights are separate issues that should not be mixed. The junta itself, backed by a few Asian autocrats, asserts that it respects human rights in an "Asian" or "Burmese" context and those internationally recognized standards do not apply. Among these critical human rights issues is the detention of opposition figures by the SPDC. This was discussed in a 1998 State department briefing:

> Resolution of the political impasse in Burma will require real, substantive dialogue with the democratic opposition, including Aung San Suu Kyi and representatives of the ethnic groups. Arbitrary detentions are unjustifiable and will only worsen rather than solve the political crisis.

> We have protested these actions to the Burmese Government through our embassy in Rangoon. We will continue to work with like-minded countries to press the Burmese Government to take positive action, including the release of the individuals and the initiation of a genuine dialogue with Aung San Suu Kyi and other NLD leaders.[5]

The explosion in April of a parcel bomb at the house of a senior official in Burma's military-led government was the most significant terrorist event in Burma in 1997. The blast killed the adult daughter of Lieutenant-General Tin Oo, Secretary Number Two of the ruling State Law and Order Restoration Council. No group or individual claimed responsibility for the attack, but the Government of Burma attributes the act to Burmese antigovernment activists in Japan; the package bore Japanese stamps and postmarks. The Burmese expatriate and student community in Japan denies any involvement in the incident.

⊙ TERRORISM BYTE 9–2

BURMA, THE SOUTH AFRICA OF THE NINETIES

This small South-East Asian country, also known as Myanmar, has a democratically elected government, elected in May 1990 by 82 percent of the vote. The government, however, was prevented from taking office by a group of generals who call themselves SLORC, or State Law and Order Restoration Council. SLORC enforces its will by rape, forced labor, and torture. The democratically elected Prime Minister, Aung San Suu Kyi, winner of the 1991 Nobel Peace Prize, was under house arrest until 1996 (she remains under virtual house arrest, with her phone lines cut periodically, and unable to leave her house without fear of being physically attacked).

Burma has been a closed country for decades. In recent years, SLORC has begun encouraging both foreign investment and tourism. 1996 was declared "Visit Myanmar Year," and Western and Japanese companies, particularly oil companies, began pouring money into the country. Unocal, along with the French oil company Total, is building a major gas pipeline there. SLORC is helping keep costs low for the pipeline by using forced labor to build access roads. And SLORC either turns a blind eye or, more likely, actively helps while heroin pours out of Burma and onto our streets. Burma is the world's number one producer of heroin.

Many companies, including Levi-Strauss, Eddie Bauer, Liz Claiborne, Amoco, Reebok, Petro-Canada and Smith & Hawken have either refused to do business with SLORC or pulled out of Burma once they realized what was going on. A growing number of city and state governments in the U.S., including San Francisco, Oakland, New York City and the state of Massachusetts, refuse to do business with companies which have invested in Burma. In May 1997, the U.S. Government banned all new American investment in Burma. The U.S. Senate is considering even stronger measures.

Source: Patterns of Global Terrorism, 1997. United States Department of State, April 1998.

Does Constructive Engagement Work?

Investments in Burma by companies who claim that they can only influence the Burmese regime by investing in the country are under attack. South African Bishop Desmond Tutu and six other Nobel Prize winners, including the Dalai Lama, were refused entry to Burma in 1993, had the following to say on the subject of **constructive engagement**:

> As a South African, I can claim some expertise on the subject of constructive engagement. For years, some governments claimed that the best way to deal with the apartheid regime in South Africa was by continuing to talk and trade. This gradualist approach, they said, would persuade the white-minority regime to share power and end its flagrant abuses.

> Today the world knows what a failure that policy was. These ties gave the apartheid regime the political will and economic sustenance to continue its repressive policies. Only when serious sanctions started to take a significant economic toll on my country did the road to real reform begin.[6]

United States President Clinton transmitted to Congress a required report on conditions in Burma and U.S. policy toward Burma for the period from March 28, 1998 to September 28, 1998. U.S. statute (Public Law 104–208) requires that such reports be given to Congress every six months. That Congressional report, as summarized below, was highly critical:

> Plan for Implementation of Section 570 of Public Law 104–208 (Omnibus Appropriations Act, Fiscal Year 1997)

> CONDITIONS IN BURMA AND U.S. POLICY TOWARD BURMA FOR THE PERIOD MARCH 28, 1998–SEPTEMBER 28, 1998

> "The people of Burma continue to live under a highly repressive, authoritarian military regime that is widely condemned for its serious human rights abuses," the report says.

> "The reorganization and renaming of Burma's ruling military junta in November 1997, through which the former State Law and Order Restoration Council (SLORC) became the State Peace and Development Council (SPDC) did not herald significant policy changes."

> "The regime has made no progress in the past six months in moving toward greater democratization, nor has it made any progress toward fundamental improvement in the quality of life of the people of Burma. To the contrary, conditions have worsened with the regime rounding up and detaining over 900 opposition National League for Democracy (NLD) officials and supporters, including 200 Members-elect of Parliament," the report continues.

> According to the report, the Burmese economy is deteriorating due to "SPDC economic mismanagement, combined with spill-over effects from the Asian financial crisis."

"The government is reportedly virtually bankrupt with regard to foreign exchange reserves, holding an amount equal to only several weeks of imports. Inflation is increasing, while the kyat continues its downward slide against the dollar. Imported foodstuffs are growing more and more difficult to obtain. Both gasoline and diesel fuel are rationed to three gallons per vehicle per day. The military junta continues to dominate the political, economic and social life of the country in the same oppressive, heavy-handed way that it has since seizing power in September 1988 after harshly suppressing massive pro-democracy demonstrations," the report says.

"As a result of sanctions and the ongoing financial crisis in much of the rest of Southeast Asia, approvals of new foreign direct investment in Burma fell by 65 percent in FY 97/98, contributing to the financial collapse of the Burmese economy. U.S. and European investors continue to pull out of Burma due to the unfavorable political situation. While the government's own mismanagement contributes to the problem, the SPDC is unlikely to find a way out of the crisis unless political developments in Burma permit an easing of restrictions on lending by international financial institutions," the report continues.

U.S. policy toward Burma seeks progress in three key areas: democracy, human rights, and counter-narcotics, the report states.

"We have taken strong measures to pressure the SPDC to end its repression and move towards democratic government," the report says. "Since 1989, the United States has been unable to certify that Burma has cooperated in efforts against narcotics. The U.S. has suspended economic aid, withdrawn Burma from the General System of Preferences (GSP) and Overseas Private Investment Corporation (OPIC) programs, implemented an arms embargo, successfully opposed assistance from international financial institutions, downgraded our representation from Ambassador to Charge, d'Affaires, imposed visa restrictions on senior officials and their families, and instituted a ban on new investment by U.S. persons."

The United States remains engaged in multilateral diplomacy to encourage the Association of Southeast Asian Nations (ASEAN), Japan, Korea, China, the European Union (EU), and other nations to take similar steps and/or other actions to encourage progress by the SPDC, according to the report.[7]

Accounting for about 90 percent of Southeast Asian production and about half of the world's supply, Burma is the world's leading producer of illicit opium. Recent reports suggest increased methamphetamine production and distribution from Burma as well. Although the Burmese government has expanded its counternarcotics efforts over the past few years, the impact has been limited. While part of the problem is that the Burmese government does not control many of the ethnic groups that traffic in drugs, the government also does not make sufficient efforts at interdiction. There is also some evidence of corrupt elements in the military that may be aiding the traffickers, and there are signs that the Burmese encourage traffickers to invest in a multitude of development projects throughout the country.

The U.S. remains concerned about the commitment of the Burmese government to fight narcotics and about the potential damage that opium cultivation in Burma can inflict on the United States and the rest of the world. Against this backdrop, we have supported a small program, the Old Soldiers Project of 101 Veterans, Inc., in Burma to replace opium poppy cultivation with substitute, economically viable alternative crops. Despite impressive strides in a short period of time the Old Soldiers Project has not received permission from the Burmese Government to continue, and the project was suspended on September 15. [8]

Burma is a poor country, with an average per capita GDP of approximately $406, at a weighted exchange rate, perhaps double that in terms of purchasing power parity. Progress on market reforms has been mixed and uneven. Beginning in 1988 the government partly opened the economy to permit expansion of the private sector and to attract foreign investment. Though modest economic improvement ensued, since 1993 the pace of economic reform has slowed, and major obstacles to further reform persist. These include disproportionate military spending, extensive overt and covert state involvement in economic activity, state monopolization of leading exports, a bloated bureaucracy prone to arbitrary and opaque governance, poor education and physical infrastructure. In addition, due to international opposition and to the SPDC's unwillingness to cooperate fully with the IMF, SPDC access to external credit from the IMF, World Bank, and Asian Development Bank continues to be blocked by sanctions. In September 1998, the World Bank announced that Burma had defaulted on its loan repayments. The laundering of drug profits in Burma's legitimate economy is thought by some analysts to be extensive.

At the ASEAN meetings in Manila, in July 1998, U.S. Secretary of State Albright, with Foreign Minister McKinnon of New Zealand, led a discussion of the political impasse in Burma, which included representatives from Austria, Australia, Canada, Germany, Korea, Japan, the U.K. and Burmese Foreign Minister Ohn Gyaw. The ministers expressed their concerns over the deteriorating conditions in Burma and demanded a speedy, peaceful resolution to the situation and pressed for the immediate commencement of an SPDC dialogue with the democratic opposition, to include Aung San Suu Kyi. Secretary Albright has continued to actively promote international engagement with the SPDC toward an improved human rights climate.

It is clear that the SPDC is not eager to release its chokehold on the Burmese people, and the world's attention is often drawn away from such remote areas. The report to the U.S. government is seen a good first move in a game of chess that seems to be using the people of Burma as pawns. It is to be seen whether or not preoccupation with problems in Bosnia, Israel and Iraq will distract prompt diplomatic action by the major powers to right the situation in Burma.

In South Asia, many of the factions involved in the Afghanistan civil war, including large numbers of Egyptians, Algerians, Palestinians, and Saudis, continued to provide haven to terrorists by facilitating the operation of training camps in areas under their control. The factions remain engaged in a struggle for political and military supremacy over their countries and regions.

SOUTHEAST ASIA

Incidents of terrorism in Southeast Asia increased in 1997. Continuing defections from the Khmer Rouge to Cambodian forces reduced the threat from the terrorist group, but guerrillas in the Cambodian provinces have been responsible for deadly attacks on foreigners. The unstable political situation in Cambodia has led to marked political violence. The most significant act of terrorism there was a grenade attack on an opposition political rally in March, which left nineteen persons dead and more than one hundred injured, including a U.S. citizen. In October, the Secretary of State designated the Khmer Rouge as a foreign terrorist organization pursuant to the Antiterrorism and Effective Death Penalty Act of 1996.

CAMBODIA

Cambodia is located on the Gulf of Thailand, between Thailand and Vietnam. It is a tiny country, slightly smaller than Oklahoma. The country is a land of paddies and forests and dominated by the Mekong River. It has a population of about 11 million, ethnically composed of Khmer (90 percent), Vietnamese (5 percent), Chinese (1 percent), and other (4 percent) distribution. The religious preference is overwhelmingly Theravada Buddhist (95 percent). Cambodia was called Kampuchea under the disastrous rule of the Khmer Rouge

The Cambodian economy has been virtually destroyed by decades of war, but it is slowly recovering. Government leaders are moving toward restoring fiscal and monetary discipline and have established good working relations with international financial institutions. Growth, starting from a low base, was strong between 1991–96. Despite such positive developments, the reconstruction effort faces many tough challenges because of the persistence of internal political divisions and the related lack of confidence of foreign investors. Rural Cambodia, where 90 percent of about 9.5 million of the Khmer live, remains mired in poverty. The almost total lack of basic infrastructure in the countryside will hinder development and contributes to a growing imbalance in growth between urban and rural areas over the near term. Moreover, the government's lack of experience in administering economic and technical assistance programs and rampant corruption among officials slows the growth of critical public sector investment. The decline of inflation from the 1992 rate of more than 50 percent is one of the bright spots in Cambodia's return to a peacetime period. In a somewhat interesting and unusual move, the **Khmer Royal Armed Forces (KRAF)** was created in 1993 by the merger of the Cambodian People's Armed Forces and the two noncommunist resistance armies. (KRAF is also known as the Royal Cambodian Armed Forces, or RCAF).

Offshore islands and sections of the boundary with Vietnam remain in dispute and the maritime boundary with Vietnam is not clearly defined. Also, parts of border with Thailand are now in dispute, as its boundaries are also not clearly defined. Golden Triangle heroin being routed to the West gives Cambodia the possibility of becoming a major money-laundering center. High-level narcotics-related corruption reportedly involves the government, military, and police. There are small-scale opium, heroin, and amphetamine production operations in the country and a larger production system of high-grade marijuana for the international market.

Hard-liners based in the Khmer Rouge stronghold at Anlong Veng regularly launched guerrilla-style attacks on government troops in several provinces. Guerrillas are also suspected in two deadly attacks against ethnic Vietnamese civilians in Cambodia, but they have denied playing a role in the disappearance of two Filipino and two Malaysian employees of a logging company in 1997.

The death of former **Khmer Rouge** leader Pol Pot on April 15, 1998, in the Thai-Cambodian border area brings to an end one of the most chilling and bloody chapters of the twentieth century. During Pol Pot's three and a half years of rule over Cambodia, from 1975 to 1978, the Khmer Rouge killed as many as two million people through mass executions, starvation and slave labor. The genocide in Cambodia was the outcome of a complex historical development in which the pernicious ideo-

POL POT

The political activity of Pol Pot (Saloth Sar) (19XX–1998) began in post-World War II France, when Cambodia was part of its Indochina colony. The son of a relatively well-off peasant family, he received a government scholarship in1949 to study in Paris, where he gravitated with a number of his friends to the Stalinist circles around the French Communist Party. He returned to Phnom Penh in 1953, worked as a teacher and was involved in the start of the embryonic Communist Party in Cambodia. Police repression under the government of Prince Norodom Sihanouk, the country's first post-colonial ruler, forced the party leaders to flee the capital in 1963 and seek sanctuary in the remote rural areas of the country.

It was only after the American intervention in Cambodia during the Vietnam War that Pol Pot and the Khmer Rouge began to get wider support. From a badly organized, rag-tag force of less than 5,000 men in 1970, the Khmer Rouge expanded to an army of around 70,000. In April 1975, the Lon Nol dictatorship collapsed and Pol Pot came to power.

The peasant-based army and Khmer Rouge leaders carried out policies of an anti-working-class character, which had far more in common with fascism than socialism. With an economy in shambles, Pol Pot was unable and unwilling to organize the feeding of the cities; he ordered the evacuation of Pnomh Penh and other towns. The entire urban population of workers, intellectuals, civil servants, small shopkeepers and others were driven into the countryside to labor under very harsh conditions on irrigation schemes and other grandiose projects aimed at elevating agricultural production.

As highlighted by the film, "The Killing Fields," hundreds of thousands died of overwork, hunger and disease. Many more were executed in the course of the pogroms against all culture and intellectual life. Others died in the vicious factional disputes that erupted within the Khmer Rouge when its economic plans fell to pieces.

Shattering urban economic life and even traditional peasant agriculture finally led the Khmer Rouge to rely more on culturally and socially primitive layers of those living an essentially tribal existence. Under Pol Pot's leadership, the Khmer Rouge conducted a campaign of genocide in which an estimated more than 2 million people were killed during its four years in power in the late 1970s.

Source: An extract from "The Death of Pol Pot." SAIS/Asia Society Cambodia Policy Study Group. Internet.

---

logical influence of Stalinism came together with the military bloodbath carried out against the people of Indochina. Pol Pot will be little mourned by the people of Cambodia.

The fate of British mine-clearing expert Christopher Howes, allegedly kidnapped by the Khmer Rouge in March 1996, remains unresolved. Unconfirmed reporting suggested Howes was with forces loyal to Pol Pot, and some Cambodian officials expressed fears publicly that he had been killed. In May, Khmer Rouge leader Khieu Samphan denied any knowledge of Howes' whereabouts.

Incidents of terrorism in East Asia increased in 1997. Continuing defections from the Khmer Rouge to Cambodian forces reduced the threat from the terrorist group, but guerrillas in the Cambodian provinces have been responsible for deadly attacks on foreigners. The unstable political situation in Cambodia has led to marked political violence. In October, the Secretary of State designated the Khmer Rouge as a foreign terrorist organization pursuant to the Antiterrorism and Effective Death Penalty Act of 1996.[9]

The Khmer Rouge is a Communist insurgency that is trying to destabilize the Cambodian Government. Under Pol Pot's leadership, the Khmer Rouge conducted a campaign of genocide in which more than 2 million people were killed during its four years in power in the late 1970s. The Khmer Rouge is still engaged in a low-level insurgency against the Cambodian Government. Although its victims are mainly Cambodian villagers, the Khmer Rouge has occasionally kidnapped and killed foreigners traveling in remote rural areas. One to two thousand members of the Khmer Rouge operate in outlying provinces in Cambodia, particularly in pockets along the Thailand border. The Khmer Rouge may not be considered by many as a serious threat to destabilization of Cambodia yet again. But, some seventeen years and three Cambodian regimes later, the National Army of Democratic Kampuchea, as the Khmer Rouge military is known, continues to wage warfare and terrorism from scattered jungle bases of operation in an attempt to regain control of Cambodia and resume their utopian experiment. Although there have been large-scale defections from the Khmer Rouge to Cambodian Government forces since 1996, and the group suffered a significant split in 1997, it still may be considered dangerous.

THAILAND

The ancient Kingdom of Thailand (Sometimes referred to as Siam, but usually just Thailand) borders on the Andaman Sea and the Gulf of Thailand; southeast of Burma. It is slightly more than twice the size of Wyoming. This peaceful country has a population of almost 60 million. The ethnic groupings are Thai 75 percent, Chinese 14 percent, and other 11 percent. Religious affiliations are Buddhism 95 percent, Muslim 3.8 percent, Christianity 0.5 percent, Hinduism 0.1 percent, other 0.6 percent, who all seem to be harmonious. Thailand has had independence since 1238 A.D. and has never been colonized. A new constitution was approved in 1991 and amended in 1992.

One of the more advanced developing countries in Asia, Thailand depends on exports of manufactured goods, including high-technology goods and the development of the service sector to fuel the country's rapid growth, averaging 9 percent since 1989. Most of Thailand's recent imports have been for capital equipment and raw materials, although imports of consumer goods are beginning to rise. Thailand's 35 percent domestic savings rate is a key source of capital for the economy, and the country is also benefiting from rising investment from abroad. Prime Minister Chawalit's government is Thailand's seventh government in six years. It will probably continue Bangkok's pro-business policies and reemphasize Bangkok's traditional fiscal austerity.

The new government is beginning to address Thailand's serious infrastructure bottlenecks, especially in the transport and telecommunications sectors. Over the longer term, Bangkok must produce more college graduates with technical training and upgrade workers' skills to continue its rapid economic development. Thailand is a minor producer of opium, heroin, and marijuana. It is a major illicit transit point for heroin en route to the international drug market from Burma and Laos. Eradication efforts have reduced the area of cannabis cultivation and shifted some production to neighboring countries, and opium poppy cultivation has also been reduced. A drug money-laundering center, Thailand has a rapidly growing role in amphetamine production for regional consumption as well as increasing indigenous abuse of methamphetamine and heroin.

While there is little terrorism to report in this placid country, an appeals court in Thailand upheld the conviction and death sentence passed on an Iranian convicted of a 1994 plot to bomb the Israeli Embassy in Bangkok. The defendant, Hussein Dastgiri, has appealed to the Supreme Court. Also, Muslim separatist groups in southern Thailand carried out a series of bombings and other violent attacks in 1997. Bomb attacks in October killed seven persons, and the bombing of a Chinese religious festival in December killed three and wounded fifteen. Government authorities credited separatist groups with assassinating eleven policemen in a two-month period and blowing up a railroad in May.

VIETNAM

The Socialist Republic of Vietnam is a communist state made up from the former North and South Vietnams so well remembered from the Vietnam War. This country, war-torn for decades, is in Southeastern Asia, bordering the Gulf of Thailand, Gulf of Tonkin, and South China Sea, between China and Cambodia. It is slightly larger than New Mexico. After consolidation at the war's end, Vietnam has a population of over 75 million. The ethnic population distribution is: Vietnamese 85 percent–90 percent, Chinese 3 percent, with MuongTai, Meo, Khmer, Man and Cham making up the balance. Religions affiliations are (in descending order) Buddhist, Taoist, Roman Catholic, indigenous beliefs, Islam, Protestant, Cao Dai, Hoa Hao. Vietnam got its independence from France in 1945, when the French colonial forces were defeated. Its new constitution was approved in 1992.

Vietnam is a poor, densely populated country that has had to recover from the ravages of decades of war, the loss of financial support from the old Soviet Bloc, and the rigidities of a centrally planned economy. Substantial progress has been achieved over the past ten years in moving forward from an extremely low starting point. Economic growth continued at a strong pace with industrial output rising by 14 percent during 1996 and real GDP expanded by 9.4 percent. Foreign direct investment rose to an estimated $2.3 billion for the year, up by about 30 percent from 1995. These positive numbers, however, masked some major difficulties that are emerging in economic performance. Many domestic industries, including coal, cement, steel, and paper, reported large stockpiles of inventory and tough competition from more efficient foreign producers. Vietnam's trade deficit widened to $4 billion in 1996, up over 80 percent from just the previous year. While disbursements of aid and foreign direct investment have risen, they are not large enough to finance the rapid increase in imports and it is widely believed that Vietnam may be using short-term trade credits to bridge the gap. That is a risky strategy, one that could result in a foreign exchange crunch in the near term. Meanwhile, Vietnamese authorities continue to move very slowly toward implementing the structural reforms needed to revitalize the economy and produce more competitive, export-driven industries. Privatization of state enterprise remains bogged down in political controversy, while the country's dynamic private sector is denied both financing and access to markets. Reform of the banking sector is proceeding slowly, raising concerns that the country will be unable to tap sufficient domestic savings to maintain current high levels of growth. Administrative and legal barriers are also causing costly delays for foreign investors and are raising similar doubts about Vietnam's ability to maintain the inflow of foreign capital. Ideological bias in favor of state intervention and control of the economy is slowing progress toward a more liberalized investment environment.

Vietnam has disputes over maritime boundaries with Cambodia and is involved in complex negotiations over the Spratly Islands in the South China Sea. These are ongoing with China, Malaysia, the Philippines, Taiwan, and possibly Brunei. There are also unresolved maritime boundaries with Thailand and with China in the Gulf of Tonkin and disputed ownership of the Paracel Islands in the South China Sea, which are occupied by China but claimed by Vietnam and Taiwan. Offshore islands and sections of boundary with Cambodia are in dispute as well.

TERRORISM BRIEF 9-2
THE OLD GUARD PREVAILS

He may have won the war, but General Giap seems to have lost the plot. Now in his late eighties, the Vietnamese military hero who vanquished first the French and then the Americans recently told an audience that "caring for the nation and fighting foreign invaders are the duties of every generation" of Vietnamese. Like many of Vietnam's older generation, he probably finds it difficult to adjust to change. And yet he was called as a keynote speaker at an academic conference on international cooperation. The event, held in Hanoi in mid-July with the help of a $200,000 grant from America's Ford Foundation, was the first of its kind to be organized inside Vietnam.

More than 300 foreign scholars turned up. The foundation hopes it will open up debate in a communist country where Marxism-Leninism and "Ho Chi Minh thought" are still taught to schoolchildren. Yet General Giap's remarks were not the only sign of how far that debate still has to go. Apart from the standard summary of 4,000 years of Vietnamese history, the participants also heard from local professors about Ho Chi Minh's poetry and his "initial study on the way of writing foreign proper nouns." Foreign delegates, with their irritating tendency to come to conclusions at odds with the party line, were mostly ignored.

An American studying suburban development in Ho Chi Minh City was told that she could not hope to research the subject because she was not Vietnamese. Another American comparing rural resistance in China and Vietnam to economic reform was told there was no such thing in Vietnam—despite renewed unrest last year in the northern province of Thai Binh. Foreigners felt that they had been invited merely to provide window dressing for a feast of cultural self-congratulation. The conference overlapped with a meeting of the Party's powerful Central Committee, which concentrated on a future national cultural policy. After ten days of discussions, it declared that the object of all cultural activities was "to preserve Vietnam's cultural identity...for the building and defending of the socialist homeland."

Does this matter? When the Association of South-East Asian Nations meets in Hanoi in December, the delegates will find themselves in a country that rivals Myanmar and North Korea in its inability to speak the common intellectual language of East Asia. Despite Vietnam's attempts at economic integration with the region, it remains constrained socially and politically by the Communist Party. For example, Vietnam's universities have no political-science departments and no real experts on international relations. As a result, Vietnam is unable to take part in the academic forums on security that are increasingly a part of confidence-building in East Asia. The hope is that, with growing opportunities for Vietnamese scholars to travel abroad, and with more foreign research underway in Vietnam, that will change. Indeed, even five years ago it would have been impossible to hold any sort of international academic conference in Vietnam.

Yet the risk is that such progress will be slowed by a faltering economy: Vietnam has cut its target for economic growth this year, from 9 percent to under 7 percent because of the Asian turmoil. The signs are that the party will now try to bolster support through even more introspection and the contemplation of past glories. Indeed, its meeting ended with a call for a new campaign that would culminate in some sort of national conference in 2000. The subject will be national heroes; General Giap would be proud.

SOURCE: EDITORS, "UNCLE HO'S LEGACY," *THE ECONOMIST* (ECONOMIST NEWPAPERS, LONDON, JULY 25, 1998) P. 39.

Key growing areas in Vietnam cultivated 3,150 hectares of poppy in 1996, producing 25 tons of opium, making it a major opium producer and an increasingly important transit point for Southeast Asian heroin destined for the U.S. and Europe. Vietnam has a growing opium addiction problem, plus possible small-scale heroin production in-country. While there is little known terrorism in Vietnam, a Vietnamese court sentenced two persons to death and three others to life in prison for carrying out a grenade attack on the waterfront in Ho Chi Minh City in 1994, in which twenty persons, including ten foreigners, were injured. The five were part of the Vietnam Front for Regime Restoration, an antigovernment exile group based in the United States.

SUMMARY

The terrorism and violence generated in the areas we have covered in this chapter span the whole menu of scenarios. These range from individual acts (assassination of two presidents named Gandhi), religious hatred (the Hindus and Muslims and Sikhs), political genocide (Khmer Rouge), state terrorism (Burma) and all the way up to conventional and nuclear war possibilities. This strange and mysterious region has huge potential but many problems. Thailand alone stands calm and stable in the midst of such violence and terror. The former Indochina has suffered from wars, terror and destruction for over four decades and are beginning to make some progress, but with fits and starts. The situation between India and Pakistan, the nuclear armed giants of this region seem to be the biggest problem to face. Time will tell if these great nations, facing a situation every bit as dangerous as in the Middle East, can eventually come to some accommodation. The incredibly long histories of most of the nations in the region have created very long memories, as well as great hatreds and grudges. In the next chapter the student will observe many of the same issues and problems, which have been exacerbated by a serious economic problem on the Pacific Rim.

Terms to Remember

Indian National Congress	Kashmir and Afghanistan	HUA
SGPC	Khalistan	Afghanistan Mujahidden
ISI	LTTE	Colombo World Trade Center
SLORC	Myanmar	SPDC
constructive engagement	KRAF	Khmer Rouge
Islami Inqilabi Manaz	Shironami Gurudwara Prabandhak Committee	

Review Questions

Describe the conditions in the past that created the hatred between India and Pakistan.

How does Afghanistan stand in the friction between Pakistan and India on the Kashmir issue?

What is the major religion in Sri Lanka and how does that relate to strife in the region?

Why do you think that Cambodia had to go through such a horrible time of "the killing fields" from the Khmer Rouge?

Discuss the situation in existence in Burma and elaborate on the United States' stance regarding that problem.

Endnotes

1. Much of the background data contained in this chapter and woven into and throughout this book were extracted from web sites such as: The U.S. State Department of State *1997 Patterns of Global Terrorism* Report; The U.S. Department of State *Country Reports on Human Rights Practices*; The U.S. Department of State *Background Notes: Geographic Entities and International Organizations*; The U.S. Central Intelligence Agency *World Factbook;* and other government sources. We are, again, grateful for the presence of these sources and the information they have provided.

2. *Patterns of Global Terrorism, 1997*, United States Department of State, April 1998.

3. *Patterns of Global Terrorism, 1997*, United States Department of State, April 1998.

4. *Patterns of Global Terrorism, 1997*, United States Department of State, April 1998.

5. Press statement by James P. Rubin, Spokesman, September 8, 1998.

6. Bishop Desmond Tutu, press statement on the subject of constructive engagement.

7. The White House, Office of the Press Secretary, October 27, 1998.

8. The Secretary of State's Office's report to Congress, "Conditions in Burma and U.S. Policy Toward Burma for the Period March 28, 1997 to September 28, 1998."

9. *Patterns of Global Terrorism, 1997*, United States Department of State, April 1998.

CHAPTER 10

THE PACIFIC RIM

> *Efforts to categorize terrorism as a class or form of political violence are compli-*
> *cated by the fact that violence occurs on different levels of political interaction.*
>
> —*Martha Crenshaw*

OVERVIEW

The Pacific Rim, those countries which sweep in a long arc from Australia to Japan, has suffered a massive financial crisis. As they are major trading partners to the United States and the European Economic Community, the crisis has bought the world into turmoil. Many of these countries have also been suffering from wars, insurgencies, corrupt governments and right- and left-wing terrorists. As noted by the United States Secretary of State:

> There is a long way to go back to real equilibrium. President Clinton has outlined a clear path for ways [for] the international community—including the United States—to resolve this crisis and thwart future crises. There are lots of other ideas out there. They need careful evaluation; but time is passing, confidence is eroding quickly, and we need to act—now.
>
> America's interests are at risk, and we will continue to provide leadership in the recovery efforts. But responsibility also lies around the globe, firstly with other developed country governments, but also with those of developing countries, the private sector, and the international financial institutions. Some protest that the system is unfair. Yes, reforms to the system are necessary, but these cannot be allowed to become an excuse for avoiding the domestic reforms that are needed now.
>
> The task we all face is critical. At risk are the gains so many have worked to make over the past several decades—gains that are both economic and political. Restoring macroeconomic stability, strengthening national financial systems, improving the effi-

ciency of the international financial system, all these are tasks that will take immense amounts of energy on the part of the international community. Successfully meeting these challenges is critical to global prosperity and to each of our country's economic and political well being for years and decades to come.[1]

Complicating this problem is the impact of financial and political chaos, and the opportunities for terrorist groups to take advantage of the situation to forward their causes. This chapter will build on the previous analysis of the rest of Asia and discuss the way these individual countries are reacting in terms of their backgrounds and histories of terrorist actions. We start with the biggest country, in terms of population and production, China.

CHINA

No discussion of the Far East and the Pacific Rim can be undertaken without referring to the **People's Republic of China (PRC)**, the world's second superpower and most populous country. Bordered on the water by a coastline of over 10,000 miles, it includes the East China Sea, Korea Bay, Yellow Sea, and South China Sea. China is only slightly smaller than the United States. It protects borders along over 14,700 miles that include the countries of Afghanistan, Bhutan, India, Kazakstan, North Korea, Kyrgyzstan, Laos, Macau, Mongolia, Nepal, Pakistan, Russia (northeast), Russia (northwest), Tajikistan, and Vietnam. China is the world's fourth-largest country (after Russia, Canada, and U.S.), with a population of one and a quarter billion. The ethnic makeup of this world giant is; Han Chinese 91.9 percent; Zhuang, Uygur, Hui, Yi, Tibetan, Miao, Manchu, Mongol, Buyi, Korean, and "other" make up the remainder. While China is officially atheist, its traditionally pragmatic and eclectic. Daoism (Taoism), Buddhism, and Isalm are unofficially practiced by 2 percent to 3 percent of the population, and Christians number only about 1 percent.

China is an old and diverse society which was unified under the Qin or Ch'in Dynasty in 221 B.C. The Ch'ing Dynasty, the last, was replaced by the Chinese Republic in 1912. The People's Republic of China was established in 1949. Beginning in late 1978, the Chinese leadership has been trying to move the economy from a sluggish Soviet-style centrally planned economy to one that is more market-oriented but still within a rigid political framework of Communist Party control. To this end, the authorities switched to a system of household responsibility in agriculture in place of the old collectivization, increased the authority of local officials and plant managers in industry, permitted a wide variety of small-scale enterprise in services and light manufacturing, and opened the economy to increased foreign trade and investment.

The result has been a quadrupling of China's GDP since 1978. Agricultural output doubled in the 1980s, and industry also posted major gains, especially in coastal areas near Hong Kong and opposite Taiwan, where foreign investment helped spur output of both domestic and export goods. On the darker side, the leadership has often experienced in its hybrid system the worst results of socialism (bureaucracy, lassitude, corruption) and of capitalism (windfall gains and stepped-up inflation). Beijing thus has periodically backtracked, re-tightening central controls at intervals. In 1992–96 annual growth of GDP accelerated, particularly in the coastal areas–averaging more than 10 percent annually, according to official figures.

In late 1993, China's leadership approved additional long-term reforms aimed at giving still more play to market-oriented institutions and at strengthening the center's control over the financial system; state enterprises would continue to dominate many key industries in what was now termed "a **socialist market economy**." In 1995–96 inflation dropped sharply, reflecting tighter monetary policies and stronger measures to control food prices. At the same time, the government struggled to:

- collect revenues due from provinces, businesses, and individuals
- reduce corruption and other economic crimes
- keep afloat the large state-owned enterprises, most of which had not participated in the vigorous expansion of the economy and many of which have been losing the ability to pay full wages and pensions

From 60 to 100 million surplus rural workers are constantly adrift between the villages and the cities, many subsisting through part-time low-paying jobs. Popular resistance, change in central policy and loss of authority by rural cadres has weakened China's population control program, which is essential to maintaining growth in living standards. Another long-term threat to continued rapid economic growth is the deterioration in the environment, notably air pollution, soil erosion, and the steady fall of the water table, especially in the north. China continues to lose arable land because of erosion and economic development; furthermore, the regime gives insufficient priority to agricultural research. The next few years will witness increasing tensions between a highly centralized political system and an increasingly decentralized economic system. Rapid economic growth likely will continue but at a declining rate.[2]

China is a major transshipment route for heroin produced in the Golden Triangle and is experiencing a growing domestic drug abuse problem. There were no reported incidents of international terrorism in China in 1997, but **Uygur separatists** continued a campaign of violence. The Uygurs are a Chinese Muslim ethnic minority group concentrated in the Xinjiang autonomous region in far western China. In February 1997, Uygur separatists conducted a series of bus bombings in Urumqi that killed nine persons and wounded 74. Uygur rioting earlier in the month in the city of Yining caused as many as 200 deaths. Uygur exiles in Turkey claimed responsibility for a small pipe bomb that exploded on a bus in Beijing in March and which killed three persons and injured eight. In August, Uygur separatists were blamed for killing five persons, including two policemen. The Chinese Government executed several individuals involved in both the rioting and bombings. Beijing claims that support for the Uygurs is coming from neighboring countries, an accusation these countries deny.

In the calm since 1991, China seems to be relatively free from terrorist acts today. As this mighty country becomes less and less tightly controlled, and if the Asian economies are slow in recovering, the dissidents now in hiding may sow the seeds from which future discord or insurgent acts will bloom. With 60–100 million people without work, that potential is great. This ancient country demands careful study in the near future.

Hong Kong

Hong Kong again returned as a province of China on July 1, 1997. Hong Kong businesspersons and others had fled in droves from the island when this move was first announced several years ago, but many are returning to be where "the action is" in Asia. In a joint declaration, China promised to respect Hong Kong's existing social and economic systems and lifestyle. Hong Kong borders the South China Sea and mainland China and is about six times the size of Washington, D.C., scattered over more than 200 islands. The six and a half million people are an ethnic "mix" of Chinese 95 percent, other 5 percent. The people are religiously diverse, with the rough distribution of eclectic local religions at 90 percent and Christianity, 10 percent.

Hong Kong has long been the dynamic business and financial center of mainland Asia and a bustling free market with few tariffs or nontariff barriers. Natural resources are limited, and food and raw materials must be imported. Manufacturing and construction account for about 18 percent of GDP. Goods and services exports account for about 50 percent of GDP. Real GDP growth averaged a remarkable 8 percent. A shortage of labor continues to put upward pressure on prices and the cost of living. Prospects remain bright so long as major trading partners continue to be reasonably prosperous and so long as investors feel China will continue to support free market practices after the takeover. While terrorism has been virtually nonexistent, Hong Kong is a hub for Southeast Asian heroin trade, and is involved in transshipment and money laundering. There is also an increasing problem with indigenous amphetamine abuse.

TAIWAN (REPUBLIC OF CHINA)

The Republic of China (usually called Taiwan) borders the East China Sea, Philippine Sea, South China Sea and Taiwan Strait. It is north of the Philippines. It is a large island off the southeastern coast of China that is slightly smaller than Maryland and Delaware combined. The population of 21,699,776 is composed of Taiwanese 84 percent, mainland Chinese 14 percent and aborigine 2 percent. Religion is based on a mixture of Buddhist, Confucian, and Taoist 93 percent, Christian 4.5 percent and other 2.5 percent. Political pressure groups include the Taiwan independence movement, and various environmental groups. Debate on Taiwan independence has now become acceptable within the mainstream of domestic politics on Taiwan. Political liberalization and the increased representation of the opposition **Democratic Progressive Party (DPP)** in Taiwan's legislature have opened public debate on the island's national identity. Advocates of Taiwan independence, including within the DPP, oppose the ruling party's traditional stand that the island will eventually reunify with mainland China. Goals of the Taiwan independence movement include establishing a sovereign nation on Taiwan and entering the U.N. Other organizations supporting Taiwan independence include the World United Formosans for Independence and the Organization for Taiwan Nation.

Taiwan has a dynamic capitalist economy with considerable government guidance of investment and foreign trade and partial government ownership of some large banks and industrial firms. Real growth in GDP has averaged about 9 percent a year during the past three decades. Export growth has been even faster and has provided the impetus for industrialization. Inflation and unemployment are low. Agriculture contributes less than 4 percent to GDP, down from 35 percent in 1952. Traditional labor-intensive industries are steadily being moved off-shore and replaced with more capital and technology-intensive industries. Taiwan has become a major investor in China, Thailand, Indonesia, the Philippines, Malaysia, and Vietnam. The tightening of labor markets has led to an influx of foreign workers, both legal and illegal.

Taiwan is involved in complex dispute over the Spratly Islands with China, Malaysia, Philippines, Vietnam, and possibly Brunei; Paracel Islands occupied by China, but claimed by Vietnam and Taiwan. The Japanese-administered Senkaku-shoto (Senkaku Islands/ Diaoyu Tai) are also in disputed claims from China and

Victims of terrorist
attack on subway in
Tokyo, using sarin gas.
CP Picture Archive (AP
Photo/Asahi, Eiji Hori)

Taiwan. The island nation is tightly controlled and there is very little terrorism of any scope. Taiwan is considered an important heroin transit point and there seems to be a growing major problem with domestic consumption of methamphetamine and heroin.

JAPAN

Japan is a constitutional monarchy which became an independent state in 660 B.C. through the efforts of Emperor Jimmu. It is located in Eastern Asia, an island chain between the North Pacific Ocean and the Sea of Japan, east of the Korean Peninsula and is slightly smaller than California. With a population of over one hundred and a quarter million, Japan's appetite for fish is contributing to the depletion of these resources in Asia and elsewhere. Ethnic diversity is literally unknown in Japan, with Japanese 99.4 percent, and other 0.6 percent (mostly Korean). Religions are broken out with those who observe both Shinto and Buddhist 84 percent, and other 16 percent.

Government-industry cooperation, a strong work ethic, mastery of high technology, and a comparatively small defense allocation (roughly 1 percent of GDP) have helped Japan advance with extraordinary rapidity to the rank of second most powerful economy in the world. One notable characteristic of the economy is the collaboration of manufacturers, suppliers, and distributors in closely knit groups called **keiretsu**. A second basic feature has been the guarantee of lifetime employment for a substantial portion of the urban labor force, but this guarantee is slowly eroding. Industry, the most important sector of the economy, is heavily dependent on imported raw materials and fuels. The much smaller agricultural sector is highly subsidized and protected, with crop yields among the highest in the world. Usually self-sufficient in rice, Japan must import about 50 percent of its requirements of other grain and fodder crops. Japan maintains one of the world's largest fishing fleets and accounts for nearly 15 percent of the global catch.

For three decades overall real economic growth had been spectacular: a 10 percent average in the 1960s, a 5 percent average in the 1970s, and a 4 percent average in the 1980s. Growth slowed considerably in 1992–95, largely because of the aftereffects of overinvestment during the late 1980s and contradictory domestic policies intended to wring speculative excesses from the stock and real estate markets. Growth picked up in 1996, largely a reflection of simulative fiscal and monetary policies as well as low rates of inflation and social disorder. As a result of the expansionary fiscal policies and declining tax revenues due to the recession, Japan currently has one of the largest budget deficits as a percent of GDP among the industrialized countries. The crowding of habitable land area and the aging of the population are two other major long-run problems.

The trial of the leader of Aum Shinrikyo, the group responsible for the sarin gas attacks on the Tokyo subway system in 1995, continued. A government panel decided not to invoke an Anti-Subversive Law to ban **Aum Shinrikyo**, concluding that the group poses no future threat, although the group continued to operate and to recruit new members. In October, the Secretary of State designated Aum Shinrikyo as a foreign terrorist organization pursuant to the Antiterrorism and Effective Death Penalty Act of 1996. The trials of Aum Shinrikyo leader, Shoko Asahara, and other members of the sect continued in 1997. Prosecutors reduced the number of victims listed in the indictments against Asahara to speed up the proceedings, which entered their second year. In addition to the murder charges stemming from the March 1995 sarin nerve gas attack on the Tokyo subway system, Asahara faces 16 other charges ranging from kidnapping and murder to illegal production of drugs and weapons. Nine former Aum members pleaded guilty or received sentences from 22 months to 17 years for crimes they committed on behalf of Asahara; one Aum member was acquitted of forcibly confining other cult members.

Despite the legal proceedings against Asahara and other members, what remained of Aum following the arrests of 1996 continued to exist, operate, and even recruit new members in Japan in 1997. In January a government panel decided not to invoke the Anti-Subversive Law against Aum Shinrikyo, which would have outlawed the sect. The panel ruled that Aum posed no future threat to Japanese society because it was financially bankrupt and most of its followers wanted by the police had been arrested.

Several members of the Japanese Red Army (JRA) were arrested in 1997. Five members were convicted in Lebanon on various charges related to forgery and illegal residency and sentenced to three years in prison. Another member, Jun Nishikawa, was captured in Bolivia and deported to Japan, where he was indicted for his role in the 1977 hijacking of a Japanese Airlines flight. Four of the five JRA members arrested in February remain in custody in Lebanon. The Japanese Government is seeking extradition of the five to Tokyo to face terrorism and other charges upon their release.

Tsutomu Shirosaki was captured in 1996 and brought to the United States to stand trial for offenses arising from a rocket attack against the U.S. Embassy in Jakarta, Indonesia, in 1986. He was convicted in Washington, D.C., of assault with the intent to kill, attempted first degree murder of internationally protected persons, and attempted destruction of buildings and property in the special maritime and territorial jurisdiction of the United States. He was also convicted of committing a violent attack on the official premises of internationally protected persons. (In February 1998 he was sentenced to 30 years in prison.) Seven hardcore JRA members remain at large.

The Japanese economy is still unstable at this point and the financial and political situation, while calmed, is ripe for more antigovernment dissatisfaction. There is great potential for sophisticated attacks on both travelers and leaders.

Much of East Asia is trying to rid itself of signs of "crony capitalism." The Philippines, which has long delighted in being different, is engulfed in a storm over the resurgence of some old cronies under its new president, Joseph Estrada. Many Filipinos are still haunted by the corruption and brutality of Ferdinand Marcos, the dictator toppled by a "people power" revolution in 1986. Hence, concern rose at the sight earlier this month of Eduardo Cojuangco sweeping up to the head office of the country's brewing and food giant, San Miguel, in a Mercedes to reclaim his post as chairman after a boardroom coup. Mr. Cojuangco was Marcos's main chum and during his rule assembled a vast business empire. The two were so close that when Marcos fled Manila Mr. Cojuangco left in the helicopter with him. Though exiled to the political wilderness by two subsequent presidents, Corazon Aquino and Fidel Ramos, Mr. Cojuangco has not only moved back into the boardroom of San Miguel but is also fighting for control of a large block of shares in the company. These were seized from him in 1986 by Mrs. Aquino's administration after allegations that they had been acquired illegally through his links with Marcos. Many believe the tycoon will soon have his shares back.

Although Mr. Estrada says the affairs of San Miguel have nothing to do with him, it is hard for him to avoid controversy. Mr. Cojuangco was the chief financier behind Mr. Estrada's expensive election campaign and is now head of the president's political party. The two are so close that many wonder who is calling the shots. Mr. Estrada has also been criticized for his efforts (so far unsuccessful) to have Marcos's body moved from cold storage in the director's home town of Batac, in the northern Philippines, and buried in Heroes Cemetery in Manila. The president has also said he would try to seek a settlement with the Marcos

family—led by his redoubtable widow, Imelda—to recover money plundered from goverment coffers. This creeping rehabilitation of the Marcos family worries many Filipinos. Imelda's daughter Imee now serves as a congresswoman, and her son, Ferdinand who is usually known as "Bong Bong," is a newly elected provincial governor.

Mr. Estrada's officials have added to the controversy by saying they want to reach a settlement over a 25.6 billion peso (611 million dollars) tax-evasion case against Lucio Tan, a Chinese-Filipino tycoon also once linked to Marcos. The secretive Mr. Tan is widely reckoned to be the country's richest man. He owns Phillipines Airlines, Asia Brewery, Fortune Tobbaco, and Allied Bank. Mr. Tan was also a financial backer of Mr. Estrada's presidential campaign. But, as Edgardo Esdpiritu, the finance minister, admits, the pressure on the government to reach agreement with Mr. Tan is clear: it faces a budget deficit of 70 billion pesos and Mr. Tan's contributions would come in handy.

The problem of how to deal with the Marcoses and their cronies is turning into a far more awkward issue than expected. One of the reasons given by Mr. Estrada for abolishing the presidential commission on good government, a body established by Mrs. Aquino to reclaim assets believed to have been acquired illegally during the Marcos years, is compelling—it has not worked. Even the influential Roman Catholic Church believes it is best to draw a line through the Marcos years and move on. But having the old dictator's family and their cronies restored to positions of power and influence may prove too much for even forgiving Filipinos.

SOURCE: EDITORS, "THE MARCOS MOB IS BACK," THE ECONOMIST (ECONOMIST NEWPAPERS, LONDON, JULY 25, 1998), PP. 38–39.

PHILIPPINES

The Republic of the Philippines is situated in Southeastern Asia, on a long archipelago between the Philippine Sea and the South China Sea. It is east of Vietnam and is slightly larger than Arizona. The scattered population of over seventy-six million has an ethnic mix of Christian Malay 91.5 percent, Muslim Malay 4 percent, Chinese 1.5 percent, and other 3 percent. The major religions are: Roman Catholic 83 percent, Protestant 9 percent, Muslim 5 percent, Buddhist and other 3 percent

The Philippine economy, primarily a mixture of agriculture and light industry, continued its fourth year of recovery in 1996, led by growth in exports and investments. Officials have targeted 7.1 percent–7.8 percent growth for 1997 after achieving an estimated 5.5 percent growth in 1996. The government is continuing its economic reforms to enable the Philippines to move closer to the development of the newly industrialized countries of East Asia. The strategy includes improving infrastructure, overhauling the tax system to bolster government revenues, and moving toward further deregulation and privatization of the economy.

In the Philippines, implementation of a peace agreement with insurgent groups has reduced fighting with government forces, but former members of these insurgent groups and members of Philippine terrorist organizations continued attacks. Foreigners number among their victims. In October, the Secretary of State designated one of these terrorist organizations, the **Abu Sayyaf Group**, as a foreign terrorist organization pursuant to the Antiterrorism and Effective Death Penalty Act of 1996. In China and Indonesia, separatist violence not targeted against foreigners but having the potential to claim foreigners as collateral victims continued.

The Philippine Government began implementing terms of a peace agreement signed with the **Moro National Liberation Front (MNLF)** in 1996 and continued efforts to negotiate a peace agreement with the **Moro Islamic Liberation Front (MILF)**. The government began the process of integrating former MNLF rebels into the Philippine military. A cease-fire with the MILF reduced the fighting that peaked in the first half of 1997, but the two sides failed to agree on a more comprehensive arrangement. The MILF and the smaller Abu Sayyaf Group continue to fight for a separate Islamic state in the southern Philippines.

Muslim rebels in the southern Philippines conducted several attacks against foreigners in 1997. A Japanese businessman and three Filipino boys were kidnapped in June by members of the Abu Sayyaf Group. A rescue operation by the Philippine military freed the Japanese hostage. A German businessman was abducted in September by former members of the MNLF and was released in December only after his family agreed to pay the kidnappers some $100,000 in ransom. In separate incidents in October and November, former MNLF members abducted priests, one Irish and one Belgian, and demanded payment of funds owed them under a government rehabilitation program. The captives were released after the government agreed to expedite disbursal of the funds.

The government had mixed results in its efforts against communist rebels in 1997. Philippine police captured some key communist personnel. The government again suspended negotiations with the political arm of the communist **New People's Army (NPA)** in late 1997 following an upsurge in small-scale attacks by the NPA on police and government units. In May communist guerrillas ambushed a vehicle owned by a subcontractor of a major U.S. firm, killing two Filipino employees. In December, New People's Army rebels ambushed two army detachments and abducted 21 paramilitary troops in Davao City in Mindanao. The government pledged to revisit the issue of a dialogue with the communists if acceptable circumstances could be met. Another communist rebel group, the Alex Boncayao Brigade, is not participating in peace talks with the government.

In September a previously unknown group calling itself the Filipino Soldiers for the Nation claimed responsibility for grenade attacks at bus terminals in Manila and Bulcalan City that killed six persons and wounded sixty-five. Press reports indicated the group claimed to favor a constitutionally prohibited second term for President Ramos. The Ramos government strongly condemned the attacks and blamed them on unknown provocateurs.

The Philippine government continued its strong support for international cooperation against terrorism and actively sought to build a multilateral approach to counter-terrorism in regional and other forums. The government cooperated in providing additional personnel to protect likely targets and to identify, investigate, and act against likely terrorists. The government quickly responded when an U.S. company experienced what appeared to be an NPA attack on one of its subcontractors in Quezon, and officials at the cabinet level met with company executives to discuss what could be done to improve security.

The Moro Islamic Liberation Front rebels handed over Italian priest Luciano Benedetti to Philippine government officials in Maguindanao, Mindanao, several hours after he was released by his captors to MILF forces.

The guerrilla arm of the Communist Party of the Philippines (CPP), an avowedly Maoist group, was formed in December 1969 with the aim of overthrowing the government through protracted guerrilla warfare. Although primarily a rural-based guerrilla group, the NPA has an active urban infrastructure to carry out terrorism: it uses city-based assassination squads called sparrow units. The NPA derives most of its funding from contributions of supporters and so-called revolutionary taxes extorted from local businesses. The NPA is in disarray because of a split in the CPP, a lack of money, and successful government operations. With the U.S. military gone from the country, the NPA has engaged in urban terrorism against the police, corrupt politicians, and drug traffickers. The NPA has an estimated strength of several thousand members operating throughout the Philippines. It is unknown whether it receives any external aid.

In September 1998, a previously unknown group calling itself the **Filipino Soldiers for the Nation** claimed responsibility for grenade attacks at bus terminals in Manila and Bulcalan City that killed six persons and wounded sixty-five. The group claimed to favor a constitutionally prohibited second term for President Ramos. The Ramos government strongly condemned the attacks and blamed them on unknown provocateurs.

The Philippines has had a long and complex dispute over the Spratly Islands with China, Malaysia, Taiwan, Vietnam, and possibly Brunei. It has also laid claim to the Malaysian State of Sabah. The Philippine growers export locally produced marijuana and hashish to East Asia, the U.S., and other western markets, and the country serves as a transit point for heroin and crystal methamphetamine to Western countries.

INDONESIA

Indonesia, the former Dutch East Indies, is situated in Southeastern Asia, on an archipelago between the Indian Ocean and the Pacific Ocean. It has a varied population of almost two hundred and ten million in land area of slightly less than three times the size of Texas. Independence from the Netherlands came in 1949, when Indonesia became legally independent from the Netherlands.

Indonesia enjoyed a decade and a half of peace in the 1950–1960 timeframe, but its political fortunes shifted significantly in 1965, following a leftist coup attempt against President Sukarno, the republic's first leader. Within days, the army executed the leaders of the coup, but its aftermath brought a wave of violence. Rightist gangs, encouraged by military commanders, killed tens of thousands of alleged communists. By 1966, an estimated 500,000 people had been killed in the unrest. The events of 1965 and 1966 left President Sukarno severely weakened. In 1966, he was forced to transfer key political and military powers to then General Suharto, who had led the military defeat of the coup. In 1967, the legislative assembly named Suharto acting president, removing Sukarno from power.

With the backing of the military, Suharto quickly proclaimed a New Order in Indonesian politics, concentrating on policies of economic rehabilitation and development. Using advice from Western-educated economists, Indonesia grew steadily, transforming itself from an agricultural backwater to a highly diversified manufacturing and export-driven state. Per-capita income levels rose from $70 in 1966 to $900 in 1996, while the proportion of the population living below the poverty line declined from 60 percent to an estimated 11 percent over roughly the same period. The government instituted further economic reforms in the early 1980s, liberalizing trade and finance and expanding foreign investment and deregulation. Trade and investment boomed as a result; Indonesia's economy grew more than 7 percent annually from 1985 to 1996.

Suharto, his family, and his friends benefited greatly from the economic expansion. Critics claim the president regularly used his position to provide subsidies and regulatory relief for the companies of his children and friends. Suharto's family controls an empire valued anywhere from $16 billion to $35 billion in industries ranging from hotels and transportation, to banks and automobiles.

The country's economic prosperity, however, did little to affect the political freedom of the average Indonesian. Beginning with the 1965 coup, Suharto's security forces jailed hundreds of activists for speaking out against the government; many were eventually tortured and killed in prison.

In the mid-1970s, Suharto moved quickly to stop what he saw as a leftist move to make the colony of East Timor independent after Portugal abandoned the territory. Fearing creation of a state that could destabilize surrounding provinces, Suharto sent in troops to crush the movement and annexed East Timor. Thousands of people died during the fighting or later starved to death.

The United States cut off some military assistance to Indonesia in response to a November 1991 shooting incident in East Timor involving security forces and peaceful demonstrators. In 1996, government forces swept through East Timor again, this time after a series of guerrilla attacks on security personnel. The government takeover of the Indonesian Democratic Party's East Timor headquarters in July of that year triggered serious rioting in Jakarta. Human rights officials say that 5 died and 149 were injured in the attack. Twenty-three people were reported missing.

Despite the corruption and human rights abuses, Suharto continued to stay in power into 1998. His grip on power started deteriorating the year before, when Thailand announced the devaluation of the baht in July 1997, a move that caused the value of Indonesia's currency—the rupiah—to drop as much as 80 percent at one point. Foreign investors fled and many companies, adversely affected by the currency devaluation, went bankrupt. Like other Asian countries, Indonesia's banks were hit especially hard; by January 1998, 16 banks had their operations suspended. As the country negotiated with the International Monetary Fund over the terms of its $43 billion bailout package in early 1998, riots began to erupt over rising food prices, gradually intensifying despite violent police efforts to put them down.

In March, the **People's Consultative Assembly**, a legislative body largely appointed by the president himself, reelected Suharto to a seventh term. Student protests broke out, and calls mounted for him to step down. In May, riots and looting turned violent as tens of thousands of students demonstrated in Jakarta and other parts of the country. Hundreds perished in clashes with security forces in Jakarta. In a show of resistance, students occupied the country's parliament grounds, demanding the president's resignation. On May 21, Suharto bowed to the pressure and resigned, naming the Vice President B.J. Habibie as his successor.

Within days, Habibie pledged to lift restrictions on political parties and hold open elections as part of a package of reform measures intended to liberalize life in Indonesia and revive political activity that had been stifled for more than four decades.

The moves did little to quell the unrest. Throughout the summer of 1998, student demonstrators continued to demand the resignation of President Habibie, claiming that the government had done little to stem the country's economic crisis or spiraling high prices.

In November 1998, student-led protests for democracy in Jakarta turned violent after a harsh crackdown on demonstrators killed at least five students and two others. Rioting ensued as demonstrators burned shops across the city and set cars ablaze. At least sixteen were killed over a period of several days.[3]

To add to the mounting problems in this troubled country, a thousand fires were burning at the end of February 1998 in the rainforests of East Kalimantan, the Indonesian part of the island of Borneo. It was only three months since monsoon rains finally put out the last of the devastating fires on the island. Those fires burned from July to November 1997, destroyed 15,000 square kilometers of forest and covered a huge area of Indonesia, Malaysia, Singapore and Brunei with choking smog. The pollution forced schools and airports to close and made thousands of people ill with breathing problems. Every one of these fires was started deliberately. It was a manmade disaster, but by whom, and why?

In another major problem, the U.S. welcomed the Indonesian government's establishment of a broad-based fact-finding team last August to investigate the causes of the May riots and the rapes of ethnic Chinese women. In November, the team, which included representatives from the government, the Indonesian military (**ABRI**), the police, and nongovernment organizations, released their report. Despite "reservations" registered by some members, and the fact that investigators, victims, witnesses, and family members face anonymous death threats and other forms of intimidation, the factfinding team issued a credible, balanced report under difficult circumstances.

The report found three patterns to the riots, ranging from local and spontaneous to those aggravated by provocateurs and deliberately stimulated. This included involvement by elements of the military. The report called for further investigations and recommended that Lt. Gen. Prabowo and all others involved in cases of kidnappings of political activists be brought before a military court. The report also verified that 85 acts of violence targeted primarily against ethnic Chinese women occurred, including rapes, torture, sexual assaults, and sexual harassment during the riots.

It was declared crucial, in order to restore credibility and confidence, that the Indonesian government implement the team's recommendations, including further investigation of military leaders and others alleged to have fomented or participated in the violence. It was strongly urged that the Indonesian government take steps to prevent intimidation and threats of violence against investigators, witnesses, and their families and that those responsible for all these acts should be held accountable.[4]

Sovereignty over Timor Timur (East Timor Province) is disputed by Portugal and not recognized by the U.N.. The two islands are in ownership dispute with Malaysia. Indonesia is an illicit producer of cannabis largely for domestic use, with a possible growing role as transshipment point for Golden Triangle heroin. Separatist groups in East Timor apparently continued to target noncombatants and were involved in several bomb-making activities in 1997. In Irian Jaya, an attack allegedly by the separatist **Free Papua Organization** against a road surveying crew, in April 1997, left two civilians dead. East Timor terrorists apparently continue to target nocombatants and were involved in several bomb-making activities in 1997. If Indonesia is unable to stabilize its economy, it will become a powder keg and may see opposition groups committing escalated violence and terrorism.

Two explosions sank the Greenpeace protest ship Rainbow Warrior in Auckland, New Zealand.CP Picture Archive (AP WideWorld Photos)

AUSTRALIA

Located on the Oceania continent, the Commonwealth of Australia is slightly smaller than the United States. It is the world's smallest continent but sixth-largest country. Its population of 18,438,824 lies concentrated along the eastern and southeastern coasts. The ethnic makeup is as follows: Caucasian 95 percent, Asian 4 percent, aboriginal and other 1 percent. Religious affiliations are: Anglican 26.1 percent, Roman Catholic 26 percent, other Christian 24.3 percent. Australia became an independent member of the British Commonwealth in 1901.

Australia has a prosperous, western-style capitalist economy, with a per capita GDP above the levels found in highly industrialized west European countries. Rich in natural resources, Australia is a major exporter of agricultural products, minerals, metals, and fossil fuels. Commodities account for about 60 percent of the value of total exports, so that a downturn in world commodity prices can have a big impact on the economy. The government is pushing for increased exports of manufactured goods, but competition in international markets continues to be severe. Australia has suffered from the low growth and high unemployment characterizing the OECD countries in the early 1990s, but the economy has expanded at reasonably steady rates in recent years. In addition to high unemployment, short-term economic problems include a balancing of output growth and inflationary pressures and the stimulation of exports to offset rising imports.

Australia has had very little terrorist activity on an annual basis and it is not too difficult to explain some of the possible reasons for this. Not the least is the fact that Australia is a huge country with a population that would not be considered dense by world standards. This means that population is a tight community where anonymity for an attacker is virtually impossible. As crime is so low, there is difficulty in attackers "melting into the background." Fleeing the scene with any speed would be problematic, as air travel is subjected to a system of sophisticated checks. Escape by auto would be slow and apprehension relatively easy.

A few terrorists attacks, by our definitions, have occurred in Australia's past. In 1966, a parcel bomb exploded prematurely in a Melbourne mailroom. The intended target was believed to be a major pro-Yugoslav supporter. A letter bomb campaign from the Middle East in 1975 injured a press secretary at the Queensland State Premier's office. There was also a bombing outside the Hilton Hotel in 1978, where the Commonwealth heads of government were staying. Another was the assissination of Turkish Consul General Sarik Ariyak in December 1980. Then there was 1982 bomb extortion against Woolworth, a retail chain.

SUMMARY

The Pacific Rim has become a major trading block, both import and export, for the rest of the world. The importance of this group of nations is reflected by its impact on the trading exchanges around the globe during the recent financial crises. Governments and economies are varied in this vast area of island and continental nations. The giants, China, Japan and Korea, are changing and their populations are feeling the effects. The next chapter will take the student on a tour of Central and South America, where terrorism strikes closest to the United States. While religious and left-wing terrorism seems to prevail in the other hot spots we have discussed, the dictatorship of right-wing leaders seems to be the *"plate du jour"* for the Latin American countries.

Terms to Remember

PRC	socialist market economy	Uygur separatists
DPP	keiretsu	Aum Shinrikyo
JRA	Abu Sayyaf Group	MNLF
MILF	NPA	Filipino Soldiers for the Nation
People's Consultative Assembly	ABRI	Tasmania
	Free Papua Organization	

Review Questions

Explain why there is so little terrorism in China.

Describe the organization and operations of Aum Shinrikyo and what it is most famous for.

What do you think will ever happen in regard to Taiwan becoming rejoined with China?

The Philippines are seeing a resurgence of terrorism; what is the reason?

Australia has almost no terrorism. What do you think are the reasons for that?

Endnotes

1. Again, the authors have appreciated the background and statistical data from web sites such as: The U.S. State Department of State, *1997 Patterns of Global Terror* Report; The

U.S. Department of State, *Background Notes: Geographic Entities and International Organizations*; The U.S. Central Intelligence Agency, *World Factbook* and other government sources.

2. U.S. Department of State, Secretary Albright, "Meeting the Far East Crisis: What Should Governments Do?"

3. Extracted from article by Geoge Wehrfritz, *Newsweek*, April 13, 1998, pp. 24–30.

4. Tim Ito, washingtonpost.com staff (c) Copyright 1998, The Washington Post Company.

5. U.S. Department of State Office of the Spokesman, press statement by James P. Rubin, spokesman November 4, 1998. *Indonesia-Report by Fact-Finding Team.*

CHAPTER 11

LATIN AMERICA

Hope betrayed arrays herself in bombs.

—Graffitti, Université de Provence.

OVERVIEW

In our attempts to define terrorism, the experience of the Central and South American countries tends to have significant differences from those activities found in countries in Western Europe and the Middle East. Many of the Latin states have suffered from what was described as state terrorism, with death squads that have been brought into play by extreme right wing, authoritarian governments. A definition worth considering is that put forward by the United States Department of Defense: "the calculated use of violence or the threat of violence to inculcate fear; intended to coerce or to intimidate governments or societies in the pursuit of goals that are generally political, religious, or ideological."

This definition was carefully crafted to distinguish between terrorism and other kinds of violence. The act of terrorism is defined independently of the cause which motivates it. People employ terrorist violence in the name of many causes. The tendency to label as terrorism any violent act of which we do not approve is erroneous. Terrorism is a specific kind of violence. It therefore begs the question about the state involvement in systematic abuse of human rights and the tacit support given to unofficial death squads by military juntas in many Central and South American countries. The so-called **Banana Republics**, joked about in the early part of the twentieth century, became serious problems when they experienced revolutions and insurgencies in the 1970s and 1980s. The former Soviet Union and other left wing causes often backed these efforts in order to destabilize the area and break the support of dictators by the United States.

This chapter will start with the most prominent terror movements in Central America, from their developmental stages after the Mexican revolution of 1910, and the changes in typical terror tactics in South America. Drug dealings by the

Colombian, Mexican and other cartels (narco-terrorism), and the oppressive regimes in Uruguay, El Salvador, Argentina and others will be discussed. The horrors associated with Latin American death squads will be explored, along with the conditions, tactics and distinctive characteristics of Latin American terrorism.

CENTRAL AMERICA

MEXICO

We start with the United States' closest neighbor to the south, Mexico. In the late 1990s, this country is a far cry from a century ago. The Revolutionary Party has been in power since the revolution of 1910, and the country has undergone economic growth and seen rapid social and economic advances for middle and upper class members of Mexican society. A major issue facing the Mexican government is the land dispute surrounding the Chiapas region in southern Mexico. The Mexicans have experienced unprecedented economic growth, but there has been a failure to properly distribute wealth and a lack of social reform. As a result, Mexico remains a country of "haves and have nots." In addition to Chiapas, other regions have experienced guerrilla warfare or, as the Mexican government portrays them, terrorist movements. These are located in the regions of Oaxaca and Hidalgo, Vercruz and Puebla. Immortalized from the days of the revolution, Emilio Zapata, who was killed in 1919, is lauded by the peasantry of south Mexico as their true hero. Using Zapata as a symbol of revolutionary righteousness, the Zapatista movement is waging an armed struggle for land rights in the Chiapas region.

Zapatista National Liberation Army (ELZN)

By far the best known of the groups operating within Mexico, the **Zapatista** violently appeared on the world scene in 1994. They fomented an armed uprising against the Mexican government to protest the distribution of land in the region. This movement better fits the definition of a guerilla movement than a subversive terror organization. But the group uses terror tactics to achieve notoriety as well as political aims. The Zapatista burst onto the national scene as a result of the political and economic alliance between Mexico, the United States and Canada. In the latter two countries, the pros and cons of the North American Free Trade Agreement (NAFTA) were debated; in Mexico, some went to war over it. As we have seen in so many conflicts, the issue surrounding the uprising was land. Mexicans who farmed the land and eked out their living in that fashion were granted land for their families. This ended with NAFTA, when the Mexican government stopped the land distribution program. Armed and angry men from Chiapas came out of the hills and attacked the cities. The response from the Mexican government to this localized and popular uprising was to send in the military. Chiapas became a region patrolled and controlled by the Mexican Army. Many of the problems facing Mexico revolve around the stumbling economy in 1994 and the slow rate of recovery. The erosion of the ruling Institutional Revolutionary Party's power has also contributed to the continuing unrest.

In 1995, 30,000 Mexican soldiers intent on the destruction of the ELZN guerillas invaded the region of Chiapas. The exercise was a failure, as the ELZN disappeared into the hills of Chiapas, much like the Vietcong, who knew their regions so well. The soldiers continue to surround Realidad, believed to be the center of Zapatista operations. To appeal for their rights to the land and a cessation of the violence, Bishop Samuel Louis Garcia has acted as a mediator between the ELZN, the people of Chiapas and the Mexican authorities.

Right-Wing Violence

More disturbing are extreme right-wing attacks against the ELZN and its supporters by a movement calling itself **Peace and Justice**. This group pledges its support to the Institutional Revolutionary Party and operates as a death squad in the Chiapas region. The viciousness of the right-wing attacks seems to have the support of the military as well as the local police authorities, and this has led to beatings, murders and the mass evacuation of entire villages. Active units pledging support for the government and finding support from the police have the trappings of state-sponsored terrorism. The student will recall that this involves the systemic and purposeful creation, by a political regime, of mass fear by violent means, and/or by the threat of such violence. The purpose of the systematic exercise of such publicly visible violence is to maintain, legitimize, or strengthen the social and administrative control of the state. The activities of Peace and Justice seem destined to be part of the fabric of Mexican society for this region. By generating significant fear, this right-wing group is able to influence the Mayan Indians of Chiapas.

Popular Revolutionary Army (EPR)

The EPR organization probably ranks second in strength to the Zapatista movement. With its base and origins in the southern states of Oaxaca and Guerrero, it gains support from the mainly poverty-stricken villages of those areas. The topography of the region, forested mountains and rugged terrain, makes an ideal home base for a guerrilla force. The EPR is a left-wing group considered by the Mexicans to be several movements operating under a single banner. EPR attacks have been sporadic and often without a clearly understood objective. Armed ambushes against federal police and military convoys are the primary actions of EPR. Their strength and size has yet to be determined with any precision, but the group claims over 20,000 guerrillas in the southern states. Support for the group has also come from an outside source, which may well be responsible for arming them with modern Russian-made weaponry. In response to the logistics and training it has received from Peru's Marxist Shining Path, the EPR set up a Mexican Support Committee for the Popular War in Peru. Sustained operations have been difficult, and whether the group has the ability to employ effective tactics to disrupt or alter government policy is questionable. Attacks on the outskirts of Mexico City have occurred and communiqués have been issued to target the "fat cat" capitalist businesses.

Other movements are surfacing in the poorer regions of Mexico as a result of the country's economic woes and the perception that the poor are getting poorer and the rich getting richer. Such groups as the Revolutionary Army of Popular Insurgence, and the Armed Front for the Liberation of the Marginalized People of Guerrero, may be following the Zapatista uprising as means of gaining concessions from the government. It is unclear whether the Mexican military can contain more than one guerrilla army at a time. Currently fully occupied with the Chiapas region, it would seem incapable of handling another simultaneously.

End of the Decade

As Mexico stumbles toward the second millennium, the growing discontent and likely trouble from insurgent groups, especially in the poorer regions of the country, cannot be discounted. Unrest has reached the cities, and the abuses of paramilitary police produce the same results in cities as the Zapatista have in rural areas. Mexico currently has neither an effective means to deal with violence and corruption within the ranks of its police force, nor the capability to deter any terror organizations.

GUATEMALA

Communist influences in Guatemala during the last forty-five years have done much to further the violation of human rights to the individuals opposed to the many dictatorships and juntas that have come to power. During the cold war years, this influence was particularly strong. The United States assisted in the military overthrow of Guatemala's communist regime in 1954, but the series of right-wing military governments that followed did nothing to initiate reforms in the region; rather, they focused on campaigns against communist infiltration. With so much oppression in the country, the peasantry began to respond with such movements as the Rebel Armed Forces (FAR) which began to take shape in the early 1960s and was the precursor to the Guatemalan National Unity (URNG) which was established in 1982. The military had little success in repressing such movements and, with the arrival of **URNG**, embarked on a campaign of state-sponsored terror. The military was unleashed, death squads were formed and operated clandestinely, and military and security police openly committed murder and torture. The resulting exodus from the region gradually gained international attention. The military leaders of Guatemala were desperate to remain in power, and to this end they employed the tactics of state-sponsored terror against their own people. A "scorched earth" policy was employed in many instances as whole villages, their lands and crops were destroyed. Torture of suspected communists was commonplace and the methods of torture were gruesome in the extreme. Human rights in Guatemala and past United States support for the regime are issues for the student to ponder, as are questions regarding the level of involvement by the U.S. government in such political murders, torture and human rights abuses.

Ⓞ TERRORISM BYTE 11–2

MONSIGNOR JUAN GERARDI CONDERA

Guatemala and its rebels had signed a peace deal in 1996; however, this did not eradicate all the violence that permeates the country. On Sunday April 26, 1998, two days after he had released a report on human rights violations he was beaten to death by a lone assailant as he returned to his home. Gerardi was the Bishop of Guatemala and the coordinator of the Archbishop's Human Rights Office (ODHA). Monsignor Gerardi was the driving force behind the project for the Recovery of Historical Memory (REMHI), which he had created to shed light on the war's human rights violations. The killer had access to his house and car and was, his colleagues believe, the subject of a death squad attack. Witnesses saw unknown men in two trucks hanging around the parish house the night of the killing, another trademark of the death squads that had killed with impunity during the 36-year conflict. Geradi's report entitled "*Guatemala: Never Again*" documented 55,021 cases of human rights abuses occurring during the conflict, placing 80 percent responsibility on the Guatemalan Army.

Source: War Called Peace, "*Death of a Bishop,*" Piet van Lier 1998, Internet.

Impunity

The abuses and atrocities perpetrated in the name of the state have rested on a system of impunity, which can be defined "freedom from accountability for criminal wrongdoing or freedom from other legal sanctions." The impunity system in Guatemala is conducted by several simple mechanisms. Primarily, the state denies any state-sponsored violence and secondly, those that would have made claims of torture and rights abuse have simply "disappeared." Such disappearances make it difficult to bring any judicial action against Guatemala. In the sixteen years leading up to 1990, it is estimated that over 100,000 Guatemalans were killed and possibly another 40,000 disappeared without a trace. The government has a veneer of democracy, but its ability to control the powerful military is doubtful, especially when it comes to human rights abuses. The peace accord, finalized in 1996, brought an end to thirty-six years of internal fighting, and Guatemalans began returning to their villages from neighboring countries.

State-sponsored terrorism in Guatemala has fostered a populace with a shared set of experiences of systemic human rights violations. It is a populace not only cynical of the formal, institutional applications of justice, but one that has experienced extralegal "justice" in the fight for social control and social transformation of Guatemalan society.[1]

The Civil War

The first thorn in the side of successive oppressive military governments was the Rebel Armed Forces (FAR), which began limited guerilla operations as far back as 1962. Over the years, the movement grew among the indigenous groups and expanded to include the Guerilla Army of the Poor (EGP) in 1972 and the Organization of People in Arms (OPRA). With the merging of these three guerilla movements, all with the same causes and complaints, the Guatemalan National Unity Group (URNG) was formed. Many villages were totally destroyed and entire populations killed in the operations conducted by the military. In some part, their actions typified those used by the military in Vietnam, collectively called pacification. A "scorched earth" policy was employed. By targeting the civilian population in the Guatemalan countryside, the military assumed they would stop support of the guerilla army. Since the signing of the 1996 Peace Accords, there have been many attempts to bring justice to bear in Guatemala. Amnesty International has been prominent in detailing human rights abuses believed perpetrated by the military and the death squads. This has led to attacks against prominent church leaders in Guatemala to try to silence criticism.

By the end of 1998, climatic changes in the region prompted the government to suspend parts of their constitution. Following the wrath of Hurricane Mitch, which decimated several Central American countries, including Guatemala, the government of Alvaro Arzu suspended two Articles of the country's constitution, Articles Six and Twenty-Six. This is believed to be a direct result of the looting and violence in the cities following the hurricane and the government's fear of a resurgence of terrorism.[2] Article Six protects Guatemalans from detention or imprisonment without cause or in the absence of a court order, and Article Twenty-Six guarantees the right of freedom of travel. Such severe measures may return Guatemala to a repressive government. This volatile country should be carefully watched in the next century.

HONDURAS

As has been evidenced throughout Central America, the paranoia which gripped the United States during the Cold War years of the 1960s was played out in its support of countries ripe for communist influence. Honduras has benefited from decades of military support from the United States, and has been involved, through the 1980s, in fighting with the invading Sandinistas and in hunting down rebel Contra bases.

Morazanist Patriotic Front (FPM)

This small, extreme left-wing terror group was violently opposed to United States intervention and support of the right-wing political government in Honduras. It has targeted United States military personnel. The group, which is not particularly well organized, is believed to have been supported by Cuba. It has carried out bomb attacks on military buses carrying United States service personnel, and in 1989, claimed responsibility for an incident in which three United States servicemen were wounded. Attacks since then have been sporadic and ineffectively executed.[3]

⊙ **TERRORISM BYTE 11-3**

THE MORAZANIST PATRIOTIC FRONT (FPM)

The FPM is a radical, leftist terrorist group that first appeared in the late 1980s. Attacks on U.S., mainly military, personnel in Honduras made to protest U.S. intervention in Honduran economic and political affairs. The FPM claimed responsibility for attack on a bus in March 1990 that wounded seven U.S. servicemen. Claimed bombing of Peace Corps office in December 1988; bus bombing that wounded three U.S. servicemen in February 1989; attack on U.S. convoy in April 1989; and grenade attack that wounded seven U.S. soldiers in La Ceiba in July 1989. The strength of the FPM is unknown, but it was probably relatively small, with ties to former government of Nicaragua and possibly Cuba.

EL SALVADOR

As in Mexico, the natives of El Salvador have been engaged in an ongoing demand for land rights, dating back nearly seventy years. Much of El Salvador's economy was based on its coffee production and export, which was controlled by a select and influential group of families. The first sign of protest dates back to the first quarter of the twentieth century and a campaigner from the Central American Communist Party, Augustin Farabundo Marti. His goal, like that of the Chiapas of Mexico, was not the overthrow of the government but the redistribution of the wealth from the land on an equitable basis. By 1930, the country was under the military control of General Martinez, who sided with the society elite coffee owners. Marti was arrested in a military crackdown on his movement and was subsequently executed by firing squad. The peasants were not organized in sufficient numbers to mount any sort of insurgent response. The military sought to purge the country of peasant "subversives" and went on a killing spree which accounted for over 30,000 deaths. In 1981, there were 12,501 murders in El Salvador.

El Salvador in the late 1960s and 1970s provides yet another example of extreme right-wing terror being used as a government tool to eradicate opposition. Again death squads became the norm, and two specific groups were formed, one covert and the other overt to protect wealthy landowners and to spread fear among the peasants. The commander of the El Salvador National Guard in 1968 formed the **ORDEN**. This was an intelligence-gathering organization to amass information. It went beyond information gathering; it was also kidnapping and murdering peasants. In attempting to analyze and define terrorism, some scholars believe that the actions of death squads are not terroristic in nature. However, the actions of terrorist or guerilla organizations spread fear, disorder and uncertainty within the ruling government and the country as a whole. Repression by death squads or paramilitary groups has the same effects.

Periods of relative peace were interrupted by violence against the peasantry by the death squads, which operated both clandestinely and openly. The violence was brought to a halt in 1992 with a peace agreement. Liberal views made one a target for death squads, and even priests and nuns were murdered. Also targeted were outspoken labor leaders as well as politicians. Throughout the 1980s, fear was pervasive throughout El Salvador.

◯ TERROR BYTE 11–4

NEW WAVE OF POLITICAL TERROR

On October 31, 1993 a wave of what are considered politically motivated killings occurred. Four killings in five days, which resulted in the church warning that a new wave of political terror may be imminent, similar to that of the death squads of the 1980s. Two of the victims were leaders of the former guerilla movement, the Farabundo Marti National Liberation Front, and a couple who were believed to be former guerilla soldiers. Although there was no conclusive evidence the United Nations mission had stated that a dozen other killings were almost certainly carried out by death squads for political reasons. The assassination of Francisco Velis on a busy street in San Salvador as he took his daughter to a day care center was clearly a political crime. Velis was a former guerilla commander and a member of the governing committee of Farabundo Marti. Farabundo Marti became a political party when the civil war ended.

Source: *New York Times*, A–7, November 1, 1993.

NICARAGUA

This small Central American country of 4.5 million has been embroiled in what can best be described as a struggle between superpowers. Nicargua has had a leadership with close ties to the United States and its military training institutions for the better part of the twentieth century. The country has also been involved in the sale of drugs for weapons, and has brought into disrepute the activities of the Central Intelligence Agency (CIA). The National Guard of Nicaragua was modeled after and trained by the United States military in the years prior to WW II. The United States committed support to the regime of Anistasio Garcia and successive generations of his family up until 1979. It seemed of no particular concern to the United States administration what political ideology Garcia espoused, so long as it was not communist. In fact, he held power with corrupt associates and used repression to great effect. He was also an avid anticommunist, which very much appealed to the United States.

Anistasio's corrupt government and its repressive tactics were eventually overthrown by a Communist-inspired revolutionary movement called **Sandinista**. The Sandinista National Liberation Front (FLSN) had been waging a guerilla war against Samoza Anastasio since the start of the 1970s. The cold war was not a distant memory for the United States and military assistance was provided to the Anastgsio government to fight the Sandinistas. The Sandinistas, with Soviet assistance, seized power in 1979. Now the stage was set for the United States to support what the Nicaraguan government would call rebels, while the Soviet bloc would support the Sandinista government. The Reagan government was committed to mitigating any communist influences on its doorstep and promptly poured aid into the rebel Contra movement in its attempt to dislodge the Sandinistas.

Fund Raising

Aside from the problems of the guerilla war in Nicaragua, a far bigger scandal was being unraveled in the halls of the Pentagon. Questions arose concerning the level of involvement the government of the United States had in drug trafficking in exchange for weapons to the **Contras**. There have been many sensational journalistic pieces pointing a finger at the CIA and the administration. The Kerry Committee Report of April 1995 holds some interesting facts in its findings. The subcommittee found that the Contra drug links included:

- Involvement in narcotics trafficking by individuals associated with the Contra movement
- Participation of narcotics traffickers in Contra supply operations through business relationships with Contra organizations
- Provision of assistance to the Contras by narcotics traffickers, including cash, weapons, planes, pilots, air supply services and other materials, on a voluntary basis
- Payment to drug traffickers by the United States State Department of funds authorized by the Congress for humanitarian assistance to the Contras, in some cases after the traffickers had been indicted by federal law enforcement agencies on drug charges, in others while traffickers were under active investigation by these same agencies[5]

There is no doubt that those involved in these drug schemes on the United States side hoped to expunge any pending legal indictments in return for assistance to the rebel Contras. The level of exploitation by the drug traffickers was purely self-serving and certainly not ideologically driven.

When examining the infrastructure that was in place in the 1970s for the movement of illegal narcotics through Central America to the United States, it was a simple shift to include weapons into the operation. This was a method used by the Sandinistas to bring Cuban weapons into Nicaragua. Supply and staging areas abounded along the Nicaraguan border with Costa Rica, and most of the neighboring governments, which supported the actions of the Sandinistas, offered them safe haven and the opportunity to transfer drugs and weapons for their cause. When the Sandinistas gained power, the gun running did not cease. In fact, all that changed was the final user. The suppliers now had El Salvadoran rebels as customers, and not the Sandinistas.

One name has become synonymous with the Contras in the 1980s, Lieutenant Colonel Oliver North, who at the time "managed" Contra operations on the Southern Front. Evidence in the Kerry findings relates also to a United States national living in Costa Rica. John Hull, an Indiana farmer, had moved to Costa Rica, and bought large tracts of land. The area was known as Hulls Ranch, and happened to include six airstrips that were ideal for drugs and weapon smuggling. Hull helped the CIA with military shipments to the Contras and was also heavily involved in transshipments of drugs from Colombia. Added to this was the fact that the state department was signing contracts with companies that were either under investigation or had been indicted on narcotics smuggling charges. These companies were used to make military hardware drops to the Contra rebels.

PANAMA

Formerly under Spanish rule, this tiny strip of land between the Pacific and the Atlantic became a province of Colombia, before gaining its independence in 1903. Famous for the Panama Canal, which was under the control of the United States until the late 1970s, Panamanians have been a largely rural nation. The country has seen many varied forms of military governments over the past century, the most notorious being that of General Manuel Noriega, who became president of Panama in 1983. From the time he came to power, he ran a corrupt government and made millions of dollars from drug trafficking to the United States and from diverting aid funds. He controlled the public with strong-arm tactics and death squads. In 1988, he was indicted by a Florida grand jury on charges of racketeering and drug running. Up until 1989, Noriega continued to act with impunity. However, after the death of a United States Marine officer, when he overturned the results of a democratic election, President George Bush gave the almost unprecedented order for United States troops to invade Panama and restore the elected president. They seized Noriega and handed him over to United States marshals. He then stood trial and was sentenced to forty years in prison, where he languishes today. Some think the effort to restore democracy in Panama was more about trying to stem the endless flow of drugs into the United States and to bring Mr. Noriega to trial for his drug trafficking.

SOUTH AMERICA

COLOMBIA

To most students, the name Colombia conjures up one simple word: drugs. The U.S. Department of State characterizes the country as one of the most dangerous in the world to visit. Marijuana and cocaine have been a product of Colombia for the past forty years, but the market for drugs did not take off until the wealthy and middle classes in the U.S. began abusing them. Cocaine became the drug of choice, and the opportunity for expansion to a North American market was huge. Drugs in Colombia are controlled in two regions of the country, Medellin and Cali. These two "families" control nearly 80 percent of Columbia's distribution.

Violence and intimidation in Colombia center around the drug trade. Terrorism, therefore, becomes a byproduct of the drug trade and a means of control and power. Extortion, kidnapping, and murder are all hallmarks of the drug cartels. In a country where the economics are dictated by drug barons, anarchy is not far away. It is difficult to appreciate the enormous wealth that comes from the machinations of the drug trade. Drug barons are known to have utilized outside "sources" to assist their own internal security services. The economy of Colombia seems to be drug dependent, and eradicating the drugs from the region would be simpler if there was a legal economy able to produce an income similar to that of the drug trade. Several have been attempted, but the demand for drugs makes growing coca a better alternative.

Revolutionary Armed Forces of Colombia (FARC)

This terror group is considered the largest and best equipped of the terror organizations in Colombia. An extreme left-wing, communist-inspired movement, the **FARC** aspires to the overthrow of the Colombian government. It first came to notice in 1966 as a military wing of the Colombian Communist Party. Formed on rough military outlines, its members engage in a broad scope of activities. In a country where kidnapping is as commonplace as drinking a cup of coffee and might be considered the largest growth industry, the FARC targets the government and military. Its income is derived from drug trafficking as well as armed robberies, kidnappings and extortion. This group is anti-United States and its campaign resembles that of Cuban-style revolution. Its membership of active terrorists is believed to number around 7,000. With widespread support in rural areas, it has definite links to organized drug trafficking and also carries on external activities in Ecuador, Panama and Venezuela.[6]

The high number of attacks on military police, civil servants and members of government has given rise to a movement of death squads. Unable to effectively control the terrorists and drug barons by democratic process, some police and military officers have formed underground units, by way of a response, to target and destroy the terrorists. Colombia's drug cartels have had assistance in training their private security teams provided by mercenaries from Britain and Israel in paramilitary-style training schools uncovered by the Colombian Secret Police (DAS) near Puerto Boyaca.[7]

◯ TERRORISM BYTE 11–5

REVOLUTIONARY ARMED FORCES OF COLOMBIA (FARC)

The FARC is the largest, best trained, and best equipped guerrilla organization in Colombia. Established in 1966 as a military wing of Colombian Communist Party, its goal is to overthrow the government and ruling class. Organized along military lines; it includes at least one urban front. FARC has been anti-United States since its inception. It conducts armed attacks against Colombian political and military targets. Many members pursue criminal activities, carrying out kidnappings for profit and bank robberies. Foreign citizens often are targets of FARC kidnappings. The group has well-documented ties to narcotics traffickers.

FARC has an estimated 7,000 armed combatants and an unknown number of supporters, mostly in rural areas of Colombia, with occasional operations in Venezuela, Panama, and Ecuador. Its profitable criminal activities allow it to operate without the need for external aid.

National Liberation Army (ELN)

Formed in 1963, the ELN, smaller and less organized than FARC, carries on a campaign against the government. It is predominantly a Marxist inspired group with membership of about 3,000 fighters. Similar to FARC the group is anti-United States, and frequently engages in the profitable tactic of kidnapping. Usually the target is a businessman from a foreign company working in Colombia. In addition, it targets U.S. and foreign installations for bomb attacks.

Kidnapping

Kidnapping takes place in Columbia with such frequency that the Colombian government has an anti-kidnap program in place. Colombian law prohibits families and companies from negotiating with guerillas for release of the captives. However, in October 1998, a strange occurrence took place in a remote mountain region, when a Canadian businessman working for the Canadian-owned Terramundo Drilling Company in Colombia made an exchange of hostages. The original kidnap victim was Ed Leonard, of British Columbia. In secret dealings between the company and the guerillas Norbert Reinhart exchanged himself for the original kidnap victim on October 6, 1998. Whether the Canadian Embassy or the government took any leading role in this action is not clear; however, FARC is still holding Mr. Norbert hostage. Mr. Norbert's company is involved in mining for huge gold deposits in the region. No mention of any ransom has been made;[8] however, that is the normal course of events in this dangerous Latin American state.

Right-Wing Death Squads

The rise to prominence of the **death squads** in Colombia appears to have had the tacit support of both the government and military. Many of these defense groups sprang up in the 1960s and 1970s in response to terrorist activities against wealthy landowners by the FARC. Over the years the groups, which tended to operate in select areas, moved from defensive to offensive strategies and began to attack suspected members of FARC and to intimidate peasant villagers believed to be helping the FARC.[9] In regions such as Central Magdelena, drug cartels began buying up rich tracts of land, and this was most directly responsible for transforming the self-defense units into right-wing death squads.[10]

O TERRORISM BYTE 11–6

NATIONAL LIBERATION ARMY (ELN)—COLOMBIA

This rural-based, anti-United States, Maoist-Marxist-Leninist guerrilla group was formed in 1963. Attempted peace talks with the government ended in May 1992. The ELN periodically kidnaps foreign employees of large corporations and holds them for large ransom payments. ELN conducts frequent assaults on oil infrastructure and has inflicted major damage on pipelines. Extortion and bombings are tactics against United States and other foreign businesses, especially the petroleum industry. ELN forces coca and opium poppy cultivators to pay protection money and attacks the government's efforts to eradicate these crops. The ELN is reported to have at least 3,000 members, operating in the Colombian border regions of Venezuela. As far as it is known the ELN receives no external aid.

The student should not lose sight of the real issue in the rise of death squads and the need for terrorist actions in this country. For the Colombian drug lords, the end most certainly justifies the means. In a country so heavily dependent on the production and export of drugs, the methods used, which terrorize the populace, are not intended as means to overthrow or replace a political system. Their efforts are aimed at maintaining the status quo for their own benefit and dissuading police, judges and politicians from taking action against drug traffickers.

International Links

The Saudi dissident millionaire Usama bin Laden is not known to have any links with Latin American terrorist groups. However, one of his associates, a member of Egypt's largest militant group, Jammaa Islamiyya, was arrested in Bogota, Colombia in early November 1998. He was subsequently released by Colombian authorities and deported back to his country of origin, Ecuador. The question to carefully consider is, why would such a high ranking and high profile terrorist, be in Latin America? It may be assumed that he was either studying the United States embassy as a potential target or negotiating a meeting with FARC or ELN to set up trade deals involving drugs for weapons.

PERU

Peru is often remembered only for its fabulous Inca villages and high mountains. History tells us that an Inca chief named Tupac Amaru and his Inca followers overcame their colonial Spanish masters in the latter half of the seventeenth century. The country has been under the control of military juntas throughout much of this century, but civilian rule returned to Peru in the 1980s. Peru suffers from two sources of indigenous state terrorism with the Sendoro Luminoso (Shining Path) and the **Tupac Amaru Revolutionary Movement (MRTA)**.

Sendoro Luminoso (Shining Path)

The **Shining Path** movement has its origins in the university city of Aucayacu, in the upper Huallaga region. It is led by Abimael Guzman, who received his indoctrination and training in China in 1965, at the start of the Chinese Cultural Revolution. His time in China taught him how to set up and organize clandestine political and terrorist activities against the democratic state. On his return home, he became the leader of the pro-Chinese faction of the Peruvian Communist Party. Guzman was working high in the Andes Mountains as a university lecturer studying the exploitation suffered by Peru's Indians. He had no trouble drawing parallels with the Chinese peasants who had fought for Mao Tse Tung three decades earlier. He recruited his students into the Maoist Party and sent them to agitate in the Indian villages.[11] His movement went underground in 1976 and began its campaign of terror and insurgency in 1980.

In 1976, while the Peruvian government was trying to restore the democratic processes and the economy of the country, Guzman and his Shining Path followers were training with automatic weapons. He and his followers were of the belief that Peruvian society had to be torn down, and a classless society formed to replace it. Guzman and his followers started out as the saviors of the poor of Peru. That was to quickly change as their Marxist style became similar, in its approach to the natives, to that of the Khmer Rouge in dealing with the Cambodians. In merging the extreme teachings of Chairman Mao with the philosophy of Che Guevara[12] a dangerous hybrid emerged. Like the Khmer Rouge, Guzman and his guerillas set about the destruction of the country by intimidating villagers into joining his movement. Those who refused were killed. The group quickly became a cult of mass murderers, feared for their savagery throughout Peru. Guzman aimed to overthrow the democratic government and replace it with a Marxist dictatorship built in his own image. Over the next 14 years, their reign of terror took the lives of 25,000 Peruvians and resulted in over $20 billion in damage to the country's infrastructure.

Shining Path terrorist include a number of female operatives, and they have been known to use children to deliver bombs to public buildings and police stations. Guzman's philosophy and ideals spread farther than just in Peru; he had goals of reuniting the old Inca Empire, and his terrorists threatened not only Peru, but Ecuador, Colombia, and Bolivia. Guzman was believed to be invincible by his supporters and was called the Fourth Sword of Marxism.[13] This belief was to be dispelled by his capture in September 1992. During the 1980s, terrorist activity was so prevalent that villagers were fleeing to the urban slums of big cites such as Lima to escape the ravages of Shining Path. International observers feared that the democratic government in Peru would not be able to deal with the onslaught from Shining Path.

The Peruvian police captured Abimael Guzman in 1992. With his capture, the movement stumbled and began to disintegrate. The Peruvian government, led by President Fujimori, is determined to overcome both narcotics trafficking and terrorism in Peru and seems to have the overwhelming support of the people. Prior to Guzman's capture, several other key members of Shining Path were behind bars. No doubt information gathered during their interrogations assisted in Guzman's apprehension. Fujimori's democratic administration and the revival of the country's economy have done much to defeat the terrorist threat, which, considering the meager counterinsurgency training available to the barely equipped security police, is quite surprising.

Tupac Amaru (MRTA)

The second of Peru's terrorist movements takes its name from a legendary Inca leader. Successful police operations and arrests decimated it. With the country heading towards elections in 1993, the levels of terrorism began to pick up, and by 1996 both the MRTA and Shining Path were resorting to campaigns of terror once again. The Shining Path was not able to deliver the same number of guerillas to the campaign as previously, and the numbers of combatants was significantly lower. Following the principles of Carlos Marighella, written three decades previously, urban terrorism was beginning to take shape.

Victor Polay formed the Tupac Amaru in 1985. A traditional Marxist/Leninist movement, its goal was the overthrow of imperialism in Peru. The group had no external support and its membership was considerably lower than that of Shining Path. Polay, however, was captured in 1992 and sentenced to life in prison. In a spectacular display of support and solidarity for Polay, Tupac Amaru terrorists attacked the Japanese ambassador's residence in Lima during a diplomatic Christmas celebration in December of 1996. They took hundreds of guests, mainly diplomats, as hostages. In front of the world press corps assembled outside, Tupac Amaru demanded the release of Polay. With the strong support of the population, Fujimori stood his ground and did not give way to the threats from the terrorists. Though pressure from the government of Japan for a quick resolution to the impasse was being applied, everyone settled down to win.

The assault on the ambassador's residence took place when about 400 guests were starting a meal. The celebration was short lived, as over a dozen heavily armed guerillas stormed the grounds, firing weapons in the air. The attackers were calling themselves the Edgar Sanchez Special Forces, and were commanded by Comrade Edigirio Huerta. The assault began at about 8:00 P.M. on December 17, 1996. The situation was delicate, as a large number of foreign dignitaries and ambassadors were being held hostage, including the ambassadors of Austria, Brazil, Bulgaria, Cuba, Guatemala, Panama, Poland, Romania, South Korea, Spain and Venezuela, a truly significant group. The government of President Fujimori would now be put to the test as they had steadfastly refused to negotiate with terrorists, so the implications both political and economic would rest on the outcome.

The terrorist demands were as follows:

1. They would shoot hostages unless their demands were met
2. Release of some 500 imprisoned colleagues
3. Transfer of freed prisoners and hostages to a jungle hideout, with the last hostage to be released at the final destination
4. Payment by the Peruvian government of a "war tax" in an unspecified amount
5. An economic program to aid the Peruvian poor[14]

The End of the Crisis

After dragging on for four months, the drama was eventually brought to its climax when the Peruvian special security forces tunneled into the compound and rescued the hostages. Up until the middle of March, negotiations had been proceeding well, and the number of hostages had dwindled to seventy-one, as concessions were made. However, Fujimori would not budge on the main demand, which was the release of the imprisoned members of Tupac Amaru. At 3:20 P.M., April 22, 1997, the rescue began. The Peruvian government had authorized a rescue mission and tunneling, which had taken weeks, was now completed, allowing security forces to gain entry

Peruvian soldiers help hostages escape from the Japanese ambassador's residence in Lima, Peru. CP Picture Archive (AP Photo/ Eugene Hoshiko)

for a surprise strike. Explosions and gunfire were heard from inside the compound, and plumes of smoke curled up from the residence windows. Within forty minutes, the 140-man rescue team had secured the residence, all fourteen guerillas were dead and twenty-five hostages were injured. Two members of the rescue team died in the operation. This incident brought congratulations to the Fujimori government for his stance against terrorism from leaders around the world. But it was also a harsh reminder of the vulnerability of political leaders to terrorist attacks.[15]

BOLIVIA AND BRAZIL

Neither of these two South American nations has any significant domestic terrorism problems at this time. Although Bolivia has a subversive and antiwestern group called the Tupac Katari Guerilla Army (EGTK), its actions have been extremely limited. Like so many other Latin areas, Bolivia and Brazil have seen military governments during the 1960s and 1970s result in repression. Both countries have been almost free of both government and international terror. Human rights violations continue to occur as these states have the apparatus in place for torture and confinement. Efforts to bring any wrongdoers to book for repressive activities have thus far failed. Brazil has a democratic constitution which prohibits the inhumane treatment of prisoners and detainees. When a military coup toppled the Bolivian government in 1980, the usual array of journalists, opposition politicians and trade unionists were detained by the secret police, the *Servicio Especial Seguridad* (SES). However, most detainees were only held for a short period of time. The National Intelligence Service (SNI) in Brazil has practiced torture.

Brazil is famous in international terrorist circles for the pamphlet *Mini-Manual of the Urban Guerrilla*, written by Carlos Marighella in 1969. On Tuesday, November 4, 1969, he was assassinated in São Paulo. On that day, two missions were simultaneously interrupted. The first was that of a man who for nearly forty years had been involved in shaping theories for the struggle against the dominant system. The second was that of a determined **urban guerrilla**. Marighella was killed in an ambush as he was about to begin rural guerrilla warfare, the next step in his liberation cycle. He had the unique position of having made valuable contributions to the revolutionary cause in both theory and practice. During the last year of his life, as a parallel to the action he undertook, he wrote intensively to support his theories about the liberation of Brazil.

Mini-Manual of the Urban Guerrilla, which is presented, in part, in a Terrorism Brief elsewhere in this chapter, has special importance. The work examines the conditions, characteristics, necessities, and methods of guerrilla war and the urban guerrilla, and demonstrates Marighella's sense of detail, organization, and mental clarity. It also shows that Marighella was endowed with inexhaustible confidence and a youthfulness that belied his fifty-eight years. For the experiences described in its pages and for its detailed foresight, the *Mini-Manual of the Urban Guerrilla* became one of the principal books of every man who, in the battle against the bourgeoisie and imperialism, takes the road of armed rebellion.[16]

URUGUAY

In comparison to other Latin American states, Uruguay seemed to have an advantage with a prosperous economy, built upon its sugar growing and export market. However, as has been evidenced in other regions of the world, the onset of severe economic downturns has led to the rise of worker parties, student revolts and such. This was the scenario with Uruguay, when the economy crashed in the late 1950s. With the collapse came unrest, high unemployment and inflation. The sugar workers had already organized labor unions to speak on their behalf, and by the end of the 1950s the union was being led and influenced by extreme elements demanding social reforms and justice. Confrontation was the ultimate result.

National Liberation Movement (MLN): The Tupamaros

This movement grew out of the disillusionment of unionists, who marched on Montevideo, the capital, in 1962. The confrontations with police ended in numerous arrests. The government was unsympathetic to union demands, and rather than listen to their claims, portrayed union members as insurgents and guerillas. A law student who was arrested during one of the clashes rose to form the MLN. Raul Sendic emerged from a brief spell in prison bitter and determined to fight back. The government imposed more restrictions on rights and freedoms, which forged the beginnings of terrorism in Uruguay. Largely an agricultural country, Uruguay is situated on the Atlantic Ocean and borders the River Plate. To mount an effective campaign, the group decided that its base and battleground would be the streets of Montevideo. The aim of the MLN was not to replace the government, but to force issues and change policy for the redistribution of wealth. Although the MLN espoused Marxist theories, it did not engage in rhetoric at the expense of support from the public. By the end of the 1960s, the Tupamaros had grown significantly, and were believed to number more than 2,000. The combatants had no doubt studied the *Mini-Manual of the Urban Guerilla*, and their tactics tended to mirror Marighella's teachings. For support and supplies they depended on bank robberies and kidnapping officials for ransom. Their methods became an example for other terror groups operating in urban centers of the world.

The police in Uruguay were unable to stop the growing surge of the Tupamaros. With the democratic fabric now in tatters, the police resorted to torture to extract information and to deter would-be Tupamaros. Many suspected members of the MLN ended up in the country's top security prison, the *Penal de Libertad* under

KIDNAPPING OF SIR GEOFFREY JACKSON

A charismatic and highly intellectual diplomat, Sir Geoffrey Jackson had been acutely aware that he was being followed and watched by Tupamaros as early as March 1971. Kidnapping has always been a tool of the terrorists, only for Sir Geoffrey it was unclear how or when this was going to take place. The following year his official vehicle was rammed in a narrow street and the eight-month ordeal of being confined to a basement "people's prison" had begun. From the very outset Sir Geoffrey and the British Foreign Office had made it absolutely clear that there would be no bargaining with the kidnappers. For the Tupamaros this was developing into a dilemma; if they killed the Ambassador they would gain nothing and to simply release him would not allow them to "save face." A prison riot, which saw the release of over 100 Tupamaros, was the excuse that was needed for them to release Sir Geoffrey.

Source: Richard Clutterbuck, *Guerrillas and Terrorists*, p. 99, Faber and Faber, London, 1977.

the control of the county's secret police, the *Organismo Coordinador de Actividades Anti-Subversivas*.[7] Methods of torture were cruel, inhuman and effective, and included rapes, burning, electrical shocks and sleep deprivation.

The end for the Tupamaros was not as might have been expected. The chaos they had brought to the cities had forced the government into a more vigorous application of repressive measures. In other words, in classic fashion, the Tupamaros' brand of terror forced the government to respond with its own brand of terror. However, the Tupamaros sought respectability and began to align with left-wing political movements to replace the government at the polling booth. This was a disaster, as left-wing constituents did not favor terrorism and the socialist ticket failed. As socialists, they should have expected support from the working classes, but MLN was made up mainly of middle class Uruguayans. With the failure of the political movement, a strong right-wing military government came into power. Its draconian measures in curbing the Tupamaros were endorsed by the populace, and resulted in mass arrests and the end of MLN. The kidnapping of the British ambassador in Montevideo in 1972 ultimately shattered the myth that the Tupamaros were invincible. Shortly after his release from captivity a general election was held and the Frente Amplio, a strong political supporter of the Tupamaros, was decimated at the polls. The government was returned to office with a clear mandate to end terrorism.

The Tupamaros served as an example of how to organize an effective strike force of terrorists in an urban environment, using the city for cover, following the advice of the *Mini-Manual of the Urban Guerrilla*. Other such terror groups have profited from this example in Northern Ireland and in West Germany. The tactics employed by these middle-class terrorists, as saviors of the poor of Montevideo, did not translate into popular support for the movement. To some extent their organization was built on small independent units, and this cell-like structure is also a hallmark of the Irish Republican Army.

ARGENTINA

Argentina has suffered through systematic human rights violations under the political will and control of strict military juntas since the mid-1970s. In order to escape the problems at home, the Argentine military government called on the historic claims of the nation to the Malvinas Islands (Falkland Islands) deep in the South Atlantic. Argentina had for the past century claimed title to the islands, which were populated by British families. Before the battle for the Falklands, Argentine's military had attempted to "remove" all political opponents to its regime. This was achieved by clandestine arrests, which were followed by the complete disappearance of those arrested. Bodies which had been dumped in the ocean and were pulled up in fishing nets showing signs of brutalization and torture.

Before WW II, Argentina had close ties to Germany. However, in 1945 the new government of General Farrell severed its links and joined the Allies in the defeat of Germany.

Two of the most celebrated names associated with South American politics are those of Colonel Juan Domingo Peron and his wife, Eva. Peron was almost certainly responsible for initiating the use of what is now termed "death squads" in Argentina. His vision, on coming to power as president in 1946, was to industrialize the nation at the expense of the agricultural industry, which had been the economic mainstay for most of the century. With industrialization and heavy government spending came inflation at a staggering rate never before seen in Argentina. Left-wing political opposition to Peron's activities mounted, and as the 1950s arrived, Argentina was sliding down a dangerous slope, where food shortages and protests were the order of the day. In response, Peron nationalized the press and took total control over what was printed in the media. In 1949, he had created his own secret police force known as the **CERT**. CERT and its later version, the *Division de Informacion Politicas Antidemocratic* (DIPA) hid within its ranks a group designed for torture and repression called the Triple A or the Argentine Anti-Communist Alliance. Peron was deposed in 1955, three years after the death of Eva Peron.

The Triple A (AAA)

This was an extreme right-wing death squad which functioned clandestinely at the beginning of the 1970s and consisted of members of the Argentine military and police. Many people suspected of being left-wing sympathizers were abducted, usually in the early hours of the morning. The captors would explain that they were government agents. Death camps were set up apart from the normal prison structures of the country, making it almost impossible for relatives to locate those taken, let alone establish the agency which had detained them. There were forty-seven of these secret camps, which were similar to the concentration camps built by the Nazis.[18] As the years of unceasing military repression grew, so did the pressure from the Red Cross and Amnesty International to make the military juntas accountable for those missing. In a remarkable piece of legislation passed by the Argentine government in 1979, those who were missing were presumed dead unless it could be proved otherwise.

The Battle for the Falklands

In 1982, the Argentine military machine invaded the British Falkland Islands and sparked a reaction of gunboat diplomacy from Margaret Thatcher, the "Iron Lady" of British politics. Scenes on television showed the Union Jack being lowered over government buildings, then replaced by the flag of Argentina. This, coupled with pictures of the British troops in the act of surrender, did much to raise British anger against the "Argies." No doubt existed among the military junta that the British would surrender the islands peacefully to the Argentines. However, they were soon to learn

The chronic structural crisis characteristic of Brazil today, and its resultant political instability, are what have brought about the upsurge of revolutionary war in the country. The urban guerrilla is a man who fights the military dictatorship with arms, using unconventional methods. A political revolutionary and an ardent patriot, he is a fighter for his country's liberation, a friend of the people and of freedom. The area in which the urban guerrilla acts is in the large Brazilian cities. There are also bandits, commonly known as outlaws, who work in the big cities. Many times, assaults by outlaws are taken as actions by urban guerrillas. The urban guerrilla, however, differs radically from the outlaw. The outlaw benefits personally from the action, and attacks indiscriminately without distinguishing between the exploited and the exploiters, which is why there are so many ordinary men and women among his victims. The urban guerrilla follows a political goal and only attacks the government, the big capitalists, and the foreign imperialists, particularly North Americans.

Another element just as prejudicial as the outlaw and also operating in the urban area is the right-wing counterrevolutionary who creates confusion, assaults banks, hurls bombs, kidnaps, assassinates, and commits the worst imaginable crimes against urban guerrillas, revolutionary priests, students, and citizens who oppose fascism and seek liberty. The urban guerrilla is an implacable enemy of the government and systematically inflicts damage on the authorities and on the men who dominate the country and exercise power. The principal task of the urban guerrilla is to distract, to wear out, to demoralize the militarists, the military dictatorship and its repressive forces, and also to attack and destroy the wealth and property of the North Americans, the foreign managers, and the Brazilian upper class.

The urban guerrilla is not afraid of dismantling and destroying the present Brazilian economic, political, and social system, for his aim is to help the rural guerrilla and to collaborate in the creation of a totally new and revolutionary social and political structure, with the armed people in power. The urban guerrilla must have a certain minimal political understanding. To gain that he must read certain printed or mimeographed works such as:

- *Guerrilla Warfare* by Che Guevara
- Memories of a Terrorist
- Some Questions about the Brazilian
   Guerrilla Operations and Tactics
   On Strategic Problems and Principles
- Certain Tactical Principles for Comrades Undertaking Guerrilla Operations
- Organizational Questions
- *O Guerrilheiro*, newspaper of the Brazilian revolutionary groups.

Personal Qualities of the Urban Guerrilla

His bravery and decisive nature characterize the urban guerrilla. He must be a good tactician and a good shot. The urban guerrilla must be a person of great astuteness to compensate for the fact that he is not sufficiently strong in arms, ammunition, and equipment. The career militarists or the government police have modern arms and transport, and can go about anywhere freely, using the force of their power. The urban guerilla does not have such resources at his disposal and leads a clandestine existence. Sometimes he is a convicted person or is out on parole and is obliged to use false documents.

Nevertheless, the urban guerrilla has a certain advantage over the conventional military or the police. It is that, while the military and the police act on behalf of the enemy, whom the people hate, the urban guerrilla defends a just cause, which is the people's cause.

The urban guerrilla's arms are inferior to the enemy's, but from a moral point of view, the urban guerrilla has an undeniable superiority. This moral superiority is what sustains the urban guerrilla. Thanks to it, the urban guerrilla can accomplish his principal duty, which is to attack and to survive. The urban guerrilla has to capture or divert arms from the enemy to be able to fight. Because his arms are not uniform, since what he has are expropriated or have fallen into hands in different ways, the urban guerrilla faces the problem of a variety of arms and a shortage of ammunition. Moreover, he has no place to practice shooting and marksmanship. These difficulties have to be surmounted, forcing the urban guerrilla to be imaginative and creative, qualities without which it would be impossible for him to carry out his role as a revolutionary.

The urban guerrilla must possess initiative, mobility, and flexibility, as well as versatility and a command of any situation. Initiative especially is an indispensable quality. It is not always possible to foresee everything. And the urban guerrilla cannot let himself become confused, or wait for orders. His duty is to act, to find adequate solutions for each problem he faces, and not to retreat. It is better to err acting than to do nothing for fear of erring. Without initiative there is no urban guerrilla warfare.

SOURCE: CARLOS MARIGHELLA, *MINI-MANUAL OF THE URBAN GUERILLA*, (PAMPHLET, 1969), PP. 1–2.

that the Thatcher government was in no mood to surrender British territory.

What followed was the rapid deployment of England's military might to the south Atlantic in the largest operation of its kind until that time. With superior weaponry and aircraft, the Royal Navy was the first to score a hit in this conflict. HMS Conqueror, a Navy submarine, had quietly slipped southwards to take on the Argentine Navy. Arriving on station in the exclusion zone imposed by Britain, the sub torpedoed and sank the Argentinean battleship *Belgrano*, with a massive loss of life. This had a twofold effect. The battleship would obviously play no part in the conflict, and the death of nearly 2,000 Argentinean servicemen served to undermine support for the junta. Once British Marines and guardsmen, backed up by Gurkhas, landed on the island, the superior skills of the British war machine quickly brought Argentina to its knees in surrender. With the disastrous foray in the Falklands, it was only a matter of time before democracy returned to Argentina. Those who had been involved in torture, including senior members of government, were investigated and sentenced to long terms in prison.

Montoneros

One of the military junta's main targets were the **Montoneros** and their supporters. Set up as a left-wing Peronist movement after the death of Juan Peron, they were active from 1975–1979. The Montoneros were violently opposed to the military takeover of the Argentine government. They attempted to organize the union movement as a cohort for their activities, but a brutal crackdown by the junta prevented any effective action in the cities and the group had to settle for actions in the countryside. Their tactics were hit-and-run, using bombings and shootings. By 1979, the group had been totally destroyed.[19] This is yet another example of an extreme right-wing military government resorting to terrorism of its own to remain in control, using torture, murder and widespread intimidation.

CHILE

As the century of military dictatorships in Central, Southern and Latin America draws to a close, the only active terror group in Chile is a splinter group called the Manuel Rodriguez Patriotic Front (FPMR). Active in the 1980s was the **Lautaro Youth Movement**, which was a mixed bag of disillusioned youths, leftist elements, and criminals.

One of the most significant influences in Chile over the past twenty years was General Augusto Pinochet, a military dictator of fascist principles, who is today considered by many in Chile to be an elder statesman of the country. Few dictators ever successfully reach happy retirement, but Pinochet is one who has "gone the distance," despite appalling acts during his tenure. Pinochet swept to power during a bloody military coup in 1973, which removed the Marxist regime responsible for the mismanagement of the country and its economy over a three-year period.

The Marxist leader Salvador Allende had been the first democratically elected Marxist president to head a nation in the western Hemisphere. Allende came to power in 1970, on a ticket promising social programs for Chileans. His government took immediate control of the country's copper mines and banking system. His huge increase in the minimum wage structure and attempts to keep the cost of consumer products at a low level fueled runaway inflation. Inflation between 1971 and 1973 rose by nearly 400 percent. The government was besieged on all sides. Violent

MANUEL RODRIGUEZ PATRIOTIC FRONT (FPMR)

Originally the FPMR was founded in 1983 as the armed wing of the Chilean Communist Party and was named for the hero of Chile's war of independence against Spain. The group splintered into two factions in the late 1980s, and one faction became a political party in 1991. The dissident wing FPMR/D is Chile's only remaining active terrorist group.

FPMR/D attacked civilians and international targets, including the United States and US business interests as well as Mormon churches. In 1993 FPMR/D bombed two McDonald's restaurants and attempted to bomb a Kentucky Fried Chicken restaurant. Successful government counterterrorism operations have significantly undercut the organization. However, the FPMR staged a dramatic escape from prison using a helicopter in December 1996.

Presently, the FPMR/D is believed to have between 50 and 100 members. It is believed to still be operating in Chile. It does not receive any external aid.

protests began in the streets of Santiago. The military, assisted by the CIA, overthrew the Allende government on September 11, 1973. Allende was arrested and died in custody. Reports on the circumstances of his death vary from torture, execution and suicide.

The Pinochet Years

The military takeover, followed by the installation of a yet another junta, was not widely accepted. Fighting broke out between right-wing supporters of Pinochet and the extreme left communist elements. The junta cracked down hard on all opposition by dissolving the congress, restricting the freedom of the press, and privatizing what had formerly been nationalized industries. Pinochet banned all political opposition parties and ran the country as a dictatorship. The trigger point for the attempted coup was not a momentary aberration on the part of Pinochet; in fact many of the high ranking military generals actually served in the Allende cabinet. What caused the problems for the military was the introduction of left-wing extremism into the fabric of Chile's society. Allende had placed communist reactionaries in the armed forces to incite rebellion, and over 14,000 foreign agitators moved into Chile, with his blessing. These included Cuban DGI agents, who were in Chile to reorganize internal security for Allende, as well as Soviet, Czech and North Korean military instructors and arms suppliers and hard-line Spanish Communist Party members. Their intent was to organize revolutionary brigades to take on the established military. The 1970s were a decade of change for Central and South America, and insurgent terror groups and guerilla movements were on the move from Montevideo to Managua.[20]

To stem the flow of left-wing subversives, the Pinochet junta carried out mass arrests and used torture to gain both information and confessions. He arrested not only Chileans, but also foreign subversive elements. These are actions for which the international communities want him held accountable. Executions were commonplace in Chile, and the targets were leftist politicians, trade unionists, and other activists. Many simply disappeared, never to be heard from again. The junta engaged a semi-official death squad organization to do some of its dirty work. The *Avengers of the Martyrs* were a fascist paramilitary movement comprised mainly of military and police/security personnel. To make sure the security and paramilitary groups could conduct business in an unfettered manner a decree was passed by the military to effectively remove the legal processes and protections. The Decree Law on Amnesty gave total and unequivocal immunity from arrest and prosecution to all security forces of the Pinochet coup.

The Pinochet military regime laid the foundation for a vibrant South American economy and passed it on to the democratic government that followed. Pinochet had turned Chile from a second-rate third world country into a strong market economy, one that is being emulated in 1990s. Military dictators usually leave in the same violent manner with which they arrive in power, but General Pinochet is considered by many in Chile to be a hero of the people.

On a recent visit to Britain for back surgery, Pinochet was arrested in his hospital bed. At the age of eighty-three, he now faces claims of torture inflicted by his regime and requests for his extradition. The highest court in Britain dealt a stunning blow to Pinochet, and in a stand for international law and justice, the British have hammered a nail into a portion of his coffin. Pinochet and the democratic government of Chile claimed he had diplomatic immunity as a former head of state and was therefore not subject to arrest and extradition. In the majority decision handed down in November 1998, Lord Nicholls commented that "the Vienna Convention on diplomatic relations may confer immunity in respect of acts performed in the exercise of functions which international law recognizes as functions of a head of state irrespective of the terms of his domestic constitution." Lord Nicholls further commented that " it hardly needs saying that the torture of his own subjects, or of aliens, would not be regarded by international law as a function of a head of state."[21] Reactions to the decision in Santiago have led to waves of protest as well as outpourings of relief. Whether the democracy that Pinochet has resurrected in Chile can survive remains to be seen. Certainly any frailty of the system may invite left-wing advances on the power base of government and a return to Marxism. As his eighty-third birthday is spent in custody, the way is clear for Pinochet's extradition to face charges of torture and murder.

VENEZUELA

Venezuela might be considered a democratic oasis in a desert of military dictatorships. Unlike much of Latin America this country has had a history of democratic government since 1958, with lessening interference by the military. Venezuela suffers minor incursions by Colombian terrorists in the border villages and towns. Kidnapping and extortion are the main activities of both the National Liberation Army (ELN) and the Colombian People's Liberation Army (EPL).

Since the independence movement led by Venezuela's favorite son, Simon Bolivar, in the early 1800s, the country had been the home to a succession of military dictators. Venezuela began to prosper with the discovery of petroleum, which became its main source of revenue. Mismanagement and corruption ended the military dictatorship of General Gomez in 1935, when the democratic movement, supported by the army, overthrew him and established a democratic government. The country has been ruled by two parties since 1958, the Acción Democratica (AD) and the Christian Democratic Party (COPIE). Each has had its share of periods in office. However, economic downturns have stalled government action on behalf of many poverty-stricken Venezuelans. Although there is no active terror movement in the country, there are definite signs that reforms will be needed if democracy is to endure. The government has utilized severe measures to control the country in tough economic times, and the former leader of the 1992 military coup, Lieutenant Colonel

CP Archive (AP Photo/Jose Caruci)

TERRORISM PLAYER 11–3

CARLOS THE JACKAL

Ilich Ramirez Sanchez, born October 12, 1949 in Caracas, Venezuela, is better known as simply Carlos or Carlos the Jackal. Ilich grew up with his family in Caracas and became, at 14 years of age, the leader of the Communist Youth Movement of Venezuela. To most of the world in the late 1960s and throughout the 1970s, his very name became synonymous with terrorism. Considered the "Scarlet Pimpernel" of international terrorism, he is responsible for some of the most notable terror attacks of this century. The OPEC hostage crisis of 1972, the U.S. embassy hostage-taking in Tehran, the Munich Olympic Games massacre 1968 are but a small number. Carlos did his work wherever he liked and for whomever he liked. He was to receive further education at the Patrice Lumumba University in Moscow and is believed to have received his terror training from the Soviet Union. His involvement with the world's sponsors of

(continued)

Hugo Chavez, has made a successful leap into the current political system. General elections were held in December 1998, and Chavez won the presidency with a plurality of 56.5 percent, for a five-year term. As President Chavez begins to set up his government, however, we must all carefully follow events to detect if there might be a return to a military dictatorship.[22]

Many of the problems facing the existing government involve corruption at the highest levels as well as drug smuggling and money laundering. The United States is one of Venezuela's main import and export partners and has, on the surface, made an effort to deter drug traffic. With poverty so widespread and little light at the end of the economic tunnel, a different style of government might well emerge after the elections.

SUMMARY

Central and South America have been under strong right-wing military rule for many decades of the twentieth century. They have also suffered the ravages of death squads. In studying the causes of terrorism and guerrilla activity throughout Latin America, there are trends which become apparent. In Mexico, El Salvador, Chile and Uruguay, much that took place was related to land claims, in countries where the few wealthy landowners had immense influence in the ruling political and military governments. In protecting those interests, the extreme right death squads operated with impunity. Violations of human rights and prosecution of those responsible continue to the present. General Pinochet, the former Chilean dictator, awaits trial under international law, at the age of eighty-three. Argentina is recovering from the stringent rule of the military juntas of the 1980s and crushing humiliation and defeat in the Falkland Islands at the hands of the British. The loss of loved ones to death squads will continue to plague the citizens of new democracies as they strive to move forward. Our next chapter will take us to familiar climes as we examine North America and the Caribbean islands.

Terms to Remember

Banana Republics	Zapatistas	Peace and Justice
URNG	ORDEN	FPMR
Sandinistas	FARC	death squads
MRTA	Contras	Shining Path
urban guerillas	Tupomaros	CERT
Montoneros	Lautaro Youth Movement	

Review Questions

Explain why Columbia is such a difficult country to rid of drugs and terrorism.

Describe how the death squads were used and the reasons for them in Venezuela.

Who were the Sandinistas, and how were they a factor in the United States policy in Central America?

Describe the actions of the Zapatistas in Mexico and the basis for their complaints.

international terror, Qaddafi, Assad, for example, are common knowledge. Wanted by police agencies throughout western Europe, he was eventually arrested and convicted for the murder of a French policeman in 1998 and sentenced to a long prison term in France. It is thought that by the end of the decade the need for his particular expertise had waned on the international terror market. He had been residing in Syria prior to his arrest.

DAVID YALLOP, TRACKING THE JACKAL, RANDOM HOUSE, LONDON, 1993.

Trace the origins of the Shining Path in Peru and their methods for influencing the government and bordering states.

Endnotes

1. Frank M. Afflitto, Abstract from a paper presented at the Conference of the American Society of Criminology, November 20, 1997. San Diego, California.
2. Global Intelligence Update, The Internet. Stratford Inc. November 1998.
3. *Patterns of Global Terrorism*, United States Department of State, Publication 10321.
4. Jonathan R. White, *Terrorism, an Introduction* (Brooks Cole Publishing, Belmont California), p. 157.
5. *Kerry Committee Report*, April 19, 1995.
6. *Patterns of Global Terrorism, 1997*, United States Department of State, April 1998.
7. Stan Yarbo, "Death Squads Seek Negotiations," *The Christian Science Monitor*, June 18, 1990, p. 3.
8. Jeremy McDermott, *The Vancouver Sun*, Southam Press, November 18, 1998.
9. Yarbo, *The Christian Science Monitor*, November 18, 1998.
10. Ibid.
11. Sam Dillon, "As Peru Votes, Insurgent's Mystique Casts Shadow" (*Miami Herald*, Miami Herald Publishing Company, June 10, 1990), pp. 1A, 26A.
12. Jonathan R. White, *Terrorism, an Introduction* (West/Wadsworth Publishing Co., Belmont Ca. 1998), p. 62.
13. "The Shining Path Comes Back," *The Economist*, August 17, 1996, p. 35.
14. Gabriel Escobar, "Peruvian Guerrillas Hold Hundreds Hostage" (*Washington Post Foreign Service*), December 19,1996, the Internet.
15. CNN Interactive World News, "One Hostage Killed in Daring Peru Rescue" (*CNN*, April 22, 1997, Cable News Network Inc.).
16. N. A. Keck, CPP, ASIS presentation, May 16, 1996.
17. Bruce Quarrie, *The World's Secret Police* (Octopus Books Ltd., London 1986), p. 48.
18. Ibid., p. 21.
19. White, *Terrorism, an Introduction*, p. 48.
20. Arnaud de Borchgrave, "Demonized for Foiling a Left-wing Plot," *The Washington Times*, October 27, 1998, p. A–15.
21. International News, *The Globe and Mail*, Vancouver, Canada. Thursday, November 26, 1998.
22. Steven Gutkin, *Associated Press*, November 28, 1998.

CHAPTER 12

NORTH AMERICA AND THE CARIBBEAN

"We cannot sit home and hope that trouble will somehow pass us by. And if we are going to build the kind of world we want for our children and ourselves we must take the lead in designing it, not wait for others to set the parameters for us."

—Secretary Madeline K. Allbright

OVERVIEW

Over the last twenty-five years, North America's television screens have displayed major terrorists bombings, hijackings and murders taking place in faraway lands for seemingly bizarre reasons. Many viewers were intrigued, but most were complacent. The idea of a major terrorist attack in the United States or Canada was simply unimaginable. There were survivalist fringe groups and various other types of protesters, but they were not perceived to be as menacing as the radical elements in the Middle East and Europe. Such head-in-the-sand thinking came to an abrupt halt in February 1993. On that day, the shocking television pictures of terrorist violence came not from Beirut, Londonderry or Jerusalem, but from New York City! When a truck bomb shattered the World Trade Center, it sounded a clear wake-up call to the United States and its neighbors.

This chapter will introduce the student to the growing cancer of domestic and foreign-sponsored terrorism in the United States, then discuss major problems with terrorism in the rest of North America and the Caribbean. Terrorism in this region is not nearly the problem it has become in other portions of the globe. Still, the relative openness of societies in this region, and the ease with which terrorist acts can be organized and executed, by both domestic terror groups and those sponsored from abroad are issues requiring close examination. We begin with the United States, the most prosperous and powerful country in the world and therefore a prime target for jealousy, hate and anger.

THE UNITED STATES OF AMERICA

The United States is a big country, but not as big as most Americans think it is. It is half the size of Russia and slightly larger than China. It is about two and one-half times the size of Western Europe, but half the size of South America and three-tenths the size of Africa. The United States shares a long border with its northern neighbor, Canada, of over 6,000 miles. To the south, it has another long border of over 2,000 miles with Mexico. In terms of preventing terrorism, smuggling and drug trafficking opportunities, that is an awesome amount of territory to protect. When you add American coastlines of about 13,000 miles, the difficulty escalates rapidly.

International terrorism in the United States is generally not considered a critical problem yet. There are, nevertheless, indications that if a foreign terrorist group became angry enough at the United States, and was so determined, it could present a serious threat to the population. The **World Trade Center** bombing was a "first alert" for Americans to the danger of foreign terrorism. But as the news went on to other headline stories, the American public slipped back into complacency. Then, in April 1995, another shocker filled the airwaves and television screens, with the image of the **Alfred P. Murrah Federal Building** in Oklahoma City shattered by a devastating blast. A huge truck bomb had destroyed that building, leaving 168 people dead and more than 500 others injured. When early reports indicated that the bomber might have been from the Middle East, anger rose to a fever pitch. The

The World Trade Center bombing woke up America to the vulnerability to terrorism in a free country. (AP/WideWorld Photos)

arrest of Timothy McVeigh and his subsequent trial and conviction, as well as the arrest and conviction of his friend Terry Nichols, rattled the nation. When it was revealed that both were members of right-wing local militias, it was clear that this terrible act had been committed by *domestic* terrorists. Those two events and many others since have caused the United States to alter perceptions of where terrorist threats lie and reorganize efforts to counter them.

The levels of terrorism experienced in places such as Beirut, Paris, London, Islamabad and Munich do not engender major concern among Americans or impact the American lifestyle. Public belief in threats from foreign terrorism is not enhanced when a violent act occurs and the media credits it to a foreign operative, only to discover that this assumption was erroneous. When the "talking heads" on television move on to another story after revealing that the incident was not one of foreign terrorism, confusion and skepticism result. Two especially relevant examples are:

- The bombing of the van of Navy Captain Will Rogers III, former captain of the U.S.S. Vincennes, the Aegis missile-equipped U.S. warship that mistakenly shot down an Iranian airliner during the Iran-Iraq war
- The mysterious "Middle Eastern" man who was brought back to the United States for questioning in regard to the bombing of the Alfred P. Murrah Federal Building in Oklahoma City

In both cases, the media jumped to the conclusion that these bombings were planned and executed by foreign terrorists. When facts to the contrary surfaced, it became more difficult for the public to accept material presented by the media in regard to terrorism.

The U.S. has not been subjected to as much political violence as nations in the Middle East, Ireland and Asia. Some examples of political extremists in America are the **Symbionese Liberation Front (SLA)**, the Weathermen, the Black Panthers and the Unabomber. **Domestic terrorist activities** have been few and far between. On the other hand, the IRA's ongoing slaughter of innocent women and children with car bombs is unremitting. Now, however, the United States has seen that it is not immune to acts identifiable as those of foreign terrorists. The World Trade Center explosion was perhaps only the first salvo of external terrorist and politically motivated activities targeting random victims. Such strikes are intended to incite public fear as well as make a statement.

But terrorism in the United States is not limited to those with nondomestic agendas. Witness the attack on the federal building in Oklahoma City, Oklahoma. The terrorists in this case were members of a paramilitary survivalist militia from Michigan. They had a festering anger over the United States government's bungling of the **Waco Massacre** of the Davidians, a fringe religious group headed by David Koresh.

The United States has been and still is a violent country, a relative youngster in the family of nations, often carrying on the frontier tradition. Even the American War of Independence involved fighting the troops of the British Crown in ways that were contrary to the prevailing so-called "civilized rules" of warfare. The "redcoats" marched in straight lines, impeccably dressed, while the rag-tag American "minutemen" fought in guerilla fashion and ambushed them from behind rocks and trees. This kind of fighting won them a nation and changed warfare forever. Later, when the Americans fought their own Civil War, a far inferior band of southern rebels held off the northern armies for almost five years, using unconventional tactics and terror whenever it was needed.

TERRORISM BRIEF 12-1
BRANCH DAVIDIANS (STUDENTS OF THE SEVEN SEALS)

This was a sect that had split away from the Seventh-Day Adventist church. Under leader David Koresh, it was a destructive doomsday cult whose membership experienced a major loss of life in Waco, Texas.

History of the Church

The group that became popularly known as the Branch Davidians was a splinter sect that broke away from the Seventh-Day Adventist Church (SDA) in 1929. The SDA church is well known for belief in the imminent return of Jesus Christ to earth, for special vegetarian dietary restrictions and for retention of Saturday as the Sabbath. Victor Houteff, who had joined the SDA church in 1919, founded the breakaway sect.

The group called themselves Students of the Seven Seals (meaning students of the scroll protected by the seven seals). The term "Branch Davidians" (BD) was derived from the expression "Get off the dead shepherd's rod and move onto a living branch." It was not generally used by the membership, but became the name most commonly used by the public and media.

Vernon Howell joined the group as a handyman in 1981 and eventually became its leader. In 1990 Howell changed his name to David (after King David of the Israelites) Koresh (after the Babylonian King Cyrus). In 1992, Koresh renamed Mt. Carmel Ranch Apocalypse because of his belief that the final, encompassing battle of Armageddon mentioned in the Bible would start at the BD compound.

What is Known about Waco

A major tragedy occurred at Ranch Apocalypse in Waco in the spring of 1993. There is a consensus that the sequence of events was as follows:

- The ATF decided to arrest David Koresh on firearm violations. He could have been easily arrested away from the compound while jogging or while visiting Waco. But apparently it was necessary for them to arrest him at the compound near the guns in order to have a chance of winning a court case.

- A group of seventy-six armed ATF agents entered the compound on February 28th and attempted to serve a search warrant.

- A shot was heard; it is unclear whether it was an accidental firing by an ATF agent, or an intentional or accidental discharge from within the buildings.

- In the resultant firefight, six Davidians and four ATF agents died; at least one Davidian and 24 agents were wounded.

- The ATF withdrew, the FBI took charge, and a fifty-one-day siege followed.

David Koresh, Leader of the Branch DividiansCP Picture Archive (AP Photo)

- Based on a report from a psychiatrist at the Baylor College of Medicine, the FBI believed that the Branch Davidian children were being sexually and physically abused inside the compound. (The FBI has since acknowledged that the report is false. It is apparently based on false memories implanted in the children.)

- The FBI consulted a number of experts on new religious movements with knowledge about destructive cults, who warned of a high probability of mass murder or suicide if aggressive action was taken.

- The FBI also consulted a number of psychiatrists, who had no specialized experience with doomsday cults, who assured the FBI that the chances of major loss of life were slim. The Bureau decided that it was safe to attack the compound with tear gas.

- The FBI seems to have ignored the religious experts and accepted the beliefs of the psychiatrists. The FBI emergency response team had been at the site for almost two months. If the siege lasted much longer, then the team would be in need of refresher training; there was no replacement team.

- On April 19, 1993, specially adapted tanks approached the building to penetrate the walls and inject a form of tear gas inside.

- A group of fires started almost simultaneously in different locations within the compound; they combined to form a great conflagration.

- Eight followers were able to escape during the attack; many were severely burned. Koresh and about seventy-five of his followers died of stab wounds, gun shots, and from the effects of smoke and flames. This included twenty-one children. Five followers were convicted of voluntary manslaughter and firearms violations. Two others were convicted of arms charges.

- Later, a famous video was distributed which appears to show a flame-throwing tank igniting the compound. This has been proven to be a fake, a forged picture of a flame superimposed in a film laboratory on top of actual footage of the tanks at Waco. The latter was taken about two hours before the fire.

- Whenever a high profile and tragic event occurs (e.g., the assassination of President Kennedy, the bombing at Oklahoma City, etc.) facts become mixed with fantasies. Waco is no exception, the truth will probably remain unknown.

Link to the Oklahoma City Bombing

The Federal Building in Oklahoma City was bombed on April 19, 1995, precisely on the second anniversary of the disaster at Waco. Timothy McVeigh was charged and convicted as the person primarily responsible for the bombing. According to his former army buddy, McVeigh was primarily motivated by a desire to avenge the 1993 government siege at Waco. McVeigh allegedly believed that the "orders were issued" for the attack on the Davidians at Waco from the Federal Building in Oklahoma City. He was wrong.

SOURCE: EXTRACTED FROM THE BRITANNICA-NEWSWEEK INTERNET WEB SITE.

In the late 1920s, in the days of prohibition, gangs and mobsters preyed on society and each other with deadly violence. Mobsters gunning down those who opposed or interfered with their bootlegging traumatized all that witnessed such carnage. These were not just criminal but also terrorist acts. Terror strikes at the basic need for safety in anyone who hears about it or observes it. Serial killers are unwitting terrorists when their deeds are publicized. Street gangs in American cities today use **drive-by shootings** as a tactic for creating fear and terror. These demonstrations keep their rivals in check and neighborhood citizens from reporting these and other crimes against their communities to the police. The same kinds of fear-inducing methods have long been the favorite tactics of the Cosa Nostra. From killings in schools and fast food restaurants to motorcycle gangs terrorizing an entire town, all forms of violence can become a means of inciting terror.

With a population of almost 268,000,000 in mid-1997, the United States remains a "nation of immigrants," people who came to a great and prosperous land, legally and illegally, from the four corners of the earth. They came in hope of finding a better life. As far as terrorism was concerned, many of these immigrants escaped from it to come to a place where such actions were unthinkable. As we have now seen, the history of the United States does not support that premise. Many forms of terror have scarred its brief but bloody past and even mar its present.

The United States has the most powerful, diverse, and technologically advanced economy in the world. It boasts a per capita annual income of $28,600, the highest among the major industrialized nations. In this market-oriented economy, private individuals and business firms make most of the decisions, and government buys needed goods and services predominantly in the private marketplace. American business firms enjoy considerably greater flexibility than their counterparts in western Europe and Japan in decisions to expand capital plant, lay off surplus workers, and develop new products.

In all economic sectors, United States firms are at or near the forefront in technological advances, especially in computers, medical services, aerospace and military hardware. However, the advantage has narrowed since the end of World War II. The rapid development of technology largely explains the evolution of a two-tiered labor market. This occurs when those at the bottom lack the education and the professional/technical skills of those at the top and cannot get the positions which have equitable pay, health insurance coverage and other benefits. The years 1994–1998 witnessed moderate gains in real output, low inflation rates, and a drop in unemployment to below 6 percent. However, this **two-tiered system** could open the door for discontent among those unable to share in the full portion of the American dream. It has already led a number of individuals and groups to vent their frustrations through violence. In all likelihood, the most serious threat to the United States is not foreign, but domestic terror.

DOMESTIC TERRORISM

The face of domestic terrorism in the United States continues to change. The FBI identified a further decline in traditional left-wing domestic extremism, and an increase in activities among extremists associated with right-wing groups and special interest radical organizations.

Left-Wing Terrorism

Over several decades, left wing extremist groups posed the predominant domestic terrorist threat in the United States. In the 1980s, the FBI neutralized many of these groups by arresting key members who were conducting criminal activity. The failure of communism and the fall of the former Soviet Union deprived many leftist groups of a coherent ideology or tangible support. As a result, membership and belief in the "cause" waned.

The United States still faces a threat from some left-wing extremists, including several Puerto Rican terrorist groups. Although Puerto Rico voted to remain within the U.S. Commonwealth in 1993, some extremists still plan and conduct minor terrorist acts to draw attention to their support for independence.

The bombing of the Alfred Murrah Federal Building in Oklahoma City left 168 people dead and another 500 injured in April, 1995. AP WideWorld Photos)

Right-Wing Terrorism

Right-wing extremist groups, on the other end of the political spectrum, generally adhere to an antigovernment or racist ideology and continue to attract new members. Many of these recruits feel displaced by rapid changes in the U.S. culture and economy, or are seeking some form of personal affirmation. As American society continues to change, the potential for escalating hate crimes by extremist right wing groups is an increasing concern. Of particular note is that state and local law enforcement organizations consider a wider range of activities to be terrorist, or potentially terrorist, than does the FBI. Official FBI statistics point to low levels of terrorist activity and attribute many recent incidents to Puerto Rican nationalists. They do not count many threatening acts by skinheads, street gangs and drug dealers. States and municipalities, however, do not hesitate to identify right wing (Neo-Nazi, the Ku Klux Klan, anti-Semitic, anti-federalist and militias) and issue-specific (anti-abortion, animal rights, environmentalist) organizations as the most threatening potential terrorist sources in the United States.

The militia movement in the United States was brought to blinding light by the admissions of Timothy McVeigh and Terry Nichols. These paramilitary, rabid antigovernment groups also continue to attract supporters. Several factors have contributed to an increase in this generally antigovernment mood. In a changing political environment, issues such as gun-control legislation, United Nations involvement in international affairs, and clashes between dissidents and law enforcement are cornerstones of militia ideology. Combined with extremist zeal, these issues may become incendiary. Some militia members firmly believe that the U.S. government is conspiring to create a "new world order," in which international boundaries will be dissolved and the United Nations will rule the world. Others believe the federal government has gotten either too powerful or simply illegal. Many of these militants continue to conduct paramilitary training and stockpile weapons in preparation for armed confrontation with the government. A few of these extreme militias pose a serious terrorist threat. Counterterrorism efforts by the United States will be covered in the following chapter.

Special Interest Extremists

Special interest extremists continued to commit politically oriented crimes. Violent anti-abortion advocates are responsible for almost all of these acts.

The Department of Justice's **Task Force on Violence Against Abortion Providers (TFVAAP)** decreased the number of abortion-related crimes from the high 1994 levels. Although the number of incidents declined, the TFVAAP still investigated more than 100 violations of the **Freedom of Access to Clinic Entrances (FACE) Act.**

Two of the most prominent abortion-related events in 1995 included the following:

> On February 22, 1995, Dr. Elizabeth Karlin, a physician in Madison, Wisconsin, received two death threat letters. Vincent Whitaker, an inmate at a local county jail who was serving a 67-year sentence for reckless injury with a motor vehicle, later admitted writing the letters.

> On September 12, 1995, Whitaker was tried and convicted of two counts of the FACE Act and sending threats through the U.S. Mail. On November 21, 1995, Whitaker was sentenced to an additional 63 months' imprisonment.

The Militia of Montana is an educational organization dedicated to the preservation of the freedoms of ALL Citizens of the State of Montana and of the United States of America.

The best defense against the usurpation of these freedoms by the tyranny of a run-away, out of control government is a well-informed and well-prepared Unorganized Militia of the Citizens of the State of Montana and of the other States of the Federal Union.

A popular government without popular information, or the means of acquiring it, is but a prologue to a farce or a tragedy, or perhaps both. Knowledge will forever govern ignorance, and a people who mean to be their own governors must arm themselves with the power which knowledge gives. –James Madison

James Madison and the other framers of the Constitution knew that in the future that if our Constitution was not interpreted in the context and according to the history in which it was drafted, we would not have a proper understanding of the original intent of our founding fathers, or in the words of Madison, primary author and the supreme expert on the Constitution:

Do not separate text from historical background. If you do, you will have perverted and subverted the Constitution, which can only end in a distorted, bastardized form of illegitimate government.

The Militia of Montana urges the reader of this page to seek out the TRUTH, taking nothing for granted, for it is the TRUTH which will keep us FREE.

The Distinction Between the National Guard and the Constitutional Unorganized Militia

Most Americans today believe that the National Guard is the Militia reserved to the states in the State Constitutions and the Constitution of the United States of America.

Nothing could be further from the TRUTH.

The National Guard did not exist from the beginnings of the Republic until 1903 when it was instituted and created by Congress as the Act of January 21, 1903, known by the name of its sponsor as "The Dick Act."

In 1982 the Senate Judiciary Committee Subcommittee on the Constitution stated in Senate Document 2807:

That the National Guard is not the "Militia" referred to in the Second Amendment is even clearer today. Congress had organized the National Guard under its power to "raise and support armies" and not its power to "Provide for organizing, arming and disciplining the militia." The modern National Guard was specifically intended to avoid status as the constitutional militia, a distinction recognized by 10 U.S.C. 311(a).

Title 32 U.S.C. in July 1918 completely altered the definition of the militia and its service, who controls it and what it is. The difference between the National Guard and Regular Army was swept away, and became a personnel pay folder classification only, thus nationalizing the entire National Guard into the Regular Standing Armies of the United States.

All the arms, munitions, armament and equipment of the National Guard is owned and controlled by the federal government, not by "the people" as clearly stipulated in the Second Amendment.

The Unorganized Militia consists of all able-bodied persons of the nation and of the states between the ages of 18 and 44, and is exclusive of all members of the organized militia, i.e., the Armed Forces of the Federal Government of the United States and of the National Guards of the various states of the Union.

Article II

A well regulated Militia being necessary to the security of a free State, the right of the people to keep and bear Arms shall not be infringed.

It is of great interest to note that in the ensuing years since this Amendment was ratified that two commas have been inserted, after the words "Militia" and "Arms," providing misconstruction of a very explicit restriction on the legislatures and the government. These commas appear in virtually all presentations of the 2nd Amendment today, including the official NARA presentation. The correct wording as presented to the States for ratification is shown in the "True Bill" and the Original Congressional Engrossing of the Proposed Amendments.

Early publications of the Laws and Constitutions of the the United States DO NOT show these commas, i.e., the Bioren and Duane publication, "The Laws of the United States of America, from the 4th of March, 1789 to the 4th of March, 1815," available in the archives of Yale University, and the "The Constitutions of the United States", which I own and cherish, published in 1809 during Jefferson's administration by "Exeter: Printed by Charles Norris & Co for Edward Little & Co. Booksellers & Stationers, Newburyport."

This volume contains the Declaration of Independence, Articles of Confederation, State constitutions for New Hampshire, Massachusetts, Rhode Island (which was still operating under the King's Charter until 1843), Connecticut, New York, New Jersey, Pennsylvania, Delaware, Maryland, Virginia, North Carolina, South Carolina, Georgia, Vermont, Tennessee, Kentucky, and Ohio. It also has the "Government of the Northwest Territory", "An Act to Divide the Northwest Territory into two separate governments", "An Act Concerning the District of Columbia" and supplements, "An Act to incorporate the inhabitants of the City of Washington in the District of Columbia" and supplements, and finally "An Act erecting Louisiana into two Territories, and providing for the Temporary government thereof."

The Bioren and Duane edition of 1815 was published by an Act of Congress. This publication, in five volumes, represents the first authorized edition of the Laws of the United States and the U.S. Constitution issued following the destruction of the Library of Congress and the other records of the government by the British army in 1814. The lawmakers then seated as the Thirteenth Congress authorized the spending for this special edition on February 16th, 1815.

The Founders of our Nation and the Framers of the Constitution were well aware of the dangers of the tyranny and treason of a run-away governmental bureaucracy and had a very PRIMARY reason for the inclusion of the Second Amendment to the Constitution. Let's let them speak for themselves:

Firearms stand next in importance to the Constitution itself. They are the American people's liberty teeth and keystone under independence. From the hour the Pilgrims landed, to the present day, events occurrences and tendencies prove that to ensure peace, security and happiness, the rifle and pistol are equally indispensable. The very atmosphere of firearms everywhere restrains evil interference—they deserve a place of honor with all that's good.

—George Washington, Commanding General of the Continental Army, Father of Our Country and First President of the United States, in his address to 2nd Session of 1st Congress.

The strongest reason for the people to retain the right to keep and bear arms is, as a last resort, to protect themselves against tyranny in Government.

—Thomas Jefferson, author of the *Declaration of Independence*, and President of the United States

The highest number to which a standing army can be carried in any country does not exceed one hundredth part of the souls, or one twenty-fifth part of the number able to bear arms. This portion would not yield, in the United States, an army of more than twenty-five or thirty thousand men. To these would be opposed a militia amounting to near half a million citizens with arms in there hands, officered by men chosen from among themselves, fighting for their common liberties and united and conducted by governments possessing their affections and confidence. It may well be doubted whether a militia thus circumstanced could ever be conquered by such a proportion of regular troops. Besides the advantage of being armed, it forms a barrier against the enterprises of ambition, more insurmountable than any which a simple government of any form can admit of. The gov-

ernments of Europe are afraid to trust the people with arms. If they did, the people would surely shake off the yoke of tyranny, as America did. Let us not insult the free and gallant citizens of America with the suspicion that they would be less able to defend the rights of which they would be in actual possession than the debased subjects of arbitrary power would be to rescue theirs from the hands of their oppressors.

—James Madison, principal author of Constitution, principal writer of *The Federalist Papers*, President of the United States, Mainstream Revolutionary and Militant

What, Sir, is the use of a militia? It is to prevent the establishment of a standing army, the bane of liberty. ...Whenever Governments mean to invade the rights and liberties of the people, they always attempt to destroy the militia, in order to rise an army upon their ruins.

—Rep. Elbridge Gerry of Massachusetts, spoken during floor debate over the Second Amendment, I Annals of Congress at 750, August 17, 1789

It is not the function of the government to keep the citizen from falling into error; it is the function of the citizen to keep the government from falling into error.

—U.S. Supreme Court Justice Robert H. Parker, Chief Prosecutor for the United States of America at the Nuremberg Trials

Of those persons which oppose the upholding of the Second Amendment, a principal lobbyist for the "Brady Bill," in an excerpt from the January, 1984 issue of the National Educator, page 3, reveals that Sarah Brady is Chairman of Handgun Control, Inc., and while lobbying liberal Senator Howard Metzenbaum about gun control legislation, said to him:

Our task of creating a SOCIALIST America can only succeed when those who would resist us have been TOTALLY DISARMED. (emphasis added)

We owe a debt of gratitude to the Historical Society of Wisconsin, for they spent a great deal of time searching for this January, 1994 issue of the National Educator.

The Conspirators to form a Socialist New World Government and the United Nations are still at work treasonously subverting the Constitution in order to enslave the Citizens of the State of Montana, The United States of America and the World in a socialist union.

Thank you and Sincerely,
Randy L. Trochmann, Co-founder, Militia of Montana

SOURCE: OFFICIAL MILITIA OF MONTANA WEBSITE

In August 1995, John Salvi–the suspected murderer of two receptionists during a December 30, 1994, shooting spree at an abortion clinic in Brookline, Massachusetts–was declared competent to stand trial. Salvi is charged under Massachusetts law with the murders of Shannon Lowney and Lee Ann Nichols, and five other counts of aggravated assault.[1]

The Civil Rights Division of the Department of Justice, through the TFVAAP, investigates any instance in which customers or providers of reproductive health services are criminally threatened, obstructed, or injured while seeking or providing services.

International Terrorism

Foreign terrorists view the United States as a priority target. They and their supporters continue to live in and travel with great ease throughout the country. Ironically, the drug abusing population of the United States continues to finance terrorism around the world through consumption of the entire spectrum of illegal drugs. American dollars fill the war chests of terrorists around the world. They purchase cocaine shipped from Colombia through Mexico and the Caribbean, as well as black-tar heroin, marijuana, and increasingly, methamphetamine. The American user is also a major consumer of high-quality Southeast Asia heroin from the Golden Triangle. America is also a producer of marijuana, depressants, stimulants, hallucinogens, methamphetamine and so-called designer drugs. This creates a multibillion dollar need for drug money-laundering centers.

PUERTO RICO

The Commonwealth of Puerto Rico is closely intertwined with the United States. The island's inhabitants possess all the rights and obligations of United States citizens, except for the right to vote in presidential elections and the obligation to pay federal taxes. The United States also governs the Virgin Islands, Guam, and American Samoa. Puerto Rico is slightly less than three times the size of Rhode Island. Taino Indians, who inhabited the territory originally, called the island Boriken or Borinquen, a word that with various modifications is still popularly used to designate the people and island of Puerto Rico. The Taino Indians, who came from South America, inhabited the major portion of the island when the Spaniards arrived.

While the post-Colombian native language is Spanish, both Spanish and English are now the official languages. Language has been a central issue in Puerto Rican education and culture since 1898. Until 1930, U.S. authorities insisted upon making English the language of instruction in the schools, the intent being to produce English-speaking students of American culture. Strong resistance to the policy finally brought a change to Spanish as the basic school language, with English becoming a second language studied by all students. In 1991, the Puerto Rican legislature, following the lead of the pro-commonwealth Popular Democratic Party and the governor, Rafael Hernández Colon, endorsed a bill that made Spanish the island's official language, thus reversing a 1902 law that gave both Spanish and English official recognition. In 1993, the pro-statehood governor, Pedro J. Rossello, signed legislation restoring equal status to Spanish and English for the population of close to 3,900,000. Puerto Rico's population density of 1,100 people per square mile is among the world's highest; only Bangladesh, the Maldives, Barbados, Taiwan, South Korea and the city-states of Hong Kong and Singapore are more crowded.

It is estimated that some 2 million Puerto Ricans have migrated to the United States. Had these people remained in Puerto Rico, the island would be so densely populated that there would be virtually no room for people to live. Because of the massive migration to the mainland, more Puerto Ricans are said to live in New York City than in San Juan.

In addition to the slaves imported from Africa (Sudan, Congo, Senegal, Guinea, Sierra Leone, and the Gold, Ivory, and Grain Coasts), other ethnic groups brought to work on the plantations joined the island's racial mix. Fleeing Simón Bolívar's independence movements in South America, Spanish loyalists fled to Puerto Rico, a fiercely conservative Spanish colony during the early 1800s. French families also flocked here from both Louisiana and Haiti. As changing governments or violent revolutions depressed the economies of Scotland and Ireland, many farmers from those countries also journeyed to Puerto Rico in search of a better life.

While the Puerto Ricans have had a fairly peaceful existence, there have been some situations that came close to terrorism. The most notable included an action where a quasi-terrorist group, the **Macheteros**, blew up eleven jet fighters of Puerto Rico's National Guard near San Juan. Ronald Fernandez, Professor of Sociology and author of *Los Macheteros: The Violent Struggle for Puerto Rican Independence,* has spent the last seven years researching Puerto Rico. He writes of the Macheteros' frustrations and susceptibility to lashing out:

> On August 25, 1989, Filiberto Ojeda Rios, acting as his own attorney, gave his closing argument to the jury in a U.S. court in San Juan. The indictment, drawn in the name of the United States of America, charged that Ojeda Rios had shot at and assaulted agents of the Federal Bureau of Investigation. The prosecutor had been appointed by President Reagan, the judge by President Carter, and the American flag stood in the courtroom, but the jury was Puerto Rican.
>
> Far from denying his actions, Ojeda Rios embraced them, and asked the jury to uphold the right of the Puerto Rican people to use force, in self defense, against the unwanted, foreign presence of the United States of America.
>
> There are no American heroes [in this book,] nor is there a happy ending. Yet it is imperative for Americans to know our own contribution to the perpetuation of colonialism, particularly as some prepare to celebrate Columbus Day 1992. When the sun rises on October 12, 1992 marking 500 years of colonialism, Americans would do well to take a look at Puerto Rico and the destruction wrought there in the name of "democracy." The island today has a per-capita income of one-half that of Mississippi, the poorest state in the United States. Its rates of suicide, mental illness, drug addiction, crime, alcoholism, and sterilization of women are among the highest in the world.[2]

Highlighted is the hotly contested issue of the continuing status of Puerto Rico. In 1991, in an islandwide vote, Puerto Ricans rejected an amendment that would have "reviewed" their commonwealth status. In the referendum, commonwealth status was reaffirmed by a very close vote. The results were as follows: with Statehood, 788,296 (46.3 percent); Commonwealth, 826,326 (48.6 percent); Independence, 75,620 (04.4 percent); Nulls, 10,748 (00.7 percent). This issue has caused a lot of tempers to flare, but falls short of provoking terrorist groups.

The United States still seems to be "the land of the free and the home of the brave." But its very freedom, in a world of terrorism, can be its "Achilles heel." As

Flames engulf the Branch Davidian compound, April 19, 1993, in Waco, Texas. CP Picture Archive (Susan Weems)

the world economic situation continues to destabilize and the American economy stays strong, the gap between those who can get ahead and those that can't widens. As that gap grows, the disenfranchised movements in the United States, and around the globe, will become a more active threat to its peace and tranquility.

CANADA

Canada defines the most northern reaches of North America and extends all the way to the Arctic Ocean. It is a good neighbor of the United States and Canadians are more like Americans that different from them. This huge country, bordering the North Atlantic Ocean and North Pacific Ocean, is slightly larger than the United States (it is the second largest country in the world behind Russia), but has a population of only about 30,400,000. The permafrost in the northern territories is a major obstacle to development, as are the cyclonic storms that form east of the Rocky Mountains. The mixing of air masses from the Arctic, Pacific, and North American interior produce most of Canada's rain and snow.

As a member of the British Commonwealth, Canada's chief of state, since February 6, 1952, is Her Majesty Queen Elizabeth II, represented by an appointed governor general. The head of government is the elected prime minister. An affluent, high-tech industrial society, Canada today closely resembles the United States in per capita output, market-oriented economic system, and patterns of production. Since World War II, the impressive growth of the manufacturing, mining, and service sectors has transformed the nation from a largely rural and fishing economy into one primarily industrial and urban. Canada began the 1990s in recession, and real rates of growth have averaged only 1.1 percent so far this decade. Because of slower growth, Canada still faces high unemployment, especially in Quebec and the Maritime Provinces. With its natural resources, skilled labor force, and modern capital plant, however, Canada will surely enjoy better economic prospects in the future. The continuing constitutional impasse between English- and French-speaking areas is raising the possibility of a split in the confederation, and makes foreign investors somewhat edgy.

As Juliet O'Neill, of the *Ottawa Citizen*, said in 1996, "You're more likely to be struck down by lightning or die in a car crash than find yourself victim of a terrorist attack in Canada."[3] Your authors searched hard and long to find some examples of serious and violent terrorism in Canada. But very few such acts were discovered. In the three decades since terrorism has dominated the headlines and is constantly on the evening news, terrorist acts in Canada can be counted in single digits. The FLQ (*Front de liberation du Québec*) crisis in 1970 was the first, followed by the mid-1980s Armenian attacks on Turkish diplomats in Ottawa. And lastly, Sikh terrorists were allegedly involved in the crash of an Air India jet from Toronto which blew up over the coast of Ireland, killing 329 passengers, mostly Canadians. On the same day, in June 1985, an explosion occurred in the baggage hall at Tokyo Airport. Baggage had just arrived on a Canadian Pacific airliner from Vancouver. The limited data on terrorism and violence showed criminal use of explosives at the very low incidence rate of two cases per 100,000 people. It appears that in "the peaceable kingdom" of Canada, spectacular violence is rare and terrorism is something expected to be seen happening on television, to other people in other countries.

A major concern is that Canada may be being used as a base for organizing, fundraising, consciousness-raising, transport and logistics for international terrorists among the many refugees who have come there. These groups range from Tamil Tigers and Islamic fundamentalists to Protestant and Catholic Irish paramilitaries and Latin American and Asian activists. Canada stays on the alert for homegrown terrorism from what they refer to as "issue group extremists." Examples of these are animal rights activists, armed Indians, anti-abortion radicals, neo-fascist bikers and skinheads.

Of course, potential violence stemming from disputes over land and politics, should Quebec someday choose separation in a referendum, is always on the agenda of Canadian counterterrorism agencies. Among tactics used by low-level terrorist groups in recent years are consumer scare threats, mail bombs, shootings, and vandalism. Canada has some problems with illicit production of cannabis for the domestic drug market, where use of hydroponics technology permits growers to plant large quantities of high-quality marijuana indoors. With its links to the Far East and a very long coastline, Canada has a growing role as a transit point for heroin and cocaine entering the United States market.

Front du Liberation de Québec (FLQ)

Liberal young Quebecers were eager for change and the right to establish a separate French-speaking sovereign state within Canada. The turbulent days of the radical 1960s saw terrorism come to Central Canada in the shape of a separatist movement, the *Front du Liberation de Québec* (FLQ). From its beginnings in 1963, its aim was the separation of the Province of Quebec from English-speaking Canada. Canada is part of the British Commonwealth, and therefore pays allegiance to the Crown. French-speaking Quebec in the 1960s wanted status as a sovereign country within Canada. The debate on a separation still continues to this day. In the 1960s, the radical and left-wing FLQ espoused a workers' revolution as a means of achieving that goal. Along with many French-speaking Canadians, the FLQ strongly resented the control that English Canada exerted on both politics and the economy in the Province of Quebec. The *Parti Québecois*, still a political party today, has actively pursued the agenda of separation.

The political boost that the FLQ needed came from an unexpected source. On a visit to Montreal in 1967, the President of France, General Charles De Gaulle, in a now famous speech, ended with the phrase *"vive le Québec libre"* (long live free

Seargeant Major Walter R. Leja, a Canadian Army engineer, lies injured after a FLQ bomb exploded in his hands on May 17, 1963, in Montreal. CP Picture Archive.

Quebec). Throughout the 1960s, Anglophone areas of Montreal were targets for bomb attacks by the FLQ.[4] More than 200 explosions took place between 1963 and 1970, with the Quebec government and the federal government seemingly powerless to intervene. The FLQ used robberies to finance their operations and to strike at Anglophone businesses. The terrorist event which spelled the end for the FLQ was the kidnapping of the British Trade Commissioner, James Cross, and the Province of Quebec's Labor Minister, Pierre Laporte. The kidnappings were of little value to the FLQ but gave the Prime Minister, Pierre Trudeau, the weapon he needed to use a firm hand against all subversive elements, not only in Quebec, but throughout the rest of Canada. The two VIP's were kidnapped in October 1970. The body of Laporte was found days later in the trunk of a car. Canadians were appalled that the FLQ would go to such lengths. The brutal murder turned public and political opinion sharply against them. James Cross was located in a suburb of Montreal by the Royal Canadian Mounted Police (RCMP). After protracted negotiations, the kidnappers were allowed to fly to Cuba in exchange for his release. They had also demanded the release of colleagues serving prison sentences for FLQ offenses, but these demands were not met.

One of the founders of the FLQ, Raymond Villeneuve, was convicted of planting a number of bombs and sentenced to twelve years in prison. A national referendum, held in Canada in October 1995, saw a narrow defeat for the separation movement; however, Villenueve had by now been released from prison and was assisting a new, younger breed of Quebec separatists bent on tearing up the constitution. The *Movement de Liberation Nationale du Québec* is extremely small, consisting of about two dozen diehard activists and former militant members of the defunct FLQ.[5] The presence of this terrorist movement, the only one of note in normally peaceful Canada, demonstrates that this country was not totally immune to such social violence.

CUBA

The island Republic of Cuba is the largest country in Caribbean. It is located between the Caribbean Sea and the North Atlantic Ocean, just ninety miles south of Florida, and is slightly smaller than Pennsylvania. The U.S. Naval Base at

Guantanamo Bay is leased by the United States and remains part of Cuba, and only mutual agreement or United States abandonment can terminate the lease. This has been a serious bone of contention in United States/Cuban relations for decades. The population of this communist state is almost 11,000,000. Its ethnic makeup is unique and diverse, with 51 percent mulatto, 37 percent white, 11 percent black and 1 percent Chinese.

The state is the primary player in the Cuban economy and controls practically all foreign trade. The government has undertaken several reforms in recent years to stem excess liquidity, increase labor incentives, and alleviate serious shortages of food, consumer goods, and services. The liberalized agricultural markets introduced in October 1994, at which state and private farmers sell above-quota production at unrestricted prices, have broadened legal consumption alternatives and reduced black market prices. Government efforts to lower subsidies to unprofitable enterprises and to shrink the money supply caused the peso's black market value to move from a peak of 120 to the dollar in the summer of 1994 to a low of 20–21 to the dollar at the end of 1996. New taxes helped drive down the number of legally registered self-employed workers from 208,000 in January 1996 to 180,000 by December. Havana announced that GDP declined by 35 percent during 1989–1993, the result of lost Soviet aid and domestic inefficiencies. The drop in GDP was turned around in 1994, when Cuba reported a 0.7 percent growth. Government officials claimed that GDP increased by 2.5 percent in 1995 and 7.8 percent in 1996. Export earnings rose an estimated 40 percent in 1996 to $2.1 billion. This trend is a sign that Cuba may be making a move back into the economy of the region. Some say this is largely on the strength of increased sugar shipment to Russia and higher nickel production through a joint venture with a Canadian firm. With the economic recovery, imports rose for the second straight year, growing by an estimated 26 percent to $3.5 billion. The economy, however, experienced another downturn, and living standards for the average Cuban have not improved significantly.

Fidel Castro

Kim Il-Sung , Deng Xiaoping, Peron, Khrushchev, Kadar, Franco and Tito are dictators long departed. Fidel Castro, the longest-serving leader of any country in the modern world, has all but destroyed Cuba with iron-fisted leadership, yet remains in power.

Born on August 13, 1926, Castro led a revolt against the dictator Batista and became the President of Cuba in 1959. He remains as solidly ensconced in his palace in Havana as he was forty years ago. Recent data suggest that nearly half the Cuban workforce is unemployed and most Cubans live on a bare subsistence of only 1,400 calories a day. Foreign investment, which peaked at $563 million in 1994, was as low as $30 million in 1998. Worst of all, Cuba has lost its long position as the world's largest producer of sugar. Barely 3 million tons are being produced, an all-time low.

Castro is a "classic" dictator, in that he emerged not from the historical center of his society but from its periphery. His father was a rough and deceitful "gallego" from the impoverished north of Spain. Castro came from a background similar to Napoleon, Hitler and Stalin. He has a perversely captivating combination of seductiveness and violence. As a boy, he tried to burn down his parents' house and burn up his father's car. Legend says that young Fidel would regularly hang over a canyon while the trains thundered by. Above all, he is the perfect Machiavellian, naturally mastering every technique of political, physical and psychological manipulation over the Cuban people, his troops and leaders around the world.

The disastrous Bay of Pigs invasion of April 1961 started on April 15 with the bombing of Cuba by what appeared to be defecting Cuban air force pilots. At 6:00 A.M. on that Saturday, two B-26 aircraft with Cuban markings bombed three Cuban military bases. Seven people were killed at Camp Libertad and forty-seven people were killed at other sites on the island.

The B-26s left Cuba and flew to Miami, creating the appearance of a defection to the United States. Both planes were badly damaged and their tanks were nearly empty. The Cuban government, in exile in New York City, released a statement saying that the bombings in Cuba were "carried out by Cubans inside Cuba."

Then, in the early hours of April 17, the assault on the Bay of Pigs began, with an invading force of about 1,500 Cuban exiles. It immediately became obvious that the troops would have problems in the area chosen for them to land. The Bay of Pigs is a swampy marshland area which would be difficult for any troops. The Cuban air force sank the command vessel *Marsopa* and the supply ship *Houston*. The 5th battalion was lost on the *Houston*, as were the supplies for the landing teams and eight other vessels. The operation soon broke down as the other supply ships were kept at bay by Castro's air force, which easily won superiority over the invading force. His fast moving T-33s, although unimpressive by today's standards, made short work of the slow moving B-26s. The invaders lost ten of their twelve aircraft. With air power firmly in control of Castro's forces, the end was near for the invading army.

Over the next seventy-two hours, the Cubans pushed the invaders back to their landing zone at Playa Girón. Some began to surrender while others fled into the hills. A total of 114 men were killed in the abortive action, while thirty-six died as prisoners in Cuban cells.

Others were to live out twenty years or more in those cells, plotting to topple the government of Castro.

On the international scene, the Bay of Pigs invasion led to increased tensions between the United States and the Soviet Union. During the invasion, messages were exchanged between John Kennedy and Nikita Khrushchev regarding the events in Cuba. Khrushchev accused the Americans of being involved in the invasion and stated in one of his messages that:

> A so-called small war can produce a chain reaction in all parts of the world...we shall render the Cuban people and their Government all necessary assistance in beating back the armed attack on Cuba.

Though this crisis passed, it set the stage for the next major crisis over Soviet nuclear missiles in Cuba, and led to the Soviets increasing their military support for Castro.

The long-term ramifications of the Bay of Pigs invasion and failure seem to be that, thirty-four years later, Castro is still in power. As with many wars, even a cold one, the leader is able to rally his people around him against an aggressor. Now that he is no longer receiving help from the Soviet Union things are beginning to change. He has opened up the Cuban economy for some investment, mainly in telecommunications, oil exploration, and joint ventures. In an attempt to stay in power, he is trying to adapt his country to the new reality of the world. Rather than suppressing the educated elite, he is giving them a place in guiding Cuba. The question is, will they eventually want more power and a right to control Cuba's fate without Castro's guidance and support? If the collapse of past regimes is any indication, they will eventually want more power.

Source: Department of State Website 1999

While he was at a Jesuit high school, Castro became fascinated as he read about the European fascists. From Mussolini, he took hysterical rhetorical gestures. From Hitler, he borrowed the sociology of revolution. Hitler had created a power base from the alienated and devastated German lower classes. Castro created his own base from the poor workers and farmers. When he marched into Havana, in January of 1959, he began using his unique system of revolutionary control to bring down the upper and middle classes through seizing their lands, removal of their privileges and terror. He managed to eliminate any competitors for power, by sending them to places where they would surely die (Che Guevara in Bolivia, 1967; Frank Pais on the streets of revolutionary Santiago de Cuba, 1957), or by executing them (General Ochoa in Havana, 1989).

Meanwhile, his military and intelligence organizations assured, and still assure, his physical control over the island. Castro has been extraordinarily adept at using the traditional Cuban fear of the "Miami Cubans" and the hated "Americanos" to hold his own people ignorant and in check.[6]

"Hatred is an element of struggle; relentless hatred of the enemy that impels us over and beyond the natural limitations of man and transforms us into effective, violent, selective, and cold killing machines. Our soldiers must be thus; a people without hatred cannot vanquish a brutal enemy." Thus spoke **Che Guevara**, one of the most radical of Castro's entourage in 1967. As mentioned above, he was sent by Castro to die in Bolivia. Guevara advocated hatred, or as he put it, "relentless hatred" to "impel us over and beyond the natural limitations of man." This use of hatred to encourage the dehumanization of one's enemy is but another manifestation of the doctrine found throughout the centuries to justify mass murder and torture. It has apparently been used to great success in Cuba, keeping Castro in power for forty years.

THE DOMINICAN REPUBLIC AND HAITI

These two small countries share an island and have been involved in strife, war, rebellion and terrorism in the Caribbean to some extent, although minor. We shall examine them briefly as a possible source of future problems in that region. First we look at the Dominican Republic.

The Dominican Republic

The Dominican Republic is located on the eastern two-thirds of the island of Hispaniola, between the Caribbean Sea and the North Atlantic Ocean, and is bordered by Haiti. It is slightly more than twice the size of New Hampshire, with a population of almost 7,900,000. The ethnic mix is a reflection of past developments, with white 16 percent, black 11 percent, and mixed 73 percent. The population is 95 percent Roman Catholic.

Economic reforms launched in late 1994 contributed to exchange rate stabilization, reduced inflation, and strong GDP growth in 1995–96. In 1996, there was increased mineral and petroleum exploration, and a new investment law that allows for repatriation of capital dividends has drawn more investment to the island. Upon coming to power in August 1996, President Fernandez inherited a trouble-ridden economy, hampered by a pressured peso, a large external debt, nearly bankrupt state-owned enterprises, and a manufacturing sector hindered by daily power outages. In December, Fernandez presented a bold economic reform package—which included such reforms as the devaluation of the peso, income tax cuts, a 50 percent increase in sales taxes, reduced import tariffs, and increased gasoline prices—in an attempt to create a market-oriented economy that could compete internationally. The legislature, however, has been slow to act on several of the economic measures. The Dominican per capita purchasing power is $3,670, three times that of neighboring Haiti.

The Dominican Republic's History of Pain and Politics

Continued violence and instability in the Dominican Republic prompted United States President William H. Taft to dispatch a commission to Santo Domingo on September 24, 1912, to mediate among the warring factions. The presence of a 750-

member force of United States Marines apparently convinced the Dominicans of the seriousness of Washington's threats to intervene directly in the conflict.

Archbishop Nouel was assigned as provisional president, but he was unable to mediate successfully between the ambitions of rival Horacistas and Jimenistas and he stepped down. His successor was equally unable to restrain the hostilities, and a new American president, Woodrow Wilson, had to intervene. Taft had cajoled the combatants with hints of military action, but Wilson delivered an ultimatum: elect a president or the United States will impose one. Comparatively fair elections returned Jiménez to the presidency. He tried to broaden support, but the internecine conflicts that resulted had quite the opposite effect.

United States forces had already occupied Haiti by this time, and the first Marines soon landed. They established effective control of the country within two months and proclaimed a military government. Reactions of many Dominicans were largely positive. Most Dominicans, however, greatly resented the loss of their sovereignty to foreigners, few of whom spoke Spanish or displayed genuine concern for the welfare of their republic.

From 1917 to 1921, the United States forces battled a guerrilla movement in that area known as the "gavilleros." The guerrillas enjoyed considerable support among the population, and they benefited from a superior knowledge of the terrain. However, the gavilleros eventually yielded to the occupying forces' determined, often brutal, counterinsurgent methods.

After World War I, public opinion in the United States began to run against the occupation. Warren G. Harding, who succeeded Wilson in March, 1921, had campaigned against the occupations of both Haiti and the Dominican Republic. In June 1921, United States representatives presented a withdrawal proposal, known as the Harding Plan, which included elections under United States supervision. Popular reaction to the plan was overwhelmingly negative. In the presidential election of March 15, 1924, Horacio Vásquez Lajara handily won the presidency and a comfortable majority in both houses of congress and the republic returned to Dominican hands.[7]

The Vásquez administration still shines in Dominican history like a star amid a gathering storm. Vásquez was also a veteran of political infighting. In an effort to undercut his primary rival he agreed, in 1927, to extend his term from four to six years, which effectively invalidated the constitution of 1924.

Trujillo occupied a strong position in this contest. The commander of the national army, he established his power base behind the scenes and was ready, by 1930, to assume control of the country. This uncertainty prompted Rafael Estrella Ureña to proclaim a revolution. Estrella marched on the capital, while army forces remained in their barracks, as Trujillo declared "neutrality." The ailing Vásquez fled the capital and Estrella assumed the provisional presidency.

In the May elections, it became clear that Trujillo would be the only candidate the army would allow, and army personnel harassed and intimidated electoral officials and eliminated potential opponents. The new dictator announced his election with 95 percent of the vote. The dictator proceeded to rule the country like a feudal lord for thirty-one years and held the office of president from 1930 to 1938 and from 1942 to 1952.

Ideologically, Trujillo leaned toward fascism. The trappings of his personality cult, the size and architectural mediocrity of his building projects, and the level of repressive control exercised by the state invited comparison with the style of his contemporaries, Hitler in Germany and Mussolini in Italy. Cold War winds from Washington persuaded Castro to crack down and to outlaw the Dominican Communist Party (*Partido Communista Dominicano*–PCD).

It was his adventurous foreign policy that drew the ire of other governments and led directly to his downfall. In October 1937, Trujillo ordered the massacre of Haitians living in the Dominican Republic in retaliation for execution by the Haitian government of his most valued covert agents in that country. The Dominican army slaughtered as many as 20,000 unarmed men, women, and children. The Trujillo regime became increasingly isolated from the governments of other nations. Cuba's Fidel Castro aided a small, abortive invasion attempt by dissident Dominicans in 1959. Trujillo, however, expressed greater concern over Venezuela's President Rómulo Betancourt (1959–64). Trujillo developed an obsessive personal hatred of Betancourt and supported numerous plots to overthrow him. This led the Venezuelan government to take its case against Trujillo to the Organization of American States (OAS). An infuriated Trujillo ordered the assassination of Betancourt. The attempt, on June 24, 1960, injured, but did not kill, the Venezuelan president, but inflamed world opinion against Trujillo. The members of the OAS, expressing this outrage, voted unanimously to sever diplomatic relations and to impose economic sanctions on the Dominican Republic.

Civil War and United States Intervention, 1965

A coup effectively negated the 1962 elections by installing a civilian junta, known as the Triumvirate. The initial head of the Triumvirate, Emilio de los Santos, resigned and was replaced by Donald Reid Cabral. The widespread dissatisfaction with Reid and his government resulted in a revolution in April 1965.

The vanguard of the 1965 revolution, the perredeistas (members of the PRD) and other supporters of Bosch, called themselves Constitutionalists (a reference to their support for the 1963 constitution). A combination of reformist military and aroused civilian combatants, they took to the streets on April 24, seized the National Palace, and installed Rafael Molina Ureña as provisional president. The revolution took on the dimensions of a civil war when conservative military forces, led by army general Elías Wessín y Wessín, struck back against the Constitutionalists on April 25. These conservative forces called themselves Loyalists. Despite tank assaults and bombing runs by Loyalist forces, however, the Constitutionalists held their positions in the capital; they appeared poised to branch out and to secure control of the entire country.

On April 28th, the United States intervened in the civil war. President Lyndon B. Johnson ordered in forces that eventually totaled 20,000 to secure Santo Domingo and to restore order. Johnson had acted in the stated belief that the Constitutionalists were dominated by communists and that they therefore could not be allowed to come to power. The intervention was subsequently granted some measure of hemispheric approval by the creation of an OAS-sponsored peace force, which supplemented the United States military presence in the republic. An initial interim government was headed by Héctor García Godoy, who assumed a provisional presidency. Violent skirmishes between Loyalists and Constitutionalists went on sporadically as, once again, elections were organized.

Joaquín Balaguer Ricardo won handily, garnering 57 percent of the vote in balloting held July 1, 1966. His Reformist Party (*Partido Reformista*–PR) also captured majorities in the Congress. Balaguer went on to serve as president for twelve years. A relative nonentity under Trujillo, he demonstrated, once in power, the astuteness with which he had studied the techniques of the late dictator. Even though as a conservative he theoretically was more secure against military machinations, he actively sought to head off opposition from the armed forces by rewarding officers loyal to him, purging those he suspected, and rotating everyone's assignments on a regular and frequent basis. He curtailed nonmilitary opposition through selective (compared to the Trujillo years) repression by the National Police. His reelection in 1970 and in 1974 was accomplished largely through intimidation. The PRD, the only viable, broad-based opposition party, boycotted both.

The contemporary political system of the Dominican Republic dates from 1978. That year Balaguer, who had governed the country in an authoritarian, but paternalistic, manner for the preceding twelve years, was forced, because of domestic and international pressures, to yield the presidency to Guzmán, a wealthy rancher and candidate of the PRD, who had clearly won the election. Guzmán governed democratically and with full respect for human rights, but he committed suicide in 1982, apparently because of evidence of corruption reaching into his own family. The vice president, Majluta, took over temporarily until a new government, which actually had been elected before Guzmán's suicide, could be inaugurated.

The 1982 election was fair, honest, and competitive. It was won by Jorge, a lawyer who, like Guzmán, was a member of the PRD. But whereas Guzmán had represented the conservative wing of the party, Jorge represented its centrist, or social-democratic, wing.

President Jorge continued, like Guzmán, to govern in a democratic matter. His government respected civil liberties and honored human rights. Jorge had promised to expand the democratic reforms begun by his predecessor in the areas of agrarian reform, social justice, and modernization. He campaigned on the slogan, and entered office with the intention of bringing, "economic democracy" to the country to go with its now flourishing political democracy.

But 1982, the year of Jorge's inauguration, was the year the bottom dropped out of the Dominican economy. The country began to feel the full impact of the second oil price rise, induced by the **Organization of Petroleum Exporting Countries (OPEC)**; recession in the United States and Western Europe dried up the market for Dominican exports; and the international debt crisis also hit home strongly. These conditions forced Jorge to abandon his ambitious reform agenda in favor of austerity, belt tightening and a cutback in services. The nation witnessed the wrenching dilemma of a reform democrat, a socialist, who had to give up his entire social-democratic program in order to impose severely restrictive economic policies, the burden of which, as usual, fell most heavily on the shoulders of the poor—precisely those people who had been Jorge's main constituents. Jorge's popularity plummeted, and in 1985 riots broke out in response to his austerity measures, riots that the police put down with considerable loss of civilian life.

To his credit, Jorge succeeded in putting in place a sorely needed budget-balancing program that offered hope of getting the country out of its severe economic troubles. The steep decline in the president's popularity, however, prompted even members of his own party in the congress and elsewhere to turn against him. In addition, increasing evidence of corruption in the public bureaucracy began to surface; as the austerity measures pinched, there was little extra money in the system, and the low-level patronage that had always existed began to be perceived as blatant, high-level graft. As Jorge's popularity declined, so did that of his entire government and his party.

New elections were held in 1986. President Jorge's deeply divided PRD eventually nominated Majluta, Guzmán's vice president, who four years earlier had served a short stint as interim president. Majluta was of Lebanese background, a longtime PRD stalwart, and a businessman who was tainted with the corruption of the previous administrations. Balaguer, who, though old and legally blind, still enjoyed widespread popularity, opposed him. Many associated Balaguer with the economic boom of the 1970s; in addition, he was widely admired as a shrewd, resourceful, and skilled politician. In a very closely contested election, Balaguer won with 41 percent of the vote to Majluta's 39 percent. Another former president, Bosch, candidate of the leftist Dominican Liberation Party (Partido de la Liberación Dominicana–PLD), garnered 18 percent.

In office, Balaguer proved as adept as before, although now slowed by age and infirmity. He juggled assignments within the armed forces to assure its loyalty and support; followed policies that pleased the economic elite, while at the same time doling out land and patronage to the peasants; and fostered greater contact with Cuba, while simultaneously keeping United States support. He listened to advice from all quarters, but kept his own counsel, kept his subordinates off guard and insecure so they could not develop a base from which to challenge the president himself, and refused to designate a successor while keeping all his own options open. Balaguer delegated some limited power and patronage to subordinates, but he kept most of the reins of power in his own hands; he let cabinet and autonomous agency heads have a bit of responsibility, while he maintained control of the all important matters of patronage, money, and the military. Whatever one thinks of his policies, Balaguer must be considered one of the cleverest presidents in Dominican history.

Haiti

The Republic of Haiti occupies the western third of the island of Hispaniola, bordering on the west of the Dominican Republic It is slightly smaller than Maryland but has a population that is predominantly black (95 percent), with mulatto and white comprising only 5 percent. More than six and a half million people are crowded into half the land space of their neighbor, the Dominican Republic. Haitians are predominantly Roman Catholic (80 percent), yet an overwhelming majority also practice voodoo.

About 75 percent of the population live in abject poverty. Nearly 70 percent of all Haitians depend on the agriculture sector, which consists mainly of small-scale subsistence farming and employs about two-thirds of the economically active work force. The country has experienced little or no job creation since President Preval took office in February 1996. Failures to reach agreements with international sponsors have denied Haiti badly needed budget and development assistance. Meeting aid conditions in 1997 will be especially challenging in the face of mounting popular criticism of reforms.

François **"Papa Doc"** Duvalier was the absolute dictator of Haiti from 1957 to 1971. His nickname came from his career as a physician. He became director general of the Haitian national public health service in 1946 and subsequently served as minister of health and of labor. After opposing Paul Magloire's coup in 1950, he hid in the interior, practicing medicine, until a general political amnesty was granted in 1956. In 1957, with army backing, "Papa Doc" was overwhelmingly elected president. Reelected in a sham election in 1961, he declared himself president for life in 1964. His regime, the longest in Haiti's history, was a brutal reign of terror; political opponents were summarily executed, and the notorious Tonton Macoutes (secret police) kept the populace in a state of abject terror. Under Duvalier, the economy of Haiti continued to deteriorate, and the illiteracy rate remained at about 90 percent. Duvalier nevertheless maintained his hold over Haiti. His practice of voodooism encouraged rumors among the people that he possessed supernatural powers. He died in 1971, after arranging for his son, Jean-Claude, "Baby Doc," to succeed him.

Jean-Bertrand Aristide became president of Haiti in December 1990, elected in a landslide, only to be ousted seven months after taking office. He went into exile in Venezuela and later the United States. Three years later, a 20,000-member United States led multinational force intervened to forcibly disband the army and restore Aristide to power.

President Aristide was a radical Catholic priest who defended liberal theology. He worked among Haiti's poor and was part of a group of progressive priests who opposed the Duvalier dictatorship. Expelled from his religious order in 1988 because of his revolutionary teachings, he became the candidate of a coalition of leftist parties in the 1990 presidential elections and was elected with an overwhelming majority. Party infighting plagued Aristide toward the end of his five-year term, however, and has continued for the new administration of René Préval, who took over in February 1998.[8]

In the relative safety of the new U.N. protected Haiti, Aristide recently launched an umbrella movement to invigorate and unify the governing Lavalas coalition. Many Haitians still have hopes of seeing Aristide back in the National Palace in the year 2000. Aristide has insisted that his latest efforts are not a challenge to Preval, a friend and activist whom Aristide belatedly endorsed for president last year. By law, Aristide could not seek a consecutive term as president of Haiti.

It must be emphasized that the appearance of safety in this battered nation is not necessarily reality; in 1998, unknown gunmen opened fire on the National Palace and police headquarters in the latest apparent effort to try to destabilize Haiti's new government. At least one person was killed, a civilian working at the police station, and a policeman was slightly injured. U.N. soldiers and Haitian police officers returned fire but no casualties were reported. U.N. helicopters also took to the air and patrolled the city. There have been death threats against Préval, former president Aristide and several liberal Haitian legislators. The distinctive sounds of gunfire ring out almost nightly in Port-au-Prince, the Haitian capital.

Préval has blamed the attacks on soldiers from the army that ousted Aristide in 1991 and was disbanded after an American-led military intervention restored the exiled Aristide in October 1994. Préval also has speculated that the subversion could be connected to his controversial plan to privatize some state-owned enterprises. The fate of this beleaguered, poor and downtrodden country is far from settled. The state terrorism created by the two despotic Duvaliers, a combination of violence and voodoo, has left a legacy of former state terrorists ready to leap into the vacuum created by the departure of the U.N. operation. Time will tell if this dire prospect will become reality.[9]

SUMMARY

North America's experience with international terrorism on the home front is a new phenomenon for the security forces to deal with. Local paramilitary-style militia, the Ku Klux Klan, hate groups and organized gangs have been around for many decades; however, it was the last decade of the twentieth century that brought the international horrors of terrorist bombs home to Americans. Whole generations of British and European cities have grown up with terrorism on their doorsteps, so the World Trade Center bombing brought the U.S. onto the international map of terrorist attacks. Much U.S. attention is given to the fringe groups, such as the Branch Davidians, and individuals such as the Unabomber. From an international viewpoint the U.S. sees itself as being vulnerable to attack, particularly from Islamic fundamentalists, wherever there are U.S. personnel and interests. This now, of course, includes assaults within the borders of the U.S. Canada on the other hand, thanks to its liberal policies on immigration, has seen an influx from third world countries of thousands of "refugees." No doubt most are genuine, but some have escaped from oppressive regimes only to foster and promote terrorism from within Canada. This has been evidenced by the downing of an Air India Boeing 747 off the southern coast of the Republic of Ireland. Canada's only brush with an organized front using terror tactics has been the central Canadian experience with the FLQ. Whether the cause of separation will see any resurgence of an FLQ-styled organization is not apparent at the end of this decade. Sporadic problems in the Caribbean and Cuba continue to flare and most of the terrorist and insurgent problems in the islands have been as a result of economic downturns and inefficient and corrupt governments. Cuba remains firmly under the control and dictates of Fidel Castro, and his power continues to covertly influence other Latin American states.

Terms to Remember

World Trade Center	domestic terrorist acts	Alfred P. Murrah Federal Building
SLA	Waco Massacre	drive-by shootings
two-tiered system	New World Order	TFVAAP
FACE	Macheteros	FLQ
Che Guevara	OPEC	Papa Doc

Review Questions

Describe the terrorist events that brought major international and domestic terrorism home to the United States.

Describe the motives of the Canadian FLQ movement and its major acts of terrorism.

Why is there a movement on Puerto Rico for independence?

Describe the problems in Haiti and why it is having so much trouble surviving.

Discuss why Fidel Castro has been able to maintain power in Cuba for so long?

Endnotes

1. In this chapter much was extracted from web sites such as: the The U.S. State Department of State, *1997 Patterns of Global Terror* Report; The U.S. Department of State, *Country Reports on Human Rights Practices*; The U.S. Department of State, *Background Notes: Geographic Entities and International Organizations*; The U.S. Central Intelligence Agency, *World Factbook* and other government sources. We are continually and eternally grateful for these modern and the information they have provided to work into our writing.

2. The U.S. Department of State, *Background Notes: Geographic Entities and International Organizations*; The U.S. Central Intelligence Agency, *World Factbook* and other government sources.

3. Excerpted from *The Ottawa Citizen*, August 3, 1996, by Juliet O'Neill, Foreign Affairs.

4. George Rosie, *The Directory of International Terrorism*, (Paragon House, New York 1987), p. 123.

5. Canadian Press, December 3, 1995, "Neo-FLQ Group to fight for breakup," the Internet.

6. Copyright (c) 1998 Universal Press Syndicate. All rights reserved.

7. Offices of the General Customs Receivership, Santo Domingo, 1907, Courtesy National Archives.

8. *The Columbia Encyclopedia*, Fifth Edition Copyright (c)1993, Columbia University Press. Licensed from Inso Corporation.

9. Michael Norton, Associated Press Writer, August 19, 1996, Port-au-Prince, Haiti (AP).

PART 3

COUNTERTERRORISM

Terrorism in Korea in 1986. Required careful safeguards for VIP protection. Courtesy of U.S. Department of Defense.

CHAPTER 13

COUNTERING TERRORISM

Terrorists don't play golf on Sundays; we won't play golf on Sundays.

—Field Marshall Templar

OVERVIEW

One of the most fascinating subjects on the topic of terrorism is the means by which governments deal with both indigenous and international terrorism. In this chapter the student will learn about nations that use different tactics and methods to deal with terrorist issues and see how the democracies of the world mix military with civilian police operations. The methods used to gain information on suspected terror groups will also be discussed, with some of the most effective and recognized response units for countering terrorism.

The student will be shown how difficult it is for covert operations by forces against terrorism to respect suspected terrorists' civil liberties, and how easily such efforts conflict with their mission in a democratic society. The need for inter-agency and intra-agency cooperation and the free flow of information between those agencies will be examined, particularly in the aftermath of such incidents as those at Waco and Ruby Ridge.

The student will understand the need is for nations to have a trained and specifically designated organization that is responsible for responding to terrorist incidents as well as maintaining civil liberties on a scale acceptable to the public in general. We will examine the important part the media plays, as does the public, in the critical intelligence gathering role. The student will gain an appreciation of how an effective counterterrorism agency must gain the acceptance of the public it serves in its efforts to stem the flow of terrorist activity.

THE ROLES FOR COUNTERTERRORISM

Are the actions of subversive groups and insurgents terrorist or criminal? In many countries legislation has been enacted not only to ban membership in terror organizations, but to allow for certain suspensions of civil rights to facilitate law enforcement. To implement such actions successfully in a western democracy requires that the government ensure that such legislation requires renewal on a regular basis. In the United Kingdom, the legislation restricting the Irish Republican Army and other terrorist groups required the government to regularly justify its need for such drastic powers, or it would automatically lapse.

The tactics of terrorists which strike fear in the public for political gain are well documented. This has been clearly shown in the U.K., where the Provisional IRA has waged a campaign of indiscriminate violence against the authorities as well as innocent civilians. One of the earliest terror incidents in Great Britain was the attack on the Parachute Regiment Officers Mess in Aldershot, in the south of England. It was viewed by many as reprisal for the Bloody Sunday massacre by British paratroopers in Northern Ireland (see Chapter 4). The reaction depicted in local and national press coverage and on the television news was complete outrage at such a senseless act. Immediately after the bombing, there were sporadic incidents against local Irish families, who were intimidated and even assaulted. The same reaction occurred after the Guilford and Birmingham bombings. Calls for restraint from both ends of the British political and religious spectrum went out quickly, and defused a major outpouring of hatred against the several million Irish citizens who have coexisted peacefully alongside their English, Welsh and Scottish neighbors.

Maintaining Order

The example of the Irish "troubles" has been remarkable in many respects. In Britain and Northern Ireland, the role of the police had always been very public, and the typical British "bobby" was always on hand to assist. During the terrorist campaign of bombing on the mainland of Britain, the police did not resort to a system of rigid rules and control. As has been evidenced in many Latin American countries, threats and intimidation by terrorist actions have too often been met by even harsher measures inflicted by military police. In the British experience, terror against the public in general reached almost epidemic proportions in the 1970s. But order and calm prevailed and the public outrage was contained. Rather than form vigilante groups to hunt down suspected terrorists, the public and media were fully supportive of police actions. The police were shown, on TV news coverage, as the front line troops, always the first on the scene of whatever new atrocity that had been perpetrated by the IRA. London in the 1970s became a virtual battleground, but sound police tactics and investigative techniques did far more to bring criminal terrorists to justice than the suspension of civil liberties might have done.

In many countries throughout the world, armed and aggressive police are a reality. That was not the case in Great Britain, where police were unarmed throughout the IRA crisis. The police adhered to their role of identifying, tracking down and apprehending terrorists as they would any criminal. Police investigations are all about the necessity to gather information, intelligence and ultimately evidence. Britain's Special Branch, which deals with terrorists, took the lead in gathering intelligence on subversive Irish groups operating in Northern Ireland and Great Britain. Success in such efforts, however, involves a cooperation between police, the public and the media. As has been seen in the United States, cooperation between agencies may be strained. Some jealously guard not only sources, but information as well. Usually, the public is the last to know the true story. There are no simple right or wrong tactics in combating terrorists. There are, however, many examples of how and how not to deal with terrorist situations.

The **Balcombe Street** siege was a botched IRA action in which a group of armed terrorists held an elderly couple hostage in their central London home. The standoff, which was captured by television for all to see, was handled effectively and decisively by the Metropolitan Police. What may also have caused the terrorists to give up was the leaked briefing to the press that the SAS were en route to assist the police and the terrorists wanted nothing to do with that elite paramilitary organization. (We will discuss the SAS later on in this chapter.) The most open display of police weaponry is seen at London's Heathrow Airport, which has been the site of numerous false alarms as well as actual bombings and mortar attacks. The message is clearly sent that the police are ready to respond with overwhelming force.

Repression

To determine whether repressive actions by the state against terror are effective, one only has to examine the Soviet Union before the fall of that communist regime. Very few, if any, terrorist attacks were either recorded or reported in the former Soviet Union, which had a thriving community of secret police and thousands of informers in every sector of business and society. This made it very difficult, if not impossible, for subversive ideas to become reality. The KGB would almost certainly snuff out such plots before they became action. Yet, with the breakup of the Soviet Union, we have witnessed criminal activity as well as terrorism on a massive scale. The question to be asked is, why did that happen in this society? The fall of the Soviet Union was so sudden, and the Russian Federation of States underwent such rapid change, that it brought about the collapse of their structured and well-supported police service. In a vast empire that had relied on a state police for all forms of investigations and tactics, both overt and covert, there was now chaos. Now the time was right for criminal and subversive elements to move in and take advantage of weak controls. The drastic reduction in the need for nuclear weapons capability created a ready market in which radical terroristic governments could acquire nuclear devices, especially if they could pay the highest price.

Great Britain in the 1990s is a different battleground altogether. With ever-increasing demands on civilian police forces, they have adopted a "Big Brother" approach to their duties, maintaining a watchful eye on the communities they serve. Closed circuit television cameras to monitor the heart of the major cities, as well as the network of major motorway systems, have aided in the search for serious criminals. Civil libertarians and extreme left-wing agitators may argue an invasion of privacy but the police have had undisputed success in tracking down terrorists in London who abandon vehicles packed with explosives.

To many observers, it would have been an acceptable solution, in the wake of the IRA bombing campaign, to unleash the army against what were perceived to be vicious and callous terrorists. One must keep in mind that an army's main role is that of national defense, not policing. The use of the U.S. Marines in Somalia demonstrated the futility of policing with a military combat unit. In Northern Ireland, when the local Royal Ulster Constabulary was unable to protect Catholics from Protestant terrorism, the army was called in to "assist." That assistance to the Catholic community was also the rallying call for the underequipped Irish Republican Army of the day. As matters further deteriorated at the end of the 1960s, the army was brought into a policing role that involved searches of houses for weapons. At the very least, their actions were heavy handed, and the soldiers became objects of hatred and scorn for the local Catholics they were attempting to protect.

Northern Ireland

Without using the ultimate weapon of imposing martial law in Northern Ireland, the British government used a statutory instrument to control the lawlessness of the terror groups operating against the security forces in the province. Special powers to deal with the present emergency came into effect in 1973. The Northern Ireland (Emergency Provisions) Act empowered the military to have a greater impact in dealing with the urban terrorists. "No go" areas in parts of **Belfast and Londonderry** had been springing up and fostering terrorists and supplying safe houses. The Emergency Provisions gave sweeping powers that would permit the searching of houses without the necessity of warrants from the civil courts. These searches were authorized to take place at any time and the security forces could detain and question anyone for up to four hours. These methods allowed the military to build up a significant data base of information on the people of Northern Ireland. In the five years from 1972 to 1976, nearly 250,000 houses were searched by the army, uncovering 5,800 weapons and 661,000 rounds of ammunition. Added to these powers was the internment of active members of terrorist organizations. Hundreds of Irishmen were interned in the 1970s and, in hindsight, brought the Provisional IRA to the brink of defeat. Nearly all its executive and operations groups are either serving prison sentences or interned.[1] The IRA's call for a Christmas truce in 1974 was made from a position of extreme weakness. After all, there was no way IRA demands for total withdrawal of the British from Northern Ireland and general amnesty for all convicted terrorists would be met. It would be another twenty-four years before the IRA terrorists would walk out of prison as part of the Good Friday Agreement of 1998.

Legislation

Many operational methods and legislated practices can be put into place, but in a true and solid democracy there is the necessity to ensure that civil liberties are not abrogated to such an extent that the public is duly affected by its restrictive nature. Over the past thirty years there have been significant pieces of legislation and internationally recognized conventions aimed at curbing the activities of terrorists as well as countering their actions. The first major terror attacks attracting attention on a global scale involved hijacking of commercial airlines by terrorists from the PLO. Those attacks and the ineptitude of most governments in handling such crises prompted international anti-hijacking legislation to be drafted. These terrorist acts also prompted a more fundamental approach by one of the target states, Israel.

Israel was one of the first states to provide trained and armed "sky marshals" on all their aircraft around the world. Wherever there was an El Al flight, specially trained staff carried out stringent physical and profile security checks on every passenger boarding the flight. So effective was the El Al approach to handling security issues that the terrorists had to find a "soft underbelly" to attack. This, in several instances, was a ground-level attack at airport check-in counters. There were also attempts to shoot down the aircraft by means of RPG-7 rockets, as was the case with the failed attack by Black September terrorists at Orly Airport in France.

The fundamental principle of international legislative instruments such as the Chicago Convention, and in particular **Annex 17**, was that they required member states to safeguard global air transportation from acts of unlawful interference. The Convention applied a common set of standards for the security of international civil aviation.

HIJACKINGS

The terrorist hijackings by the **PLO**, and subsequently, many other terrorist groups with connections to the Middle East, which occurred at the end of the 1960s, changed the face of aviation for the rest of the century. For the terrorists, a hijacked aircraft became a way to attract the worldwide media coverage that the group craved. This allowed them to present an agenda or message about their cause instantly and universally. For the respective governments and the traveling public, the horror became too much to deal with. Measures to counteract these depredations were hastily drawn up and passenger screening for hand-carried baggage was born. Security is in many ways a reactive function, and this is clearly seen in the aviation industry.

To say that the airline industry "shuts the stable door after the horse has gone," would seem an inappropriate platitude. Following the bombing of Pan Am 103, the member states agreed on stringent sets of policy and procedures to screen all checked baggage. To the traveling public, that would seem an entirely credible action in light of such an atrocity. Airports, as everyone is aware, are busy and often cramped locations designed and built in the decades before security of passengers and aircraft had been considered an issue. A demand had now added the additional layer of baggage security to an already overtaxed system. The biggest problem facing the airlines was, Who is going to pay for all this? In the long run, it would of course be the traveling public. Developing effective explosive detection equipment which could handle the massive baggage throughout was also part of the immediate challenge for airports and aviation security experts.

The United Kingdom installed baggage-screening equipment at both Glasgow and Manchester Airports as test sites for systems that were new to the marketplace. Since that time, billions of development dollars, pounds, francs and others units of currency have been spent. Most have been expended on adding to airport infrastructure over the past ten years since **Pan Am 103**. And there has been no similar incident of the bomb that killed 270 passengers and crew over Scotland. What can be drawn from that scenario? To the well-organized terrorist, that particular door had now been almost completely closed, with more attention being paid to matching passengers with their bags and to the screening of hold baggage. However, in countering any further terrorist actions with regard to civil aviation, the experts had to begin to think terrorists. Rather than waiting for an attack to occur and then responding to it, governments set up programs to specifically look at soft areas which might become targets for terrorists.

Airports are, by their very nature, open and public places. As a result, the opportunity for terrorists to leave bombs in such public places always exits. Only awareness, vigilance and response by the public and police can help prevent disaster. But what about security in other sectors of the aviation industry? What about mail and airfreight carriers? How secure is that area of transport? At present, these must be considered as high-risk problems for carriers. Placing all airfreight into a decompression chamber is cumbersome, expensive and time-consuming. Other methods to protect against sabotage of freight and mail will have to be devised before this area is no longer considered a viable target for terrorists. The same stringent techniques and developments in the profiling of passengers and their baggage must, in due course, be applied to airfreight. The student must remember that it is impossible to have a totally secure airport or airline. The object of equipment and procedures designed to detect and remove such threats will act as a significant deterrent to the terrorist.

European Civil Aviation Conference (ECAC)

Nations are responsible for implementing effective aviation security systems for flights leaving their country. Terrorism is an international issue striking anywhere within hours by modern air transport. Therefore, it is necessary to have an international body to work with governments to develop measures, standards and recommended practices. That body is the **ECAC** and it operates with the active support of the International Civil Aviation Organization (ICAO). ECAC which was formed more than twenty years ago, has the following three principles in the area of aviation security:

1. That the threat of unlawful interference with civil aviation in its many forms of violence is likely to persist
2. That **ICAO** Standards and Recommended Practices in aviation security have to take into account the widely varying provisions available for their implementation in more than 180 Contracting States of ICAO
3. Mutual understanding and close and constant cooperation between all State authorities concerned are necessary to achieve and maintain a high standard of aviation security.[2]

Combating Terrorists

One of the first considerations of any would-be hijacker is the amount of mass media publicity he or she can expect. Certainly hijacking an aircraft and demanding that it be flown to JFK Airport in New York, or to London's Heathrow Airport, would gain worldwide media attention. And because of the size and complexity of these airports, the ensuing chaos and disruption to the traveling public would be horrendous. Consider, if you will, that in combating a hijacking it is imperative to have the option to "direct" the hijacked aircraft to an airport of choice. Authorities must be able to handle the incident without disrupting the major airports and airline systems of the world.

Stanstead

London's third airport is little known to the international traveler, who will normally arrive at the gateway airports of Heathrow, on the outskirts of London, or Gatwick, about one hour south of London. Stanstead, located to the east of London, has become the venue of choice for authorities dealing with a hijacked aircraft. This supposes, of course, that they are able to hoodwink the terrorist into believing the plane is actually landing at Heathrow. The airport was first used to receive a hijacked aircraft in 1975, when a BAC1-11 was hijacked on an internal flight between Manchester in the North of England and London. The incident took place as the aircraft was approaching Heathrow and the pilot managed to divert, without the hijackers' knowledge, to Stanstead. The hijacker then demanded money and to be flown to France. By the time the pilot had flown around and then landed at Stanstead, the hijacker was convinced he was in France. Few police were available in those days to cover Stanstead airport, and the lessons they learned as a result were incorporated into the training of the **Special Air Service (SAS)** regiment for dealing with terrorist hijackings in the future.

Security operations were lacking in the following areas:

- Number of police on hand to deal with an emergency of this magnitude
- Designated emergency rendezvous points for emergency services
- Communications between pilot and ground
- A designated command post for the operation

The requirement to train and maintain a level of response became of great importance. A second hijacking, originating in central Africa in 1982, ended up with an Air Tanzania Boeing 727 landing, after a circuitous route around Europe, at Stanstead. On this occasion, the response was a combined police and military operation with the elite SAS in attendance to mount a hostage rescue if police negotiations failed. While police negotiated, a team of SAS embarked on similarly configured British Airways 737 and flew directly from Heathrow to **Stanstead**. As a result of protracted negotiations involving the Tanzanian High Commissioner, the siege was brought to a peaceful conclusion some twenty-four hours later. What was also apparent in this incident was the role of the media and its release of sensational and newsbreaking pictures to an eager public. Photographs of armed police lying near the aircraft could have been a considerable problem for the negotiators had they reached the hijackers. In any democratic society, the value of the press and its principle focus of news gathering must be weighed against the impact on the situation at hand. Close cooperation with the media is an issue that must be addressed in terror and hijacking incidents where they are present.

In August 1996, a **Sudan Airways A310** Airbus which originated in Khartoum was hijacked by an Iraqi group demanding that the plane be flown to Italy. Because of insufficient fuel, the aircraft had to land in Cyprus, refuel and then take off for London. Stanstead, having learned valuable lessons in the preceding twenty years, was ready and waiting to receive the aircraft. This particular hijacking was to end peacefully, and Stanstead remains the airport of choice for receiving terrorist-controlled flights into the U.K.[3]

The Media

Interfering with the media's "right to know" is of course frowned upon. However, there must be limits placed on the release of pictures and information while an incident is in process. As preservers of order in the fabric of democracy, the police and military are bound to come into conflict with the media about the control and dissemination of information. One example of such conflict occurred during the Falklands War, when the media were given briefings by the government and the content of news was tightly censored so as not to give critical information to the enemy. During the Gulf War, the commander himself, General Norman Schwarzkopf, conducted press briefings. These briefings contained diluted information that the military chiefs allowed for media release. The press was not allowed on the field of battle during the invasion operations. In a terror incident taking place in a city, it is not possible to control media coverage in the first phase of the action. The bombing of the Federal Building in Oklahoma City brought television crews to the scene at almost the same time rescue and police services were arriving. Graphic television coverage of the heroic deeds of fire fighters and police officers goes a long way toward winning public acceptance of the methods they may subsequently use to catch terrorists. Police are seen as the front line against terrorism, as part of the community, and therefore better appreciated.

Media coverage can also have negative effects in combating terror, even when government censors have neutralized information. Again, this was illustrated in the Falklands War, when the government media spokesman let it slip that the Argentinean bombs were not exploding because they were not being deployed correctly. One might not think this problematic; however, the **BBC** coverage was available to Argentinans, who made adjustments for their failure and recalibrated their weaponry. Who knows how many brave men and women died as a result? Another media mistake involved a hijacked American airliner at Beirut International Airport in 1985. A rescue unit of Delta Force commandos was dispatched to the region, only to be thwarted by news coverage of their imminent arrival, which allowed the hijackers time to hide and move their captives throughout Beirut. Many analysts have discussed and reviewed the effects of media coverage on terrorist actions. And many conclusions both for media coverage and against can surely be reached. The media, however, must understand that it should remain at arm's length so as not to become a tool of the terrorist. Much media coverage is aimed at showing the horrors of the unfolding situation. The motivational drives of the terrorists are seldom considered and dramatic effect often becomes the main goal. When that happens, the media inadvertently serves the purposes of the terrorist, giving them precisely the attention they seek.

After all, as mentioned in several chapters, terrorist actions are all about sending a message. Their preferred method of sending the message is via the broadest media coverage. No doubt studies might conclude that sensational pictures of terrorist events do nothing to get "the message" out to the public and in fact, may fuel public anger. In a free society, the media and the government will invariably clash on what should get coverage and what should not. However, much of what is reported will generally be acquired through government sources, who may appear to be manipulating the media.

Government censorship of the press undoubtedly occurs in many countries. And where military dictatorships or totalitarian governments are in power, they totally control the media. With the clamor for some form of restriction on the press, the media have themselves begun to set standards, and to establish codes of conduct. Freedom of the press is preserved, but the need of various agencies responding to a crisis are also considered. It is increasingly apparent that these agencies must be able to function unhindered by an overzealous media.

Policy

As the end of the millenium nears, the reaction of Western governments to terrorist activity has been to come up with methods of responding to such activities swiftly and effectively. This has been enhanced by the use of military and spy satellites to track down the terrorist. Is the problem of defining and dealing with terrorism a police or military problem? Certainly the bombing of United States embassies in Nairobi and Dar es Salaam in the summer of 1998 was very difficult for the local

Exiled Saudi dissident Osama bin Laden, accused of masterminding the twin bombing of the U.S. embassies in Tanzania and Kenya. CP Picture Archive (AP Photo)

police to deal with. In trying to come to terms with an enemy not residing within its own borders, the United States decided on a preemptive military strike at the bases of suspected terrorists in both the Sudan and Pakistan. Were they violating sovereign territory of two other countries? The primary target was **Usama bin Laden**, suspected of being behind the two bombings. After the bombings, and the retaliatory strikes by the United States, one wonders who will fire the next shot in anger. No doubt the forces of Islamic fundamentalism will gather strength and expand their base of support for more actions against the United States and its principal allies in the west.

International cooperation in dealing with world terrorism was addressed at the **Lyon Summit** Conference in 1996. Ministers responsible for state security agreed on a framework of some twenty-five measures. The agreement focused on the following main points:

1. Adopting internal measures to prevent terrorism, by improving counter-terrorism cooperation and capabilities. By adopting this strategy governments could focus on training of counterterrorism personnel to prevent all kinds of terrorism actions including the use of chemical, biological and toxic substance attacks.

2. Accelerating the research and development of methods to detect explosives and other harmful substances that cause death or injury, and also to develop standards for marking explosives in order to identify their origin in post-blast investigations.

3. In respect to prosecution and deterrence, the agreement noted that where sufficient justification existed according to national laws, that states must investigate organizations, groups and associations, including those with charitable, social or cultural goals, which may serve as a cover for terrorist operations. (An example of such a group would be **NORAID**, which supports and collects funds for the IRA in the United States).

"Operation Nimrod", May 5th, 1980 – the SAS termites the siege of the Iranian Embassy in London. CP Picture Archive (AP Wirephoto/Dave Caulkin)

4. Adopt laws for the restriction and control of weapons and explosives, including export controls, to prevent their use by terrorist organizations.

5. Review and amend all current anti-terror legislation.

6. In dealing with political asylum issues, states must ensure that the rights and freedoms of a country are not taken advantage of by terrorists who seek to fund, plan and commit terrorist acts.

7. Facilitate the exchange of information through central authorities to provide speedy coordination of requests. Direct exchange of information between agencies should be encouraged.

8. The exchange of information should specifically identify:

- The actions and movement of persons or groups suspected of belonging to or being connected with terrorist networks
- Travel documents suspected of being forgeries
- Trafficking in arms, explosives or sensitive materials
- The use of communications technologies by terrorist groups
- The threat of new types of terrorist activities including those using chemical, biological, or nuclear materials and toxic substances[4]

International police cooperation has existed through the efforts of the International Criminal Police Organization (Interpol) for several decades. Terrorism is considered by INTERPOL to be "a crime, characterized by violence or intimidation, usually against innocent victims in order to obtain a political or social objective." **INTERPOL** distinguishes between terrorism and organized crime by commenting that organized crime has a profit motive, whereas terrorism's goals are not primarily for financial, but rather for ideological, gains.

INTELLIGENCE GATHERING

Intelligence gathering for terrorist offenses is the domain of police forces throughout the world. Many forces grudgingly share information, and when several spectacular

IRA attacks occurred in London in the early 1990s, the intelligence gathering operations were transferred from the police to the arm of British intelligence known as **MI5**. MI5's analysis encompassed not only IRA terrorists, but all groups that could pose a threat. In March 1996, the British Government published a report by the Parliamentary Committee on Security and Intelligence that about 39 percent of resources went toward compiling data on the membership, infrastructure and methods used by terrorist groups through long-term penetration. With an adequate budget, MI5 could devote time to infiltrating subversive organizations. When cases of terrorism are brought to trial on evidence painstakingly gathered by both police and MI5, it would be counterproductive for a spy to appear on the witness stand to give testimony. Collaboration between these agencies is essential, and there has been successful cooperation between the British police and the intelligence community.

COUNTERTERRORISM UNITS

GREAT BRITAIN

In the world of counterterrorism operations few are as effective as the British SAS. Terrorism in the twentieth century has taken place primarily in the fifty-year period after World War II; therefore, counterterror and counterinsurgency units have also developed since the war. However, the SAS was formed during WWII, by an eccentric Scot, David Stirling, who was ably assisted by a commando officer, Captain Robert Laycock. Conventional army theoreticians during the war frowned upon the activities being proposed by the unconventional Stirling. At 6' 5", he was an impressive figure of a man, and he believed passionately that there was an important role for "special operations" behind enemy lines. Once in Egypt, he teamed up with a Welsh Guardsman, an Australian named Jock Lewis, and these three men created the Special Air Service. Protocol was the order of the day, and for Second Lieutenant Stirling to communicate his ideas to the general commanding Middle East operations would require going through a long chain of command. Stirling thought the war would be over before his ideas reached the general. By accident, he met with the Deputy Commander, General Ritchie, who was so impressed with the Lieutenant's ideas that they were soon put into practice for operations behind German lines in North Africa. This first unit was named "L Detachment, Special Air Service Brigade" and the SAS was born.

Special Air Service (SAS)

The SAS of the 1990s is a far cry from that of the war years, and it has developed into what is arguably one of the best counterterror units in the world. Many counterterrorism organizations around the world have been modeled after the SAS.

The SAS regiment is headquartered in Hereford in the west of England, but with government spending cuts, it is destined for a new home at Royal Air Force base at Creedenhill. The Special Air Service is made up of a Special Projects Team, and it is from this team that the Counter Revolutionary Warfare Squadron has been formed to handle both foreign and domestic terrorism issues. Training for the SAS is continuous, with one squadron always on standby to leave at a moment's notice to deal with a terrorist situation. An Operations Research unit supports all SAS projects and has developed weaponry specific to the needs of the Regiment. This unit developed the stun grenade widely used by counterterrorism units around the world. They also developed night vision goggles and special ladders for aircraft and train assaults.

As a peacetime unit, the SAS has been primarily involved in dealing with the IRA. The Provisional IRA referred to the British application of the SAS in Northern Ireland as death squads sent to terminate Irishmen. Unfortunately for the Provisional IRA, the SAS was extremely effective in the urban warfare of Northern Ireland. The speed and efficiency with which the unit carried out operations stunned the Irish terrorist community. SAS activity is not restricted to the United Kingdom, however, and it is believed that the regiment has been involved in operations against Libya. Adding to the mystique surrounding this elite regiment is the anonymity of its members. A hostage drama at the Iranian embassy in London was covered by a plethora of news cameras from around the world, which captured the sudden and dramatic rescue by armed men dressed in black fatigues. The success of that raid, which led to the death of all but one of the terrorists, placed Britain firmly in the spotlight as a country which did not deal lightly with terrorists and was prepared to use whatever force was necessary to end a crisis. It is important to note that this operation had been under the control of the civil police authorities until the go-ahead was given for the SAS assault. This was the first time the public saw the SAS in action, and although there was an outpouring of indignation from extremists, the vast majority of Britons strongly supported the actions of the elite SAS team.

The SAS has been used against the IRA and throughout Europe. An IRA unit had been followed to Gibraltar in 1988, where, intelligence sources indicated, the terrorists would detonate a bomb during a military parade. The SAS carried out an attack on the three IRA members, and according to witness reports gunned them down in cold blood. The subsequent outcry seemed too much for a democracy to handle, with claims of a "shoot to kill" policy being adopted by the government. The IRA now had "martyrs" to bury at home in Northern Ireland and the opportunity to haul the British government before the European Court of Justice, which condemned the assault. This court decision showed that caution was required, lest counterterrorist forces go too far. Of course, for the IRA it meant they had the right to not only to shoot first, but to kill as well! The SAS is on good terms with numerous countries, as it has actively assisted in training many antiterrorism units around the globe. It is believed that the SAS is present, either officially or unofficially, at every terror incident, to view how it was handled and to determine what went well and what went wrong. Thorough debriefs are held, and every minute detail of the operation is analyzed. The SAS also provided assistance to the Peruvian government when terrorists took control of the Japanese ambassador's residence in Lima in 1996.

Special Boat Squadron (SBS)

The British Royal Navy has its own counterterrorism unit to rival the SAS. This unit is highly trained to respond to maritime acts of terrorism, though it has not been widely used. The unit has responded with the SAS, most notably during a bomb threat to the ocean liner Queen Elizabeth II in the North Atlantic. Specifically designed for naval operations, the unit was deployed prior to the arrival of the Naval Task Force off the Falkland Islands at the outbreak of the war between Great Britain and Argentina.

SAS Associates

Because of the effectiveness of the regiment and its legendary exploits since WW II, other commonwealth countries have modeled their counterterrorism units on the SAS. The Australian SAS and the New Zealand SAS have even adopted the same name as the British regiment.

AUSTRALIA

Tactical Assault Group (TAG) and Special Air Service Regiment (SASR)

The above units were originally formed in 1957, and comprise Australia's response to any outbreak of domestic terror. The Australian SAS was originally a single company. By 1964, two additional companies had been added and the unit was renamed the Special Air Service Regiment. The regiment saw military action in Borneo, and with the outbreak of the Vietnam War was instrumental in training the Australian army for its role in Southeast Asia. By the time the Vietnam War ended, the **SASR** had achieved some impressive results in the area of "special operations." Since Vietnam, Australia has not seen terrorist activity at home and the unit has been scaled down. Like its British counterpart, it engages in training and assists other units in the west. SASR has staff based at Fort Bragg and Little Creek in the United States. A specialist unit is also available for seaborne counterterror response, called the **Offshore Installations Assault Group (OAG)**. Since its creation, the SASR has lost a total of seventeen men: six were killed on active duty in Vietnam, three in operations in Borneo, and eight during a training exercise near Townsville in 1996.

RHODESIA

Rhodesian SAS

The Rhodesian SAS is part of the original regiment which was disbanded at the end of WWII. That regiment was so effective that German radio stations referred to David Stirling with respect and fear. Rhodesians have a long and proud history of engagements on foreign soil. One WWII Rhodesian, Mike Sadler, served with the SAS in North Africa and was considered the best navigator in the vast Western Desert.[5] When the war was over, the members of the SAS were returned to their respective countries. The regiment was almost disbanded, but survived as a territorial unit.

After the war with Germany and Japan was won, the next problem facing the allied powers was the rise of communism in the Far East. It was the Malayan crisis of 1951 which established reasons for retaining a Rhodesian SAS regiment for actions at home and abroad. The Commonwealth countries were asked to supply volunteers for a force to be dispatched to Malaya to handle the entrenched communist terrorists in the region. It was commanded by Major "Mad Mike" Calvert, who had been given the go-ahead to form a self-sustaining warfare unit, trained for jungle conditions. Its mission would be the continued disruption of communist terror activity. Major Calvert flew to Rhodesia to meet with the contingent of one hundred men and briefed them on the Malayan operation. The unit from Rhodesia would become C Squadron 22 SAS (Malayan Scouts).[6]

The Malayan emergency was to last until the end of that decade, and the Rhodesian SAS remained on station for two years. On returning to Africa, the unit was disbanded and the men returned to their civilian lives. However, the lessons learned in that Far East operation were valuable in the country's struggle for identity and independence during the 1960s. At the beginning of the 1960s, Rhodesia's army was in need of specialized expansion and development. Following an assessment, it was decided that the Special Air Service Squadron would be established as a branch of the Rhodesian army. Training would be conducted under the auspices of the British SAS at Sterling Lines in Hereford, England. The Rhodesian military has a long and successful history of graduates at the Sandhurst Military Academy in Berkshire, England, and several cadets have been awarded the coveted Sword of Honor. Among those selected to join the newly formed Rhodesian SAS were remnants of the old Malaya task force of C Squadron.[7]

The Rhodesian SAS was exceptionally well trained and schooled in jungle warfare techniques and its troops were accomplished paratroopers. The squadron assisted the 22 SAS Regiment in operations with the British army in the Crater District of Aden (now Yemen) during that crisis. The 1960s were a time of rationalization and decolonization. Great Britain was divesting itself of major parts of its empire and Africa was in massive turmoil, as other European empires were doing the same. The break-up of parts of Rhodesia began: The northern part became Zambia, and Nyasaland became independent Malawi. In 1964, Ian Smith, a former WWII fighter pilot, became prime minister of the country and was determined to take Rhodesia to full independence from Britain. Politics would play a role in the gradual demise of the SAS in Rhodesia. When Ian Smith was unable to persuade the British government to grant independence to Rhodesia, he declared a Unilateral Declaration of Independence (UDI). This resulted in sanctions by Britain and a full trade embargo by the United Nations. The following fourteen years of turmoil in the region would end with a Black Nationalist government in power and the dissolution of the SAS. On December 31, 1980 the Rhodesian SAS disbanded and its members fled to South Africa, taking with them the memorial to their war dead.

SPAIN

Grupo Especial de Operaciones (GEO)

Spain, which has had problems with the ETA terrorist group and GRAO, was late in establishing an effective counterterrorism unit. In 1978, following the successes of the German GSG-9, Spain sought help from Germany in setting up GEO. One of Spain's difficulties was finding fiscal and political resources with which to staff the unit. Spain has both left-wing and right-wing terrorist problems, so there was a desperate need for members of any elite unit to be apolitical. Spain's **GEO** is not well known outside the country but is a highly trained and effective force. Although Spain has a thriving munitions industry of its own, the GEO uses the same close assault weapons as their counterparts in GSG-9, favoring the Heckler and Koch MP5. As secretive as their comrades in both the SAS and GSG-9, GEO has had some unsung successes in dealing with terrorists. In May 1981, twenty-four right-wing terrorists had occupied the Central Bank of Barcelona and taken over 200 hostages. The bank was stormed by GEO using their standard assault weapon, the MP5. Only one of the hostages was injured, ten of the terrorists were captured and one terrorist was killed. The remainder fled the bank with the hostages in the ensuing confusion.[8]

Guarda Civil

Spain's second unit which handles hostage-taking and terrorist activity operates within the structure of the *Guarda Civil* (National Police). The *Unidad Especial de Intervencion* (UEI) is responsible to the ministries of the interior and defense and forms part of Spain's national police force. Like the GEO, it is deployed across the country and has had notable successes in rescuing kidnap and hostage victims from both ETA and Grappo.

THE PERSIAN GULF

Cobras (Sultan of Oman Special Forces [SSF])

Continuing traditions, with close ties to the Royal Military Academy at Sandhurst, the SAS provided training and logistical support for friendly Middle East countries. The tiny sultanate of Oman has seen very little terrorist activity, but, when the region started to destabilize with pro-communist guerillas under the **Popular Front for the Liberation of Oman (PFLO)**, the sultan requested assistance from Britain. The rebellion in Oman lasted almost thirteen years, 1962–1975. During that time, the British SAS was actively involved in counterterrorism operations with the sultan's army. However, the sultan was not prepared for the kind of terror and insurgent tactics the guerrillas would use. The SAS was more than happy to oblige and was instrumental in bringing down the forces opposing the sultan. When the fighting was over, Sultan Qaboos made the decision that his country would never again be without a response unit for insurgency and terrorism.

The British SAS gave support and training in the setup of the SSF for the sultan. The Cobras, based in Dhofar, are now considered the most elite force in the Persian Gulf region. Cobra teams are set up along the same military lines as the SAS, and are on a constant fifteen-minute standby. From their bases in Dhofar and Muscat they have provided assistance to neighboring Kuwait. In a peculiar setup, the Cobras are subordiante to the Omani police, who are less equipped and trained. The police retain jurisdictional control of incidents. Jealousy and interservice rivalry have not helped efforts to maintain this effective force in the Gulf.

FRANCE

Groupment d'intervention de la Gendarmerie Nationale (GIGN)

Unlike the British SAS, the elite counterterrorism response force in France was created following terrorist attacks at the Munich Olympic Games and the takeover of the Saudi Embassy in Paris. The GIGN is a police unit, not a military one. The recruits to this unit come from the ranks of the paramilitary police service, the *Gendarmerie Nationale* (National Police). All members undergo eight months of rigorous training which is similar to that of the SAS and includes parachute qualification. On successful completion, they are based at the Maison Alfort near Paris. As a police unit, the GIGN is called on to deal with criminal incidents as well as terrorist attacks. The unit is heavily armed with the Heckler and Koch MP5 sub-machine gun as well as an assortment of sophisticated handguns. The GIGN are also trained in negotiating and recognizing psychological weaknesses and changes in the state of mind of the terrorist. Like the SAS, GIGN shuns publicity. They have had remarkable success in rescuing kidnap victims. Their most widely know action was the storming of an Air France Airbus at Marseilles, which resulted in the death of all thirteen hijackers.

NETHERLANDS

Bijondere Bijstands Eenheid (BBE)

Qua Patet Orbis (The Whole World Over) is the motto of the Netherlands Marine Corps. "Sending in the Marines" has always been an option for Western governments and is an often used phrase. In the case of the Netherlands, that is exactly what takes place in handling hostage-taking and terrorist actions. The Netherlands has one of the oldest military organizations in the world with the Dutch Marine Corps, which was founded on December 10, 1665. Today's modern Royal Netherlands Marine Corps numbers about 2,800. The corps is split into two separate areas for operational purposes, one group in the Netherlands for NATO duties and the other stationed in Aruba in the Dutch Antillies. The Marines represent a strike force that can respond to any terrorist situation that presents itself. A section of the Marine Corps is devoted to counterterrorism functions and is called the BBE. Translated, this has the literal meaning, "different circumstances unit." The Dutch government, like those of other west European countries, does not negotiate with terrorists, and although the country is not beset with severe terrorist problems, one issue that has resulted in conflict relates to Dutch colonialism in Indonesia. The region known as South Molucca, seeking independence in its own right from Indonesia, put pressure on the Dutch government by hijacking a train in 1975. The hijackers were members of the Free South Moluccan Youth Organization (VZJ).

The Netherlands' response was to send in the marines (BBE). On this occasion, as with others involving the South Moluccans, the siege was ended by extreme force resulting in the death of the terrorists and minor injuries to the rescuers and the rescued. Each attack unit of the BBE consists of two 33-man platoons, each comprised of four assault teams. They are further broken down into 5-man units. The unit's functions are similar to those of the British SAS and it is assisted with maritime operations from the seventh Special Boat Squadron, another elite unit made up of four 6-man intervention teams.

NORWAY

Forsvarets Spesialkommando (FSK) Special Defense Commando

Norway's elite military response unit was formed in 1982, primarily as a defensive unit to deal with terrorist attacks against its many North Sea oil rigs. It is also responsible for the close protection of the Norwegian Royal Family, the national assembly and other government officials. The **FSK** is a branch unit of the Norwegian Army Jegercommand. This is another unit that has used the example of the SAS, and the start of the unit involved five years of close involvement with them. The two units have continued to maintain close ties and often train together on exercises. The close nature of the two units brought the FSK some unwanted publicity when it was reported in the Norwegian press that they had been involved in SAS operations against the IRA in Northern Ireland in 1994, a report that has been strenuously denied by both governments. FSK has also seen service overseas when it was dispatched to the Kashmir to help locate a Norwegian being held captive by Al-Faran guerillas.

GERMANY

Grenzschutzgruppe 9 (GSG9)

GSG9 stands alongside the major elite terrorist responders in the world today as one of the most successful units. The unit was formed following the disaster at the Munich Olympic Games. After the horrendous events of the Olympics, the Germans were not prepared to allow such atrocities to happen again. In the case of the Olympics it was the soft target with worldwide media coverage that the Black September movement was after. In the two decades after the end of the war, Germany had taken pains not to produce any elitist force for any purpose. This unit was formed and fully operational by April 1973, six months after the Munich massacre. Unlike the SAS, this unit would become part of the Federal Border Police service and not part of the German military. Membership has the requirement that each is a volunteer and a member of the Border Police. Those in the German army who wish to volunteer must first resign from the army and join the Border Police.

The group is split into three definable units. **GSG-9/1**, with one hundred members, is responsible for counterterrorism; GSG-9/2 for maritime counterterrorism, and GSG-9/3, each with fifty members, deals with airborne situations. The federal government supplies GSG-9 with the best and most advanced equipment available, and the five-man units are outfitted with two sets of combat gear, one for day and the other for nighttime operations.

The architect of GSG-9 was the charismatic Colonel Ulrich Wegener, and not long after the training of the three newly created units was complete, they were called upon to effect a rescue attempt of truly significant proportions. Colonel Wegener firmly believed that a successful anti-terrorist unit must have small, tightly knit groups of men capable of infinite stealth and, when needed, extreme ferocity.

ISRAEL

Sayeret Mat'Kal

Sayeret Mat'kal is also known as the General Staff Reconnaissance Unit 269 and was founded in 1957. This unit has been in the forefront of every anti- and counterterrorism strategy since its inception. It is the unit that is also dedicated to handling hostage-taking incidents. In wartime, this unit takes on the role of intelligence gathering. The Sayeret Mat'kal actively does the bidding of the Israeli government and has hunted down and executed known terrorists. After the Munich massacre, it was mandated to track down and kill those involved.

TERRORISM PLAYER 13-1

WOLFGANG GRAMS

In June 1994 the GSG-9 counterterrorism unit attempted to apprehend the leader of the Red Army Faction (RAF), Wolfgang Grams. Reports surfacing from the arrest indicated that he had been killed in a shootout with the GSG-9 troopers; however, there has been speculation that he may have been summarily executed by the unit after he had been subdued. In an incredible epilogue to that incident, the RAF firebombed the home of one of the unit members of GSG-9 involved in the incident. Strict secrecy as to the GSG-9 membership leads to the conclusion that information at a high level must have been leaked for such an attack to have happened.

RAID ON MOGADISHU

GSG-9 had their first taste of real action and a chance to prove to the people of Germany and the world that they were a force to be reckoned with on October 13, 1977 when Lufthansa Flight LH181 took off from the holiday island of Majorca, under the command of Captain Jurgen Schumann. Shortly after takeoff the captain announced to air traffic control that his aircraft had been hijacked and he was altering course for Rome. The hijacker frantically demanded the release of the leaders of the Baader-Meinhof gang languishing in prison in Germany and a sum of about $15 million for the release of the Boeing 737 and its 79 passengers and crew. On arriving at Rome the captain was able to drop four cigars from a cockpit window to signal that there were four terrorists on the aircraft. The 737 refueled and took off headed for Cyprus on a journey that would see the aircraft fly around the Middle East before reaching its final destination of Mogadishu in Somalia. Immediately after receiving notification of the hijacking, the GSG-9 shadowed the aircraft to its final destination. Before reaching Mogadishu, the captain of the aircraft had been shot dead by the leader of the hijackers, Zohair Youssef Akache, calling himself "Captain Mahmoud." On arriving at Mogadishu, Mahmoud threatened to blow up the aircraft if his ransom and prisoner release demands were not met. To emphasize his point he had the Captain's body thrown onto the tarmac. To stall for time the negotiators told Mahmoud they were in the process of releasing 11 of the prisoners in Germany. This gave the GSG-9 time to prepare for the assault on the aircraft. After surveying the aircraft the information gained indicated that Mahmoud and another terrorist were located in the cockpit but the exact whereabouts of the others was not confirmed. The final briefing complete and Colonel Wegener informed the unit that once he was inside the aircraft he would shout, "heads down" and anyone left standing would be shot and killed. Two members of Britain's SAS were with GSG-9 to offer assistance. A distraction of a burning barrel was placed in the runway in front of the aircraft, this alerted the hijackers and also distracted them. Explosive charges were placed on the aircraft doors and detonated as the burning drum distracted the terrorists. With the doors now blown open the two SAS men threw in their stun grenades to temporarily disorient the people in the cabin. In a five-minute period from 0207 to 0212 all the terrorist had been either killed or seriously wounded. Several of the passengers were slightly injured in the rescue. Following the success of Mogadishu the unit has not been called on to complete the same type of rescue, although it is actively involved in the pursuit of home-grown terrorists in Germany.

Source: Leroy Thompson, GSG-9.

COLONEL ULRICH WEGENER

Ulrich Wegener joined the Federal Border Police in 1958, and his impeccable credentials made him the obvious choice to lead GSG-9. His training with both the FBI and the Israeli Secret Service gave him expert knowledge on terrorism. He is believed to have been involved with the Israeli raid at Entebbe in 1976. Wegener's orders had been to create a small and highly flexible anti-terrorist unit that could be used and deployed at a moment's notice. Following his success at Mogadishu he was promoted to Brigadier and given ultimate control over the Federal Border Police.

Source: Leroy Thompson, GSG-9.

OPERATION SPRING YOUTH

The Sayeret Mat'kal is also an offensive anti-terror unit and has used every possible means at its disposal in the protection of Israeli interests. It carries out actions that for nearly every other Western power would be unacceptable; however, to the embattled Israelis their actions are accepted as a requirement in the protection of the state. On April 9–10, 1973 Sayeret infiltrated into Beirut, which had to be considered extremely hostile territory, and assassinated the leaders of the Black September organization. This action was carried out successfully at three separate locations in West Beirut.

EGYPT AIR 648

The incident at Malta Airport in 1985 is an example of what can go wrong even with a well trained and equipped anti-terror unit. The lessons learned from this debacle, which ended with fifty-four dead passengers, is testament to the paramount need to have as much intelligence as possible about the target group before an assault is mounted. In addition, snipers outside the aircraft mistook escaping passengers for terrorists and gunned some of them down. In September 1985, an Egypt Air flight was hijacked to Malta and the Egyptian government dispatched Force 777 to the island to assist with the hostage rescue operations. The Maltese government gave the go-

ahead for Force 777 to take action against the terrorists. The assault began at about 8:00 P.M. and lasted for more than a minute and a half, which is nearly four times longer than most anti-terror groups will take to storm an aircraft and release hostages. The series of mistakes, miscalculations, and lack of intelligence and planning resulted in the death of the passengers.

Source: Extracts from Leroy Thompson, "The Rescuers, The World's Top Anti- Terrorist Units," Paladin Press.

Hostage Rescue Units (HRU)

These types of units are in operation throughout the world. Most countries have teams designated, trained and equipped to deal with hostage-taking crises, and the protection of VIP's and government officials. Units have been formed in the Philippines named the Aviation Security Commando (AVESCOM). In Thailand, it is the responsibility of the Royal Thai Air Force. In India, the extremely efficient and well trained Special Counterterrorist Unit (SCU) is considered to be the best in Asia. Malaysia uses the Special Strike Unit of the Royal Malay Police and Sri Lanka the Army Commando Squadron. In the Middle East, Bahrain and Saudi Arabia have units trained by the British SAS and the French GIGN, respectively. The Hashemite Kingdom of Jordan maintains the 101st Special Forces Battalion, which also provides sky marshals for Alia, the national airline of Jordan. Egypt has had two failures in hostage rescue in recent decades. Both of the incidents occurred in the Mediterranean. Egypt uses the Saiqa unit for counterterror operations, as well as Force 777, created in 1978.

The countries of Latin and South America use sections of the military and federal police services for the HRU functions in most cases.

UNITED STATES OF AMERICA

The United States has only in the last decade begun to experience at home what most European and Middle East countries have been experiencing for nearly four decades. Hostage rescue, kidnapping and their negotiation have long been the province of the Federal Bureau of Investigation (FBI), assisted by special police squads that are formed in almost every jurisdiction in the United States. These units are termed Special Weapons and Tactical Units (**SWAT**). The FBI is the United States federal agency responsible for information and intelligence gathering at home, which is not, as many believe, the domain of the Central Intelligence Agency. The CIA is mandated for intelligence and field operations outside the United States for protecting her interests. With varying gun laws throughout the United States, weapons offences are a daily diet for the state police, with SWAT teams regularly called upon to deal with many criminal activities, particularly bank hold-ups. With the hostage crisis in Tehran in the 1970s the need arose to have dedicated and well trained tactical teams to deal with subversive activities both at home and abroad.

Delta Force was the brainchild of Charles Beckwith in the 1970s. Beckwith realized that the United States did not have the same capability for hostage rescue and counterterrorism response as the Europeans and proposed establishing an elite unit from the ranks of the U.S. Special Forces. The unit created was as selective and disciplined as the British SAS, which Beckwith himself had experienced in the 1960s. The seizure of the U.S. Embassy in Tehran, in November 1979, placed the Delta Force on standby to handle the rescue and evacuation of the hostages. Considerable intelligence gathering and logistical planning went into the plans to rescue the hostages, which would see the Delta team front and center. The mission was to fail, due to dust storms and with one of the helicopters crashing into a C-130 plane carrying munitions, resulting in the death of eight members of the Marine Corps. The members of Delta Force managed to escape injury and returned to the U.S. without completing their mission. After the abortive mission to Iran, a Special Operations Group was initiated, and from that came the creation, in 1980, of **SEAL Team Six**. SEAL Team Six is the Navy's equivalent to the Delta Force and is responsible for handling counterterrorism in any maritime environment. Its beginnings directly resulted from the failure of the Tehran operation which had been designated "Eagle Claw." The name SEAL Team Six was chosen as ploy to confuse the Soviets as to exactly how many SEAL units the U.S. had in operation at the time. All of the SEAL platoons were trained in counterterrorism. SEAL Six went through an extensive training regimen that involved training overseas with members of the SAS, GSG-9, GIGN and other counterterrorism organizations. SEAL Team Six would undergo further changes to its structure, including a name change due to its poor reputation within the Navy. SEAL Team Six was embarrassed by its founding member, Commander Richard Marcinko, who was charged with an assortment of offenses ranging from fraud to bribery and was sentenced to a brief term of imprisonment. Following this fiasco, the unit designation was changed to The Naval Special Warfare Development Group. Structured on the same lines as the SAS and numbering approximately 200 men, the **NSWDG** covers a wide spectrum of abilities, much the same as the SAS and the SBS. Unlike their European counterparts, they have not had the opportunity to prove themselves, as the SAS had at Prince's Gate or the GSG-9 had at Mogadishu, although they have been in operations both covert and overt since the 1980s.

In 1985, they were on standby in the Mediterranean during the Achille Lauro hijacking that claimed the life of Leon Klinghoffer, but they were not called into use. In the same year, the unit was used during the U.S. invasion of Grenada to rescue the governor of the island, Sir Paul Scoon. During that operation, four SEALs were drowned during the helicopter insertion offshore. In a more criminal response operation for the U.S. government, they were involved alongside the Delta Force to locate and capture Manuel Noriega from Panama in 1990. Following a coup in Haiti in 1991, it is believed the unit was involved in rescuing deposed President Aristide. The SEALs were used for the initial landings in Somalia in 1992, when they came ashore in scuba gear to a throng of media with video cameras and floodlights which broadcast their invasion, live, around the world. This was another example of poor understanding between operational forces and the media.

The U.S. has also used, in domestic situations, the Alcohol Tobacco and Firearms (ATF) unit for dealing with criminals stockpiling illegal weapons. A major operation was covered for weeks by the news media when the ATF went to execute a warrant against the Branch Davidians led by David Koresch in Waco, Texas. The ensuing gun battle and a long standoff later resulted in an assault by the ATF during which everyone inside the compound was incinerated. It was discovered after the event, however, that many had been killed or committed suicide before the flames overtook the buildings.

SUMMARY

In reviewing this chapter, the salient point to remember is that the authorities have immense power at their fingertips and need to use it cautiously and judiciously. Specialized counterterrorism units have been used as a response mechanism and may be viewed as a well-advertised deterrent by governments unwilling to deal with terrorists. As can be seen with Northern Ireland, both police and specialized units have been deployed in a common cause of fighting terrorism. Special military powers to restrict, control, search and intern suspected members of illegal or proscribed organizations have also been instituted. In democracy, specialist units like the SAS, GIGN, and GSG-9 can operate effectively and have the support of the government and the public they serve. It is also necessary and prudent to have strict guidelines and controls for the use of such counterterrorism units. In Northern Ireland, the accusations of "shoot to kill" and "death squads" were hurled by the IRA in a desperate attempt by the subversive group to halt the activities of a response mechanism which was too effective for their purposes. In the final chapter, we shall make a general summation of terrorism as it is today and threats to be vigilant about at the start of the twenty-first century.

Terms to Remember

Balcombe Street	Belfast and Londonderry	Annex 17
PLO	Pan Am 103	ECAC
ICAO	SAS	Stanstead
Sudan Airways A310	BBC	Usama bin Laden
Lyon Summit	NORAID	INTERPOL
MI5	SBS	TAG
SASR	OAG	GEO
HRU	GIGN	BBE
YZJ	FSK	SWAT
Delta	PFLO	GSG-9/1
SEAL Team Six	NSWDG	

Review Questions

Describe the reasons for establishing counterterrorism specialized units in England and Ireland.

What social and media value does the practice of honest and open discussion about terrorism have for police and counter terrorism units?

Discuss the role of the European Civil Aviation Conference (ECAC) and how it acts to protect the air traveler.

Explain how the British SAS helped a number of nations learn counterterrorism techniques.

What can be done to make a better team of the public, police, special teams and the media?

End Notes

1. Paul Wilkinson, *Terrorism and the Liberal State* (New York University Press, 1977), p. 155.
2. Alan Pangborn, "How Far Has Europe Come Since Pan Am 103?" (*Intersec*, Three Bridges Publishing, May 5, 1996), Vol. 6, p. 195.
3. Gerry Edwards, "Hijackers' Gateway," (*Intersec*, Three Bridges Publishing, April 1998) Vol. 8, Issue 4, p. 168.
4. Summary of the Ministerial Conference on Terrorism, Paris, France, July 30, 1996.
5. Barbara Cole, *The Elite: The Story of the Rhodesian Special Air Service* (Three Knights Publishing, Transkei, 1984), p. 6.
6. Ibid., p. 9.
7. Ibid., p. 15.
8. Leroy Thompson, *The Rescuer* (Paladin Press, Colorado 1986), p. 84.

CHAPTER 14

TERRORISM IN THE TWENTY-FIRST CENTURY

Predicting stuff is difficult, especially when it's about the future.

—Pogo

OVERVIEW

The quote above, written by cartoonist Walt Kelly in the 1950s for his great comic strip, is so perfect in the turbulent world of today that we had to share it with students who may have no memory of that great satirist. In the world of terrorism, predictions are often more wrong than correct. When we started this book, the hopes for future peace between Northern Ireland and Britain were high, and an accord was even signed. As we watched the news tonight, the shooting and burning of cars were escalating and riot police lined the streets. By the time this book is off the presses and in the bookstores, who knows where that situation will stand? The Israelis and the PLO had just had the successful Wye meetings as we were finishing this manuscript. Trying to discern what motivates governments, religious zealots, and terrorists is definitely not an exact science. The best we can do is give the student a look at what has happened in past conflicts involving serious terroristic violence and hope this background will provide some clues about the future from a social, economic, religious, psychological, and economic standpoint. While the past may be prologue, trying to plan for the future using only the past as a guide is as dangerous as driving a truck by looking only in the rearview mirror. You could be in for one heck of a crash.

How do we conclude a book that has engrossed our minds and our time for so long? It seems that all we can do now is examine what we see as some of the most critical issues that have emerged in regard to terrorism and make some modest comments as to the warning signs to watch for. Many of these topics are extensions of those we have covered in previous chapters. We will start with the problems associated with terrorism and weapons of mass destruction.

TERRORISM GETS A LARGER STAGE

United States Embassies Become Targets

Shock and horror rocked the United States public as not one, but *two* U.S. embassies were struck by terrorists in central Africa. On August 7, 1997, the citizens of the United States got another wake-up call about terrorism. Americans and American institutions had long been favorite targets for terrorists; however there had only been two other major attacks outside the country in the 1990s. A truck bomb killed nineteen U.S. troops living at a base near Dhaahran, Saudi Arabia in June, 1996. In June 1998, rocket-propelled grenades exploded near the U.S. Embassy in Beirut, Lebanon, with no injuries. When car bombs exploded outside the United States Embassy in Nairobi, Kenya and Dar es Salaam, Tanzania any remaining illusion of security on embassy grounds was shattered. Together, the bombings killed over eighty people and injured more than 1,700 others. Among the dead were at least eight Americans in Nairobi. Five local employees of the U.S. Embassy died in the Dar es Salaam blast. President Clinton spoke to the American people in strong language: "We will use all the means at our disposal to bring those responsible to justice, no matter what or how long it takes."

The most likely suspects were well-established terrorist groups from outside Kenya and Tanzania, and they probably chose those countries because they knew there was lax security. According to government reports, terrorism had actually been declining. In 1997, the number rose only slightly (304). Most of these were minor attacks on soft American targets overseas.

Rescuers carry the body of another bombing victim from the ruins of the destroyed Ufundi House which was next to the U.S. Embassy in Nairobi, Kenya. *Associated Press (AP)*

Terrorist organizations in the past have rushed to take credit for an event. Sometimes, several groups compete for credit. But of late, perhaps related to the retaliatory raid on Libya, terrorists are less likely than ever before to take responsibility for their acts. Experts agree that the most likely financier and orchestrator of the embassy bombings is Usama bin Ladin. He was suspected of using the Egyptian terror group, Islamic Jihad or the Lebanon-based Hezbollah, or both. Bin Ladin is alleged to control a personal fortune estimated at $250 million and spends it freely on his personal war against America. He combines financial muscle with religious fanaticism, a deadly cocktail. Bin Ladin and a coalition of Islamic extremist groups had earlier issued a fatwa (similar to that issued on Rushdie in Iran). Its wording was chilling: "To kill the Americans and their allies—civilian and military—is an individual duty for every Muslim who can do it, in any country in which it is possible to do it."

As recently as May 1998, the United States had asked bin Ladin's hosts and protectors in Afghanistan, the Taliban, to turn him over to them, but to no avail. Because of a deteriorating security situation in war-torn Sudan, the U.S. embassy staff from that country had been operating out of the Nairobi embassy since February 1996, and this may have provided the motive for bin Ladin to strike in Kenya. In a frightening side issue, the car containing the explosive was parked inside the embassy compound—meaning that it had somehow passed by security guards. Security may have been lax because neither Kenya nor Tanzania was considered a dangerous location.

Among the injured was United States Ambassador to Kenya, Prudence Bushnell, cut by flying glass but still working with locals and embassy staff to rescue the injured. Because the explosions took place at midmorning, the streets around both embassies were busy and hundreds were hurt. The hue and cry immediately went up for greater security to be provided to U.S. sites overseas. The problem with that scenario is that, if you only beef up one type of target, it just alerts terrorists to select easier ones. Less secure facilities, even in relatively safe regions, produce opportunities for terrorism leaders who always take the path of least resistance. And it is feared that tougher security at embassies may merely make United States tourists and other civilians abroad the "softest" targets. The curtain is not yet down on these attacks.

The United States retaliated in early August with missile strikes on terrorist training camps in Afghanistan and air strikes on a suspected chemical plant in the Sudan. It was reported that twenty were killed in the Afghanistan raid, and the chemical plant in Sudan was destroyed. The U.S. Secretary of State is quoted as saying, "This will be a long-time struggle, but we are in for the duration." Meanwhile bin Laden is receiving safe haven from his allies, the Taliban, in Afghanistan at an unknown location.

NEW GULF WAR?

In August 1998, Iraq slammed the United States and Britain over their calls for a change in Baghdad's regime. U.N. arms inspectors hastily pulled out of Baghdad when strikes against Iraq appeared inevitable. A long weekend was cut short for members of the U.N. Special Commission (UNSCOM). Inspectors from the International Atomic Energy Agency would not return if the Iraqi government tried again to limit or block their work. United States and British forces remain prepared to unleash another devastating military barrage on Baghdad if Saddam shuts down the inspectors—again. The promises of good behavior were echoed by Saddam's puppet scientific advisor. But on August 5, Iraq limited the inspectors' work to routine monitoring of specific Iraqi-designated locations.

Saddam protested loudly that he had seen no sign that the U.N. intended to lift economic sanctions. This fell on deaf ears, which had heard that song before. Then, with planes in the air streaking toward Iraq, Hussein capitulated. The Iraqi commitment to fully cooperate was later tested and resulted in another delay tactic in the weeks that followed. Saddam continues to berate them as being spies for the United States and Israel. About thirty to forty sites in Iraq were kept under UNSCOM's constant "technical surveillance," for confirmation and verification efforts to determine whether Iraq is building long-range missiles for carrying chemical, biological and nuclear weapons. UNSCOM also is deeply interested in Iraq's production of the nerve gas VX and whether it has been loaded into warheads. U.S. diplomats stressed that Iraqi compliance with U.N. resolutions requiring elimination of all weapons of mass destruction, and even that would not automatically lead to the lifting of sanctions. In addition to the weapons inspectors, about 120 U.N. humanitarian aid workers came back after a 600-mile drive from Amman, Jordan.

Despite this cat and mouse, another Gulf War with Iraq was inevitable. Saddam Hussein did break his promises again and blocked weapons inspections. It is difficult for a dictator like Hussein to admit that if he would simply comply with the U.N. directives, he could become a member of the family of nations again. It appears that he is incapable of keeping a promise and has no regard for the safety of his people. Like a rat backed into a corner, he is especially dangerous now. That could have serious consequences not only for Iraq, but for the U.S.

American and British forces were already standing ready to hit Iraq instantly and are determined to "shoot first and negotiate later." France, Russia and other countries formerly protective of Saddam now agreed that punitive strikes should be launched. British Prime Minister Tony Blair has become more hawkish than anyone after having to call off the first bombing and missile raids with only fifteen minutes to spare. After Saddam responded by promising to back off, President Clinton decided not go to war and possibly kill thousands of innocent Iraqis. But U.S. Secretary of State Albright, who was in Malaysia at the time, wanted to press ahead with the attack. Tony Blair said, "We are looking with the Americans now at ways in which we can bolster the opposition and improve the possibility of removing Saddam

An Israeli police officer uses a fire extinguisher shortly after a car bomb exploded in Jerusalem's Mahane Yehuda market.
Associated Press (AP)

altogether," making it clear that he had lost patience with the Iraqi leader but not the Iraqi people. "On the contrary," he said, "we support the desire of the overwhelming majority of them for freedom from Saddam Hussein."

When Saddam remained unmoving in his stance, the planning of "Operation Desert Fox" began. The American and British leaders remain in favor of maintaining a tough line against Iraq until the complete destruction of its country's biological and chemical weapons capability has been achieved. John Major, who was British Prime Minister at the time of the Gulf War, agreed that Tony Blair had been right in committing British forces to take part in a "punitive" exercise against Iraq. It would be unforgivable if Britain did not take action to ensure that Saddam could not use his weapons against neighboring states.

When all avenues had been exhausted, and the start of the Muslim month of Ramadan approached, a decision was made. From December 16 to December 19, 1998, the planes and missiles of Desert Fox pounded targets in Iraq. More cruise missiles were fired than in the Gulf War. The B-1 Lancer bomber was used for the first time in combat. The assault stopped on the first day of Ramadan and strict "no-fly" zones were reestablished in the north and south of Iraq. Antiaircraft positions were constantly focusing their target radars at the Desert Fox air patrols and Iraqi fighters who were defying the no-fly. Desert Fox was not another Gulf War, but it seems inevitable that Saddam Hussein will continue to provoke the rest of the world until he satisfies what seems to be a death wish.

HOLY TERROR

Terrorism motivated by religious imperatives is growing quickly, increasing the number of killings and reducing the restraints on mass, indiscriminate murder. So great is this change, according to Bruce Hoffman, that we may have to revise our notions of the stereotypical terrorist organization. Hoffman explained that traditional terrorist groups could be characterized as groups that engage in conspiracy as a full-time avocation, living underground and constantly planning and plotting terrorist attacks, perhaps under the direct control or at the behest of a foreign government. The seemingly amateurish World Trade Center bombers, however, may be the model of a new kind of terrorist group: a more or less ad hoc amalgamation of like-minded individuals, who merely gravitate toward one another for a specific, perhaps even one-time, operation. This new breed of part-time terrorists may represent an even greater threat than its predecessors have.

"Holy terror" and the purely so-called "secular terror" have radically different value systems, mechanisms for justifying their acts, and concepts of morality. For the religious terrorist, violence is a divine duty. Whereas secular terrorists generally regard indiscriminate violence as immoral and counterproductive, religious terrorists view such violence as both morally justified and necessary. Also, whereas secular terrorists attempt to appeal to a constituency composed of sympathizers and the aggrieved people they claim to speak for, religious terrorists act for no audience but themselves. This absence of a constituency, combined with an extreme sense of alienation, means that such terrorists can justify almost limitless violence against virtually any target who is not a member of their own religious belief or sect.

Religious or ethnic fanaticism could more easily allow terrorists to overcome the psychological barriers to mass murder than a radical political agenda has in the past. Many white supremacists actually welcome the prospect of nuclear war or terrorism. They see it as an opportunity to eliminate their avowed "enemies" and permit the fulfillment of their objectives to create a new world order peopled exclusively by the white race. Any doubts about the seriousness of such hate groups were dispelled when police and federal agents raided a white supremacist compound in rural Arkansas in April 1984, and discovered a stockpile of some thirty gallons of cyanide to be used to poison municipal water supplies.

The targets and tactics of "holy terror" operations that have occurred or been attempted during the past decade lead to the possibility of far more destructive acts. Ominous examples already abound:

- Poisoning of water supplies of major urban centers—not only American white supremacists, but also terrorists in India are alleged to have made such plans
- Dispersal of toxic chemicals through internal building ventilation system, which has been attempted by white supremacist skinheads in Arizona
- Indiscriminate, wanton attacks on busy urban centers—accounting for 1,400 injuries and deaths in Bombay last winter, alleged to be the work of Muslim terrorists
- Attacks on power grids to disrupt electrical service to large population areas—conducted by a Black Muslim sect in Colorado
- Poisoning of food—undertaken in Oregon by followers of the Baghwan Rajneesh to influence a local election

The approach of the year 2000, the literal millennium, may inspire religious terrorists to increased violence as they attempt to implement their own visions of Armageddon.[1] This type of blind allegiance to some obscure right-wing, white supremacist dogma is a real concern as we approach the new century. This is one of the areas that must be watched closely, even as we concentrate on the Middle East. If we ignore the militias and the network they have across the nation, we do so at our own peril. It is clear that this movement is growing rapidly. The student need only type in the word "militia" on the browser and they will find dozens of the examples like those shown in Chapter 12.

TECHNO TERRORISM

While the Internet offers great opportunity for good and is the fastest growing business sector the world has ever seen, it must be aligned with commercial market forces and operate on an international basis. Some observers believe that encryption software must be developed so that industrial and other espionage is prevented. The proliferation of strong encryption will have the effect opposite that envisioned by the administration. That is, it will help fight crime by keeping information secure in the new borderless world.

Testifying before a Senate committee, Jerry Berman, executive director of the Center for Democracy and Technology, thinks that data security demands strong encryption to foil threats wherever they are in the world. And good data security and privacy policies must recognize that the Bill of Rights in the U.S. Constitution is nothing more than a local law. As the Internet user reaches the unnerving conclusion that terrorism, like the Internet, recognizes no national boundaries, law enforcement officials will seek more ways to ferret it out.

In the past, investigators have wielded telephone wiretaps against terrorists, but the Clinton administration points to the recent use of encrypted files by child pornographers, militia members and spies to avoid discovery. Grave crimes, such as a plot to shoot down several airliners over Chicago, have been foiled by the use of wiretaps. Had the FBI been unable to read those transmissions, a major tragedy might have occurred. There have also been calls for regulation of Internet content, such as the administration's ill-fated attempt to curb child pornography via the Communications Decency Act.

Senator Dianne Feinstein (D-Calif.) introduced a bill that would make it illegal to distribute explosives-making information "by any means," including online, if the distributor intends or knows the information would be used in committing a crime. Perhaps this will become an important law enforcement tool. Encryption that is difficult to decipher should not be distributed to anyone. It's almost the same argument as that for gun control. The good citizen doesn't need a background check, but how can you distinguish that person from a bank robber without one? This area is another that must be watched closely, since the vast network of the right-wing militias and racist organizations can be used covertly and encrypted today.

PRO-LIFE TERRORISM

On January 3, 1997, the peace of the new year was shattered by bomb blasts and injuries at the Northside Family Services Clinic in Atlanta, Georgia, rekindling fears and memories of the bombing at the Summer Olympics in that stately southern city. The first blast occurred at 9:30 A.M., while the second blast was set and deliberately delayed to catch federal agents, firemen, ambulance attendants, and clinic workers as they responded to the scene forty-five minutes later. The second blast resulted in major and minor injuries and serious damage to the five-story building less than a week before the twenty-eighth anniversary of the Supreme Court's decision in *Roe* v. *Wade*, which had legalized abortion. Was this explosion simply individual rage and violence or was it a terrorist act? This question will be the major thrust of this section.

The Task Force on Terrorism concluded that terrorism "is a technique, a way of engaging in certain types of criminal activity, so as to attain particular ends." This would be a process by which a group would create "an overwhelming fear for coercive purposes," such fear to be raised not only in the immediate victims but also within the audience of community or society. It seems that this definition fits nicely within the parameters of the violence against abortion clinics by extremist members of the pro-life movements across the nation. The technique used in the Atlanta bombings is one well known from the efforts of terrorist groups like the Irish Republican Army (IRA). This method is referred to by experts on terrorism as the "congregate effect." The goal is to get people to gather around or near the first bombing and then explode the second or third device with devastating impact. Such planning is not typical of a random act of violence by a single dissident.

As we discussed in Chapter 1, terrorism is defined by the FBI as: the unlawful use of force or violence against persons or property to intimidate or coerce a government, the civilian population, or any segment thereof, in furtherance of political or social objectives. Again, the acts of violence against abortion clinics by those who wish to have the Supreme Court reverse *Roe* v. *Wade* seem to fall neatly within this definition as well.

"Limited political" and "subrevolutionary" terrorism are the terms applied to those acts in which the goal is to influence, through coercive fear, certain public policies or practices. While violence, harassment, disruptions, arson and bombings, demonstrations and action plan documents *in toto* squarely fit the Federal Bureau of Investigation's definition, the Department of Justice has concluded that abortion clin-

New Woman All Women Health Care clinic in Birmingham, Alabama was hit by a bomb blast early Thursday, January 29, 1998. It was the first fatal clinic bombing in U.S. history. *Associated Press (AP)*

ic violence is not terrorism and that there is no national conspiracy to engage in terrorism. It is not clear whether the FBI addressed the question of regional or local conspiracies in this decision, although the Justice Department continues to investigate the alleged conspiracy among anti-abortion activists and to indict activists on federal conspiracy and arson charges.

A Social Construction of Abortion Clinic Violence/Terrorism

The United States has been undergoing a religious revival since at least 1977, in part due to the approaching millennium and in part due to a reactionary movement fueled by fear of crime, anti-Semitism, racism, political demagoguery, and a desire to make the past become the future. The New Right has emerged, with its goal of political and cultural hegemony in the United States. Anti-abortionists, in particular define abortion as a "violation of their moral precepts." The movement gained momentum in the 1980s, with the election of pro-life presidents Reagan and Bush.

The movement can be characterized as:

- Adopting a "pro-family" stance
- Stressing parental rights
- Emphasizing strong families
- Expressing moral indignation of abortion, perceived as murder
- Stressing the patriarchal family as the ideal model

- Emphasizing a fear of changes occurring in the family systems
- Decrying the alleged decline in the traditional American family

Thus, this is a backlash movement, and the heart of the effort is to fight the shifts and changes underway in American culture by focusing concerns on reproductive control, including abortion, women's rights, and male domination over women's bodies. For pro-life extremists, those not holding the same moral and religious beliefs are viewed in dualistic terms: good-bad, saved-damned, chosen-evil, God's children-spawn of Satan. Such moral absolutes permit causal attribution, assigning to one's opponents both malicious intent as well as evil character. Such a mindset encourages and validates the use of force against opponents ("sinners"). Indeed, it is a moral requirement to punish offenders using whatever force necessary to restrain the wicked and make them virtuous. This could include violence against persons and property, as well as threats of violence (verbal statements, confrontations at abortion clinics, telephoning a mother of an abortion clinic patient and stating that their yet unborn grandchild is going to be killed by the pregnant daughter, etc.).

The anti-abortion movement and the New Right interact and network in many ways, including media evangelism, workshops, books, training sessions, Bible colleges, and demonstration events. While some movement speakers state that their followers ought not to engage in violence, they also argue that it is to be expected, since "truly moral" people have no other recourse, having been pushed to these extremes. Thus one could argue that frustration and anomie are underlying causes of abortion clinic violence and demonstrations.

Abortion and Religious Political Organizations

Although abortion clinic demonstrators come from a wide swath of society, it could be argued that most demonstrators are middle-class, religiously influenced and motivated by millenarianism, post-millenniumism eschatology, the *parousia* (second-coming), and a long-range hope for the revitalization of the Church and re-Christianization of American society. The four major religious strategy groups are the Lambs of Christ, Operation Rescue, Pro-Life Action League, and Missionaries to the Pre-Born. Other groups exist (Rescue America, for example), but no one knows the relative composition or influence of these groups. Since academic study of the more radical factions of the pro-life movement is at best scanty, research lags behind events, although diverse written materials are abundant.

The major groups, their seminal leaders, and examples of their strategic literature are:

- Lambs of Christ, founded by "Father Doe" (Father Norman Weslin)
- Operation Rescue, founded by Randall Terry
- Pro-Life Action League, headed by Joseph Scheidler
- Missionaries to the Unborn, headed by Joseph Foreman with Matt Trewhella as chief strategist.

The basic concern is with abortion clinic bombings, killings and disturbances. But we call attention to the fairly coherent body of literature and existing personal narratives that have not been carefully examined by scholarly inquiries or students of terrorism, Jeffrey Kaplan being one exception to this criticism.

Abortion Clinic Violence and Disruption

The National Abortion Federation compiles national statistics forwarded by family planning programs and abortion service providers. Relying on voluntary reporting creates many of the same problems associated with the Uniform Crime Reports and data should be interpreted as minimal estimates of the extent of abortion clinic violence and disruptions. For example, data are gathered on "stalking," defined as the "persistent following, threatening, and harassing of an abortion provider, staff member, or patient away from the clinic." Stalking may be so frequent that some staff may relegate it to "routine behavior" and not report the incidents. Harassing calls at any hour of the day or night may also be underreported. There is no equivalent of the National Crime Victimization Survey to permit estimates of the extent of underreporting.

Examples of anti-abortion activities likely to be underreported in the data gathered by the National Abortion Federation include the following:

- Beheading of a cat of a clinic worker
- Spray painting the van of a county councilwoman with the word "baby killer" to coerce her to vote to terminate the lease of a Planned Parenthood agency
- Poisoning dogs of a physician who performs abortions in his office
- Threatening a clinic worker by holding a sledge hammer over her head
- Holding red meat up before a physician's children while asking why their father "kills babies"
- Shooting a judge
- Picketing physicians' and council members' homes
- Slashing tires of clinic workers
- Telephoning patients in the middle of the night and yelling "baby killer"
- Calling parents of clinic patients to accuse their daughters of sexual and moral misconduct ("whore," "tramp," "slut," "pin cushion," "Ms. Community Chest," etc.)

It is estimated that many similar such acts go unreported.

Such harassment techniques are fear-inducing. Private practices and public policies are influenced by such coordinated efforts. It would not exceed the limits of logic to argue that religious-political terrorists are attempting to impose their moral beliefs and religious practices on a nation by the use of and the threat of the use of violence to gain sufficient power to affect political institutions, especially local and state lawmaking bodies.

There is evidence of persistent action against abortion providers, and some suggestion of decline in overall incidents in the last two years. Murder and attempted murder are more recent developments; invasion and vandalism are down in numbers. A summary statement might be that such incidents have been influenced by *Roe v. Wade*, the U.S. Supreme Court's later reaffirmation of that case, and a 1994 federal law guaranteeing access to clinics that provide abortions (Freedom of Access to Clinic Entrances), as well as a 1994 U.S. Supreme Court decision upholding the legality of "buffer zones" to keep protesters away from clinics. Violence and disruptions continue but at a reduced level of incidence.

Future Scenarios

It is clear that after a somewhat calmer 1996, the level of violence at abortion clinics and providers may be rising again. There was a drop in incidents of violence against abortion providers in 1996, but a sharp increase in the number of incidents of disruption. When you combine these two categories, it becomes clear that the total increase in incidents is *threefold*.

Protesters in general have undertaken new strategies for removing abortion providers and reducing opportunities for abortion. After having failed to secure a reversal of *Roe* v. *Wade* and facing U.S. Supreme Court affirmation of buffer zones, anti-abortion strategists may have concluded that more might be gained by focusing activities on local and state governments. These include challenging the tax-exempt status of Planned Parenthood organizations by searching for legal flaws in the wording of charters and bylaws, seeking revocation of property-tax exemptions of non-profit organizations, pushing local statutes and ordinances, and encouraging passage of anti-abortion laws. The National Abortion Federation points out that there is no evidence that militant antiabortion activism has stopped women from having abortions. Nonetheless, it has caused untold trauma, unnecessary and unconscionable health risks, and the loss of personal dignity and privacy for hundreds of thousands of women. It also points out several factors at work in the 21 percent decline in antiabortion violence in 1996:

- The deterrent effect of the passage and enforcement of the Freedom of Access to Clinic Entrances Act
- Control of both houses of Congress and many state legislatures by conservative forces which advanced an antichoice agenda, which may have appeased some anti-abortion extremists
- Increased expenditures by abortion providers on security systems, programs, and staff training
- Utilization of legal tools such as injunctions, buffer zones, and restraining orders

Editors of *The New York Times* were less sanguine on the erosion of the constitutional right to choose abortion, noting that hospital abortion is now so expensive that women must go to physicians' offices or specialized abortion clinics. Protesters' harassment and violence have led many physicians to stop performing abortions and a spate of new laws may have further closed off a woman's right to choose abortion. The changing legal environment on local and state levels cited by the editors included:

- Some 84 percent of counties in the nation do not have abortion providers
- Eleven states require women to undergo a bifurcated procedure: physician counseling and a 24-hour waiting period before abortion. (This could permit local activists to trace license plate numbers after the first visit and contact families of the patients before they come in for the abortion.)
- In 1995, legislators in twenty-two states introduced legislation requiring mandatory waiting periods
- Twenty-eight states require women under age eighteen to get consent of one or both parents. (This could contribute to teenagers deferring abortions until

later when abortions would be more complicated and potentially more dangerous to the patient's health.)

- Thirty-seven states deny Medicaid coverage for abortions, even if necessary to preserve the woman's health
- Mississippi requires both the bifurcated process as well as consent of both parents, and that physicians who advertise abortion services (and perform more than nine a month) to widen their hallways and hire more staff to qualify as surgical centers. Physicians must also provide patients with color photographs of fetuses at two-week stages of development.[2]

The editors argued that pro-life think tanks are continuously drafting proposed new laws, which state legislators introduce around the country. They conclude that such development in the states has received little attention since middle-class women's access to abortion has largely been unhampered, but such efforts have heavily impacted poor, young, small-town and rural women who cannot afford to overcome the bifurcated hurdle, track down absent fathers to secure permission for abortion, find overnight baby sitters, and commute to a large city and pay for hotel costs. Antiabortion activists no doubt take comfort in achievements to date to limit constitutional rights to choose.

The battlefield in America's abortion struggle may be redrawn with the introduction of RU-486 (mifepristone), approved September 18, 1996 for nonsurgical abortion in the very early stage of pregnancy (and by women who would not choose a surgical termination). Yet treatment protocol would require three visits to the physician's office (first for counseling and mifepristone, a second visit 36-48 hours later for administration of prostaglandin, and a third visit to assure the abortion is complete). It is likely that more middle class women might follow this protocol, and that poorer women will still face hurdles in their efforts to seek abortions. No doubt alternative markets will arise to provide the pills, but poorer women may opt to avoid the confirmation (third) visit to the physician's office.

There is little reason to suspect that anti-abortion activists, currently with ready access names and addresses of license plate owners, will not also have ready access to names of physicians willing to administer the RU-486 nonsurgical abortion option. As Rebecca Lindstedt of the American Life League stated: "It won't be difficult to find out who is prescribing RU-486 in Topeka, Kansas." Presumably these physicians (and the pharmaceutical manufacturers) would then receive the attentions of anti-abortionists.

Our concern has been with the use of violence and the threat of violence to induce fear among targeted victims and a larger audience to achieve limited social and religious goals. We postulate that these acts, in the aggregate, are not only unlawful but should be defined as domestic terrorism. Persistent abortion clinic violence, ranging from arson, to murder of staff, to the carefully planned terrorist-style bombing of the Atlanta clinic seems to us to clearly fit the definition of terrorism as enunciated by the Federal Bureau of Investigation. The FBI, however, has decided that antiabortion violence is not terrorism, possibly for political or other reasons. To be more generous, this may be for such administrative reasons as wanting to focus attention on international or offshore terrorism, or to downplay the real or imagined existence of domestic terrorists to the public. By not defining abortion clinic violence as terrorism, the FBI has shifted responsibility for bombing and arson investigation to the Department of the Treasury and the Bureau of Alcohol, Tobacco and Firearms, a smaller agency with considerably fewer resources than the FBI. Perhaps the federal government can now begin to refocus attention on this extremely violent behavior as a true form of domestic terrorism.

Finally, we raise the question of subversion of constitutionally guaranteed federal rights. The Fourteenth Amendment of the U.S. Constitution defines residents as being citizens of both the federal government and the state in which they reside. It expressly forbids states from making any ordinance, law or regulation that abridges the federal rights of citizens. If there is a constitutional right to abortion and the effects (whether by "color" or "usage") of local, county or state government clearly abridge that right, is there a colorable issue that might be considered by federal courts? If one defines anti-abortion terrorism as an effort to impose a set of religious beliefs on others, is there a colorable question of separation of church and state? Students of constitutional history may later consider this pre-millennium era as an odious period of challenge to and denial of liberty.

TERRORISTS FOR SALE OR EXCHANGE

In an ideal world, governments would deal with any terrorists they apprehended themselves. Alternately, if requested to do so and good reason was given, they would hand them over to the government of the country where their crimes had been committed, for trial with the barest of formalities or delays. And they should fully expect reciprocal treatment. Unfortunately, this seldom happens, because one man's terrorist is another man's freedom fighter, and suspicious governments seldom give away something for nothing. All want to retain a few bargaining terrorist chips, just in case. A terrorist in hand often has value.

Years ago, the expression "he has a price on his head" was clearly understood: it meant that a person was "wanted" by the justice authorities, either having escaped from legal custody, or on the run, allegedly having committed a crime. A cash reward was offered for his apprehension and conviction, especially in the days before modern police forces appeared, to induce the public to bring the criminal to justice. Cash rewards for these purposes brought about bounty hunters, a practice which still lingers in some countries. Nowadays, the expression that "every government has its price" might be more apt, particularly when dealing with the extradition of terrorists.

Extradition has always been a delicate subject, touching as it does on national sovereignty, seeming at times to be regarded more as a personal favor to the government asking for it, than a routine, moral international transaction. One has long suspected that there must be secret exchange channels, as all such transactions are carried out with the utmost discretion, and are publicly denied.

Cash Will Do Nicely

In August 1994, the French government "bought" the notorious Carlos the Jackal from the Sudanese government for a reputed $2 million. The French only admitted that he had been arrested "outside the legal framework." Carlos (Ilyich Ramirez Sanchez) was a star terrorist captive, wanted for killing eighty-three people in a series of terrorist attacks, several in France. In December 1975, he led the terrorist team that kidnapped eleven OPEC oil ministers in Vienna.

Carlos had long been sheltered in Middle Eastern states, courtesy of the KGB, but with the ending of the Cold War he became an embarrassment. He was subsequently ejected from Syria, refused entry by Yemen and Libya, and forced to accept asylum in Sudan. Carlos now resides in a French prison, having just been convicted for killing two gendarmes. The French thought they made a good bargain; perhaps so did the Sudanese government.

The Carlos incident established the fact that terrorists have a monetary value. We may be able to look forward to "transactions" involving elderly, formerly active international terrorists, such as Abu Nidal or bin Laden and others of his generation, who made international headlines in the 1970s, 1980s and 1990s. Bringing them to trial for a price, when certain governments still sheltering some of them need a cash infusion, could be tempting. Such show trials could provide a major boost to the morale of national security services. Lower profile terrorists might be obtained for lower prices, a process that might have been in operation for some time for all we know, as secrecy surrounds it. Either the media were well ahead of the diplomats in the Carlos case, or the French government deliberately sought publicity.

During the Western hostage saga in Lebanon (1984–1992), most of those held were eventually ransomed. Often huge sums of money were paid for the release of employees by wealthy international concerns, since it is against government policy to deal directly with terrorists. The last two German hostages (Kemptner and Strubig) were only freed after the two Hamadei brothers, who had been involved in hijacking and kidnapping, were released from German detention, this being a person-for-person exchange. In June 1995, the German government paid a reputed $1million to the poverty-stricken Yemeni government for the extradition of Johannes Weinrich, a colleague of Carlos in his heyday. After twenty years on the run, he was wanted for murder and explosions in Berlin, and is now in prison in Germany. One wonders who may be next.

Bounty Hunting

While the much-publicized Carlos incident may have alerted the world to the cash value of a terrorist, some states, especially the U.S., have long been offering cash rewards for the apprehension of criminals in order to tempt bounty hunters, many of which have been successful. No film about the "Old West" is complete without its "Wanted: Reward" poster in the background.

In October 1985, the Italian cruise ship the Achille Lauro was hijacked in the Mediterranean, and one United States citizen was killed. The situation was resolved with the help of the Egyptian government, which provided an aircraft for escaping terrorists. Under President Reagan's "you can run but you can't hide" policy, U.S. aircraft forced the plane down in Italy, where the leader, Abu Abbas, a Palestinian terrorist mastermind, was allowed to escape to Yugoslavia. The other terrorists involved stood trial and were convicted in Italy. One, Magied al-Mulkil, was sentenced to thirty years imprisonment and later jumped his parole for good behavior, whereupon the U.S. government immediately offered a $2 million reward for his recapture. After the recent terrorist massacre at Luxor (Egypt) in November 1996, the Egyptian government condemned the British government for harboring Islamic fundamentalist terrorist leaders thought to be responsible. The pot often calls the kettle black.

The United States offered a reward of $2 million (which seems to be the going rate for a top terrorist) for the apprehension of Ramzi Ahmad Yousef. He was the mastermind and "evil genius" behind the conspiracy to blow up the World Trade Center in New York and other buildings and bridges. He was thought to be in

Pakistan. Yousef was located by the CIA, which issued thousands of small green (an Islamic color) matchboxes, with his likeness on one side of them and details of how to obtain the reward on the other. They smoke a lot in Pakistan, and this did the trick. Yousef is now in an American prison.

One hopes that the CIA will issue its green matchboxes by the hundreds of thousands in Afghanistan, where many Islamic fundamentalist terrorists, including bin Ladin, are reputed to have sought refuge with the Taliban in the hope that money, lots of it, may overcome religious scruples. Now that the Taliban's income from drug trafficking is much reduced, it is becoming short of ready cash and may have some Islamic fundamentalist terrorists to sell.

The Exchange Market

Through fact and fiction during the Cold War, we came to accept that spies were sometimes exchanged, so why not "wanted" terrorists too? In the turbulent Middle East, terrorists have sometimes been selectively exchanged under cover of Red Cross prisoner-of-war transfers. Exchanging hostages is an ancient military custom, revived during the Lebanese Civil War (1975–92), when warring factions had their own private prisons where hostages were held as security insurance, for vengeance and for selective exchange.

Israel has, on occasion, indulged in kidnapping raids to seize terrorist leaders, such as Sheikh Abdul Rahman Obeid and Mustafa Dirani. This practice is known locally as "cross-border terrorism." According to the Israeli press, the Israeli government offered to release forty-seven Palestinians, including certain political prisoners loosely referred to as terrorists, for the freeing of one captured Israeli soldier. There have been other instances when "Arab guerrillas," meaning terrorists, have been released in exchange for Israelis who have been taken prisoner.

Two Mossad agents were caught after failing to assassinate Khaled Mishal, a Hamas leader in Amman (Jordan), and four others took refuge in the Israeli Embassy in Amman, all having forged Canadian passports. In exchange for the safe return of the Mossad agents, Israel had to release Sheikh Ahmad Yassin, imprisoned spiritual leader of the Hamas terrorist organization, which had been exploding suicide bombs in Israel. Israelis have made a few selective key terrorist exchanges over the years, censorship invariably concealing precise details.

A Sliding Scale

High prices have been demanded and obtained for the release of certain terrorist-held hostages, but the success of these extortion plans depended on someone's ability to pay large sums of money, governments excepted. Wealthy commercial concerns might be prepared to meet a terrorist's demands for the release of one of their employees, but would hesitate to embark upon such an illegal and secretive process. However, a few have done so, but as indirectly as possible. Not all were wealthy, but many were able to raise lesser sums of money, so it is probable that there was a terrorists' sliding scale of ransom demands, a sort of actuary's table, understood only by terrorist masterminds and their intermediaries.

Comparatively few hostages are killed, as lucrative prospects seem to outweigh political scruples and vengeance. This unfortunately does happen sometimes, particularly when terrorists quarrel among themselves over possession of the hostage and what to do with him or her. On occasion, one terrorist group will snatch a kidnapped hostage from another. Generally, terrorist groups more often quarrel with each other over spoils and territory than political dogma.

Occasionally, hostages have been sold or bartered between groups. One example is Rod Arad, an Israeli airman shot down over Lebanon, and taken hostage by a small Shia terrorist group known as the Faithful Resistance. Led by Mustafa Dirani, the group, according to some intelligence sources, held Arad for two years before selling him to the Iranian Pasdaran organization for $300,000. Hopes are that Arad may still be alive somewhere in Iran.

Shelf-Life Expired

In February last year, when the Lebanese army was reasserting its control over parts of the lawless Bekaa Valley, it cleaned out a nest of miscellaneous international terrorists, including five members of the Japanese Red Army. They were all former prisoners of the Israelis who had been freed in a mass Red Cross-organized Arab-Israeli exchange. One was Kozo Okamoto, the surviving terrorist of the May 1972 massacre at Lod Airport, in which over twenty people had been killed and more than eighty injured. Another was Kazuo Tohira, the group's master passport forger. The JRA members had disappeared from public view and notice.

Japan showed no interest in them at all, as their shelf-life had expired and Japanese authorities were reluctant to resurrect the emotions of past terrorist dramas. In July, the Lebanese government was reduced to charging the five JRA terrorists with illegal entry into Lebanon, and they were sentenced to three years' imprisonment, after which they were to be deported. The Lebanese government seems to be the loser, having to pay for their upkeep in prison, and probably an airline ticket, if it can persuade the Japanese government to eventually accept them.

Open Negotiation

Communications between terrorist hostage-takers and those who ultimately pay the ransoms is invariably shrouded in secrecy. An exception seems to be the case in Chechenya, where a twenty-one month separatist war (1994–1996) between Russia and Chechenya left an open expanse of no man's land between the two hostile military forces, across which illicit contacts and trade flourish. Russian mothers seeking missing soldier sons have been placing notices on general information boards in the area, giving details and asking for information about them. These well-read notice boards are also being used by terrorist go-betweens for communication (not always in code), quoting demands for ransom and how negotiations may begin.

Terrorist leaders in Chechenya have already kidnapped several international aid and humanitarian workers, demanding food, medical supplies and money in return for their release. An unofficial exchange of military prisoners seems to be conducted through the notice boards, while military authorities look the other way, as the end result is often to their benefit. Russian authorities admit that a prosperous market in kidnapping for ransom exists in Chechenya. What of the future? Sadly, one must forecast more of the same, with governments forever seeking to extradite wanted terrorists, and terrorists forever seeking valuable hostages. Market forces influence the prices and we can predict a lot more terrorists being turned in for thirty pieces of silver.[3]

SUMMARY

Well, we have come to the end of the tale we have spun for the student. As is clear, we have only touched the tip of the iceberg and have not used nearly as much material as we would liked to have done. In this chapter, we have touched on just a few of the issues facing our tottering world in the twenty-first century. It will be up to the next generation to try to find ways to eliminate the conditions that separate people, ethnically, religiously, racially, tribally, politically, traditionally and, last but not least, economically. Only when there is less of a gap between the haves and have nots can we hope to build bridges. We hope that this book has opened a window through which students will see the evening news from a far different perspective. If we have whetted the student's appetite for knowing more about how violence and terrorism came about, we are pleased and will feel that all this writing has been worth it.

Endnotes

1. RAND researcher Bruce Hoffman, Winter 1994 issue of the Rand Newsletter.
2. Harry E. Allen and Clifford E. Simonsen, "Abortion Clinic Violence and Terrorism," paper prepared for presentation at the annual meeting of the Southern Criminal Justice Association, September 27, 1996, Savannah, GA.
3. Edgar O'Balance, "Terrorists for Sale or Exchange," *Intersec: The Journal of International Security* (Three Bridges Publishing, Surrey, January 1998), Vol. 8, Issue 1, pp. 9–10, 12.